THE GHOST IN HAMLET (T. R. GOULD).

# SHAKESPEARE'S

## TRAGEDY OF

# HAMLET, PRINCE OF DENMARK.

# SHAKESPEARE'S

## TRAGEDY OF

# HAMLET, PRINCE OF DENMARK.

EDITED, WITH NOTES,

BY

WILLIAM J. ROLFE, LITT. D.,

FORMERLY HRAD MASTER OF THE KIGH SCHOOL, CAMBRIDGE, MASS.

ISBN: 978-93-5128-898-5(PB)

First Published in 1892
Indian Reprint in 2017

*Published by*

Kalpaz Publications
C-30, Satyawati Nagar,
Delhi – 110052
E-mail: kalpaz@hotmail.com
Website: kalpazpublications.com
Ph.: +91-9212142040

**Cataloging in Publication Data—DK**
Courtesy: D.K. Agencies (P) Ltd. <docinfo@dkagencies.com>

**Shakespeare, William,** 1564-1616, **author.**
Shakespeare's tragedy of Hamlet, Prince of Denmark / edited, with notes by William J. Rolfe.
pages cm
Play.
Reprint. Originally published: 1892.
ISBN 9789351288985

1. Hamlet (Legendary character)—Drama. 2. Princes—Denmark—Drama. I. Rolfe, W. J. (William James), 1827-1910, editor. II. Title.

PR2807.A2R65 2017 DDC 822.33 23

# PREFACE.

THE text of this edition of *Hamlet* is based upon a careful collation of the quarto of 1604 and the folio of 1623 with the other early editions and the leading modern ones. All the important *variæ lectiones* are given in the Notes; so that the reader, if he considers my text too "conservative," has all the materials necessary for making one to suit himself.

In the Notes my indebtedness to Furness is acknowledged on almost every page, and yet is by no means fully recorded. His edition furnishes an abstract and epitome of the vast literature of *Hamlet*, and is indispensable to the teacher and the critical scholar. He found it no easy task to condense his material into two octavo volumes; and in carrying out my more modest plan I have found a like difficulty in keeping within my limited space. The play is one of the longest (about twice as long as *Macbeth*), and the amount that has been written about it far exceeds that on any other of Shakespeare's works. Furness does not exaggerate when he says: "No one of mortal mould (save Him 'whose blessed feet were nailed for our advantage to the bitter cross') ever trod this earth, commanding such absorbing interest as this Hamlet, this mere creation of a poet's brain. No syllable that he whispers, no word let fall by any one near him, but is caught and pondered as no words ever have been, except of Holy Writ. Upon no throne built by mortal hands has ever 'beat so fierce a light' as upon that airy fabric reared at Elsinore."[1]

THE CLOPTON MONUMENT, STRATFORD CHURCH.

# CONTENTS.

PAGE

Introduction to Hamlet ........ 9

I. The History of the Play ........ 9

II. The Sources of the Plot ........ 12

III. Critical Comments on the Play ........ 14

HAMLET ........ 39

Act I ........ 41

" II ........ 70

" III ........ 93

" IV ........ 122

" V ........ 144

Notes ........ 167

# INTRODUCTION TO HAMLET.

## I. THE HISTORY OF THE PLAY.

THE earliest known edition of *Hamlet* appeared in quarto form in 1603, with the following title-page:

THE | Tragicall Historie of | HAMLET | *Prince of Denmarke* | By William Shake-speare. | As it hath beene diuerse times acted by his Highnesse ser- | uants in the Cittie of London: as also in the two V- | niuersities of Cambridge and Oxford, and else-where | At London printed for N. L. and Iohn Trundell. | 1603.

In the preceding year (July 26, 1602) James Roberts the printer had entered in the Stationers' Register "A booke called *the Revenge of HAMLETT Prince of Denmarke as yt was latelie acted by the Lord Chamberleyne his servantes.*" The quarto of 1603 may have been printed by Roberts, though his name does not appear on the title-page. He certainly printed the second quarto, published by the same "N. L." (Nicholas Ling) in 1604, with the following title-page:

*THE* | Tragicall Historie of | HAMLET, | *Prince of Denmarke.* | By William Shakespeare. | Newly imprinted and enlarged to almost as much | againe as it was, according to the true and perfect | Coppie. | AT LONDON, | Printed by I. R. for N. L. and are to be sold at his | shoppe vnder St. Dunstons Church in | Fleetstreet. 1604.

The relation of the first quarto to the second has been much disputed. Collier, White, and some other critics believe that the former is merely an imperfect report of the play as published in the latter; that it was printed, either from short-hand notes taken at the theatre, or from a stage-copy cut down for representation and perhaps corrupted by the insertion of stuff from an earlier play on the same subject. The second quarto, on the other hand, was an authorized edition of the play from "the true and perfect copy."

Other critics—among whom are Caldecott, Knight, Staunton, and Dyce — believe that the first quarto represents, though in a corrupt form, the first draught of the play, while the second gives it as remodelled and enlarged by the author. It is not necessary to suppose that the former was written near the time when it was published; it was more likely an early production of the poet. After the revision the original copy could be more easily obtained for surreptitious publication, and it may have been printed in haste to "head off" an authorized edition of the remodelled play.

Another theory, and a very plausible one, is that of Messrs.

Clark and Wright, brought out in the "Clarendon Press" edition of the play; namely, "that there was an old play on the story of *Hamlet*, some portions of which are still preserved in the quarto of 1603; that about the year 1602 Shakespeare took this and began to remodel it, as he had done with other plays; that the quarto of 1603 represents the play after it had been retouched by him to a certain extent, but before his alterations were complete; and that in the quarto of 1604 we have for the first time the *Hamlet* of Shakespeare."

For a *résumé* of the discussion of this interesting question (which will probably never be settled) see Furness's *Hamlet*, vol. ii. pp. 12–33.

The third quarto, published in 1605, is a reprint of the second; the title-page being identical except in date, and the variations in the text slight and unimportant. A fourth quarto, "Printed for *Iohn Smethwicke*" and "to be sold at his shoppe in Saint *Dunstons* church yeard in Fleetstreet," appeared in 1611; and a fifth, undated, was afterwards issued by the same publisher.* No other editions appeared during the lifetime of Shakespeare, or before the publication of the folio of 1623. The text of the latter varies considerably from that of the quartos, as will be seen by our *Notes*, in which the more important differences are recorded. Collier thinks that "if the *Hamlet* in the first folio were not composed from some hitherto unknown quarto,† it was derived from a manuscript

* Malone believes that this edition was printed in 1607, and Halliwell is inclined to place it "before 1609;" but, as the Cambridge editors show, its orthography is more modern than that of the quarto of 1611, from which it was probably printed.

† It is not impossible that there may have been such a quarto. No copy of the quarto of 1603 was known until 1823, when one was found by Sir Henry Bunbury. A second was picked up in 1856 by a Dublin bookseller, who paid a shilling for it. The former, which lacks the last page, was afterwards sold to the Duke of Devonshire for £230; the latter, which wants the title-page, was bought by Mr. Halliwell for £120, and

obtained by Heminge and Condell from the theatre." The standard text of the play is chiefly made up by a collation of the second quarto and the first folio.

## II. THE SOURCES OF THE PLOT.

There was certainly an old play on the subject of Hamlet, and some critics believe that it was an early production of Shakespeare's. The first allusion to it that has been discovered is in an *Epistle* "To the Gentleman Students of both Universities," by Thomas Nash, prefixed to Greene's *Menaphon*, printed in 1589. Referring to the playwrights of that day, Nash says: "It is a common practice now a daies amongst a sort of shifting companions,* that runne through every arte and thrive by none to leave the trade of *Noverint*† whereto they were borne, and busie themselves with the indevours of art, that could scarcelie latinize their necke-verse if they should have neede; yet English Seneca read by candle-light yeeldes manie good sentences, as *Bloud is a begger*, and so foorth: and if you intreate him faire in a frostie morning, he will affoord you whole *Hamlets*, I should say Handfulls of tragical speaches."

In Henslowe's *Diary* the following entry occurs:

9 of June 1594, Rd at hamlet . . . viiij$^{s}$

Five lines above the entry is this memorandum: "In the name of God Amen, beginninge at Newington, my Lord Admeralle and my Lorde chamberlen men, as foloweth, 1594." At this date, Shakespeare was one of the company of actors known as "the Lord Chamberlain's men."

Again, in Lodge's *Wits miserie, and the Worlds madnesse,*

is now in the British Museum. These are the only copies of the first quarto that have come down to our day.

* For the contemptuous use of *companion* (=fellow), cf. *J. C.* iv. 3. 138: "Companion, hence!" and see *Temp.* p. 131, or *M. N. D.* p. 125.

† That is, of attorney; from the Latin formula with which deeds began: "*Noverint universi*"=our "Know all men," etc.

published in 1596, we have an allusion to "y[e] ghost which cried so miserally [*sic*] at y[e] theator, like an oisterwife, *Hamlet reuenge.*"

There is also an old German play on the story of Hamlet, *Der Bestrafte Brudermord*, which some critics suppose to have been acted by English players in Germany as early as 1603 (though there seems to be no authentic record of any performance earlier than 1626, and the text that has come down to us cannot be traced farther back than 1710), and which may have been based on the pre-Shakespearian play. In the quarto of 1603 Polonius appears as "Corambis," and in the German play as "Corambus." As there is no evidence that the German writer made any use of the quarto, it is not improbable that he drew from the earlier drama.*

It is impossible to say what use Shakespeare made of this old English play (we do not believe that it was a youthful production of his own), as it seems to be hopelessly lost, and we cannot guess how much of it, if anything, survives in diluted form in the German play just mentioned. Of another source from which he probably derived his material we have better knowledge: namely, *The Hystorie of Hamblet*, translated from the *Histoires Tragiques* of Francis de Belleforest. The story of Hamlet is found in the fifth volume, which was printed at Paris in 1570. The English version was probably made soon after, though the only edition now extant is that of 1608.†

The poet has followed the *Hystorie* in some of its main incidents—the murder of Hamlet's father by his uncle, the marriage of his mother with the murderer, his feigned madness, his killing of Polonius, his interview with his mother, his voyage to England, his return, and his revenge—but not

* For a translation of the German play and a discussion of its relations to the history of Shakespeare's *Hamlet*, see Furness, vol. ii. pp. 114–142.

† Reprinted (with the exception of the last two chapters, of which S. made no use) by Furness, vol. ii. pp. 91–113.

in the *dénouement.* In the *Hystorie* Hamlet, after his uncle's death, becomes king of Denmark, visits England again, marries two wives, by one of whom he is betrayed into the power of his maternal uncle Wiglerus, and is finally slain in battle.*

It may be added that Belleforest got the story from the *Historia Danica* of Saxo Grammaticus, written about the close of the 12th century, though the earliest existing edition of it is that of Paris, 1514.

## III. CRITICAL COMMENTS ON THE PLAY.

[*From Goethe's "Wilhelm Meister."*†]

I sought for every indication of what the character of Hamlet was before the death of his father; I took note of all that this interesting youth had been, independently of that sad event, independently of the subsequent terrible occurrences, and I imagined what he might have been without them.

Tender and nobly descended, this royal flower grew up under the direct influences of majesty; the idea of the right and of princely dignity, the feeling for the good and the graceful, with the consciousness of his high birth, were unfolded in him together. He was a prince, a born prince. Pleasing in figure, polished by nature, courteous from the heart, he was to be the model of youth and the delight of the world. . . .

Figure to yourself this youth, this son of princes, conceive him vividly, bring his condition before your eyes, and then observe him when he learns that his father's spirit walks; stand by him in the terrible night when the venerable Ghost itself appears before him. A horrid shudder seizes him; he speaks to the mysterious form; he sees it beckon him; he

* Elze (see Furness, vol. ii. p. 89) gives some very plausible reasons for supposing that the *Hystorie* is of later date than the old play of *Hamlet.*

† Carlyle's translation, as quoted with slight variations by Furness in his *Hamlet*, vol. ii. p. 272 fol.

follows it and hearkens. The fearful accusation of his uncle rings in his ears; the summons to revenge and the piercing reiterated prayer, "Remember me."

And when the Ghost has vanished, who is it we see standing before us? A young hero panting for vengeance? A born prince, feeling himself favoured in being summoned to punish the usurper of his crown? No! Amazement and sorrow overwhelm the solitary young man; he becomes bitter against smiling villains, swears never to forget the departed, and concludes with the significant ejaculation:

> "The time is out of joint; O cursed spite,
> That ever I was born to set it right!"

In these words, I imagine, is the key to Hamlet's whole procedure, and to me it is clear that Shakespeare sought to depict a great deed laid upon a soul unequal to the performance of it. In this view I find the piece composed throughout. Here is an oak-tree planted in a costly vase, which should have received into its bosom only lovely flowers; the roots spread out, the vase is shivered to pieces.

A beautiful, pure, and most moral nature, without the strength of nerve which makes the hero, sinks beneath a burden which it can neither bear nor throw off; every duty is holy to him,—this too hard. The impossible is required of him,—not the impossible in itself, but the impossible to him. How he winds, turns, agonizes, advances, and recoils, ever reminded, ever reminding himself, and at last almost loses his purpose from his thoughts, without ever again recovering his peace of mind. . . .

It pleases, it flatters us greatly, to see a hero who acts of himself, who loves and hates us as his heart prompts, undertaking and executing, thrusting aside all hindrances, and accomplishing a great purpose. Historians and poets would fain persuade us that so proud a lot may fall to man. In *Hamlet* we are taught otherwise; the hero has no plan, but the piece is full of plan. Here is no villain upon whom vengeance is inflicted according to a certain scheme, rigidly and in a peculiar manner carried out. No, a horrid deed occurs; it sweeps on in its consequences, dragging the guiltless along with it; the perpetrator appears as if he would avoid the abyss to which he is destined, and he plunges in just then when he thinks happily to fulfil his career. For it is the property of a deed of horror that the evil spreads out over the innocent, as it is of a good action to extend its benefits to the undeserving, while frequently the author of one or of the other is neither punished nor rewarded. Here in this play of ours, how strange! Purgatory sends its spirit, and demands revenge; in vain! Neither earthly nor infernal thing may bring about what is reserved for Fate alone. The hour of judgment comes. The bad falls with the good. One race is mowed away, and another springs up. . . .

Hamlet is endowed more properly with sentiment than with a character; it is events alone that push him on; and accordingly the piece has somewhat the amplification of a novel. But as it is Fate that draws the plan, as the piece proceeds from a deed of terror, and the hero is steadily driven on to a deed of terror, the work is tragic in its highest sense, and admits of no other than a tragic end.

[*From Schlegel's "Dramatic Literature."**]

*Hamlet* is singular in its kind: a tragedy of thought inspired by continual and never-satisfied meditation on human destiny and the dark perplexity of the events of this world, and calculated to call forth the very same meditation in the minds of the spectators. This enigmatical work resembles those irrational equations in which a fraction of unknown magnitude always remains, that will in no way admit of solution. Much has been said, much written, on this piece, and

* *Lectures on Dramatic Art and Literature*, by A. W. Schlegel; Black's translation, revised by Morrison (London: 1846), p. 404 fol.

yet no thinking man who anew expresses himself on it will (in his view of the connection and the signification of all the parts) entirely coincide with his predecessors. . . .

The only circumstance from which this piece might be judged to be less suited to the stage than other tragedies of Shakespeare is that in the last scenes the main action either stands still or appears to retrograde. This, however, was inevitable, and lay in the nature of the subject. The whole is intended to show that a calculating consideration, which exhausts all the relations and possible consequences of a deed, must cripple the power of acting; as Hamlet himself expresses it:

> "And thus the native hue of resolution
> Is sicklied o'er with the pale cast of thought;
> And enterprises of great pith and moment,
> With this regard, their currents turn awry,
> And lose the name of action."

With respect to Hamlet's character, I cannot, as I understand the poet's views, pronounce altogether so favourable a sentence upon it as Goethe does. He is, it is true, of a highly cultivated mind, a prince of royal manners, endowed with the finest sense of propriety, susceptible of noble ambition, and open in the highest degree to an enthusiastic admiration of that excellence in others of which he himself is deficient. He acts the part of madness with unrivalled power, convincing the persons who are sent to examine into his supposed loss of reason merely by telling them unwelcome truths and rallying them with the most caustic wit. But in the resolutions which he so often embraces and always leaves unexecuted, his weakness is too apparent: he does himself only justice when he implies that there is no greater dissimilarity than between himself and Hercules. He is not solely impelled by necessity to artifice and dissimulation: he has a natural inclination for crooked ways; he is a hypocrite towards himself; his far-fetched scruples are often mere pretexts to cover his want of determination: thoughts, as he says, on a different occasion, which have

> —— "but one part wisdom
> And ever three parts coward."

He has been chiefly condemned both for his harshness in repulsing the love of Ophelia, which he himself had cherished, and for his insensibility at her death. But he is too much overwhelmed with his own sorrow to have any compassion to spare for others; besides, his outward indifference gives us by no means the measure of his internal perturbation. On the other hand, we evidently perceive in him a malicious joy, when he has succeeded in getting rid of his enemies, more through necessity and accident, which alone are able to impel him to quick and decisive measures, than by the merit of his own courage, as he himself confesses after the murder of Polonius, and with respect to Rosencrantz and Guildenstern. Hamlet has no firm belief either in himself or in anything else: from expressions of religious confidence he passes over to sceptical doubts; he believes in the ghost of his father, as long as he sees it, but as soon as it has disappeared, it appears to him almost in the light of a deception. He has even gone so far as to say, "there is nothing either good or bad, but thinking makes it so;" with him the poet loses himself here in labyrinths of thought, in which neither end nor beginning is discoverable. The stars themselves, from the course of events, afford no answer to the question so urgently proposed to them. A voice from another world, commissioned, it would appear, by Heaven, demands vengeance for a monstrous enormity, and the demand remains without effect; the criminals are at last punished, but, as it were, by an accidental blow, and not in the solemn way requisite to convey to the world a warning example of justice; irresolute foresight, cunning treachery, and impetuous rage hurry on to a common destruction; the less guilty and the innocent are equally involved in the general ruin. The destiny of humanity is there exhibited as a gigantic Sphinx, which threatens to precipitate into the abyss of scepticism all who are unable to solve her dreadful enigmas.

[*From Coleridge's "Notes and Lectures upon Shakespeare."**]

I believe the character of Hamlet may be traced to Shakespeare's deep and accurate science in mental philosophy. Indeed, that this character must have some connection with the common fundamental laws of our nature may be assumed from the fact that Hamlet has been the darling of every country in which the literature of England has been fostered. In order to understand him, it is essential that we should reflect on the constitution of our own minds. Man is distinguished from the brute animals in proportion as thought prevails over sense: but in the healthy processes of the mind, a balance is constantly maintained between the impressions from outward objects and the inward operations of the intellect:—for if there be an overbalance in the contemplative faculty, man thereby becomes the creature of mere meditation, and loses his natural power of action. Now one of Shakespeare's modes of creating characters is, to conceive any one intellectual or moral faculty in morbid excess, and then to place himself, Shakespeare, thus mutilated or diseased, under given circumstances. In Hamlet he seems to have wished to exemplify the moral necessity of a due balance between our attention to the objects of our senses, and our meditation on the workings of our minds,—an *equilibrium* between the real and the imaginary worlds. In Hamlet this balance is disturbed: his thoughts, and the images of his fancy, are far more vivid than his actual perceptions, and his very perceptions, instantly passing through the *medium* of his contemplations, acquire, as they pass, a form and a color not naturally their own. Hence we see a great, an almost

* Coleridge's Works (Harper's ed.), vol. iv. p. 145 fol.

enormous, intellectual activity, and a proportionate aversion to real action, consequent upon it, with all its symptoms and accompanying qualities. This character Shakespeare places in circumstances under which it is obliged to act on the spur of the moment:—Hamlet is brave and careless of death: but he vacillates from sensibility, and procrastinates from thought, and loses the power of action in the energy of resolve. Thus it is that this tragedy presents a direct contrast to that of Macbeth; the one proceeds with the utmost slowness, the other with a crowded and breathless rapidity.

The effect of this overbalance of the imaginative power is beautifully illustrated in the everlasting broodings and superfluous activities of Hamlet's mind, which, unseated from its healthy relation, is constantly occupied with the world within, and abstracted from the world without,—giving substance to shadows, and throwing a mist over all commonplace actualities. It is the nature of thought to be indefinite;—definiteness belongs to external imagery alone. Hence it is that the sense of sublimity arises, not from the sight of an outward object, but from the beholder's reflection upon it;—not from the sensuous impression, but from the imaginative reflex. Few have seen a celebrated waterfall without feeling something akin to disappointment: it is only subsequently that the image comes back full into the mind, and brings with it a train of grand or beautiful associations. Hamlet feels this; his senses are in a state of trance, and he looks upon external things as hieroglyphics. His soliloquy—

> "Oh that this too, too solid flesh would melt," etc.,

springs from that craving after the indefinite—for that which is not—which most easily besets men of genius; and the self-delusion common to this temper of mind is finely exemplified in the character which Hamlet gives of himself:—

> "It cannot be
> But I am pigeon-liver'd, and lack gall
> To make oppression bitter."

He mistakes the seeing his chains for the breaking of them, delays action till action is of no use, and dies the victim of mere circumstance and accident.

[*From* "*Letters on Shakespeare*," *Blackwood's Magazine*, *Feb.* 1818.*]

There is in the ebb and flow of Shakespeare's soul all the grandeur of a mighty operation of nature; and when we think or speak of him, it should be with humility where we do not understand, and a conviction that it is rather to the narrowness of our own ken than to any failing in the art of the great magician, that we ought to attribute any sense of imperfection and of weakness which may assail us during the contemplation of his created worlds. . . .

Shakespeare himself, had he even been as great a critic as a poet, could not have written a regular dissertation upon Hamlet. So ideal, and yet so real an existence could have been shadowed out only in the colours of poetry. When a character deals solely or chiefly with this world and its events, when it acts and is acted upon by objects that have a palpable existence, we see it distinctly, as if it were cast in a material mould, as if it partoök of the fixed and settled lineaments of the things on which it lavishes its sensibilities and its passions. We see in such cases the vision of an individual soul, as we see the vision of an individual countenance. We can describe both, and can let a stranger into our knowledge. But how tell in words, so pure, so fine, so ideal an abstraction as Hamlet? We can, indeed, figure to ourselves generally his princely form, that outshone all others in manly beauty, and adorn it with the consummation of

* These "Letters on Shakespeare" are signed "T. C.." and are probably, as Furness surmises, by the poet Campbell.

all liberal accomplishment. We can behold in every look, every gesture, every motion, the future king,—

> "The courtier's, soldier's, scholar's eye, tongue, sword,
> Th' expectancy and rose of the fair state;
> The glass of fashion, and the mould of form,
> Th' observ'd of all observers."

But when we would penetrate into his spirit, meditate on those things on which he meditates, accompany him even unto the brink of eternity, fluctuate with him on the ghastly sea of despair, soar with him into the purest and serenest regions of human thought, feel with him the curse of beholding iniquity, and the troubled delight of thinking on innocence, and gentleness, and beauty; come with him from all the glorious dreams cherished by a noble spirit in the halls of wisdom and philosophy, of a sudden into the gloomy courts of sin, and incest, and murder; shudder with him over the broken and shattered fragments of all the fairest creations of his fancy,—be borne with him at once, from calm, and lofty, and delighted speculations, into the very heart of fear, and horror, and tribulations—have the agonies and the guilt of our mortal world brought into immediate contact with the world beyond the grave, and the influence of an awful shadow hanging forever on our thoughts,—be present at a fearful combat between all the stirred-up passions of humanity in the soul of one man, a combat in which one and all of these passions are alternately victorious and overcome; I say, that when we are thus placed and acted upon, how is it possible to draw a character of this sublime drama, or of the mysterious being who is its moving spirit? In him, his character and his situation, there is a concentration of all the interests that belong to humanity. There is scarcely a trait of frailty or of grandeur, which may have endeared to us our most beloved friends in real life, that is not to be found in Hamlet. Undoubtedly Shakespeare loved him beyond all his other creations. Soon as he appears on the stage we are satisfied; when absent we long for his return. This is the only play which exists almost altogether in the character of one single person. Who ever knew a Hamlet in real life? yet who, ideal as the character is, feels not its reality? This is the wonder. We love him not, we think of him not, because he was witty, because he was melancholy, because he was filial; but we love him because he existed, and was himself. This is the sum total of the impression. I believe that, of every other character, either in tragic or epic poetry, the story makes part of the conception; but of Hamlet, the deep and permanent interest is the conception of himself. This seems to belong, not to the character being more perfectly drawn, but to there being a more intense conception of individual human life than perhaps in any other human composition; that is, a being with springs of thought, and feeling, and action, deeper than we can search. These springs rise from an unknown depth, and in that depth there seems to be a oneness of being which we cannot distinctly behold, but which we believe to be there; and thus irreconcilable circumstances, floating on the surface of his actions, have not the effect of making us doubt the truth of the general picture.

[*From Mrs. Jameson's "Characteristics of Women."**]

Ophelia—poor Ophelia! Oh, far too soft, too good, too fair to be cast among the briers of this working-day world, and fall and bleed upon the thorns of life! What shall be said of her? for eloquence is mute before her! Like a strain of sad, sweet music which comes floating by us on the wings of night and silence, and which we rather feel than hear—like the exhalation of the violet dying even upon the sense it charms—like the snow-flake dissolved in air before it has caught a stain of earth—like the light surf severed from the

* American ed. (Boston, 1857), p. 189 fol.

billow, which a breath disperses—such is the character of Ophelia: so exquisitely delicate, it seems as if a touch would profane it; so sanctified in our thoughts by the last and worst of human woes, that we scarcely dare to consider it too deeply. The love of Ophelia, which she never once confesses, is like a secret which we have stolen from her, and which ought to die upon our hearts as upon her own. Her sorrows ask not words, but tears; and her madness has precisely the same effect that would be produced by the spectacle of real insanity, if brought before us: we feel inclined to turn away, and veil our eyes in reverential pity and too painful sympathy.

Beyond every character that Shakespeare has drawn (Hamlet alone excepted), that of Ophelia makes us forget the poet in his own creation. Whenever we bring her to mind, it is with the same exclusive sense of her real existence, without reference to the wondrous power which called her into life. The effect (and what an effect!) is produced by means so simple, by strokes so few and so unobtrusive, that we take no thought of them. It is so purely natural and unsophisticated, yet so profound in its pathos, that, as Hazlitt observes, it takes us back to the old ballads; we forget that, in its perfect artlessness, it is the supreme and consummate triumph of art.

The situation of Ophelia in the story is that of a young girl who, at an early age, is brought from a life of privacy into the circle of a court—a court such as we read of in those early times, at once rude, magnificent, and corrupted. She is placed immediately about the person of the queen, and is apparently her favourite attendant. The affection of the wicked queen for this gentle and innocent creature is one of those beautiful redeeming touches, one of those penetrating glances into the secret springs of natural and feminine feeling which we find only in Shakespeare. Gertrude, who is not so wholly abandoned but that there remains within her heart some sense of the virtue she has forfeited, seems to look with a kind yet melancholy complacency on the lovely being she has destined for the bride of her son; and the scene in which she is introduced as scattering flowers on the grave of Ophelia is one of those effects of contrast in poetry, in character, and in feeling, at once natural and unexpected; which fill the eye, and make the heart swell and tremble within itself—like the nightingales singing in the grove of the Furies in Sophocles.*

It is the helplessness of Ophelia, arising merely from her innocence, and pictured without any indication of weakness, which melts us with such profound pity. She is so young, that neither her mind nor her person has attained maturity; she is not aware of the nature of her own feelings; they are prematurely developed in their full force before she has strength to bear them; and love and grief together rend and shatter the frail texture of her existence, like the burning fluid poured into a crystal vase. She says very little, and what she does say seems rather intended to hide than to reveal the emotions of her heart; yet in those few words we are made as perfectly acquainted with her character, and with what is passing in her mind, as if she had thrown forth her soul with all the glowing eloquence of Juliet. Passion with Juliet seems innate, a part of her being, "as dwells the gathered lightning in the cloud;" and we never fancy her but with the dark, splendid eyes and Titian-like complexion of the South. While in Ophelia we recognize as distinctly the pensive, fair-haired, blue-eyed daughter of the North, whose heart seems to vibrate to the passion she has inspired, more conscious of being loved than of loving; and yet, alas! loving in the silent depths of her young heart far more than she is loved.

When her brother warns her against Hamlet's importunities—

* In the Œdipus Coloneus.

"For Hamlet and the trifling of his favour,
Hold it a fashion and a toy in blood,
A violet in the youth of primy nature,
Forward, not permanent, sweet, not lasting,
The perfume and suppliance of a minute—
No more!"

she replies with a kind of half consciousness—

"No more but so?
*Laertes.* Think it no more."

He concludes his admonition with that most beautiful passage, in which the soundest sense, the most excellent advice, is conveyed in a strain of the most exquisite poetry:

"The chariest maid is prodigal enough.
If she unmask her beauty to the moon;
Virtue itself scapes not calumnious strokes.
The canker galls the infants of the spring,
Too oft before their buttons be disclos'd;
And in the morn and liquid dew of youth
Contagious blastments are most imminent."

When her father, immediately afterwards, catechises her on the same subject, he extorts from her, in short sentences, uttered with bashful reluctance, the confession of Hamlet's love for her, but not a word of her love for him. The whole scene is managed with inexpressible delicacy: it is one of those instances, common in Shakespeare, in which we are allowed to perceive what is passing in the mind of a person without any consciousness on his part. Only Ophelia herself is unaware that while she is admitting the extent of Hamlet's courtship, she is also betraying how deep is the impression it has made, how entire the love with which it is returned. . . .

We do not see him as a lover, nor as Ophelia first beheld him; for the days when he importuned her with love were before the opening of the drama—before his father's spirit revisited the earth; but we behold him at once in a sea of troubles, of perplexities, of agonies, of terrors. Without remorse, he endures all its horrors; without guilt, he endures all its shame. A loathing of the crime he is called on to revenge, which revenge is again abhorrent to his nature, has set him at strife with himself; the supernatural visitation has perturbed his soul to its inmost depths; all things else, all interests, all hopes, all affections, appear as futile, when the majestic shadow comes lamenting from its place of torment "to shake him with thoughts beyond the reaches of his soul!" His love for Ophelia is then ranked by himself among those trivial, fond records which he has deeply sworn to erase from his heart and brain. He has no thought to link his terrible destiny with hers: he cannot marry her: he cannot reveal to her, young, gentle, innocent as she is, the terrific influences which have changed the whole current of his life and purposes. In his distraction he overacts the painful part to which he had tasked himself; he is like that judge of the Areopagus who, being occupied with graver matters, flung from him the little bird which had sought refuge in his bosom, and with such angry violence that unwittingly he killed it.

In the scene with Hamlet (iii. 1), in which he madly outrages her and upbraids himself, Ophelia says very little: there are two short sentences in which she replies to his wild, abrupt discourse:

"*Hamlet.* I did love you once.
"*Ophelia.* Indeed, my lord, you made me believe so.
"*Hamlet.* You should not have believed me; for virtue cannot so inoculate our old stock, but we shall relish of it. I loved you not.
"*Ophelia.* I was the more deceiv'd."

Those who ever heard Mrs. Siddons read the play of *Hamlet* cannot forget the world of meaning, of love, of sorrow, of despair conveyed in these two simple phrases. Here, and in the soliloquy afterwards, where she says—

"And I of ladies most deject and wretched,
That suck'd the honey of his music vows,"

are the only allusions to herself and her own feelings in the course of the play; and these, uttered almost without consciousness on her own part, contain the revelation of a life of love, and disclose the secret burden of a heart bursting with its own unuttered grief. She believes Hamlet crazed; she is repulsed, she is forsaken, she is outraged, where she had bestowed her young heart, with all its hopes and wishes; her father is slain by the hand of her lover, as it is supposed, in a paroxysm of insanity: she is entangled inextricably in a web of horrors which she cannot even comprehend, and the result seems inevitable.

Of her subsequent madness, what can be said? What an affecting—what an astonishing picture of a mind utterly, hopelessly wrecked!—past hope—past cure! There is the frenzy of excited passion—there is the madness caused by intense and continued thought—there is the delirium of fevered nerves; but Ophelia's madness is distinct from these: it is not the suspension, but the utter destruction of the reasoning powers; it is the total imbecility which, as medical people well know, frequently follows some terrible shock to the spirits. Constance is frantic; Lear is mad; Ophelia is *insane*. Her sweet mind lies in fragments before us—a pitiful spectacle! Her wild, rambling fancies; her aimless, broken speeches; her quick transitions from gayety to sadness—each equally purposeless and causeless; her snatches of old ballads, such as perhaps her nurse sung her to sleep with in her infancy—are all so true to the life that we forget to wonder, and can only weep. It belonged to Shakespeare alone so to temper such a picture that we can endure to dwell upon it:

"Thought and affliction, passion, hell itself,
She turns to favour and to prettiness."

[*From the London "Quarterly Review."**]

The universality of Shakespeare's genius is in some sort reflected in Hamlet. He has a mind wise and witty, abstract and practical; the utmost reach of philosophical contemplation is mingled with the most penetrating sagacity in the affairs of life; playful jest, biting satire, sparkling repartee, with the darkest and deepest thoughts that can agitate man. He exercises all his various faculties with surprising readiness. He passes without an effort "from grave to gay, from lively to severe,"—from his every-day character to personated lunacy. He divines, with the rapidity of lightning, the nature and motives of those who are brought into contact with him, fits in a moment his bearing and retorts to their individual peculiarities; is equally at home whether he is mocking Polonius with hidden raillery, or dissipating Ophelia's dream of love, or crushing the sponges with sarcasm and invective, or talking euphuism with Osric, and satirizing while he talks it; whether he is uttering wise maxims, or welcoming the players with facetious graciousness—probing the inmost souls of others, or sounding the mysteries of his own. His philosophy stands out conspicuous among the brilliant faculties which contend for the mastery. It is the quality which gives weight and dignity to the rest. It intermingles with all his actions. He traces the most trifling incidents up to their general laws. His natural disposition is to lose himself in contemplation. He goes thinking out of the world. The commonest ideas that pass through his mind are invested with a wonderful freshness and originality. His meditations in the church-yard are on the trite notion that all ambition leads but to the grave. But what condensation, what variety, what picturesqueness, what intense unmitigated gloom! It is the finest sermon that was ever preached against the vanities of life.

* Vol. lxxix. (1847), p. 333 fol.

So far, we imagine, all are agreed. But the motives which induce Hamlet to defer his revenge are still, and perhaps will ever remain, debatable ground. The favourite doctrine of late is, that the thinking part of Hamlet predominated over the active—that he was as weak and vacillating in performance as he was great in speculation. If this theory were borne out by his general conduct, it would no doubt amply account for his procrastination; but there is nothing to countenance and much to refute the idea. Shakespeare has endowed him with a vast energy of will. There could be no sterner resolve than to abandon every purpose of existence that he might devote himself unfettered to his revenge; nor was ever resolution better observed. He breaks through his passion for Ophelia, and keeps it down, under the most trying circumstances, with such inflexible firmness that an eloquent critic has seriously questioned whether his attachment was real. The determination of his character appears again at the death of Polonius. An indecisive mind would have been shocked, if not terrified, at the deed. Hamlet dismisses him with a few contemptuous words as a man would brush away a fly. He talks with even greater indifference of Rosencrantz and Guildenstern, whom he sends "to sudden death, not shriving-time allowed." He has on these, and, indeed, on all occasions, a short and absolute way which only belongs to resolute souls. The features developed in his very hesitation to kill the King are inconsistent with the notion that his hand refuses to perform what his head contrives. He is always trying to persuade himself into a conviction that it is his duty, instead of seeking for evasions.* He is

* His reasons for not killing the King when he is praying have been held to be an excuse. But if Shakespeare had anticipated the criticism, he could not have guarded against it more effectually. Hamlet has just uttered the soliloquy—

"Now could I drink hot blood,
And do such bitter business as the day
Would quake to look on."

seized with a savage joy when the play supplies him with indubitable proof of his uncle's guilt. His language then to Horatio is—

> "Is 't not perfect conscience
> To quit him with this arm?"

He wants, it is clear, neither will nor nerve to strike the blow. There is perhaps one supposition that will satisfy all the phenomena, and it has, to us, the recommendation that we think it is the solution suggested by Shakespeare himself. Hamlet, in a soliloquy, charges the delay on—

> "Bestial oblivion, or some craven scruple
> Of thinking too precisely on th' event."

The oblivion is merely the effect of the primary cause—"the craven scruple"—the conscience which renders him a coward. His uncle, after all, is king; he is the brother of his father, and the husband of his mother, and it was inevitable that he should shrink, in his cooler moments, from becoming his assassin. His hatred to his uncle, who has disgraced his family and disappointed his ambition, gives him personal inducements to revenge, which further blunt his purpose by leading him to doubt the purity of his motives. The admonition of the Ghost to him is, not to taint his mind in the prosecution of his end; and no sooner has the Ghost vanished than Hamlet, invoking the aid of supernatural powers, exclaims—

> "O all you host of heaven! O earth! What else?
> And shall I couple hell?—O fie!"

In this frame he passes his uncle's closet, and is for once, at least, equal to any emergency. His first thought is to kill him at his devotions; his second, that in that case Claudius will go to heaven. Instantly his father's sufferings rise into his mind; he contrasts the happy future of the criminal with the purgatory of the victim, and the contemplation exasperates him into a genuine desire for a fuller revenge. The threat relieves him from the reproach of inactivity, and he falls back into his former self.

But the hell, whose support he rejects, is forever returning to his mind and startling his conscience. It is this that makes him wish for the confirmation of the play, for evil spirits may have abused him. It is this which begets the apathy he terms oblivion, for inaction affords relief to doubt. It is this which produces his inconsistencies, for conscience calls him different ways, and when he obeys in one direction he is haunted by the feeling that he should have gone in the other. If he contemplated the performance of a deed which looks outwardly more like murder than judicial retribution, he trembles lest, after all, he should be perpetrating an unnatural crime; or if, on the other hand, he turns to view his uncle's misdeeds, he fancies there is more of cowardly scrupulosity than justice in his backwardness, and he abounds in self-reproaches at the weakness of his hesitation. And thus he might forever have halted between two opinions, if the King himself, by filling up the measure of his iniquities, had not swept away his scruples.

[*From Dowden's "Shakspere."**]

When *Hamlet* was written, Shakspere had passed through his years of apprenticeship, and become a master-dramatist. In point of style the play stands midway between his early and his latest works. The studious superintendence of the poet over the development of his thought and imaginings, very apparent in Shakspere's early writings, now conceals itself; but the action of imagination and thought has not yet become embarrassing in its swiftness and multiplicity of direction.† Rapid dialogue in verse, admirable for its

* *Shakspere: a Critical Study of his Mind and Art,* by Edward Dowden (2d ed. London, 1876), p. 125 fol.

† The characteristics of Shakspere's latest style are described by Mr. Spedding in the following masterly piece of criticism: "The opening of [*Henry VIII.*] . . . seemed to have the full stamp of Shakspere, in his latest manner: the same life, and reality, and freshness; the same

combination of verisimilitude with artistic metrical effects, occurs in the scene in which Hamlet questions his friends respecting the appearance of the ghost (i. 2); the soliloquies of Hamlet are excellent examples of the slow, dwelling verse which Shakspere appropriates to the utterance of thought in solitude; and nowhere did Shakspere write a nobler piece of prose than the speech in which Hamlet describes to Rosencrantz and Guildenstern his melancholy. But such particulars as these do not constitute the chief evidence which proves that the poet had now attained maturity. The mystery, the baffling, vital obscurity of the play, and in particular of the character of its chief person, make it evident that Shakspere had left far behind him that early stage of development when an artist obtrudes his intentions, or, distrusting his own ability to keep sight of one uniform design, deliberately and with effort holds that design persistently before him. When Shakspere completed *Hamlet*, he must have trusted himself and trusted his audience; he trusts himself to enter into relation with his subject, highly complex as that subject was, in a pure, emotional manner. *Hamlet* might so easily have been manufactured into an enigma, or a puzzle; and then the puzzle, if sufficient pains were bestowed, could be completely taken to pieces and explained. But Shakspere created it a mystery, and therefore it is forever suggestive; forever suggestive, and never wholly explicable.

It must not be supposed, then, that any *idea*, any magic phrase, will solve the difficulties presented by the play, or

rapid and abrupt turns of thought, so quick that language can hardly follow fast enough; the same impatient activity of intellect and fancy, which, having once disclosed an idea, cannot wait to work it orderly out; the same daring confidence in the resources of language, which plunges headlong into a sentence without knowing how it is to come forth; the same careless metre, which disdains to produce its harmonious effects by the ordinary devices, yet is evidently subject to a master of harmony; the same entire freedom from book-language and commonplace."

suddenly illuminate everything in it which is obscure. The obscurity itself is a vital part of the work of art which deals not with a problem but with a life; and in that life, the history of a soul which moved through shadowy borderlands between the night and day, there is much (as in many a life that is real) to elude and baffle inquiry. It is a remarkable circumstance that while the length of the play in the second quarto considerably exceeds its length in the earlier form of 1603, and thus materials for the interpretation of Shakspere's purpose in the play are offered in greater abundance, the obscurity does not diminish, but, on the contrary, deepens, and if some questions appear to be solved, other questions in greater number spring into existence. . . .

Goethe, in the celebrated criticism upon this play in his *Wilhelm Meister*, has only offered a half interpretation of its difficulties; and subsequent criticism, under the influence of Goethe, has exhibited a tendency too exclusively subjective. "To me," wrote Goethe, "it is clear that Shakspere meant . . . to represent the effects of a great action laid upon a soul unfit for the performance of it," etc. [see p. 15 above].

This is one half of the truth; but only one half. In several of the tragedies of Shakspere the tragic disturbance of character and life is caused by the subjection of the chief person of the drama to some dominant passion essentially antipathetic to his nature, though proceeding from some inherent weakness or imperfection,—a passion from which the victim cannot deliver himself, and which finally works out his destruction. Thus Othello, whose nature is instinctively trustful, and confiding with a noble childlike trust, a man

> "Of a free and open nature
> That thinks men honest that but seem so,"

a man "not easily jealous"—Othello is inoculated with the poison of jealousy and suspicion, and the poison maddens and destroys him. Macbeth, made for subordination, is the victim of a terrible and unnatural ambition. Lear, ignorant of true love, yet with a supreme need of loving and being loved, is compelled to hatred, and drives from his presence the one being who could have satisfied the hunger of his heart. . . . We may reasonably conjecture that the Hamlet of the old play—a play at least as old as that group of bloody tragedies inspired by the earlier works of Marlowe—was actually what Shakspere's Hamlet, with a bitter pleasure in misrepresenting his own nature, describes himself as being, "very proud, revengeful, ambitious." . . . But Shakspere, in accordance with his dramatic method, and his interest as artist in complex rather than simple phenomena of human passion and experience, when re-creating the character of the Danish Prince, fashions him as a man to whom persistent action, and in an especial degree the duty of deliberate revenge, is peculiarly antipathetic. Under the pitiless burden imposed upon him Hamlet trembles, totters, falls. Thus far Goethe is right.

But the tragic *nodus* in Shakspere's first tragedy—*Romeo and Juliet*—was not wholly of a subjective character. The two lovers are in harmony with one another, and with the purest and highest impulses of their own hearts. The discord comes from the outer world; they are a pair of "star-crossed lovers." . . . The world fought against Romeo and Juliet, and they fell in the unequal strife. Now Goethe failed to observe, or did not observe sufficiently, that this is also the case with Hamlet:

> "The time is out of joint; O cursed spite,
> That ever I was born to set it right!"

Hamlet is called upon to assert moral order in a world of moral confusion and obscurity. . . . All the strength which he possesses would have become organized and available had his world been one of honesty, of happiness, of human love. But a world of deceit, of espionage, of selfishness, surrounds him; his idealism, at thirty years of age, almost takes the form of pessimism; his life and his heart become sterile; he loses the energy which sound and joyous feeling supplies; and in the wide-spreading waste of corruption which lies around him, he is tempted to understand and detest things rather than accomplish some limited practical service. . . .

If Goethe's study of the play, admirable as it was, misled criticism in one way by directing attention too exclusively upon the inner nature of Hamlet, the studies by Schlegel and by Coleridge tended to mislead criticism in another by attaching an exaggerated importance to one element of Hamlet's character. "The whole," wrote Schlegel, "is intended to show that a calculating consideration, which exhausts all the relations and possible consequences of a deed, must cripple the power of acting." It is true that Hamlet's power of acting was crippled by his habit of "thinking too precisely on the event;" and it is true, as Coleridge said, that in Hamlet we see "a great, an almost enormous intellectual activity, and a proportionate aversion to real action consequent upon it." But Hamlet is not merely or chiefly intellectual; the emotional side of his character is quite as important as the intellectual; his malady is as deep-seated in his sensibilities and in his heart as it is in the brain. If all his feelings translate themselves into thoughts, it is no less true that all his thoughts are impregnated with feeling. To represent Hamlet as a man of preponderating power of reflection, and to disregard his craving, sensitive heart, is to make the whole play incoherent and unintelligible.

It is Hamlet's intellect, however, together with his deep and abiding sense of the moral qualities of things, which distinguishes him, upon the glance of a moment, from the hero of Shakspere's first tragedy, Romeo. If Romeo fail to retain a sense of fact and of the real world because the fact, as it were, melts away and disappears in a solvent of delicious emotion, Hamlet equally loses a sense of fact because with him each object and event transforms and expands itself into an idea. When the play opens he has reached the age of thirty years—the age, it has been said, when the ideality of youth ought to become one with and inform the practical tendencies of manhood—and he has received culture of every kind except the culture of active life. During the reign of the strong-willed elder Hamlet there was no call to action for his meditative son. He has slipped on into years of full manhood still a haunter of the university, a student of philosophies, an amateur in art, a ponderer on the things of life and death, who has never formed a resolution or executed a deed.

This long course of thinking, apart from action, has destroyed Hamlet's very capacity for belief; since in belief there exists a certain element contributed by the will. Hamlet cannot adjust the infinite part of him to the finite; the one invades the other and infects it; or rather the finite dislimns and dissolves, and leaves him only the presence of the idea. He cannot make real to himself the actual world, even while he supposes himself a materialist; he cannot steadily keep alive within himself a sense of the importance of any positive, limited thing,—a deed, for example. Things in their actual, phenomenal aspect flit before him as transitory, accidental, and unreal. And the absolute truth of things is so hard to attain, and only, if at all, is to be attained in the *mind.* Accordingly Hamlet can lay hold of nothing with calm, resolved energy; he cannot even retain a thought in indefeasible possession. Thus all through the play he wavers between materialism and spiritualism, between belief in immortality and disbelief, between reliance upon Providence and a bowing under fate. . . .

Yet it has been truly said that only one who feels Hamlet's strength should venture to speak of Hamlet's weakness. That in spite of difficulties without, and inward difficulties, he still clings to his terrible duty—letting it go indeed for a time, but returning to it again, and in the end accomplishing it—implies strength. He is not incapable of vigorous action,—if only he be allowed no chance of thinking the fact away into an idea. He is the first to board the pirate; he stabs Polonius through the arras; he suddenly alters the sealed commission, and sends his schoolfellows to the English headsman; he finally executes justice upon the king. But all his action is sudden and fragmentary; it is not continuous and coherent. . . .

Does Hamlet finally attain deliverance from his disease of will? Shakspere has left the answer to that question doubtful. Probably if anything could supply the link which was wanting between the purpose and the deed, it was the achievement of some supreme action. The last moments of Hamlet's life are well spent, and for energy and foresight are the noblest moments of his existence: he snatches the poisoned bowl from Horatio, and saves his friend; he gives his dying voice for Fortinbras, and saves his country. The rest is silence:—

> "Had I but time—as this fell sergeant, death,
> Is strict in his arrest—O, I could tell you!"

But he has not told. Let us not too readily assume that we "know the stops" of Hamlet, that we can "pluck out the heart of his mystery."

One thing, however, we *do* know—that the man who wrote the play of *Hamlet* had obtained a thorough comprehension of Hamlet's malady. And assured, as we are by abundant evidence, that Shakspere transformed with energetic will his knowledge into fact, we may be confident that when *Hamlet* was written Shakspere had gained a further stage in his culture of self-control, and that he had become not only adult as an author, but had entered upon the full maturity of his manhood.

# HAMLET, PRINCE OF DENMARK.

## *DRAMATIS PERSONÆ.*

CLAUDIUS, king of Denmark.
HAMLET, son to the late, and nephew to the present king.
POLONIUS, lord chamberlain.
HORATIO, friend to Hamlet.
LAERTES, son to Polonius.

VOLTIMAND,
CORNELIUS,
ROSENCRANTZ,
GUILDENSTERN,
OSRIC,
A Gentleman, } courtiers.

A Priest.

MARCELLUS,
BERNARDO, } officers.

FRANCISCO, a soldier.
REYNALDO, servant to Polonius.
Players.
Two Clowns, grave-diggers.
FORTINBRAS, prince of Norway.
A Captain.
English Ambassadors.

GERTRUDE, queen of Denmark, and mother to Hamlet.
OPHELIA, daughter to Polonius.

Lords, Ladies, Officers, Soldiers, Sailors, Messengers, and other Attendants.

Ghost of Hamlet's father.

SCENE : *Elsinore.*

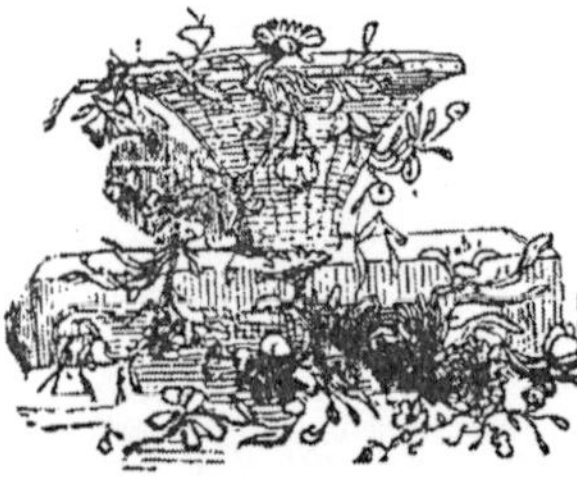

THE PLATFORM AT ELSINORE.

# ACT I.

## SCENE I. *Elsinore. A Platform before the Castle.*

FRANCISCO *at his post. Enter to him* BERNARDO.

*Bernardo.* Who 's there?
*Francisco.* Nay, answer me; stand, and unfold yourself.
*Bernardo.* Long live the king!
*Francisco.* Bernardo?

*Bernardo.* He.

*Francisco.* You come most carefully upon your hour.

*Bernardo.* 'T is now struck twelve; get thee to bed, Francisco.

*Francisco.* For this relief much thanks; 't is bitter cold,
And I am sick at heart.

*Bernardo.* Have you had quiet guard?

*Francisco.* Not a mouse stirring.

*Bernardo.* Well, good night.
If you do meet Horatio and Marcellus,
The rivals of my watch, bid them make haste.

*Francisco.* I think I hear them.—Stand, ho! Who is there?

*Enter* HORATIO *and* MARCELLUS.

*Horatio.* Friends to this ground.

*Marcellus.* And liegemen to the Dane.

*Francisco.* Give you good night.

*Marcellus.* O, farewell, honest soldier:
Who hath reliev'd you?

*Francisco.* Bernardo has my place.
Give you good night. [*Exit.*

*Marcellus.* Holla! Bernardo!

*Bernardo.* Say,—
What, is Horatio there?

*Horatio.* A piece of him.

*Bernardo.* Welcome, Horatio; welcome, good Marcellus.

*Marcellus.* What, has this thing appear'd again to-night?

*Bernardo.* I have seen nothing.

*Marcellus.* Horatio says 't is but our fantasy,
And will not let belief take hold of him
Touching this dreaded sight, twice seen of us;
Therefore I have entreated him along
With us to watch the minutes of this night,
That if again this apparition come,
He may approve our eyes and speak to it.

*Horatio.* Tush, tush, 't will not appear.
*Bernardo.* Sit down awhile;
And let us once again assail your ears,
That are so fortified against our story,
What we two nights have seen.
*Horatio.* Well, sit we down,
And let us hear Bernardo speak of this.
*Bernardo.* Last night of all,
When yond same star that 's westward from the pole
Had made his course to illume that part of heaven
Where now it burns, Marcellus and myself,
The bell then beating one,—

*Enter* GHOST.

*Marcellus.* Peace, break thee off; look, where it comes again!
*Bernardo.* In the same figure, like the king that 's dead.
*Marcellus.* Thou art a scholar; speak to it, Horatio.
*Bernardo.* Looks it not like the king? mark it, Horatio.
*Horatio.* Most like; it harrows me with fear and wonder.
*Bernardo.* It would be spoke to.
*Marcellus.* Question it, Horatio.
*Horatio.* What art thou that usurp'st this time of night,
Together with that fair and warlike form
In which the majesty of buried Denmark
Did sometimes march? by heaven I charge thee, speak!
*Marcellus.* It is offended.
*Bernardo.* See, it stalks away!
*Horatio.* Stay! speak, speak! I charge thee, speak!
[*Exit Ghost.*
*Marcellus.* 'T is gone, and will not answer.
*Bernardo.* How now, Horatio! you tremble and look pale;
Is not this something more than fantasy?
What think you on 't?
*Horatio.* Before my God, I might not this believe

Without the sensible and true avouch
Of mine own eyes.
*Marcellus.* Is it not like the king?
*Horatio.* As thou art to thyself:
Such was the very armour he had on
When he the ambitious Norway combated;
So frown'd he once, when, in an angry parle,
He smote the sledded Polacks on the ice.
'T is strange.
*Marcellus.* Thus twice before, and jump at this dead hour,
With martial stalk hath he gone by our watch.
*Horatio.* In what particular thought to work I know not;
But in the gross and scope of my opinion,
This bodes some strange eruption to our state.
*Marcellus.* Good now, sit down, and tell me, he that knows,
Why this same strict and most observant watch
So nightly toils the subject of the land,
And why such daily cast of brazen cannon,
And foreign mart for implements of war;
Why such impress of shipwrights, whose sore task
Does not divide the Sunday from the week;
What might be toward, that this sweaty haste
Doth make the night joint-labourer with the day:
Who is 't that can inform me?
*Horatio.* That can I;
At least, the whisper goes so. Our last king,
Whose image even but now appear'd to us,
Was, as you know, by Fortinbras of Norway,
Thereto prick'd on by a most emulate pride,
Dar'd to the combat; in which our valiant Hamlet—
For so this side of our known world esteem'd him—
Did slay this Fortinbras; who, by a seal'd compact,
Well ratified by law and heraldry,
Did forfeit, with his life, all those his lands
Which he stood seiz'd of, to the conqueror:

Against the which a moiety competent
Was gaged by our king; which had return'd
To the inheritance of Fortinbras,
Had he been vanquisher; as, by the same covenant
And carriage of the article design'd,
His fell to Hamlet. Now, sir, young Fortinbras,
Of unimproved mettle hot and full,
Hath in the skirts of Norway here and there
Shark'd up a list of lawless resolutes,
For food and diet, to some enterprise
That hath a stomach in 't; which is no other—
As it doth well appear unto our state—
But to recover of us, by strong hand
And terms compulsative, those foresaid lands
So by his father lost: and this, I take it,
Is the main motive of our preparations,
The source of this our watch, and the chief head
Of this post-haste and romage in the land.

*Bernardo.* I think it be no other but e'en so.
Well may it sort that this portentous figure
Comes armed through our watch, so like the king
That was and is the question of these wars.

*Horatio.* A mote it is to trouble the mind's eye.
In the most high and palmy state of Rome,
A little ere the mightiest Julius fell,
The graves stood tenantless, and the sheeted dead
Did squeak and gibber in the Roman streets:
As stars with trains of fire and dews of blood,
Disasters in the sun; and the moist star
Upon whose influence Neptune's empire stands
Was sick almost to doomsday with eclipse:
And even the like precurse of fierce events,
As harbingers preceding still the fates
And prologue to the omen coming on,
Have heaven and earth together demonstrated

Unto our climatures and countrymen.—
But soft, behold! lo, where it comes again!

*Re-enter* GHOST.

I 'll cross it, though it blast me.—Stay, illusion!
If thou hast any sound, or use of voice,
Speak to me;
If there be any good thing to be done,
That may to thee do ease and grace to me,
Speak to me;
If thou art privy to thy country's fate,
Which, happily, foreknowing may avoid,
O, speak!
Or if thou hast uphoarded in thy life
Extorted treasure in the womb of earth,
For which, they say, you spirits oft walk in death,
[*The cock crows.*
Speak of it; stay, and speak!—Stop it, Marcellus.

*Marcellus.* Shall I strike at it with my partisan?

*Horatio.* Do, if it will not stand.

*Bernardo.* 'T is here!

*Horatio.* 'T is here!

*Marcellus.* 'T is gone! [*Exit Ghost.*
We do it wrong, being so majestical,
To offer it the show of violence;
For it is, as the air, invulnerable,
And our vain blows malicious mockery.

*Bernardo.* It was about to speak, when the cock crew.

*Horatio.* And then it started like a guilty thing
Upon a fearful summons. I have heard,
The cock, that is the trumpet to the morn,
Doth with his lofty and shrill-sounding throat
Awake the god of day; and at his warning,
Whether in sea or fire, in earth or air,
The extravagant and erring spirit hies

To his confine: and of the truth herein
This present object made probation.
*Marcellus.* It faded on the crowing of the cock.
Some say that ever 'gainst that season comes
Wherein our Saviour's birth is celebrated,
The bird of dawning singeth all night long;
And then, they say, no spirit can walk abroad,
The nights are wholesome, then no planets strike,
No fairy takes, nor witch hath power to charm,
So hallow'd and so gracious is the time.
*Horatio.* So have I heard and do in part believe it.
But, look, the morn, in russet mantle clad,
Walks o'er the dew of yon high eastern hill.
Break we our watch up; and, by my advice,
Let us impart what we have seen to-night
Unto young Hamlet; for, upon my life,
This spirit, dumb to us, will speak to him.
Do you consent we shall acquaint him with it,
As needful in our loves, fitting our duty?
*Marcellus.* Let 's do 't, I pray; and I this morning know
Where we shall find him most conveniently. [*Exeunt.*

SCENE II. *A Room of State in the Castle.*

*Enter the* KING, QUEEN, HAMLET, POLONIUS, LAERTES, VOLTIMAND, CORNELIUS, Lords, *and* Attendants.

*King.* Though yet of Hamlet our dear brother's death
The memory be green, and that it us befitted
To bear our hearts in grief, and our whole kingdom
To be contracted in one brow of woe,
Yet so far hath discretion fought with nature
That we with wisest sorrow think on him,
Together with remembrance of ourselves.
Therefore our sometime sister, now our queen,
The imperial jointress of this warlike state,

Have we, as 't were with a defeated joy,—
With one auspicious and one dropping eye,
With mirth in funeral and with dirge in marriage,
In equal scale weighing delight and dole,—
Taken to wife; nor have we herein barr'd
Your better wisdoms, which have freely gone
With this affair along. For all, our thanks.
Now follows, that you know, young Fortinbras,
Holding a weak supposal of our worth,
Or thinking by our late dear brother's death
Our state to be disjoint and out of frame,
Colleagued with the dream of his advantage,
He hath not fail'd to pester us with message,
Importing the surrender of those lands
Lost by his father, with all bonds of law,
To our most valiant brother. So much for him.
Now for ourself, and for this time of meeting
Thus much the business is: we have here writ
To Norway, uncle of young Fortinbras,—
Who, impotent and bed-rid, scarcely hears
Of this his nephew's purpose,—to suppress
His further gait herein; in that the levies,
The lists, and full proportions, are all made
Out of his subject; and we here dispatch
You, good Cornelius, and you, Voltimand,
For bearers of this greeting to old Norway,
Giving to you no further personal power
To business with the king more than the scope
Of these dilated articles allow.
Farewell, and let your haste commend your duty.

*Cornelius.* }
*Voltimand.* } In that and all things will we show our duty.

*King.* We doubt it nothing; heartily farewell.—
[*Exeunt Voltimand and Cornelius.*

And now, Laertes, what 's the news with you?

You told us of some suit; what is 't, Laertes?
You cannot speak of reason to the Dane,
And lose your voice; what wouldst thou beg, Laertes,
That shall not be my offer, not thy asking?
The head is not more native to the heart,
The hand more instrumental to the mouth,
Than is the throne of Denmark to thy father.
What wouldst thou have, Laertes?

*Laertes.* Dread my lord,
Your leave and favour to return to France;
From whence though willingly I came to Denmark,
To show my duty in your coronation,
Yet now, I must confess, that duty done,
My thoughts and wishes bend again toward France
And bow them to your gracious leave and pardon.

*King.* Have you your father's leave?—What says Polonius?

*Polonius.* He hath, my lord, wrung from me my slow leave
By laboursome petition, and at last
Upon his will I seal'd my hard consent;
I do beseech you, give him leave to go.

*King.* Take thy fair hour, Laertes; time be thine,
And thy best graces spend it at thy will!—
But now, my cousin Hamlet, and my son,—

*Hamlet.* [*Aside*] A little more than kin, and less than kind.

*King.* How is it that the clouds still hang on you?

*Hamlet.* Not so, my lord; I am too much i' the sun.

*Queen.* Good Hamlet, cast thy nighted colour off,
And let thine eye look like a friend on Denmark.
Do not for ever with thy vailed lids
Seek for thy noble father in the dust.
Thou know'st 't is common; all that lives must die,
Passing through nature to eternity.

*Hamlet.* Ay, madam, it is common.

*Queen.* If it be,
Why seems it so particular with thee?
*Hamlet.* Seems, madam! nay, it is; I know not 'seems.'
'T is not alone my inky cloak, good mother,
Nor customary suits of solemn black,
Nor windy suspiration of forc'd breath,
No, nor the fruitful river in the eye,
Nor the dejected haviour of the visage,
Together with all forms, moods, shows of grief,
That can denote me truly; these indeed seem,
For they are actions that a man might play:
But I have that within which passeth show;
These but the trappings and the suits of woe.
*King.* 'T is sweet and commendable in your nature, Hamlet,
To give these mourning duties to your father:
But, you must know, your father lost a father;
That father lost, lost his; and the survivor bound
In filial obligation for some term
To do obsequious sorrow: but to persever
In obstinate condolement is a course
Of impious stubbornness; 't is unmanly grief;
It shows a will most incorrect to heaven,
A heart unfortified, a mind impatient,
An understanding simple and unschool'd:
For what we know must be and is as common
As any the most vulgar thing to sense,
Why should we in our peevish opposition
Take it to heart? Fie! 't is a fault to heaven,
A fault against the dead, a fault to nature,
To reason most absurd; whose common theme
Is death of fathers, and who still hath cried,
From the first corse till he that died to-day,
'This must be so.' We pray you, throw to earth
This unprevailing woe, and think of us

As of a father; for let the world take note,
You are the most immediate to our throne,
And with no less nobility of love
Than that which dearest father bears his son
Do I impart toward you. For your intent
In going back to school in Wittenberg,
It is most retrograde to our desire;
And we beseech you, bend you to remain
Here, in the cheer and comfort of our eye,
Our chiefest courtier, cousin, and our son.

*Queen.* Let not thy mother lose her prayers, Hamlet:
I pray thee, stay with us; go not to Wittenberg.

*Hamlet.* I shall in all my best obey you, madam.

*King.* Why, 't is a loving and a fair reply;
Be as ourself in Denmark.—Madam, come;
This gentle and unforc'd accord of Hamlet
Sits smiling to my heart: in grace whereof,
No jocund health that Denmark drinks to-day,
But the great cannon to the clouds shall tell,
And the king's rouse the heavens shall bruit again,
Respeaking earthly thunder.—Come away.

[*Exeunt all but Hamlet.*

*Hamlet.* O that this too, too solid flesh would melt,
Thaw, and resolve itself into a dew!
Or that the Everlasting had not fix'd
His canon 'gainst self-slaughter! O God! O God!
How weary, stale, flat, and unprofitable
Seem to me all the uses of this world!
Fie on 't! O fie! 't is an unweeded garden,
That grows to seed; things rank and gross in nature
Possess it merely. That it should come to this!
But two months dead! nay, not so much, not two:
So excellent a king; that was, to this,
Hyperion to a satyr; so loving to my mother
That he might not beteem the winds of heaven

Visit her face too roughly. Heaven and earth!
Must I remember? why, she would hang on him,
As if increase of appetite had grown
By what it fed on; and yet, within a month—
Let me not think on 't—Frailty, thy name is woman!—
A little month, or ere those shoes were old
With which she follow'd my poor father's body,
Like Niobe, all tears,—why she, even she—
O God! a beast, that wants discourse of reason,
Would have mourn'd longer—married with my uncle,
My father's brother, but no more like my father
Than I to Hercules. Within a month?
Ere yet the salt of most unrighteous tears
Had left the flushing in her galled eyes,
She married. O most wicked speed, to post
With such dexterity to incestuous sheets!
It is not, nor it cannot come to good:—
But break my heart, for I must hold my tongue.

*Enter* HORATIO, MARCELLUS, *and* BERNARDO.

*Horatio.* Hail to your lordship!
*Hamlet.* I am glad to see you well:
Horatio,—or I do forget myself.
*Horatio.* The same, my lord, and your poor servant ever.
*Hamlet.* Sir, my good friend; I 'll change that name with you:
And what make you from Wittenberg, Horatio?—
Marcellus?
*Marcellus.* My good lord—
*Hamlet.* I am very glad to see you.—[*To Bernardo.*] Good even, sir.—
But what, in faith, make you from Wittenberg?
*Horatio.* A truant disposition, good my lord.
*Hamlet.* I would not hear your enemy say so,
Nor shall you do mine ear that violence.

To make it truster of your own report
Against yourself; I know you are no truant.
But what is your affair in Elsinore?
We 'll teach you to drink deep ere you depart.
*Horatio.* My lord, I came to see your father's funeral.
*Hamlet.* I pray thee, do not mock me, fellow-student;
I think it was to see my mother's wedding.
*Horatio.* Indeed, my lord, it follow'd hard upon.
*Hamlet.* Thrift, thrift, Horatio! the funeral bak'd meats
Did coldly furnish forth the marriage tables.
Would I had met my dearest foe in heaven
Or ever I had seen that day, Horatio!
My father!—methinks I see my father.
*Horatio.* O where, my lord?
*Hamlet.* In my mind's eye, Horatio.
*Horatio.* I saw him once; he was a goodly king.
*Hamlet.* He was a man, take him for all in all,
I shall not look upon his like again.
*Horatio.* My lord, I think I saw him yesternight.
*Hamlet.* Saw? who?
*Horatio.* My lord, the king your father.
*Hamlet.* The king my father!
*Horatio.* Season your admiration for a while
With an attent ear, till I may deliver,
Upon the witness of these gentlemen,
This marvel to you.
*Hamlet.* For God's love, let me hear.
*Horatio.* Two nights together had these gentlemen,
Marcellus and Bernardo, on their watch,
In the dead vast and middle of the night,
Been thus encounter'd. A figure like your father,
Armed at point exactly, cap-a-pe,
Appears before them, and with solemn march
Goes slow and stately by them: thrice he walk'd
By their oppress'd and fear-surprised eyes,

Within his truncheon's length ; whilst they, distill'd
Almost to jelly with the act of fear,
Stand dumb, and speak not to him. This to me
In dreadful secrecy impart they did ;
And I with them the third night kept the watch :
Where, as they had deliver'd, both in time,
Form of the thing, each word made true and good,
The apparition comes. I knew your father ;
These hands are not more like.

*Hamlet.* But where was this?

*Marcellus.* My lord, upon the platform where we watch'd.

*Hamlet.* Did you not speak to it?

*Horatio.* My lord, I did ;
But answer made it none : yet once methought
It lifted up it head and did address
Itself to motion, like as it would speak ;
But even then the morning cock crew loud,
And at the sound it shrunk in haste away,
And vanish'd from our sight.

*Hamlet.* 'T is very strange.

*Horatio.* As I do live, my honour'd lord, 't is true ;
And we did think it writ down in our duty
To let you know of it.

*Hamlet.* Indeed, indeed, sirs, but this troubles me.
Hold you the watch to night?

*Marcellus.* } *Bernardo.* } We do, my lord.

*Hamlet.* Arm'd, say you?

*Marcellus.* } *Bernardo.* } Arm'd, my lord.

*Hamlet.* From top to toe?

*Marcellus.* } *Bernardo.* } My lord, from head to foot.

*Hamlet.* Then saw you not his face?

*Horatio.* O, yes, my lord ; he wore his beaver up.

*Hamlet.* What, look'd he frowningly?
*Horatio.* A countenance more in sorrow than in anger.
*Hamlet.* Pale, or red?
*Horatio.* Nay, very pale.
*Hamlet.* And fix'd his eyes upon you?
*Horatio.* Most constantly.
*Hamlet.* I would I had been there.
*Horatio.* It would have much amaz'd you.
*Hamlet.* Very like, very like. Stay'd it long?
*Horatio.* While one with moderate haste might tell a hundred.
*Marcellus.* *Bernardo.* } Longer, longer.
*Horatio.* Not when I saw 't.
*Hamlet.* His beard was grizzled? no?
*Horatio.* It was, as I have seen it in his life,
A sable silver'd.
*Hamlet.* I 'll watch to-night;
Perchance 't will walk again.
*Horatio.* I warrant it will.
*Hamlet.* If it assume my noble father's person,
I 'll speak to it, though hell itself should gape
And bid me hold my peace. I pray you all,
If you have hitherto conceal'd this sight,
Let it be tenable in your silence still;
And whatsoever else shall hap to-night,
Give it an understanding, but no tongue:
I will requite your loves. So, fare you well;
Upon the platform, 'twixt eleven and twelve,
I 'll visit you.
*All.* Our duty to your honour.
*Hamlet.* Your loves, as mine to you; farewell.—
[*Exeunt all but Hamlet.*
My father's spirit in arms! all is not well;
I doubt some foul play: would the night were come!

Till then sit still, my soul; foul deeds will rise,
Though all the earth o'erwhelm them, to men's eyes. [*Exit.*

SCENE III. *A Room in Polonius's House.*

*Enter* LAERTES *and* OPHELIA.

*Laertes.* My necessaries are embark'd; farewell:
And, sister, as the winds give benefit
And convoy is assistant, do not sleep,
But let me hear from you.

*Ophelia.* Do you doubt that?

*Laertes.* For Hamlet and the trifling of his favour,
Hold it a fashion and a toy in blood,
A violet in the youth of primy nature,
Forward, not permanent, sweet, not lasting,
The perfume and suppliance of a minute;
No more.

*Ophelia.* No more but so?

*Laertes.* Think it no more;
For nature crescent does not grow alone
In thews and bulk, but, as this temple waxes,
The inward service of the mind and soul
Grows wide withal. Perhaps he loves you now,
And now no soil nor cautel doth besmirch
The virtue of his will; but you must fear,
His greatness weigh'd, his will is not his own;
For he himself is subject to his birth.
He may not, as unvalued persons do,
Carve for himself, for on his choice depends
The safety and health of this whole state;
And therefore must his choice be circumscrib'd
Unto the voice and yielding of that body
Whereof he is the head. Then if he says he loves you,
It fits your wisdom so far to believe it
As he in his particular act and place

May give his saying deed; which is no further
Than the main voice of Denmark goes withal.
Then weigh what loss your honour may sustain,
If with too credent ear you list his songs,
Or lose your heart, or your chaste treasure open
To his unmaster'd importunity.
Fear it, Ophelia, fear it, my dear sister,
And keep you in the rear of your affection,
Out of the shot and danger of desire.
The chariest maid is prodigal enough,
If she unmask her beauty to the moon.
Virtue itself scapes not calumnious strokes;
The canker galls the infants of the spring,
Too oft before their buttons be disclos'd;
And in the morn and liquid dew of youth
Contagious blastments are most imminent.
Be wary then; best safety lies in fear:
Youth to itself rebels, though none else near.

*Ophelia.* I shall the effect of this good lesson keep,
As watchman to my heart. But, good my brother,
Do not, as some ungracious pastors do,
Show me the steep and thorny way to heaven,
Whiles, like a puff'd and reckless libertine,
Himself the primrose path of dalliance treads,
And recks not his own rede.

*Laertes.* O, fear me not.
I stay too long; but here my father comes.

*Enter* POLONIUS.

A double blessing is a double grace;
Occasion smiles upon a second leave.

*Polonius.* Yet here, Laertes! aboard, aboard, for shame!
The wind sits in the shoulder of your sail,
And you are stay'd for. There; my blessing with thee!
And these few precepts in thy memory

See thou character. Give thy thoughts no tongue,
Nor any unproportion'd thought his act.
Be thou familiar, but by no means vulgar.
Those friends thou hast, and their adoption tried,
Grapple them to thy soul with hoops of steel;
But do not dull thy palm with entertainment
Of each new-hatch'd, unfledg'd comrade. Beware
Of entrance to a quarrel, but, being in,
Bear 't that the opposed may beware of thee.
Give every man thy ear, but few thy voice;
Take each man's censure, but reserve thy judgment
Costly thy habit as thy purse can buy,
But not express'd in fancy; rich, not gaudy;
For the apparel oft proclaims the man,
And they in France of the best rank and station
Are most select and generous, chief in that.
Neither a borrower nor a lender be;
For loan oft loses both itself and friend,
And borrowing dulls the edge of husbandry.
This above all: to thine own self be true,
And it must follow, as the night the day,
Thou canst not then be false to any man.
Farewell; my blessing season this in thee!

*Laertes.* Most humbly do I take my leave, my lord.

*Polonius.* The time invites you; go, your servants tend.

*Laertes.* Farewell, Ophelia; and remember well
What I have said to you.

*Ophelia.* 'T is in my memory lock'd,
And you yourself shall keep the key of it.

*Laertes.* Farewell. [*Exit.*

*Polonius.* What is 't, Ophelia, he hath said to you?

*Ophelia.* So please you, something touching the Lord Hamlet.

*Polonius.* Marry, well bethought:
'T is told me, he hath very oft of late

Given private time to you, and you yourself
Have of your audience been most free and bounteous;
If it be so—as so 't is put on me,
And that in way of caution—I must tell you,
You do not understand yourself so clearly
As it behoves my daughter and your honour.
What is between you? give me up the truth.

*Ophelia.* He hath, my lord, of late made many tenders
Of his affection to me.

*Polonius.* Affection! pooh! you speak like a green girl,
Unsifted in such perilous circumstance.
Do you believe his tenders, as you call them?

*Ophelia.* I do not know, my lord, what I should think.

*Polonius.* Marry, I 'll teach you; think yourself a baby,
That you have ta'en these tenders for true pay,
Which are not sterling. Tender yourself more dearly;
Or—not to crack the wind of the poor phrase,
Running it thus—you 'll tender me a fool.

*Ophelia.* My lord, he hath importun'd me with love
In honourable fashion.

*Polonius.* Ay, fashion you may call it; go to, go to.

*Ophelia.* And hath given countenance to his speech, my lord,
With almost all the holy vows of heaven.

*Polonius.* Ay, springes to catch woodcocks. I do know,
When the blood burns, how prodigal the soul
Lends the tongue vows; these blazes, daughter,
Giving more light than heat, extinct in both,
Even in their promise, as it is a-making,
You must not take for fire. From this time
Be somewhat scanter of your maiden presence;
Set your entreatments at a higher rate
Than a command to parley. For Lord Hamlet,
Believe so much in him, that he is young,
And with a larger tether may he walk

Than may be given you: in few, Ophelia,
Do not believe his vows; for they are brokers,
Not of that dye which their investments show,
But mere implorators of unholy suits,
Breathing like sanctified and pious bawds,
The better to beguile. This is for all;
I would not, in plain terms, from this time forth,
Have you so slander any moment's leisure,
As to give words or talk with the Lord Hamlet.
Look to 't, I charge you; come your ways.
*Ophelia.* I shall obey, my lord. [*Exeunt.*

SCENE IV. *The Platform.*

*Enter* HAMLET, HORATIO, *and* MARCELLUS.

*Hamlet.* The air bites shrewdly; it is very cold.
*Horatio.* It is a nipping and an eager air.
*Hamlet.* What hour now?
*Horatio.* I think it lacks of twelve.
*Hamlet.* No, it is struck.
*Horatio.* Indeed? I heard it not: it then draws near the season
Wherein the spirit held his wont to walk.
[*A flourish of trumpets and ordnance shot off within.*
What does this mean, my lord?
*Hamlet.* The king doth wake to-night and takes his rouse,
Keeps wassail, and the swaggering upspring reels;
And as he drains his draughts of Rhenish down,
The kettle-drum and trumpet thus bray out
The triumph of his pledge.
*Horatio.* Is it a custom?
*Hamlet.* Ay, marry is 't;
But to my mind, though I am native here
And to the manner born, it is a custom

More honour'd in the breach than the observance.
This heavy-headed revel east and west
Makes us traduc'd and tax'd of other nations :
They clepe us drunkards, and with swinish phrase
Soil our addition ; and indeed it takes
From our achievements, though perform'd at height,
The pith and marrow of our attribute.
So, oft it chances in particular men,
That for some vicious mole of nature in them,
As, in their birth—wherein they are not guilty,
Since nature cannot choose his origin—
By the o'ergrowth of some complexion,
Oft breaking down the pales and forts of reason,
Or by some habit that too much o'er-leavens
The form of plausive manners, that these men,
Carrying, I say, the stamp of one defect,
Being nature's livery, or fortune's star,—
Their virtues else—be they as pure as grace,
As infinite as man may undergo—
Shall in the general censure take corruption
From that particular fault : the dram of eale
Doth all the noble substance of a doubt
To his own scandal.

*Horatio.* Look, my lord, it comes !

*Enter* GHOST.

*Hamlet.* Angels and ministers of grace defend us !—
Be thou a spirit of health or goblin damn'd,
Bring with thee airs from heaven or blasts from hell,
Be thy intents wicked or charitable,
Thou comest in such a questionable shape
That I will speak to thee : I 'll call thee Hamlet,
King, father ; royal Dane, O, answer me !
Let me not burst in ignorance ; but tell
Why thy canoniz'd bones, hearsed in death,

Have burst their cerements; why the sepulchre,
Wherein we saw thee quietly inurn'd,
Hath op'd his ponderous and marble jaws,
To cast thee up again. What may this mean,
That thou, dead corse, again in complete steel
Revisit'st thus the glimpses of the moon,
Making night hideous; and we fools of nature
So horridly to shake our disposition
With thoughts beyond the reaches of our souls?
Say, why is this? wherefore? what should we do?
[*Ghost beckons Hamlet.*

*Horatio.* It beckons you to go away with it,
As if it some impartment did desire
To you alone.

*Marcellus.* Look, with what courteous action
It waves you to a more removed ground:
But do not go with it.

*Horatio.* No, by no means.

*Hamlet.* It will not speak; then I will follow it.

*Horatio.* Do not, my lord.

*Hamlet.* Why, what should be the fear?
I do not set my life at a pin's fee;
And for my soul, what can it do to that,
Being a thing immortal as itself?
It waves me forth again; I'll follow it.

*Horatio.* What if it tempt you toward the flood, my lord,
Or to the dreadful summit of the cliff
That beetles o'er his base into the sea,
And there assume some other horrible form,
Which might deprive your sovereignty of reason
And draw you into madness? think of it;
The very place puts toys of desperation,
Without more motive, into every brain
That looks so many fathoms to the sea
And hears it roar beneath.

*Hamlet.* It waves me still.—
Go on; I 'll follow thee.
*Marcellus.* You shall not go, my lord.
*Hamlet.* Hold off your hands!
*Horatio.* Be rul'd; you shall not go.
*Hamlet.* My fate cries out,
And makes each petty artery in this body
As hardy as the Nemean lion's nerve.
Still am I call'd.—Unhand me, gentlemen.
By heaven, I 'll make a ghost of him that lets me!
I say, away!—Go on; I 'll follow thee.
[*Exeunt Ghost and Hamlet.*
*Horatio.* He waxes desperate with imagination.
*Marcellus.* Let 's follow; 't is not fit thus to obey him.
*Horatio.* Have after.—To what issue will this come?
*Marcellus.* Something is rotten in the state of Denmark.
*Horatio.* Heaven will direct it.
*Marcellus.* Nay, let 's follow him. [*Exeunt.*

### SCENE V. *Another Part of the Platform.*

*Enter* GHOST *and* HAMLET.

*Hamlet.* Where wilt thou lead me? speak; I 'll go no further.
*Ghost.* Mark me.
*Hamlet.* I will.
*Ghost.* My hour is almost come,
When I to sulphurous and tormenting flames
Must render up myself.
*Hamlet.* Alas, poor ghost!
*Ghost.* Pity me not, but lend thy serious hearing
To what I shall unfold.
*Hamlet.* Speak; I am bound to hear.
*Ghost.* So art thou to revenge, when thou shalt hear.
*Hamlet.* What?

*Ghost.* I am thy father's spirit,
Doom'd for a certain term to walk the night,
And for the day confin'd to fast in fires,
Till the foul crimes done in my days of nature
Are burnt and purg'd away. But that I am forbid
To tell the secrets of my prison-house,
I could a tale unfold whose lightest word
Would harrow up thy soul, freeze thy young blood,
Make thy two eyes, like stars, start from their spheres,
Thy knotted and combined locks to part,
And each particular hair to stand an end,
Like quills upon the fretful porpentine;
But this eternal blazon must not be
To ears of flesh and blood. List, list, O, list!
If thou didst ever thy dear father love—

*Hamlet.* O God!

*Ghost.* Revenge his foul and most unnatural murther.

*Hamlet.* Murther!

*Ghost.* Murther most foul, as in the best it is;
But this most foul, strange, and unnatural.

*Hamlet.* Haste me to know 't, that I, with wings as swift
As meditation or the thoughts of love,
May sweep to my revenge.

*Ghost.* I find thee apt;
And duller shouldst thou be than the fat weed
That roots itself in ease on Lethe wharf,
Wouldst thou not stir in this. Now, Hamlet, hear:
'T is given out that, sleeping in my orchard,
A serpent stung me; so the whole ear of Denmark
Is by a forged process of my death
Rankly abus'd; but know, thou noble youth,
The serpent that did sting thy father's life
Now wears his crown.

*Hamlet.* O my prophetic soul!
My uncle!

*Ghost.* Ay, that incestuous, that adulterate beast,
With witchcraft of his wit, with traitorous gifts,—
O wicked wit and gifts, that have the power
So to seduce!—won to his shameful lust
The will of my most seeming-virtuous queen;
O Hamlet, what a falling-off was there!
From me, whose love was of that dignity
That it went hand in hand even with the vow
I made to her in marriage, and to decline
Upon a wretch whose natural gifts were poor
To those of mine!
But virtue, as it never will be mov'd,
Though lewdness court it in a shape of heaven,
So lust, though to a radiant angel link'd,
Will sate itself in a celestial bed,
And prey on garbage.
But, soft! methinks I scent the morning air;
Brief let me be. Sleeping within my orchard,
My custom always in the afternoon,
Upon my secure hour thy uncle stole,
With juice of cursed hebenon in a vial,
And in the porches of my ears did pour
The leperous distilment; whose effect
Holds such an enmity with blood of man
That swift as quicksilver it courses through
The natural gates and alleys of the body,
And with a sudden vigour it doth posset
And curd, like eager droppings into milk,
The thin and wholesome blood: so did it mine;
And a most instant tetter bark'd about,
Most lazar-like, with vile and loathsome crust,
All my smooth body.
Thus was I, sleeping, by a brother's hand
Of life, of crown, of queen, at once dispatch'd;
Cut off even in the blossoms of my sin,

Unhousel'd, disappointed, unanel'd,
No reckoning made, but sent to my account
With all my imperfections on my head:
O, horrible! O, horrible! most horrible!
If thou hast nature in thee, bear it not;
Let not the royal bed of Denmark be
A couch for luxury and damned incest.
But, howsoever thou pursuest this act,
Taint not thy mind, nor let thy soul contrive
Against thy mother aught; leave her to heaven
And to those thorns that in her bosom lodge,
To prick and sting her. Fare thee well at once!
The glow-worm shows the matin to be near,
And gins to pale his uneffectual fire;
Adieu, adieu! Hamlet, remember me. [*Exit.*

*Hamlet.* O all you host of heaven! O earth! what else?
And shall I couple hell? O, fie! Hold, hold, my heart;
And you, my sinews, grow not instant old,
But bear me stiffly up. Remember thee!
Ay, thou poor ghost, while memory holds a seat
In this distracted globe. Remember thee!
Yea, from the table of my memory
I 'll wipe away all trivial fond records,
All saws of books, all forms, all pressures past,
That youth and observation copied there;
And thy commandment all alone shall live
Within the book and volume of my brain,
Unmix'd with baser matter: yes, by heaven!
O most pernicious woman!
O villain, villain, smiling, damned villain!
My tables,—meet it is I set it down,
That one may smile, and smile, and be a villain;
At least I 'm sure it may be so in Denmark.— [*Writing.*
So, uncle, there you are.—Now to my word;

It is 'Adieu, adieu! remember me.'
I have sworn 't.

*Marcellus.* } 
*Horatio.* } [*Within*] My lord, my lord!

*Marcellus.* [*Within*] Lord Hamlet!

*Horatio.* [*Within*] Heaven secure him!

*Hamlet.* So be it!

*Horatio.* [*Within*] Hillo, ho, ho, my lord!

*Hamlet.* Hillo, ho, ho, boy! come, bird, come.

*Enter* HORATIO *and* MARCELLUS.

*Marcellus.* How is 't, my noble lord?

*Horatio.* What news, my lord?

*Hamlet.* O, wonderful!

*Horatio.* Good my lord, tell it.

*Hamlet.* No; you will reveal it.

*Horatio.* Not I, my lord, by heaven.

*Marcellus.* Nor I, my lord.

*Hamlet.* How say you, then; would heart of man once think it?
But you 'll be secret?

*Horatio.* } 
*Marcellus.* } Ay, by heaven, my lord.

*Hamlet.* There 's ne'er a villain dwelling in all Denmark
But he 's an arrant knave.

*Horatio.* There needs no ghost, my lord, come from the grave
To tell us this.

*Hamlet.* Why, right: you are i' the right;
And so, without more circumstance at all,
I hold it fit that we shake hands and part:
You, as your business and desire shall point you,—
For every man has business and desire,
Such as it is;—and for mine own poor part,
Look you, I 'll go pray.

*Horatio.* These are but wild and whirling words, my lord.

*Hamlet.* I 'm sorry they offend you, heartily;
Yes, faith, heartily.

*Horatio.* There 's no offence, my lord.

*Hamlet.* Yes, by Saint Patrick, but there is, Horatio,
And much offence too. Touching this vision here,
It is an honest ghost, that let me tell you;
For your desire to know what is between us,
O'ermaster 't as you may. And now, good friends,
As you are friends, scholars, and soldiers,
Give me one poor request.

*Horatio.* What is 't, my lord? we will.

*Hamlet.* Never make known what you have seen to-night.

*Horatio.* }
*Marcellus.* } My lord, we will not.

*Hamlet.* Nay, but swear 't.

*Horatio.* In faith,
My lord, not I.

*Marcellus.* Nor I, my lord, in faith.

*Hamlet.* Upon my sword.

*Marcellus.* We have sworn, my lord, already.

*Hamlet.* Indeed, upon my sword, indeed.

*Ghost.* [*Beneath*] Swear.

*Hamlet.* Ah, ha, boy! say'st thou so? art thou there, truepenny?—
Come on—you hear this fellow in the cellarage—
Consent to swear.

*Horatio.* Propose the oath, my lord.

*Hamlet.* Never to speak of this that you have seen.
Swear by my sword.

*Ghost.* [*Beneath*] Swear.

*Hamlet.* Hic et ubique? then we 'll shift our ground.—
Come hither, gentlemen,
And lay your hands again upon my sword,

Never to speak of this that you have heard.
Swear by my sword.

*Ghost.* [*Beneath*] Swear.

*Hamlet.* Well said, old mole! canst work i' the earth so fast?
A worthy pioner!—Once more remove, good friends.

*Horatio.* O day and night, but this is wondrous strange!

*Hamlet.* And therefore as a stranger give it welcome.
There are more things in heaven and earth, Horatio,
Than are dreamt of in your philosophy.
But come;
Here, as before, never, so help you mercy,
How strange or odd soe'er I bear myself,—
As I perchance hereafter shall think meet
To put an antic disposition on,—
That you, at such times seeing me, never shall,
With arms encumber'd thus, or this head-shake,
Or by pronouncing of some doubtful phrase,
As 'Well, well, we know,' or 'We could, an if we would,'
Or 'If we list to speak,' or 'There be, an if they might,'
Or such ambiguous giving-out, to note
That you know aught of me: this not to do,
So grace and mercy at your most need help you,
Swear.

*Ghost.* [*Beneath*] Swear.

*Hamlet.* Rest, rest, perturbed spirit!—So, gentlemen,
With all my love I do commend me to you;
And what so poor a man as Hamlet is
May do, to express his love and friending to you,
God willing, shall not lack. Let us go in together;
And still your fingers on your lips, I pray.
The time is out of joint;—O cursed spite,
That ever I was born to set it right!—
Nay, come, let 's go together. [*Exeunt.*

ELSINORE.

## ACT II.

### Scene I. *A Room in Polonius's House.*

*Enter* Polonius *and* Reynaldo.

*Polonius.* Give him this money and these notes, Reynaldo.

*Reynaldo.* I will, my lord.

*Polonius.* You shall do marvellous wisely, good Reynaldo,
Before you visit him, to make inquire
Of his behaviour.

*Reynaldo.* My lord, I did intend it.

*Polonius.* Marry, well said, very well said. Look you, sir,
Inquire me first what Danskers are in Paris,
And how, and who; what means, and where they keep;
What company, at what expense; and finding

By this encompassment and drift of question
That they do know my son, come you more nearer
Than your particular demands will touch it:
Take you, as 't were, some distant knowledge of him,
As thus, 'I know his father and his friends,
And in part him,'—do you mark this, Reynaldo?
*Reynaldo.* Ay, very well, my lord.
*Polonius.* 'And in part him; but' you may say 'not well;
But, if 't be he I mean, he 's very wild,
Addicted' so and so: and there put on him
What forgeries you please; marry, none so rank
As may dishonour him; take heed of that;
But, sir, such wanton, wild, and usual slips
As are companions noted and most known
To youth and liberty.
*Reynaldo.* As gaming, my lord.
*Polonius.* Ay, or drinking, fencing, swearing, quarrelling,
Drabbing; you may go so far.
*Reynaldo.* My lord, that would dishonour him.
*Polonius.* Faith, no; as you may season it in the charge.
You must not put another scandal on him,
That he is open to incontinency;
That 's not my meaning: but breathe his faults so quaintly
That they may seem the taints of liberty,
The flash and outbreak of a fiery mind,
A savageness in unreclaimed blood,
Of general assault.
*Reynaldo.* But, my good lord,—
*Polonius.* Wherefore should you do this?
*Reynaldo.* Ay, my lord,
I would know that.
*Polonius.* Marry, sir, here 's my drift;
And, I believe, it is a fetch of warrant.
You laying these slight sullies on my son,
As 't were a thing a little soil'd i' the working,

Mark you,
Your party in converse, him you would sound,
Having ever seen in the prenominate crimes
The youth you breathe of guilty, be assur'd
He closes with you in this consequence:
'Good sir,' or so, or 'friend,' or 'gentleman,'
According to the phrase or the addition
Of man and country.

*Reynaldo.* Very good, my lord.

*Polonius.* And then, sir, does he this—he does—what was I about to say? By the mass, I was about to say something; where did I leave?

*Reynaldo.* At 'closes in the consequence,' at 'friend or so,' and 'gentleman.'

*Polonius.* At 'closes in the consequence,' ay, marry;
He closes thus: 'I know the gentleman;
I saw him yesterday, or 't other day,
Or then, or then, with such, or such, and, as you say,
There was he gaming, there o'ertook in 's rouse,
There falling out at tennis;' or perchance,
'I saw him enter such a house of sale,'
Videlicet, a brothel, or so forth.
See you now;
Your bait of falsehood takes this carp of truth;
And thus do we of wisdom and of reach,
With windlasses and with assays of bias,
By indirections find directions out:
So, by my former lecture and advice,
Shall you my son. You have me, have you not?

*Reynaldo.* My lord, I have.

*Polonius.* God be wi' you; fare you well.

*Reynaldo.* Good my lord!

*Polonius.* Observe his inclination in yourself.

*Reynaldo.* I shall, my lord.

*Polonius.* And let him ply his music.

*Reynaldo.* Well, my lord.
*Polonius.* Farewell! [*Exit Reynaldo.*

*Enter* OPHELIA.

How now, Ophelia! what 's the matter?
*Ophelia.* O, my lord, my lord, I have been so affrighted!
*Polonius.* With what, i' the name of God?
*Ophelia.* My lord, as I was sewing in my closet,
Lord Hamlet, with his doublet all unbrac'd;
No hat upon his head; his stockings foul'd,
Ungarter'd, and down-gyved to his ankle;
Pale as his shirt; his knees knocking each other;
And with a look so piteous in purport
As if he had been loosed out of hell
To speak of horrors,—he comes before me.
*Polonius.* Mad for thy love?
*Ophelia.* My lord, I do not know;
But truly, I do fear it.
*Polonius.* What said he?
*Ophelia.* He took me by the wrist and held me hard;
Then goes he to the length of all his arm,
And, with his other hand thus o'er his brow,
He falls to such perusal of my face
As he would draw it. Long stay'd he so;
At last, a little shaking of mine arm,
And thrice his head thus waving up and down,
He rais'd a sigh so piteous and profound
As it did seem to shatter all his bulk
And end his being: that done, he lets me go;
And, with his head over his shoulder turn'd,
He seem'd to find his way without his eyes;
For out o' doors he went without their help,
And, to the last, bended their light on me.
*Polonius.* Come, go with me; I will go seek the king.
This is the very ecstasy of love,

Whose violent property fordoes itself
And leads the will to desperate undertakings,
As oft as any passion under heaven
That does afflict our natures. I am sorry,—
What, have you given him any hard words of late?
*Ophelia.* No, my good lord, but, as you did command,
I did repel his letters, and denied
His access to me.
*Polonius.* That hath made him mad.
I am sorry that with better heed and judgment
I had not quoted him. I fear'd he did but trifle,
And meant to wrack thee; but beshrew my jealousy!
By heaven, it is as proper to our age
To cast beyond ourselves in our opinions
As it is common for the younger sort
To lack discretion. Come, go we to the king:
This must be known; which, being kept close, might move
More grief to hide than hate to utter love. [*Exeunt.*

## SCENE II. *A Room in the Castle.*

*Enter* KING, QUEEN, ROSENCRANTZ, GUILDENSTERN, *and* Attendants.

*King.* Welcome, dear Rosencrantz and Guildenstern!
Moreover that we much did long to see you,
The need we have to use you did provoke
Our hasty sending. Something have you heard
Of Hamlet's transformation; so I call it,
Sith nor the exterior nor the inward man
Resembles that it was. What it should be,
More than his father's death, that thus hath put him
So much from the understanding of himself,
I cannot dream of. I entreat you both,
That, being of so young days brought up with him,
And sith so neighbour'd to his youth and humour,

That you vouchsafe your rest here in our court
Some little time; so by your companies
To draw him on to pleasures, and to gather,
So much as from occasion you may glean,
Whether aught to us unknown afflicts him thus,
That, open'd, lies within our remedy.

*Queen.* Good gentlemen, he hath much talk'd of you;
And sure I am two men there are not living
To whom he more adheres. If it will please you
To show us so much gentry and good will
As to expend your time with us awhile,
For the supply and profit of our hope,
Your visitation shall receive such thanks
As fits a king's remembrance.

*Rosencrantz.* Both your majesties
Might, by the sovereign power you have of us,
Put your dread pleasures more into command
Than to entreaty.

*Guildenstern.* But we both obey,
And here give up ourselves, in the full bent
To lay our service freely at your feet,
To be commanded.

*King.* Thanks, Rosencrantz and gentle Guildenstern.

*Queen.* Thanks, Guildenstern and gentle Rosencrantz;
And I beseech you instantly to visit
My too much changed son.—Go, some of you,
And bring these gentlemen where Hamlet is.

*Guildenstern.* Heavens make our presence and our practices
Pleasant and helpful to him!

*Queen.* Ay, amen!

[*Exeunt Rosencrantz, Guildenstern, and some Attendants.*

*Enter* POLONIUS.

*Polonius.* The ambassadors from Norway, my good lord,
Are joyfully return'd.
*King.* Thou still hast been the father of good news.
*Polonius.* Have I, my lord? Assure you, my good liege,
I hold my duty, as I hold my soul,
Both to my God and to my gracious king;
And I do think, or else this brain of mine
Hunts not the trail of policy so sure
As it hath us'd to do, that I have found
The very cause of Hamlet's lunacy.
*King.* O, speak of that; that do I long to hear.
*Polonius.* Give first admittance to the ambassadors;
My news shall be the fruit to that great feast.
*King.* Thyself do grace to them, and bring them in.—
[*Exit Polonius.*
He tells me, my sweet queen, that he hath found
The head and source of all your son's distemper.
*Queen.* I doubt it is no other but the main,—
His father's death, and our o'erhasty marriage.
*King.* Well, we shall sift him.—

*Re-enter* POLONIUS, *with* VOLTIMAND *and* CORNELIUS.

Welcome, my good friends!
Say, Voltimand, what from our brother Norway?
*Voltimand.* Most fair return of greetings and desires.
Upon our first, he sent out to suppress
His nephew's levies, which to him appear'd
To be a preparation 'gainst the Polack,
But, better look'd into, he truly found
It was against your highness: whereat griev'd,
That so his sickness, age, and impotence
Was falsely borne in hand, sends out arrests
On Fortinbras; which he, in brief, obeys,

Receives rebuke from Norway, and in fine
Makes vow before his uncle never more
To give the assay of arms against your majesty.
Whereon old Norway, overcome with joy,
Gives him three thousand crowns in annual fee,
And his commission to employ those soldiers,
So levied as before, against the Polack;
With an entreaty, herein further shown, [*Giving a paper.*
That it might please you to give quiet pass
Through your dominions for this enterprise,
On such regards of safety and allowance
As therein are set down.

*King.* It likes us well;
And at our more consider'd time we'll read,
Answer, and think upon this business.
Meantime we thank you for your well-took labour.
Go to your rest; at night we'll feast together:
Most welcome home! [*Exeunt Voltimand and Cornelius.*

*Polonius.* This business is well ended.—
My liege, and madam, to expostulate
What majesty should be, what duty is,
Why day is day, night night, and time is time,
Were nothing but to waste night, day, and time.
Therefore, since brevity is the soul of wit,
And tediousness the limbs and outward flourishes,
I will be brief. Your noble son is mad:
Mad call I it; for, to define true madness,
What is 't but to be nothing else but mad?
But let that go.

*Queen.* More matter, with less art.

*Polonius.* Madam, I swear I use no art at all.
That he is mad, 't is true; 't is true 't is pity,
And pity 't is 't is true: a foolish figure;
But farewell it, for I will use no art.
Mad let us grant him, then; and now remains

That we find out the cause of this effect,
Or rather say, the cause of this defect,
For this effect defective comes by cause:
Thus it remains, and the remainder thus.
Perpend.
I have a daughter—have while she is mine—
Who, in her duty and obedience, mark,
Hath given me this; now gather, and surmise.
[Reads] '*To the celestial and my soul's idol, the most beautified Ophelia,*'—

That 's an ill phrase, a vile phrase; 'beautified' is a vile phrase: but you shall hear. Thus:
[Reads] '*In her excellent white bosom, these, etc.*'

*Queen.* Came this from Hamlet to her?

*Polonius.* Good madam, stay awhile; I will be faithful.
[Reads] '*Doubt thou the stars are fire;*
*Doubt that the sun doth move;*
*Doubt truth to be a liar;*
*But never doubt I love.*

'*O dear Ophelia, I am ill at these numbers. I have not art to reckon my groans; but that I love thee best, O most best, believe it. Adieu.*

'*Thine evermore, most dear lady, whilst this machine is to him,* HAMLET.'

This in obedience hath my daughter shown me,
And more above, hath his solicitings,
As they fell out by time, by means, and place,
All given to mine ear.

*King.* But how hath she
Receiv'd his love?

*Polonius.* What do you think of me?

*King.* As of a man faithful and honourable.

*Polonius.* I would fain prove so. But what might you think,
When I had seen this hot love on the wing—

As I perceiv'd it, I must tell you that,
Before my daughter told me—what might you,
Or my dear majesty your queen here, think,
If I had play'd the desk or table-book,
Or given my heart a winking, mute and dumb,
Or look'd upon this love with idle sight,
What might you think? No, I went round to work,
And my young mistress thus I did bespeak:
'Lord Hamlet is a prince, out of thy star;
This must not be:' and then I precepts gave her,
That she should lock herself from his resort,
Admit no messengers, receive no tokens.
Which done, she took the fruits of my advice;
And he, repulsed—a short tale to make—
Fell into a sadness, then into a fast,
Thence to a watch, thence into a weakness,
Thence to a lightness, and by this declension
Into the madness wherein now he raves,
And all we mourn for.

*King.* Do you think 't is this?

*Queen.* It may be, very likely.

*Polonius.* Hath there been such a time—I 'd fain know that—
That I have positively said ''T is so,'
When it prov'd otherwise?

*King.* Not that I know.

*Polonius.* [*Pointing to his head and shoulder*] Take this from this, if this be otherwise.
If circumstances lead me, I will find
Where truth is hid, though it were hid indeed
Within the centre.

*King.* How may we try it further?

*Polonius.* You know, sometimes he walks four hours together
Here in the lobby.

*Queen.* So he does indeed.

*Polonius.* At such a time I 'll loose my daughter to him:
Be you and I behind an arras then;
Mark the encounter; if he love her not,
And be not from his reason fallen thereon,
Let me be no assistant for a state,
But keep a farm and carters.

*King.* We will try it.

*Queen.* But, look, where sadly the poor wretch comes reading.

*Polonius.* Away, I do beseech you, both away;
I 'll board him presently.—

[*Exeunt King, Queen, and Attendants.*

*Enter* HAMLET, *reading.*

O, give me leave;
How does my good Lord Hamlet?

*Hamlet.* Well, God-a-mercy.

*Polonius.* Do you know me, my lord?

*Hamlet.* Excellent well; you are a fishmonger.

*Polonius.* Not I, my lord.

*Hamlet.* Then I would you were so honest a man.

*Polonius.* Honest, my lord!

*Hamlet.* Ay, sir; to be honest, as this world goes, is to be one man picked out of ten thousand.

*Polonius.* That 's very true, my lord.

*Hamlet.* For if the sun breed maggots in a dead dog, being a good kissing carrion,—Have you a daughter?

*Polonius.* I have, my lord.

*Hamlet.* Let her not walk i' the sun: conception is a blessing; but not as your daughter may conceive.—Friend, look to 't.

*Polonius.* [*Aside*] How say you by that? Still harping on my daughter: yet he knew me not at first; he said I was a fishmonger; he is far gone, far gone: and truly in my youth

I suffered much extremity for love; very near this. I 'll speak to him again.—What do you read, my lord?

*Hamlet.* Words, words, words.

*Polonius.* What is the matter, my lord?

*Hamlet.* Between who?

*Polonius.* I mean, the matter that you read, my lord.

*Hamlet.* Slanders, sir; for the satirical rogue says here that old men have grey beards, that their faces are wrinkled, their eyes purging thick amber and plum-tree gum, and that they have a plentiful lack of wit, together with most weak hams: all which, sir, though I most powerfully and potently believe, yet I hold it not honesty to have it thus set down; for you yourself, sir, should be old as I am, if like a crab you could go backward.

*Polonius.* [*Aside*] Though this be madness, yet there is method in 't.—Will you walk out of the air, my lord?

*Hamlet.* Into my grave?

*Polonius.* Indeed, that is out o' the air.—[*Aside*] How pregnant sometimes his replies are! a happiness that often madness hits on, which reason and sanity could not so prosperously be delivered of. I will leave him, and suddenly contrive the means of meeting between him and my daughter.—My honourable lord, I will most humbly take my leave of you.

*Hamlet.* You cannot, sir, take from me any thing that I will more willingly part withal; except my life, except my life, except my life.

*Polonius.* Fare you well, my lord.

*Hamlet.* These tedious old fools!

*Enter* ROSENCRANTZ *and* GUILDENSTERN.

*Polonius.* You go to seek the Lord Hamlet; there he is.

*Rosencrantz.* [*To Polonius*] God save you, sir!

[*Exit Polonius.*

*Guildenstern.* My honoured lord!

*Rosencrantz.* My most dear lord!

*Hamlet.* My excellent good friends! How dost thou, Guildenstern?—Ah, Rosencrantz! Good lads, how do ye both?

*Rosencrantz.* As the indifferent children of the earth.

*Guildenstern.* Happy, in that we are not over-happy;
On Fortune's cap we are not the very button.

*Hamlet.* Nor the soles of her shoe?

*Rosencrantz.* Neither, my lord.

*Hamlet.* Then you live about her waist, or in the middle of her favours? What 's the news?

*Rosencrantz.* None, my lord, but that the world 's grown honest.

*Hamlet.* Then is doomsday near; but your news is not true. Let me question more in particular; what have you, my good friends, deserved at the hands of Fortune, that she sends you to prison hither?

*Guildenstern.* Prison, my lord!

*Hamlet.* Denmark 's a prison.

*Rosencrantz.* Then is the world one.

*Hamlet.* A goodly one; in which there are many confines, wards, and dungeons, Denmark being one o' the worst.

*Rosencrantz.* We think not so, my lord.

*Hamlet.* Why, then 't is none to you; for there is nothing either good or bad, but thinking makes it so: to me it is a prison.

*Rosencrantz.* Why, then your ambition makes it one; 't is too narrow for your mind.

*Hamlet.* O God, I could be bounded in a nut-shell, and count myself a king of infinite space, were it not that I have bad dreams.

*Guildenstern.* Which dreams indeed are ambition, for the very substance of the ambitious is merely the shadow of a dream.

*Hamlet.* A dream itself is but a shadow.

*Rosencrantz.* Truly, and I hold ambition of so airy and light a quality that it is but a shadow's shadow.

*Hamlet.* Then are our beggars bodies, and our monarchs and outstretched heroes the beggars' shadows. Shall we to the court? for, by my fay, I cannot reason. 261

*Rosencrantz.* }
*Guildenstern.* } We 'll wait upon you.

*Hamlet.* No such matter: I will not sort you with the rest of my servants; for, to speak to you like an honest man, I am most dreadfully attended. But, in the beaten way of friendship, what make you at Elsinore?

*Rosencrantz.* To visit you, my lord; no other occasion.

*Hamlet.* Beggar that I am, I am even poor in thanks; but I thank you: and sure, dear friends, my thanks are too dear a halfpenny. Were you not sent for? Is it your own inclining? Is it a free visitation? Come, deal justly with me: come, come; nay, speak. 272

*Guildenstern.* What should we say, my lord?

*Hamlet.* Why, any thing, but to the purpose. You were sent for; and there is a kind of confession in your looks which your modesties have not craft enough to colour. I know the good king and queen have sent for you.

*Rosencrantz.* To what end, my lord?

*Hamlet.* That you must teach me. But let me conjure you, by the rights of our fellowship, by the consonancy of our youth, by the obligation of our ever-preserved love, and by what more dear a better proposer could charge you withal, be even and direct with me, whether you were sent for, or no? 284

*Rosencrantz.* [*Aside to Guildenstern*] What say you?

*Hamlet.* [*Aside*] Nay, then I have an eye of you.—If you love me, hold not off.

*Guildenstern.* My lord, we were sent for.

*Hamlet.* I will tell you why; so shall my anticipation prevent your discovery, and your secrecy to the king and queen moult no feather. I have of late—but wherefore I know not—lost all my mirth, forgone all custom of exercises; and indeed it goes so heavily with my disposition that this goodly frame, the earth, seems to me a sterile promontory; this most excellent canopy, the air, look you, this brave o'erhanging firmament, this majestical roof fretted with golden fire,—why, it appears no other thing to me than a foul and pestilent congregation of vapours. What a piece of work is man! how noble in reason! how infinite in faculty! in form and moving how express and admirable! in action how like an angel! in apprehension how like a god! the beauty of the world! the paragon of animals! And yet, to me, what is this quintessence of dust? man delights not me; no, nor woman neither, though by your smiling you seem to say so. 304

*Rosencrantz.* My lord, there was no such stuff in my thoughts.

*Hamlet.* Why did you laugh then, when I said 'man delights not me?'

*Rosencrantz.* To think, my lord, if you delight not in man, what lenten entertainment the players shall receive from you; we coted them on the way, and hither are they coming to offer you service. 312

*Hamlet.* He that plays the king shall be welcome; his majesty shall have tribute of me; the adventurous knight shall use his foil and target; the lover shall not sigh gratis; the humorous man shall end his part in peace; the clown shall make those laugh whose lungs are tickle o' the sere; and the lady shall say her mind freely, or the blank verse shall halt for 't. What players are they?

*Rosencrantz.* Even those you were wont to take delight in, the tragedians of the city. 321

*Hamlet.* How chances it they travel? their residence, both in reputation and profit, was better both ways.

*Rosencrantz.* I think their inhibition comes by the means of the late innovation.

*Hamlet.* Do they hold the same estimation they did when I was in the city? are they so followed?

*Rosencrantz.* No, indeed, are they not.

*Hamlet.* How comes it? do they grow rusty? 329

*Rosencrantz.* Nay, their endeavour keeps in the wonted pace; but there is, sir, an aery of children, little eyases, that cry out on the top of question, and are most tyrannically clapped for 't: these are now the fashion, and so berattle the common stages—so they call them—that many wearing rapiers are afraid of goose-quills, and dare scarce come thither. 336

*Hamlet.* What, are they children? who maintains 'em? how are they escoted? Will they pursue the quality no longer than they can sing? will they not say afterwards, if they should grow themselves to common players—as it is most like, if their means are no better—their writers do them wrong, to make them exclaim against their own succession?

*Rosencrantz.* Faith, there has been much to-do on both sides, and the nation holds it no sin to tarre them to controversy; there was for a while no money bid for argument, unless the poet and the player went to cuffs in the question.

*Hamlet.* Is 't possible? 349

*Guildenstern.* O, there has been much throwing about of brains.

*Hamlet.* Do the boys carry it away?

*Rosencrantz.* Ay, that they do, my lord; Hercules and his load too.

*Hamlet.* It is not very strange; for mine uncle is king of Denmark, and those that would make mows at him while my father lived give twenty, forty, fifty, an hundred ducats apiece for his picture in little. 'Sblood, there is something in this more than natural, if philosophy could find it out. 359

[*Flourish of trumpets within.*

*Guildenstern.* There are the players.

*Hamlet.* Gentlemen, you are welcome to Elsinore. Your hands, come; the appurtenance of welcome is fashion and ceremony: let me comply with you in this garb, lest my extent to the players, which, I tell you, must show fairly outward, should more appear like entertainment than yours. You are welcome; but my uncle-father and aunt-mother are deceived.

*Guildenstern.* In what, my dear lord?

*Hamlet.* I am but mad north-north-west; when the wind is southerly I know a hawk from a handsaw.

*Enter* POLONIUS.

*Polonius.* Well be with you, gentlemen!

*Hamlet.* Hark you, Guildenstern;—and you too;—at each ear a hearer: that great baby you see there is not yet out of his swaddling-clouts.

*Rosencrantz.* Happily he 's the second time come to them; for they say an old man is twice a child.

*Hamlet.* I will prophesy he comes to tell me of the players; mark it.—You say right, sir: o' Monday morning; 't was so indeed.

*Polonius.* My lord, I have news to tell you.

*Hamlet.* My lord, I have news to tell you. When Roscius was an actor in Rome,—

*Polonius.* The actors are come hither, my lord.

*Hamlet.* Buz, buz!

*Polonius.* Upon mine honour,—

*Hamlet.* Then came each actor on his ass,—

*Polonius.* The best actors in the world, either for tragedy, comedy, history, pastoral, pastoral-comical, historical-pastoral, tragical-historical, tragical-comical-historical-pastoral, scene individable, or poem unlimited; Seneca cannot be too heavy, nor Plautus too light. For the law of writ and the liberty, these are the only men.

*Hamlet.* O Jephthah, judge of Israel, what a treasure hadst thou!

*Polonius.* What treasure had he, my lord?

*Hamlet.* Why,

'One fair daughter, and no more,
The which he loved passing well.'

*Polonius.* [*Aside*] Still on my daughter.

*Hamlet.* Am I not i' the right, old Jephthah?

*Polonius.* If you call me Jephthah, my lord, I have a daughter that I love passing well.

*Hamlet.* Nay, that follows not.

*Polonius.* What follows, then, my lord?

*Hamlet.* Why,

'As by lot, God wot,'

and then, you know,

'It came to pass, as most like it was,'—

the first row of the pious chanson will show you more; for look, where my abridgments come.—

*Enter four or five* Players.

You are welcome, masters; welcome, all. I am glad to see ye well. Welcome, good friends.—O, my old friend! thy face is valanced since I saw thee last; comest thou to beard me in Denmark?—What, my young lady and mistress! By'r lady, your ladyship is nearer to heaven than when I saw you last, by the altitude of a chopine. Pray God, your voice, like a piece of uncurrent gold, be not cracked within the ring.—Masters, you are all welcome. We 'll e'en to 't like French falconers, fly at any thing we see; we 'll have a speech straight. Come, give us a taste of your quality; come, a passionate speech.

1 *Player.* What speech, my lord?

*Hamlet.* I heard thee speak me a speech once, but it was never acted; or, if it was, not above once, for the play, I remember, pleased not the million; 't was caviare to the general; but it was—as I received it, and others, whose judgments in such matters cried in the top of mine—an excellent play, well digested in the scenes, set down with as much modesty as cunning. I remember, one said there were no sallets in the lines to make the matter savoury, nor no matter in the phrase that might indict the author of affectation; but called it an honest method, as wholesome as sweet, and by very much more handsome than fine. One speech in it I chiefly loved: 't was Æneas' tale to Dido; and thereabout of it especially, where he speaks of Priam's slaughter. If it live in your memory, begin at this line; let me see, let me see—

The rugged Pyrrhus, like the Hyrcanian beast,—

't is not so:—it begins with 'Pyrrhus.'

The rugged Pyrrhus, he whose sable arms,
Black as his purpose, did the night resemble
When he lay couched in the ominous horse,
Hath now this dread and black complexion smear'd
With heraldry more dismal: head to foot
Now is he total gules; horridly trick'd
With blood of fathers, mothers, daughters, sons,
Bak'd and impasted with the parching streets,
That lend a tyrannous and damned light
To their lord's murther. Roasted in wrath and fire,
And thus o'er-sized with coagulate gore,
With eyes like carbuncles, the hellish Pyrrhus
Old grandsire Priam seeks.

So, proceed you.

*Polonius.* Fore God, my lord, well spoken, with good accent and good discretion.

1 *Player.* Anon he finds him
Striking too short at Greeks; his antique sword,
Rebellious to his arm, lies where it falls,
Repugnant to command: unequal match'd,
Pyrrhus at Priam drives; in rage strikes wide;
But with the whiff and wind of his fell sword

The unnerv'd father falls. Then senseless Ilium,
Seeming to feel this blow, with flaming top
Stoops to his base, and with a hideous crash
Takes prisoner Pyrrhus' ear; for, lo! his sword,
Which was declining on the milky head
Of reverend Priam, seem'd i' the air to stick:
So, as a painted tyrant, Pyrrhus stood,
And, like a neutral to his will and matter,
Did nothing.
But, as we often see, against some storm,
A silence in the heavens, the rack stand still,
The bold winds speechless, and the orb below
As hush as death, anon the dreadful thunder
Doth rend the region; so, after Pyrrhus' pause,
Aroused vengeance sets him new a-work,
And never did the Cyclops' hammers fall
On Mars's armour forg'd for proof eterne
With less remorse than Pyrrhus' bleeding sword
Now falls on Priam.
Out, out, thou strumpet, Fortune! All you gods,
In general synod, take away her power;
Break all the spokes and fellies from her wheel,
And bowl the round nave down the hill of heaven
As low as to the fiends!

*Polonius.* This is too long.

*Hamlet.* It shall to the barber's, with your beard.—Prithee, say on:—he 's for a jig or a tale of bawdry, or he sleeps.—Say on; come to Hecuba.

1 *Player.* But who, O, who had seen the mobled queen—

*Hamlet.* 'The mobled queen?'

*Polonius.* That 's good; 'mobled queen' is good.

1 *Player.* Run barefoot up and down, threatening the flames
With bisson rheum; a clout about that head
Where late the diadem stood; and for a robe,
About her lank and all o'er-teemed loins,
A blanket, in the alarm of fear caught up;

Who this had seen, with tongue in venom steep'd,
'Gainst Fortune's state would treason have pronounc'd:
But if the gods themselves did see her then,
When she saw Pyrrhus make malicious sport
In mincing with his sword her husband's limbs,
The instant burst of clamour that she made—
Unless things mortal move them not at all—
Would have made milch the burning eyes of heaven
And passion in the gods.

*Polonius.* Look, whether he has not turned his colour and has tears in 's eyes.—Pray you, no more.

*Hamlet.* 'T is well, I 'll have thee speak out the rest soon.—Good my lord, will you see the players well bestowed? Do you hear, let them be well used, for they are the abstract and brief chronicles of the time; after your death you were better have a bad epitaph than their ill report while you live.

*Polonius.* My lord, I will use them according to their desert.

*Hamlet.* God's bodykins, man, much better! Use every man after his desert, and who should scape whipping? Use them after your own honour and dignity; the less they deserve, the more merit is in your bounty. Take them in.

*Polonius.* Come, sirs.

*Hamlet.* Follow him, friends; we 'll hear a play to-morrow. [*Exit Polonius with all the Players but the First.*] Dost thou hear me, old friend; can you play the Murther of Gonzago?

1 *Player.* Ay, my lord.

*Hamlet.* We 'll ha 't to-morrow night. You could, for a need, study a speech of some dozen or sixteen lines, which I would set down and insert in 't, could you not?

1 *Player.* Ay, my lord.

*Hamlet.* Very well. Follow that lord; and look you mock him not.—[*Exit Player.*] My good friends, I 'll leave you till night; you are welcome to Elsinore.

*Rosencrantz.* Good my lord!

*Hamlet.* Ay, so, God be wi' ye!—[*Exeunt Rosencrantz and Guildenstern.*] Now I am alone.
O, what a rogue and peasant slave am I!
Is it not monstrous that this player here,
But in a fiction, in a dream of passion,
Could force his soul so to his own conceit
That from her working all his visage wann'd,
Tears in his eyes, distraction in 's aspect,
A broken voice, and his whole function suiting
With forms to his conceit? and all for nothing!
For Hecuba!
What's Hecuba to him, or he to Hecuba,
That he should weep for her? What would he do,
Had he the motive and the cue for passion
That I have? He would drown the stage with tears
And cleave the general ear with horrid speech,
Make mad the guilty and appal the free,
Confound the ignorant, and amaze indeed
The very faculties of eyes and ears.
Yet I,
A dull and muddy-mettled rascal, peak,
Like John-a-dreams, unpregnant of my cause,
And can say nothing; no, not for a king,
Upon whose property and most dear life
A damn'd defeat was made. Am I a coward?
Who calls me villain? breaks my pate across?
Plucks off my beard, and blows it in my face?
Tweaks me by the nose? gives me the lie i' the throat,
As deep as to the lungs? who does me this?
Ha!
'Swounds, I should take it; for it cannot be
But I am pigeon-liver'd and lack gall
To make oppression bitter, or ere this
I should have fatted all the region kites

With this slave's offal. Bloody, bawdy villain!
Remorseless, treacherous, lecherous, kindless villain!
O vengeance!
Why, what an ass am I! This is most brave,
That I, the son of a dear father murther'd,
Prompted to my revenge by heaven and hell,
Must, like a whore, unpack my heart with words,
And fall a-cursing, like a very drab,
A scullion!
Fie upon 't! foh! About, my brain! I have heard
That guilty creatures sitting at a play
Have by the very cunning of the scene
Been struck so to the soul that presently
They have proclaim'd their malefactions;
For murther, though it have no tongue, will speak
With most miraculous organ. I'll have these players
Play something like the murther of my father
Before mine uncle: I'll observe his looks;
I'll tent him to the quick: if he but blench,
I know my course. The spirit that I have seen
May be the devil; and the devil hath power
To assume a pleasing shape; yea, and perhaps
Out of my weakness and my melancholy,
As he is very potent with such spirits,
Abuses me to damn me. I'll have grounds
More relative than this; the play 's the thing
Wherein I'll catch the conscience of the king. [*Exit.*

## ACT III.

### SCENE I. *A Room in the Castle.*

*Enter* KING, QUEEN, POLONIUS, OPHELIA, ROSENCRANTZ, *and* GUILDENSTERN.

*King.* And can you, by no drift of circumstance,
Get from him why he puts on this confusion,
Grating so harshly all his days of quiet
With turbulent and dangerous lunacy?

*Rosencrantz.* He does confess he feels himself distracted;
But from what cause he will by no means speak.
*Guildenstern.* Nor do we find him forward to be sounded,
But, with a crafty madness, keeps aloof,
When we would bring him on to some confession
Of his true state.
*Queen.* Did he receive you well?
*Rosencrantz.* Most like a gentleman.
*Guildenstern.* But with much forcing of his disposition.
*Rosencrantz.* Niggard of question, but of our demands
Most free in his reply.
*Queen.* Did you assay him
To any pastime?
*Rosencrantz.* Madam, it so fell out that certain players
We o'er-raught on the way; of these we told him,
And there did seem in him a kind of joy
To hear of it. They are about the court,
And, as I think, they have already order
This night to play before him.
*Polonius.* 'Tis most true;
And he beseech'd me to entreat your majesties
To hear and see the matter.
*King.* With all my heart; and it doth much content me
To hear him so inclin'd.—
Good gentlemen, give him a further edge,
And drive his purpose on to these delights.
*Rosencrantz.* We shall, my lord.
[*Exeunt Rosencrantz and Guildenstern.*
*King.* Sweet Gertrude, leave us too;
For we have closely sent for Hamlet hither,
That he, as 't were by accident, may here
Affront Ophelia.
Her father and myself, lawful espials,
Will so bestow ourselves that, seeing unseen,
We may of their encounter frankly judge,

And gather by him, as he is behav'd,
If 't be the affliction of his love or no
That thus he suffers for.

*Queen.* I shall obey you.—
And for your part, Ophelia, I do wish
That your good beauties be the happy cause
Of Hamlet's wildness; so shall I hope your virtues
Will bring him to his wonted way again,
To both your honours.

*Ophelia.* Madam, I wish it may. [*Exit Queen.*

*Polonius.* Ophelia, walk you here.—Gracious, so please you,
We will bestow ourselves. [*To Ophelia*] Read on this book;
That show of such an exercise may colour
Your loneliness. We are oft to blame in this—
'T is too much prov'd—that with devotion's visage
And pious action we do sugar o'er
The devil himself.

*King.* [*Aside*] O, 't is too true!
How smart a lash that speech doth give my conscience!
The harlot's cheek, beautied with plastering art,
Is not more ugly to the thing that helps it
Than is my deed to my most painted word.
O heavy burthen!

*Polonius.* I hear him coming; let 's withdraw, my lord.
[*Exeunt King and Polonius.*

*Enter* HAMLET.

*Hamlet.* To be, or not to be,—that is the question:
Whether 't is nobler in the mind to suffer
The slings and arrows of outrageous fortune,
Or to take arms against a sea of troubles,
And by opposing end them? To die,—to sleep,—
No more; and by a sleep to say we end
The heart-ache and the thousand natural shocks
That flesh is heir to,—'t is a consummation

Devoutly to be wish'd. To die,—to sleep,—
To sleep! perchance to dream! ay, there 's the rub;
For in that sleep of death what dreams may come
When we have shuffled off this mortal coil,
Must give us pause: there 's the respect
That makes calamity of so long life;
For who would bear the whips and scorns of time,
The oppressor's wrong, the proud man's contumely,
The pangs of dispriz'd love, the law's delay,
The insolence of office, and the spurns
That patient merit of the unworthy takes,
When he himself might his quietus make
With a bare bodkin? who would fardels bear,
To grunt and sweat under a weary life,
But that the dread of something after death,
The undiscover'd country from whose bourn
No traveller returns, puzzles the will,
And makes us rather bear those ills we have
Than fly to others that we know not of?
Thus conscience does make cowards of us all;
And thus the native hue of resolution
Is sicklied o'er with the pale cast of thought,
And enterprises of great pith and moment
With this regard their currents turn awry,
And lose the name of action.—Soft you now!
The fair Ophelia!—Nymph, in thy orisons
Be all my sins remember'd.

*Ophelia.* Good my lord,
How does your honour for this many a day?

*Hamlet.* I humbly thank you; well, well, well.

*Ophelia.* My lord, I have remembrances of yours,
That I have longed long to re-deliver;
I pray you, now receive them.

*Hamlet.* No, not I;
I never gave you aught.

*Ophelia.* My honour'd lord, I know right well you did;
And with them words of so sweet breath compos'd
As made the things more rich: their perfume lost,
Take these again; for to the noble mind
Rich gifts wax poor when givers prove unkind.
There, my lord.

*Hamlet.* Ha, ha! are you honest?

*Ophelia.* My lord?

*Hamlet.* Are you fair?

*Ophelia.* What means your lordship?

*Hamlet.* That if you be honest and fair, your honesty should admit no discourse to your beauty.

*Ophelia.* Could beauty, my lord, have better commerce than with honesty?

*Hamlet.* Ay, truly; for the power of beauty will sooner transform honesty from what it is to a bawd than the force of honesty can translate beauty into his likeness: this was sometime a paradox, but now the time gives it proof. I did love you once.

*Ophelia.* Indeed, my lord, you made me believe so.

*Hamlet.* You should not have believed me; for virtue cannot so inoculate our old stock but we shall relish of it: I loved you not.

*Ophelia.* I was the more deceived.

*Hamlet.* Get thee to a nunnery; why wouldst thou be a breeder of sinners? I am myself indifferent honest; but yet I could accuse me of such things that it were better my mother had not borne me: I am very proud, revengeful, ambitious, with more offences at my beck than I have thoughts to put them in, imagination to give them shape, or time to act them in. What should such fellows as I do crawling between earth and heaven? We are arrant knaves all; believe none of us. Go thy ways to a nunnery. Where 's your father?

*Ophelia.* At home, my lord.

*Hamlet.* Let the doors be shut upon him, that he may play the fool no where but in 's own house. Farewell.

*Ophelia.* [*Aside*] O, help him, you sweet heavens!

*Hamlet.* If thou dost marry, I 'll give thee this plague for thy dowry: be thou as chaste as ice, as pure as snow, thou shalt not escape calumny. Get thee to a nunnery, go; farewell. Or, if thou wilt needs marry, marry a fool; for wise men know well enough what monsters you make of them. To a nunnery, go; and quickly too. Farewell.

*Ophelia.* [*Aside*] O heavenly powers, restore him!

*Hamlet.* I have heard of your paintings too, well enough; God has given you one face, and you make yourselves another: you jig, you amble, and you lisp, and nickname God's creatures, and make your wantonness your ignorance. Go to, I 'll no more on 't; it hath made me mad. I say, we will have no more marriages: those that are married already, all but one, shall live; the rest shall keep as they are. To a nunnery, go. [*Exit.*

*Ophelia.* O, what a noble mind is here o'erthrown!
The courtier's, scholar's, soldier's, eye, tongue, sword;
The expectancy and rose of the fair state,
The glass of fashion and the mould of form,
The observ'd of all observers, quite, quite down!
And I, of ladies most deject and wretched,
That suck'd the honey of his music vows,
Now see that noble and most sovereign reason,
Like sweet bells jangled out of tune, and harsh;
That unmatch'd form and feature of blown youth
Blasted with ecstasy: O, woe is me,
To have seen what I have seen, see what I see!

*Enter* KING *and* POLONIUS.

*King.* Love! his affections do not that way tend;
Nor what he spake, though it lack'd form a little,
Was not like madness. There 's something in his soul

O'er which his melancholy sits on brood,
And I do doubt the hatch and the disclose
Will be some danger; which for to prevent,
I have in quick determination
Thus set it down: he shall with speed to England,
For the demand of our neglected tribute.
Haply the seas and countries different
With variable objects shall expel
This something-settled matter in his heart,
Whereon his brains still beating puts him thus
From fashion of himself. What think you on 't?

*Polonius.* It shall do well; but yet do I believe
The origin and commencement of his grief
Sprung from neglected love.—How now, Ophelia!
You need not tell us what Lord Hamlet said;
We heard it all.—My lord, do as you please;
But, if you hold it fit, after the play
Let his queen mother all alone entreat him
To show his grief: let her be round with him;
And I 'll be plac'd, so please you, in the ear
Of all their conference. If she find him not,
To England send him, or confine him where
Your wisdom best shall think.

*King.* It shall be so;
Madness in great ones must not unwatch'd go. [*Exeunt.*

## SCENE II. *A Hall in the Castle.*

*Enter* HAMLET *and* Players.

*Hamlet.* Speak the speech, I pray you, as I pronounced it to you, trippingly on the tongue; but if you mouth it, as many of your players do, I had as lief the town-crier spoke my lines. Nor do not saw the air too much with your hand, thus, but use all gently; for in the very torrent, tempest, and, as I may say, the whirlwind of passion, you must acquire and beget a temperance that may give it smoothness. O, it offends me to the soul to hear a robustious periwig-pated fellow tear a passion to tatters, to very rags, to split the ears of the groundlings, who for the most part are capable of nothing but inexplicable dumb-shows and noise. I could have such a fellow whipped for o'erdoing Termagant; it out-herods Herod: pray you, avoid it.

1 *Player.* I warrant your honour.

*Hamlet.* Be not too tame neither, but let your own discretion be your tutor: suit the action to the word, the word to the action; with this special observance, that you o'erstep not the modesty of nature; for any thing so overdone is from the purpose of playing, whose end, both at the first and now, was and is, to hold, as 't were, the mirror up to nature; to show virtue her own feature, scorn her own image, and the very age and body of the time his form and pressure. Now this overdone, or come tardy off, though it make the unskilful laugh, cannot but make the judicious grieve; the censure of the which one must in your allowance o'erweigh a whole theatre of others. O, there be players that I have seen play, and heard others praise, and that highly, not to speak it profanely, that, neither having the accent of Christians nor the gait of Christian, pagan, nor man, have so strutted and bellowed that I have thought some of nature's journeymen had made men and not made them well, they imitated humanity so abominably.

1 *Player.* I hope we have reformed that indifferently with us, sir.

*Hamlet.* O, reform it altogether. And let those that play your clowns speak no more than is set down for them; for there be of them that will themselves laugh, to set on some quantity of barren spectators to laugh too, though in the mean time some necessary question of the play be then to be considered: that 's villanous, and shows a most pitiful ambition in the fool that uses it. Go, make you ready.

[*Exeunt Players.*

*Enter* POLONIUS, ROSENCRANTZ, *and* GUILDENSTERN.

How now, my lord! will the king hear this piece of work?

*Polonius.* And the queen too, and that presently.

*Hamlet.* Bid the players make haste.—[*Exit Polonius.*]
Will you two help to hasten them?

*Rosencrantz.*<br>*Guildenstern.* } We will, my lord.

[*Exeunt Rosencrantz and Guildenstern.*

*Hamlet.* What ho! Horatio!

*Enter* HORATIO.

*Horatio.* Here, sweet lord, at your service.

*Hamlet.* Horatio, thou art e'en as just a man
As e'er my conversation cop'd withal.

*Horatio.* O, my dear lord,—

*Hamlet.* Nay, do not think I flatter;
For what advancement may I hope from thee
That no revenue hast but thy good spirits,
To feed and clothe thee? Why should the poor be flatter'd?
No, let the candied tongue lick absurd pomp,
And crook the pregnant hinges of the knee
Where thrift may follow fawning. Dost thou hear?
Since my dear soul was mistress of her choice
And could of men distinguish, her election
Hath seal'd thee for herself; for thou hast been
As one, in suffering all, that suffers nothing,
A man that fortune's buffets and rewards
Hath ta'en with equal thanks: and blest are those
Whose blood and judgment are so well commingled
That they are not a pipe for Fortune's finger
To sound what stop she please. Give me that man
That is not passion's slave, and I will wear him
In my heart's core, ay, in my heart of heart,
As I do thee.—Something too much of this.—

There is a play to-night before the king;
One scene of it comes near the circumstance
Which I have told thee of my father's death.
I prithee, when thou seest that act afoot,
Even with the very comment of thy soul
Observe mine uncle; if his occulted guilt
Do not itself unkennel in one speech,
It is a damned ghost that we have seen,
And my imaginations are as foul
As Vulcan's stithy. Give him heedful note;
For I mine eyes will rivet to his face,
And after we will both our judgments join
In censure of his seeming.

*Horatio.* Well, my lord;
If he steal aught the whilst this play is playing,
And scape detecting, I will pay the theft.

*Hamlet.* They are coming to the play; I must be idle: Get you a place.

*Danish march. A flourish. Enter* KING, QUEEN, POLONIUS, OPHELIA, ROSENCRANTZ, GUILDENSTERN, *and others.*

*King.* How fares our cousin Hamlet?

*Hamlet.* Excellent, i' faith; of the chameleon's dish: I eat the air, promise-crammed; you cannot feed capons so.

*King.* I have nothing with this answer, Hamlet; these words are not mine.

*Hamlet.* No, nor mine now.—[*To Polonius*] My lord, you played once i' the university, you say?

*Polonius.* That did I, my lord, and was accounted a good actor.

*Hamlet.* What did you enact?

*Polonius.* I did enact Julius Cæsar: I was killed i' the Capitol; Brutus killed me.

*Hamlet.* It was a brute part of him to kill so capital a calf there.—Be the players ready?

*Rosencrantz.* Ay, my lord; they stay upon your patience.

*Queen.* Come hither, my dear Hamlet, sit by me.

*Hamlet.* No, good mother, here 's metal more attractive.
[*Lying down at Ophelia's feet.*

*Polonius.* [*To the King*] O, ho! do you mark that?

*Ophelia.* You are merry, my lord.

*Hamlet.* Who, I?

*Ophelia.* Ay, my lord.

*Hamlet.* O God, your only jig-maker. What should a man do but be merry? for, look you, how cheerfully my mother looks, and my father died within 's two hours.

*Ophelia.* Nay, 't is twice two months, my lord.

*Hamlet.* So long? Nay then, let the devil wear black, for I 'll have a suit of sables. O heavens! die two months ago, and not forgotten yet? Then there's hope a great man's memory may outlive his life half a year: but, by 'r lady, he must build churches, then; or else shall he suffer not thinking on, with the hobby-horse, whose epitaph is 'For, O, for, O, the hobby-horse is forgot!'

*Hautboys play. The dumb-show enters.*

*Enter a* King *and a* Queen *very lovingly; the* Queen *embracing him, and he her. She kneels, and makes show of protestation unto him. He takes her up, and declines his head upon her neck; lays him down upon a bank of flowers: she, seeing him asleep, leaves him. Anon comes in a fellow, takes off his crown, kisses it, and pours poison in the* King's *ears, and exit. The* Queen *returns, finds the* King *dead, and makes passionate action. The* Poisoner, *with some two or three* Mutes, *comes in again, seeming to lament with her. The dead body is carried away. The* Poisoner *wooes the* Queen *with gifts; she seems loath and unwilling awhile, but in the end accepts his love.* [*Exeunt.*

*Ophelia.* What means this, my lord?

*Hamlet.* Marry, this is miching mallecho; it means mischief.

*Ophelia.* Belike this show imports the argument of the play?

*Enter* Prologue.

*Hamlet.* We shall know by this fellow: the players cannot keep counsel; they 'll tell all.

*Ophelia.* Will he tell us what this show meant?

*Hamlet.* Ay, or any show that you 'll show him; be not you ashamed to show, he 'll not shame to tell you what it means.

*Ophelia.* You are naught, you are naught; I 'll mark the play.

*Prologue.* For us, and for our tragedy,
Here stooping to your clemency,
We beg your hearing patiently. [*Exit.*

*Hamlet.* Is this a prologue, or the posy of a ring?

*Ophelia.* 'T is brief, my lord.

*Hamlet.* As woman's love.

*Enter two* Players, King *and* Queen.

*Player King.* Full thirty times hath Phœbus' cart gone round
Neptune's salt wash and Tellus' orbed ground,
And thirty dozen moons with borrow'd sheen
About the world have times twelve thirties been,
Since love our hearts and Hymen did our hands
Unite commutual in most sacred bands.

*Player Queen.* So many journeys may the sun and moon
Make us again count o'er ere love be done!
But, woe is me, you are so sick of late,
So far from cheer and from your former state,
That I distrust you. Yet, though I distrust,
Discomfort you, my lord, it nothing must;
For women's fear and love holds quantity,
In neither aught, or in extremity.
Now, what my love is, proof hath made you know,
And as my love is siz'd, my fear is so;
Where love is great, the littlest doubts are fear;
Where little fears grow great, great love grows there.

*Player King.* Faith, I must leave thee, love, and shortly too;

My operant powers their functions leave to do:
And thou shalt live in this fair world behind,
Honour'd, belov'd; and haply one as kind
For husband shalt thou—

*Player Queen.* O, confound the rest!
Such love must needs be treason in my breast;
In second husband let me be accurst!
None wed the second but who kill'd the first.

*Hamlet.* [*Aside*] Wormwood, wormwood!

*Player Queen.* The instances that second marriage move
Are base respects of thrift, but none of love;
A second time I kill my husband dead,
When second husband kisses me in bed.

*Player King.* I do believe you think what now you speak,
But what we do determine oft we break.
Purpose is but the slave to memory,
Of violent birth, but poor validity;
Which now, like fruit unripe, sticks on the tree,
But fall unshaken when they mellow be.
Most necessary 't is that we forget
To pay ourselves what to ourselves is debt;
What to ourselves in passion we propose,
The passion ending, doth the purpose lose.
The violence of either grief or joy
Their own enactures with themselves destroy:
Where joy most revels, grief doth most lament;
Grief joys, joy grieves, on slender accident.
This world is not for aye, nor 't is not strange
That even our loves should with our fortunes change;
For 't is a question left us yet to prove,
Whether love lead fortune or else fortune love.
The great man down, you mark his favourites flies;
The poor advanc'd makes friends of enemies.
And hitherto doth love on fortune tend;
For who not needs shall never lack a friend,
And who in want a hollow friend doth try
Directly seasons him his enemy.
But, orderly to end where I begun,
Our wills and fates do so contrary run
That our devices still are overthrown,
Our thoughts are ours, their ends none of our own;

So think thou wilt no second husband wed,
But die thy thoughts when thy first lord is dead.

*Player Queen.* Nor earth to me give food, nor heaven light!
Sport and repose lock from me day and night!
To desperation turn my trust and hope!
An anchor's cheer in prison be my scope!
Each opposite that blanks the face of joy
Meet what I would have well and it destroy!
Both here and hence pursue me lasting strife,
If, once a widow, ever I be wife!

*Hamlet.* If she should break it now!

*Player King.* 'T is deeply sworn. Sweet, leave me here a while;
My spirits grow dull, and fain I would beguile
The tedious day with sleep. [*Sleeps.*

*Player Queen.* Sleep rock thy brain;
And never come mischance between us twain! [*Exit.*

*Hamlet.* Madam, how like you this play?

*Queen.* The lady protests too much, methinks.

*Hamlet.* O, but she 'll keep her word.

*King.* Have you heard the argument? Is there no offence in 't?

*Hamlet.* No, no, they do but jest, poison in jest; no offence i' the world.

*King.* What do you call the play?

*Hamlet.* The Mouse-trap. Marry, how? Tropically. This play is the image of a murther done in Vienna: Gonzago is the duke's name; his wife, Baptista: you shall see anon; 't is a knavish piece of work: but what o' that? your majesty and we that have free souls, it touches us not; let the galled jade wince, our withers are unwrung.—

*Enter* LUCIANUS.

This is one Lucianus, nephew to the king.

*Ophelia.* You are as good as a chorus, my lord.

*Hamlet.* I could interpret between you and your love, if I could see the puppets dallying.

*Ophelia.* You are keen, my lord, you are keen.

*Hamlet.* Begin, murtherer; pox, leave thy damnable faces, and begin. Come: the croaking raven doth bellow for revenge.

*Lucianus.* Thoughts black, hands apt, drugs fit, and time agreeing;
Confederate season, else no creature seeing;
Thou mixture rank, of midnight weeds collected,
With Hecate's ban thrice blasted, thrice infected,
Thy natural magic and dire property,
On wholesome life usurp immediately.

[*Pours the poison into the sleeper's ear.*

*Hamlet.* He poisons him i' the garden for 's estate. His name 's Gonzago; the story is extant, and writ in choice Italian. You shall see anon how the murtherer gets the love of Gonzago's wife.

*Ophelia.* The king rises!

*Hamlet.* What, frighted with false fire!

*Queen.* How fares my lord?

*Polonius.* Give o'er the play!

*King.* Give me some light!—away!

*All.* Lights, lights, lights!

[*Exeunt all but Hamlet and Horatio*

*Hamlet.* Why, let the strucken deer go weep,
The hart ungalled play;
For some must watch, while some must sleep:
So runs the world away.

Would not this, sir, and a forest of feathers—if the rest of my fortunes turn Turk with me—with two Provincial roses on my razed shoes, get me a fellowship in a cry of players, sir?

*Horatio.* Half a share.

*Hamlet.* A whole one, I.
For thou dost know, O Damon dear,
This realm dismantled was
Of Jove himself; and now reigns here
A very, very—pajock.

*Horatio.* You might have rhymed.

*Hamlet.* O good Horatio, I 'll take the ghost's word for a thousand pound. Didst perceive?

*Horatio.* Very well, my lord.

*Hamlet.* Upon the talk of the poisoning?

*Horatio.* I did very well note him.

*Hamlet.* Ah, ha! Come, some music! come, the recorders!—

For if the king like not the comedy,
Why then, belike,—he likes it not, perdy.—

Come, some music!

*Re-enter* ROSENCRANTZ *and* GUILDENSTERN.

*Guildenstern.* Good my lord, vouchsafe me a word with you.

*Hamlet.* Sir, a whole history.

*Guildenstern.* The king, sir,—

*Hamlet.* Ay, sir, what of him?

*Guildenstern.* Is in his retirement marvellous distempered.

*Hamlet.* With drink, sir?

*Guildenstern.* No, my lord, rather with choler.

*Hamlet.* Your wisdom should show itself more richer to signify this to his doctor; for, for me to put him to his purgation would perhaps plunge him into far more choler.

*Guildenstern.* Good my lord, put your discourse into some frame, and start not so wildly from my affair.

*Hamlet.* I am tame, sir; pronounce.

*Guildenstern.* The queen, your mother, in most great affliction of spirit, hath sent me to you.

*Hamlet.* You are welcome.

*Guildenstern.* Nay, good my lord, this courtesy is not of the right breed. If it shall please you to make me a wholesome answer, I will do your mother's commandment; if not, your pardon and my return shall be the end of my business.

*Hamlet.* Sir, I cannot.

*Guildenstern.* What, my lord?

*Hamlet.* Make you a wholesome answer; my wit 's diseased: but, sir, such answer as I can make, you shall command,—or, rather, as you say, my mother; therefore no more, but to the matter: my mother, you say,—

*Rosencrantz.* Then thus she says: your behaviour hath struck her into amazement and admiration.

*Hamlet.* O wonderful son, that can so astonish a mother! But is there no sequel at the heels of this mother's admiration? Impart.

*Rosencrantz.* She desires to speak with you in her closet, ere you go to bed.

*Hamlet.* We shall obey, were she ten times our mother. Have you any further trade with us?

*Rosencrantz.* My lord, you once did love me.

*Hamlet.* So I do still, by these pickers and stealers.

*Rosencrantz.* Good my lord, what is your cause of distemper? you do, surely, bar the door upon your own liberty, if you deny your griefs to your friend.

*Hamlet.* Sir, I lack advancement.

*Rosencrantz.* How can that be, when you have the voice of the king himself for your succession in Denmark?

*Hamlet.* Ay, sir, but 'while the grass grows,'—the proverb is something musty.—

*Re-enter* Players *with recorders.*

O, the recorders! let me see one.—To withdraw with you,—why do you go about to recover the wind of me, as if you would drive me into a toil?

*Guildenstern.* O, my lord, if my duty be too bold, my love is too unmannerly.

*Hamlet.* I do not well understand that. Will you play upon this pipe?

*Guildenstern.* My lord, I cannot.

*Hamlet.* I pray you.

*Guildenstern.* Believe me, I cannot.

*Hamlet.* I do beseech you.

*Guildenstern.* I know no touch of it, my lord.

*Hamlet.* 'T is as easy as lying; govern these ventages with your fingers and thumb, give it breath with your mouth, and it will discourse most eloquent music. Look you, these are the stops.

*Guildenstern.* But these cannot I command to any utterance of harmony; I have not the skill.

*Hamlet.* Why, look you now, how unworthy a thing you make of me! You would play upon me; you would seem to know my stops; you would pluck out the heart of my mystery; you would sound me from my lowest note to the top of my compass: and there is much music, excellent voice, in this little organ; yet cannot you make it speak. 'Sblood, do you think I am easier to be played on than a pipe? Call me what instrument you will, though you can fret me, you cannot play upon me.—

*Enter* POLONIUS.

God bless you, sir!

*Polonius.* My lord, the queen would speak with you, and presently.

*Hamlet.* Do you see yonder cloud that 's almost in shape of a camel?

*Polonius.* By the mass, and 't is like a camel, indeed.

*Hamlet.* Methinks it is like a weasel.

*Polonius.* It is backed like a weasel.

*Hamlet.* Or like a whale?

*Polonius.* Very like a whale.

*Hamlet.* Then will I come to my mother by and by.—[*Aside*] They fool me to the top of my bent.—I will come by and by.

*Polonius.* I will say so. [*Exit Polonius.*

*Hamlet.* By and by is easily said.—Leave me, friends.

[*Exeunt all but Hamlet.*

'T is now the very witching time of night,
When churchyards yawn, and hell itself breathes out
Contagion to this world; now could I drink hot blood,
And do such bitter business as the day
Would quake to look on. Soft! now to my mother.
O heart, lose not thy nature; let not ever
The soul of Nero enter this firm bosom;
Let me be cruel, not unnatural.
I will speak daggers to her, but use none;
My tongue and soul in this be hypocrites:
How in my words soever she be shent,
To give them seals never, my soul, consent! [*Exit.*

## SCENE III. *A Room in the Castle.*

*Enter* KING, ROSENCRANTZ, *and* GUILDENSTERN.

*King.* I like him not, nor stands it safe with us
To let his madness range. Therefore prepare you;
I your commission will forthwith dispatch,
And he to England shall along with you.
The terms of our estate may not endure
Hazard so near us as doth hourly grow
Out of his lunacies.

*Guildenstern.* We will ourselves provide;
Most holy and religious fear it is
To keep those many many bodies safe
That live and feed upon your majesty.

*Rosencrantz.* The single and peculiar life is bound
With all the strength and armour of the mind
To keep itself from noyance; but much more
That spirit upon whose weal depends and rests
The lives of many. The cease of majesty
Dies not alone, but like a gulf doth draw
What 's near it with it: it is a massy wheel,
Fix'd on the summit of the highest mount,

To whose huge spokes ten thousand lesser things
Are mortis'd and adjoin'd; which, when it falls,
Each small annexment, petty consequence,
Attends the boisterous ruin. Never alone
Did the king sigh, but with a general groan.

*King.* Arm you, I pray you, to this speedy voyage;
For we will fetters put upon this fear,
Which now goes too free-footed.

*Rosencrantz.* }
*Guildenstern.* } We will haste us.

[*Exeunt Rosencrantz and Guildenstern.*

*Enter* POLONIUS.

*Polonius.* My lord, he 's going to his mother's closet.
Behind the arras I 'll convey myself,
To hear the process; I 'll warrant she 'll tax him home:
And, as you said, and wisely was it said,
'T is meet that some more audience than a mother,
Since nature makes them partial, should o'erhear
The speech, of vantage. Fare you well, my liege;
I 'll call upon you ere you go to bed,
And tell you what I know.

*King.* Thanks, dear my lord.

[*Exit Polonius.*

O, my offence is rank, it smells to heaven;
It hath the primal eldest curse upon 't,
A brother's murther! Pray can I not,
Though inclination be as sharp as will;
My stronger guilt defeats my strong intent,
And, like a man to double business bound,
I stand in pause where I shall first begin,
And both neglect. What if this cursed hand
Were thicker than itself with brother's blood,
Is there not rain enough in the sweet heavens
To wash it white as snow? Whereto serves mercy

But to confront the visage of offence?
And what 's in prayer but this twofold force,—
To be forestalled ere we come to fall,
Or pardon'd being down? Then I 'll look up;
My fault is past. But, O, what form of prayer
Can serve my turn? 'Forgive me my foul murther?'
That cannot be; since I am still possess'd
Of those effects for which I did the murther,
My crown, mine own ambition, and my queen.
May one be pardon'd and retain the offence?
In the corrupted currents of this world
Offence's gilded hand may shove by justice,
And oft 't is seen the wicked prize itself
Buys out the law; but 't is not so above:
There is no shuffling, there the action lies
In his true nature, and we ourselves compell'd
Even to the teeth and forehead of our faults
To give in evidence. What then? what rests?
Try what repentance can: what can it not?
Yet what can it when one can not repent?
O wretched state! O bosom black as death!
O limed soul, that struggling to be free
Art more engag'd! Help, angels! Make assay!
Bow, stubborn knees; and, heart with strings of steel,
Be soft as sinews of the new-born babe!
All may be well. [*Retires and kneels*

*Enter* HAMLET.

*Hamlet.* Now might I do it pat, now he is praying;
And now I 'll do 't.—And so he goes to heaven;
And so am I reveng'd. That would be scann'd:
A villain kills my father; and for that,
I, his sole son, do this same villain send
To heaven.
O, this is hire and salary, not revenge.

He took my father grossly, full of bread,
With all his crimes broad blown, as flush as May;
And how his audit stands who knows save heaven?
But in our circumstance and course of thought,
'T is heavy with him; and am I then reveng'd,
To take him in the purging of his soul,
When he is fit and season'd for his passage?
No!
Up, sword, and know thou a more horrid hent:
When he is drunk asleep, or in his rage,
Or in the incestuous pleasure of his bed;
At gaming, swearing, or about some act
That has no relish of salvation in 't;
Then trip him, that his heels may kick at heaven,
And that his soul may be as damn'd and black
As hell, whereto it goes. My mother stays.—
This physic but prolongs thy sickly days. [*Exit.*

*King.* [*Rising*] My words fly up, my thoughts remain below;
Words without thoughts never to heaven go. [*Exit.*

SCENE IV. *The Queen's Closet.*

*Enter* QUEEN *and* POLONIUS.

*Polonius.* He will come straight. Look you lay home to him;
Tell him his pranks have been too broad to bear with,
And that your grace hath screen'd and stood between
Much heat and him. I 'll silence me even here.
Pray you, be round with him.

*Hamlet.* [*Within*] Mother! mother! mother!

*Queen.* I 'll warrant you;
Fear me not. Withdraw, I hear him coming.

[*Polonius hides behind the arras.*

*Enter* HAMLET.

*Hamlet.* Now, mother, what 's the matter?
*Queen.* Hamlet, thou hast thy father much offended.
*Hamlet.* Mother, you have my father much offended.
*Queen.* Come, come, you answer with an idle tongue.
*Hamlet.* Go, go, you question with a wicked tongue.
*Queen.* Why, how now, Hamlet!
*Hamlet.* What 's the matter now?
*Queen.* Have you forgot me?
*Hamlet.* No, by the rood, not so:
You are the queen, your husband's brother's wife;
And—would it were not so!—you are my mother.
*Queen.* Nay, then, I 'll set those to you that can speak.
*Hamlet.* Come, come, and sit you down; you shall not budge:
You go not till I set you up a glass
Where you may see the inmost part of you.
*Queen.* What wilt thou do? thou wilt not murther me?
Help, help, ho!
*Polonius.* [*Behind*] What, ho! help, help, help!
*Hamlet.* [*Drawing*] How now! a rat? Dead, for a ducat, dead! [*Makes a pass through the arras.*
*Polonius.* [*Behind*] O, I am slain! [*Falls and dies.*
*Queen.* O me, what hast thou done?
*Hamlet.* Nay, I know not;
Is it the king?
*Queen.* O, what a rash and bloody deed is this!
*Hamlet.* A bloody deed! almost as bad, good mother,
As kill a king, and marry with his brother.
*Queen.* As kill a king!
*Hamlet.* Ay, lady, 't was my word.—
[*Lifts up the arras and discovers Polonius.*
Thou wretched, rash, intruding fool, farewell!
I took thee for thy better: take thy fortune;

Thou find'st to be too busy is some danger.—
Leave wringing of your hands: peace! sit you down,
And let me wring your heart; for so I shall,
If it be made of penetrable stuff,
If damned custom have not braz'd it so
That it is proof and bulwark against sense.

*Queen.* What have I done, that thou darest wag thy tongue
In noise so rude against me?

*Hamlet.* Such an act
That blurs the grace and blush of modesty,
Calls virtue hypocrite, takes off the rose
From the fair forehead of an innocent love
And sets a blister there, makes marriage-vows
As false as dicers' oaths; O, such a deed
As from the body of contraction plucks
The very soul, and sweet religion makes
A rhapsody of words: heaven's face doth glow,
Yea, this solidity and compound mass,
With tristful visage, as against the doom,
Is thought-sick at the act.

*Queen.* Ay me, what act,
That roars so loud and thunders in the index?

*Hamlet.* Look here, upon this picture, and on this,
The counterfeit presentment of two brothers.
See, what a grace was seated on this brow:
Hyperion's curls; the front of Jove himself;
An eye like Mars, to threaten and command;
A station like the herald Mercury
New-lighted on a heaven-kissing hill;
A combination and a form indeed,
Where every god did seem to set his seal,
To give the world assurance of a man.
This was your husband. Look you now, what follows:
Here is your husband; like a mildew'd ear,

Blasting his wholesome brother. Have you eyes?
Could you on this fair mountain leave to feed,
And batten on this moor? Ha! have you eyes?
You cannot call it love, for at your age
The hey-day in the blood is tame, it 's humble,
And waits upon the judgment; and what judgment
Would step from this to this? Sense, sure, you have,
Else could you not have motion; but sure, that sense
Is apoplex'd: for madness would not err,
Nor sense to ecstasy was ne'er so thrall'd
But it reserv'd some quantity of choice,
To serve in such a difference. What devil was 't
That thus hath cozen'd you at hoodman-blind?
Eyes without feeling, feeling without sight,
Ears without hands or eyes, smelling sans all,
Or but a sickly part of one true sense
Could not so mope.
O shame! where is thy blush? Rebellious hell,
If thou canst mutine in a matron's bones,
To flaming youth let virtue be as wax,
And melt in her own fire; proclaim no shame
When the compulsive ardour gives the charge,
Since frost itself as actively doth burn,
And reason panders will.

*Queen.* O Hamlet, speak no more:
Thou turn'st mine eyes into my very soul,
And there I see such black and grained spots
As will not leave their tinct.

*Hamlet.* Nay, but to live
Stew'd in corruption,—

*Queen.* O, speak to me no more;
These words like daggers enter in mine ears:
No more, sweet Hamlet!

*Hamlet.* A murtherer and a villain;
A slave that is not twentieth part the tithe

Of your precedent lord ; a vice of kings ;
A cutpurse of the empire and the rule,
That from a shelf the precious diadem stole,
And put it in his pocket!
*Queen.* No more!
*Hamlet.* A king of shreds and patches,—

*Enter* Ghost.

Save me, and hover o'er me with your wings,
You heavenly guards!—What would your gracious figure?
*Queen.* Alas! he 's mad!
*Hamlet.* Do you not come your tardy son to chide,
That, laps'd in time and passion, lets go by
The important acting of your dread command?
O, say!
*Ghost.* Do not forget. This visitation
Is but to whet thy almost blunted purpose.
But, look, amazement on thy mother sits:
O, step between her and her fighting soul;
Conceit in weakest bodies strongest works.
Speak to her, Hamlet.
*Hamlet.* How is it with you, lady?
*Queen.* Alas, how is 't with you,
That you do bend your eye on vacancy
And with the incorporal air do hold discourse?
Forth at your eyes your spirits wildly peep;
And, as the sleeping soldiers in the alarm,
Your bedded hair, like life in excrements,
Starts up, and stands an end. O gentle son,
Upon the heat and flame of thy distemper
Sprinkle cool patience. Whereon do you look?
*Hamlet.* On him, on him! Look you, how pale he glares!
His form and cause conjoin'd, preaching to stones,
Would make them capable.—Do not look upon me;
Lest with this piteous action you convert

My stern effects: then what I have to do
Will want true colour; tears perchance for blood.

*Queen.* To whom do you speak this?

*Hamlet.* Do you see nothing there?

*Queen.* Nothing at all; yet all that is I see.

*Hamlet.* Nor did you nothing hear?

*Queen.* No, nothing but ourselves.

*Hamlet.* Why, look you there! look, how it steals away!
My father, in his habit as he liv'd!
Look, where he goes, even now, out at the portal!

[*Exit Ghost.*

*Queen.* This is the very coinage of your brain;
This bodiless creation ecstasy
Is very cunning in.

*Hamlet.* Ecstasy!
My pulse, as yours, doth temperately keep time,
And makes as healthful music: it is not madness
That I have utter'd; bring me to the test,
And I the matter will re-word, which madness
Would gambol from. Mother, for love of grace,
Lay not that flattering unction to your soul,
That not your trespass but my madness speaks;
It will but skin and film the ulcerous place,
Whilst rank corruption, mining all within,
Infects unseen. Confess yourself to heaven;
Repent what 's past, avoid what is to come;
And do not spread the compost on the weeds,
To make them ranker. Forgive me this my virtue;
For in the fatness of these pursy times
Virtue itself of vice must pardon beg,
Yea, curb and woo for leave to do him good.

*Queen.* O Hamlet, thou hast cleft my heart in twain.

*Hamlet.* O, throw away the worser part of it,
And live the purer with the other half.
Good night: but go not to mine uncle's bed;

Assume a virtue, if you have it not.
That monster, custom, who all sense doth eat,
Of habits devil, is angel yet in this,
That to the use of actions fair and good
He likewise gives a frock or livery,
That aptly is put on. Refrain to-night,
And that shall lend a kind of easiness
To the next abstinence: the next more easy;
For use almost can change the stamp of nature,
And either master the devil, or throw him out
With wondrous potency. Once more, good night:
And when you are desirous to be blest,
I 'll blessing beg of you.—For this same lord,
[*Pointing to Polonius.*
I do repent; but heaven hath pleas'd it so,
To punish me with this and this with me,
That I must be their scourge and minister.
I will bestow him, and will answer well
The death I gave him.—So, again, good night.
I must be cruel, only to be kind;
Thus bad begins, and worse remains behind.
One word more, good lady.

*Queen.* What shall I do?

*Hamlet.* Not this, by no means, that I bid you do:
Let the bloat king tempt you again to bed,
Pinch wanton on your cheek, call you his mouse;
And let him, for a pair of reechy kisses,
Or paddling in your neck with his damn'd fingers,
Make you to ravel all this matter out,
That I essentially am not in madness,
But mad in craft. 'T were good you let him know;
For who, that 's but a queen, fair, sober, wise,
Would from a paddock, from a bat, a gib,
Such dear concernings hide? who would do so?
No, in despite of sense and secrecy,

Unpeg the basket on the house's top,
Let the birds fly, and, like the famous ape,
To try conclusions, in the basket creep,
And break your own neck down.

*Queen.* Be thou assur'd, if words be made of breath,
And breath of life, I have no life to breathe
What thou hast said to me.

*Hamlet.* I must to England; you know that?

*Queen.* Alack,
I had forgot; 't is so concluded on.

*Hamlet.* There 's letters seal'd, and my two schoolfellows—
Whom I will trust as I will adders fang'd—
They bear the mandate; they must sweep my way,
And marshal me to knavery. Let it work;
For 't is the sport to have the enginer
Hoist with his own petar: and 't shall go hard
But I will delve one yard below their mines,
And blow them at the moon. O, 't is most sweet,
When in one line two crafts directly meet!
This man shall set me packing;
I 'll lug the guts into the neighbour room.
Mother, good night. Indeed this counsellor
Is now most still, most secret, and most grave,
Who was in life a foolish prating knave.—
Come, sir, to draw toward an end with you.—
Good night, mother.

[*Exeunt severally; Hamlet dragging in Polonius.*

DANISH SHIPS.

# ACT IV.

## SCENE I. *A Room in the Castle.*

*Enter* KING, QUEEN, ROSENCRANTZ, *and* GUILDENSTERN.

*King.* There 's matter in these sighs: these profound heaves
You must translate; 't is fit we understand them.
Where is your son?

*Queen.* Bestow this place on us a little while.—
[*Exeunt Rosencrantz and Guildenstern.*
Ah, my good lord, what have I seen to-night!

*King.* What, Gertrude? How does Hamlet?

*Queen.* Mad as the sea and wind, when both contend
Which is the mightier; in his lawless fit,
Behind the arras hearing something stir,
Whips out his rapier, cries, 'A rat, a rat!'

And in this brainish apprehension kills
The unseen good old man.

*King.* O heavy deed!
It had been so with us, had we been there;
His liberty is full of threats to all,
To you yourself, to us, to every one.
Alas, how shall this bloody deed be answer'd?
It will be laid to us, whose providence
Should have kept short, restrain'd, and out of haunt,
This mad young man; but so much was our love,
We would not understand what was most fit,
But, like the owner of a foul disease,
To keep it from divulging, let it feed
Even on the pith of life. Where is he gone?

*Queen.* To draw apart the body he hath kill'd;
O'er whom his very madness, like some ore
Among a mineral of metals base,
Shows itself pure. He weeps for what is done.

*King.* O Gertrude, come away!
The sun no sooner shall the mountains touch,
But we will ship him hence; and this vile deed
We must, with all our majesty and skill,
Both countenance and excuse.—Ho, Guildenstern!

*Re-enter* ROSENCRANTZ *and* GUILDENSTERN.

Friends both, go join you with some further aid;
Hamlet in madness hath Polonius slain,
And from his mother's closet hath he dragg'd him.
Go seek him out; speak fair, and bring the body
Into the chapel. I pray you, haste in this.—
[*Exeunt Rosencrantz and Guildenstern.*
Come, Gertrude, we 'll call up our wisest friends,
And let them know both what we mean to do
And what 's untimely done; so, haply, slander—
Whose whisper o'er the world's diameter,

As level as the cannon to his blank,
Transports his poison'd shot—may miss our name,
And hit the woundless air. O, come away!
My soul is full of discord and dismay. [*Exeunt.*

## SCENE II. *Another Room in the Castle.*

*Enter* HAMLET.

*Hamlet.* Safely stowed.

*Rosencrantz.* } *Guildenstern.* } [*Within*] Hamlet! Lord Hamlet!

*Hamlet.* What noise? who calls on Hamlet? O, here they come.

*Enter* ROSENCRANTZ *and* GUILDENSTERN.

*Rosencrantz.* What have you done, my lord, with the dead body?

*Hamlet.* Compounded it with dust, whereto 't is kin.

*Rosencrantz.* Tell us where 't is, that we may take it thence
And bear it to the chapel.

*Hamlet.* Do not believe it.

*Rosencrantz.* Believe what?

*Hamlet.* That I can keep your counsel and not mine own. Besides, to be demanded of a sponge, what replication should be made by the son of a king?

*Rosencrantz.* Take you me for a sponge, my lord?

*Hamlet.* Ay, sir, that soaks up the king's countenance, his rewards, his authorities. But such officers do the king best service in the end; he keeps them, as an ape doth nuts, in the corner of his jaw, first mouthed, to be last swallowed: when he needs what you have gleaned, it is but squeezing you, and, sponge, you shall be dry again.

*Rosencrantz.* I understand you not, my lord.

*Hamlet.* I am glad of it; a knavish speech sleeps in a foolish ear.

*Rosencrantz.* My lord, you must tell us where the body is, and go with us to the king.

*Hamlet.* The body is with the king, but the king is not with the body. The king is a thing—

*Guildenstern.* A thing, my lord!

*Hamlet.* Of nothing; bring me to him. Hide fox, and all after. [*Exeunt.*

## SCENE III. *Another Room in the Castle.*

*Enter* KING, *attended.*

*King.* I have sent to seek him, and to find the body.
How dangerous is it that this man goes loose!
Yet must not we put the strong law on him:
He 's lov'd of the distracted multitude,
Who like not in their judgment, but their eyes;
And where 't is so, the offender's scourge is weigh'd,
But never the offence. To bear all smooth and even,
This sudden sending him away must seem
Deliberate pause; diseases desperate grown
By desperate appliance are reliev'd,
Or not at all.—

*Enter* ROSENCRANTZ.

How now! what hath befall'n?

*Rosencrantz.* Where the dead body is bestow'd, my lord,
We cannot get from him.

*King.* But where is he?

*Rosencrantz.* Without, my lord; guarded, to know your pleasure.

*King.* Bring him before us.

*Rosencrantz.* Ho, Guildenstern! bring in my lord.

*Enter* HAMLET *and* GUILDENSTERN.

*King.* Now, Hamlet, where 's Polonius?

*Hamlet.* At supper.

*King.* At supper! where?

*Hamlet.* Not where he eats, but where he is eaten; a certain convocation of politic worms are e'en at him. Your worm is your only emperor for diet; we fat all creatures else to fat us, and we fat ourselves for maggots. Your fat king and your lean beggar is but variable service, two dishes, but to one table; that 's the end.

*King.* Alas, alas!

*Hamlet.* A man may fish with the worm that hath eat of a king, and eat of the fish that hath fed of that worm.

*King.* What dost thou mean by this?

*Hamlet.* Nothing but to show you how a king may go a progress through the guts of a beggar.

*King.* Where is Polonius?

*Hamlet.* In heaven; send thither to see: if your messenger find him not there, seek him i' the other place yourself. But indeed, if you find him not within this month, you shall nose him as you go up the stairs into the lobby.

*King.* Go seek him there. [*To some Attendants.*

*Hamlet.* He will stay till ye come. [*Exeunt Attendants.*

*King.* Hamlet, this deed, for thine especial safety,—
Which we do tender, as we dearly grieve
For that which thou hast done,—must send thee hence
With fiery quickness; therefore prepare thyself.
The bark is ready, and the wind at help,
The associates tend, and every thing is bent
For England.

*Hamlet.* For England!

*King.* Ay, Hamlet.

*Hamlet.* Good.

*King.* So is it, if thou knew'st our purposes.

*Hamlet.* I see a cherub that sees them.—But, come; for England!—Farewell, dear mother.

*King.* Thy loving father, Hamlet.

*Hamlet.* My mother: father and mother is man and wife; man and wife is one flesh; and so, my mother.—Come, for England! [*Exit.*

*King.* Follow him at foot; tempt him with speed aboard;
Delay it not; I 'll have him hence to-night.
Away! for every thing is seal'd and done
That else leans on the affair; pray you, make haste.—
[*Exeunt Rosencrantz and Guildenstern.*
And, England, if my love thou hold'st at aught—
As my great power thereof may give thee sense,
Since yet thy cicatrice looks raw and red
After the Danish sword, and thy free awe
Pays homage to us—thou may'st not coldly set
Our sovereign process; which imports at full,
By letters conjuring to that effect,
The present death of Hamlet. Do it, England;
For like the hectic in my blood he rages,
And thou must cure me: till I know 't is done,
Howe'er my haps, my joys were ne'er begun. [*Exit.*

## SCENE IV. *A Plain in Denmark.*

*Enter* FORTINBRAS, *a* Captain, *and* Soldiers, *marching.*

*Fortinbras.* Go, captain, from me greet the Danish king;
Tell him that by his license Fortinbras
Claims the conveyance of a promis'd march
Over his kingdom. You know the rendezvous.
If that his majesty would aught with us,
We shall express our duty in his eye;
And let him know so.

*Captain.* I will do 't, my lord.

*Fortinbras.* Go softly on.
[*Exeunt Fortinbras and Soldiers.*

*Enter* HAMLET, ROSENCRANTZ, GUILDENSTERN, *and others.*

*Hamlet.* Good sir, whose powers are these?
*Captain.* They are of Norway, sir.
*Hamlet.* How purpos'd, sir, I pray you?
*Captain.* Against some part of Poland.
*Hamlet.* Who commands them, sir?
*Captain.* The nephew to old Norway, Fortinbras.
*Hamlet.* Goes it against the main of Poland, sir,
Or for some frontier?
*Captain.* Truly to speak, and with no addition,
We go to gain a little patch of ground
That hath in it no profit but the name.
To pay five ducats, five, I would not farm it;
Nor will it yield to Norway or the Pole
A ranker rate, should it be sold in fee.
*Hamlet.* Why, then the Polack never will defend it.
*Captain.* Yes, 't is already garrison'd.
*Hamlet.* Two thousand souls and twenty thousand ducats
Will not debate the question of this straw;
This is the imposthume of much wealth and peace,
That inward breaks, and shows no cause without
Why the man dies.—I humbly thank you, sir.
*Captain.* God be wi' you, sir. [*Exit.*
*Rosencrantz.* Will 't please you go, my lord?
*Hamlet.* I 'll be with you straight. Go a little before.
[*Exeunt all except Hamlet.*

How all occasions do inform against me,
And spur my dull revenge! What is a man,
If his chief good and market of his time
Be but to sleep and feed? a beast, no more.
Sure, He that made us with such large discourse,
Looking before and after, gave us not
That capability and godlike reason
To fust in us unus'd. Now, whether it be

Bestial oblivion, or some craven scruple
Of thinking too precisely on the event,—
A thought which, quarter'd, hath but one part wisdom
And ever three parts coward,—I do not know
Why yet I live to say 'This thing 's to do,'
Sith I have cause and will and strength and means
To do 't. Examples gross as earth exhort me;
Witness this army of such mass and charge,
Led by a delicate and tender prince,
Whose spirit with divine ambition puff'd
Makes mouths at the invisible event,
Exposing what is mortal and unsure
To all that fortune, death, and danger dare,
Even for an egg-shell. Rightly to be great
Is not to stir without great argument,
But greatly to find quarrel in a straw
When honour 's at the stake. How stand I then,
That have a father kill'd, a mother stain'd,
Excitements of my reason and my blood,
And let all sleep, while to my shame I see
The imminent death of twenty thousand men,
That for a fantasy and trick of fame
Go to their graves like beds, fight for a plot
Whereon the numbers cannot try the cause,
Which is not tomb enough and continent
To hide the slain? O, from this time forth,
My thoughts be bloody, or be nothing worth! [*Exit*

## SCENE V. *Elsinore. A Room in the Castle.*

*Enter* QUEEN, HORATIO, *and a* Gentleman.

*Queen.* I will not speak with her.

*Gentleman.* She is importunate, indeed distract;
Her mood will needs be pitied.

*Queen.* What would she have?

*Gentleman.* She speaks much of her father; says she hears
There 's tricks i' the world; and hems, and beats her heart;
Spurns enviously at straws; speaks things in doubt,
That carry but half sense: her speech is nothing,
Yet the unshaped use of it doth move
The hearers to collection; they aim at it,
And botch the words up fit to their own thoughts;
Which, as her winks and nods and gestures yield them,
Indeed would make one think there might be thought,
Though nothing sure, yet much unhappily.

*Horatio.* 'T were good she were spoken with, for she may strew
Dangerous conjectures in ill-breeding minds.

*Queen.* Let her come in. [*Exit Horatio.*
[*Aside*] To my sick soul, as sin's true nature is,
Each toy seems prologue to some great amiss;
So full of artless jealousy is guilt,
It spills itself in fearing to be spilt.

*Re-enter* HORATIO, *with* OPHELIA.

*Ophelia.* Where is the beauteous majesty of Denmark?

*Queen.* How now, Ophelia!

*Ophelia.* [Sings] *How should I your true love know*
*From another one?*
*By his cockle hat and staff,*
*And his sandal shoon.*

*Queen.* Alas, sweet lady, what imports this song?

*Ophelia.* Say you? nay, pray you, mark.
[Sings] *He is dead and gone, lady,*
*He is dead and gone;*
*At his head a grass-green turf,*
*At his heels a stone.*

*Queen.* Nay, but, Ophelia,—

*Ophelia.* Pray you, mark.
[Sings] *White his shroud as the mountain snow,*—

*Enter* KING.

*Queen.* Alas, look here, my lord.

*Ophelia.* [Sings] *Larded with sweet flowers;*
*Which bewept to the grave did go*
*With true-love showers.*

*King.* How do you, pretty lady?

*Ophelia.* Well, God 'ield you! They say the owl was a baker's daughter. Lord, we know what we are, but know not what we may be. God be at your table!

*King.* [*Aside*] Conceit upon her father.

*Ophelia.* Pray you, let 's have no words of this; but when they ask you what it means, say you this:

[Sings] *To-morrow is Saint Valentine's day,*
*All in the morning betime,*
*And I a maid at your window,*
*To be your Valentine.*

*King.* How long hath she been thus?

*Ophelia.* I hope all will be well. We must be patient; but I cannot choose but weep, to think they should lay him i' the cold ground. My brother shall know of it; and so I thank you for your good counsel.—Come, my coach!—Good night, ladies; good night, sweet ladies; good night, good night. [*Exit.*

*King.* Follow her close; give her good watch, I pray you.— [*Exit Horatio.*
O, this is the poison of deep grief; it springs
All from her father's death. O Gertrude, Gertrude,
When sorrows come, they come not single spies,
But in battalions. First, her father slain;
Next, your son gone; and he most violent author
Of his own just remove: the people muddied,
Thick and unwholesome in their thoughts and whispers,
For good Polonius' death; and we have done but greenly,
In hugger-mugger to inter him: poor Ophelia

Divided from herself and her fair judgment,
Without the which we are pictures, or mere beasts:
Last, and as much containing as all these,
Her brother is in secret come from France,
Feeds on his wonder, keeps himself in clouds,
And wants not buzzers to infect his ear
With pestilent speeches of his father's death;
Wherein necessity, of matter beggar'd,
Will nothing stick our person to arraign
In ear and ear. O my dear Gertrude, this,
Like to a murthering-piece, in many places
Gives me superfluous death. [*A noise within.*

*Queen.* Alack, what noise is this?

*King.* Where are my Switzers? Let them guard the door.—

*Enter another* Gentleman.

What is the matter?

*Gentleman.* Save yourself, my lord;
The ocean, overpeering of his list,
Eats not the flats with more impetuous haste
Than young Laertes, in a riotous head,
O'erbears your officers. The rabble call him lord;
And, as the world were now but to begin,
Antiquity forgot, custom not known,
The ratifiers and props of every word,
They cry 'Choose we; Laertes shall be king!'
Caps, hands, and tongues, applaud it to the clouds,
'Laertes shall be king, Laertes king!'

*Queen.* How cheerfully on the false trail they cry!
O, this is counter, you false Danish dogs!

*King.* The doors are broke. [*Noise within.*

*Enter* LAERTES, *armed;* Danes *following.*

*Laertes.* Where is this king?—Sirs, stand you all without.

*Danes.* No, let 's come in.
*Laertes.* I pray you, give me leave.
*Danes.* We will, we will. [*They retire without the door.*
*Laertes.* I thank you: keep the door.—O thou vile king,
Give me my father!
*Queen.* Calmly, good Laertes.
*Laertes.* That drop of blood that 's calm proclaims me bastard,
Cries cuckold to my father, brands the harlot
Even here, between the chaste unsmirched brows
Of my true mother.
*King.* What is the cause, Laertes,
That thy rebellion looks so giant-like?—
Let him go, Gertrude; do not fear our person:
There 's such divinity doth hedge a king,
That treason can but peep to what it would,
Acts little of his will.—Tell me, Laertes,
Why thou art thus incens'd.—Let him go, Gertrude.—
Speak, man.
*Laertes.* Where is my father?
*King.* Dead.
*Queen.* But not by him.
*King.* Let him demand his fill.
*Laertes.* How came he dead? I 'll not be juggled with:
To hell, allegiance! vows, to the blackest devil!
Conscience and grace, to the profoundest pit!
I dare damnation. To this point I stand:
That both the worlds I give to negligence,
Let come what comes; only I 'll be reveng'd
Most throughly for my father.
*King.* Who shall stay you?
*Laertes.* My will, not all the world;
And for my means, I 'll husband them so well,
They shall go far with little.
*King.* Good Laertes,

If you desire to know the certainty
Of your dear father's death, is 't writ in your revenge,
That, swoopstake, you will draw both friend and foe,
Winner and loser?

*Laertes.* None but his enemies.

*King.* Will you know them then?

*Laertes.* To his good friends thus wide I 'll ope my arms;
And like the kind life-rendering pelican,
Repast them with my blood.

*King.* Why, now you speak
Like a good child and a true gentleman.
That I am guiltless of your father's death,
And am most sensibly in grief for it,
It shall as level to your judgment pierce
As day does to your eye.

*Danes.* [*Within*] Let her come in.

*Laertes.* How now! what noise is that?—

*Re-enter* OPHELIA.

O heat, dry up my brains! tears seven times salt,
Burn out the sense and virtue of mine eye!—
By heaven, thy madness shall be paid by weight,
Till our scale turn the beam. O rose of May!
Dear maid, kind sister, sweet Ophelia!—
O heavens! is 't possible, a young maid's wits
Should be as mortal as an old man's life?
Nature is fine in love, and where 't is fine
It sends some precious instance of itself
After the thing it loves.

*Ophelia.* [Sings] *They bore him barefac'd on the bier:*
*Hey non nonny, nonny, hey nonny;*
*And on his grave rains many a tear.*—
Fare you well, my dove!

*Laertes.* Hadst thou thy wits, and didst persuade revenge,
It could not move thus.

*Ophelia.* You must sing, *Down a-down, and you call him a-down-a.* O, how the wheel becomes it! It is the false steward, that stole his master's daughter.

*Laertes.* This nothing 's more than matter.

*Ophelia.* There 's rosemary, that 's for remembrance; pray you, love, remember: and there is pansies, that 's for thoughts.

*Laertes.* A document in madness, thoughts and remembrance fitted.

*Ophelia.* There 's fennel for you, and columbines; there 's rue for you; and here 's some for me; we may call it herb of grace o' Sundays; O, you must wear your rue with a difference. There 's a daisy: I would give you some violets, but they withered all when my father died; they say he made a good end,—

[Sings] *For bonny sweet Robin is all my joy.*

*Laertes.* Thought and affliction, passion, hell itself,
She turns to favour and to prettiness.

*Ophelia.* [Sings] *And will he not come again?*
*And will he not come again?*
*No, no, he is dead;*
*Go to thy death-bed,*
*He never will come again.*

*His beard was white as snow,*
*All flaxen was his poll;*
*He is gone, he is gone,*
*And we cast away moan:*
*God ha' mercy on his soul!*

And of all Christian souls, I pray God.—God be wi' ye.
[*Exit*

*Laertes.* Do you see this, O God?

*King.* Laertes, I must commune with your grief,
Or you deny me right. Go but apart,
Make choice of whom your wisest friends you will,
And they shall hear and judge 'twixt you and me.

If by direct or by collateral hand
They find us touch'd, we will our kingdom give,
Our crown, our life, and all that we call ours,
To you in satisfaction; but if not,
Be you content to lend your patience to us,
And we shall jointly labour with your soul
To give it due content.

*Laertes.* Let this be so;
His means of death, his obscure burial—
No trophy, sword, nor hatchment o'er his bones,
No noble rite nor formal ostentation—
Cry to be heard, as 't were from heaven to earth,
That I must call 't in question.

*King.* So you shall;
And where the offence is let the great axe fall.
I pray you, go with me. [*Exeunt.*

## SCENE VI. *Another Room in the Castle.*

*Enter* HORATIO *and a* Servant.

*Horatio.* What are they that would speak with me?

*Servant.* Sailors, sir; they say they have letters for you.

*Horatio.* Let them come in.— [*Exit Servant.*
I do not know from what part of the world
I should be greeted, if not from Lord Hamlet.

*Enter* Sailors.

1 *Sailor.* God bless you, sir.

*Horatio.* Let him bless thee too.

1 *Sailor.* He shall, sir, an 't please him. There 's a letter for you, sir—it comes from the ambassador that was bound for England—if your name be Horatio, as I am let to know it is.

*Horatio.* [Reads] '*Horatio, when thou shalt have overlooked this, give these fellows some means to the king; they have letters for him. Ere we were two days old at sea, a pirate of very warlike appointment gave us chase. Finding ourselves too slow of sail, we put on a compelled valour; in the grapple I boarded them: on the instant they got clear of our ship; so I alone became their prisoner. They have dealt with me like thieves of mercy: but they knew what they did; I am to do a good turn for them. Let the king have the letters I have sent; and repair thou to me with as much speed as thou wouldst fly death. I have words to speak in thine ear will make thee dumb; yet are they much too light for the bore of the matter. These good fellows will bring thee where I am. Rosencrantz and Guildenstern hold their course for England; of them I have much to tell thee. Farewell. He that thou knowest thine,* HAMLET.'

Come, I will make you way for these your letters;
And do 't the speedier, that you may direct me
To him from whom you brought them. [*Exeunt.*

### SCENE VII. *Another Room in the Castle.*

*Enter* KING *and* LAERTES.

*King.* Now must your conscience my acquittance seal,
And you must put me in your heart for friend,
Sith you have heard, and with a knowing ear,
That he which hath your noble father slain
Pursued my life.

*Laertes.* It well appears; but tell me
Why you proceeded not against these feats,
So crimeful and so capital in nature,
As by your safety, wisdom, all things else,
You mainly were stirr'd up.

*King.* O, for two special reasons,
Which may to you perhaps seem much unsinew'd,
But yet to me they are strong. The queen his mother
Lives almost by his looks; and for myself—
My virtue or my plague, be it either which—

She 's so conjunctive to my life and soul,
That, as the star moves not but in his sphere,
I could not but by her. The other motive,
Why to a public count I might not go,
Is the great love the general gender bear him;
Who, dipping all his faults in their affection,
Would, like the spring that turneth wood to stone,
Convert his gyves to graces: so that my arrows,
Too slightly timber'd for so loud a wind,
Would have reverted to my bow again,
And not where I had aim'd them.

*Laertes.* And so have I a noble father lost;
A sister driven into desperate terms,
Whose worth, if praises may go back again,
Stood challenger on mount of all the age
For her perfections: but my revenge will come.

*King.* Break not your sleeps for that; you must not think
That we are made of stuff so flat and dull
That we can let our beard be shook with danger,
And think it pastime. You shortly shall hear more:
I lov'd your father, and we love ourself;
And that, I hope, will teach you to imagine—

*Enter a* Messenger.

How now! what news?

*Messenger.* Letters, my lord, from Hamlet:
This to your majesty; this to the queen.

*King.* From Hamlet! who brought them?

*Messenger.* Sailors, my lord, they say; I saw them not:
They were given to me by Claudio; he receiv'd them.
Of him that brought them.

*King.* Laertes, you shall hear them.—
Leave us. [*Exit Messenger.*

[Reads] '*High and mighty, You shall know I am set naked on your kingdom. To-morrow shall I beg leave to see your*

*kingly eyes; when I shall, first asking your pardon thereunto,
recount the occasion of my sudden and more strange return.*

HAMLET.'

What should this mean? Are all the rest come back?
Or is it some abuse, and no such thing?

*Laertes.* Know you the hand?

*King.* 'T is Hamlet's character. 'Naked!'
And in a postscript here, he says 'alone.'
Can you advise me?

*Laertes.* I 'm lost in it, my lord. But let him come;
It warms the very sickness in my heart,
That I shall live and tell him to his teeth,
'Thus didest thou.'

*King.* If it be so, Laertes—
As how should it be so? how otherwise?—
Will you be rul'd by me?

*Laertes.* Ay, my lord;
So you will not o'errule me to a peace.

*King.* To thine own peace. If he be now return'd,
As checking at his voyage, and that he means
No more to undertake it, I will work him
To an exploit now ripe in my device,
Under the which he shall not choose but fall;
And for his death no wind of blame shall breathe,
But even his mother shall uncharge the practice
And call it accident.

*Laertes.* My lord, I will be rul'd;
The rather, if you could devise it so
That I might be the organ.

*King.* It falls right.
You have been talk'd of since your travel much,
And that in Hamlet's hearing, for a quality
Wherein, they say, you shine; your sum of parts
Did not together pluck such envy from him
As did that one, and that, in my regard,
Of the unworthiest siege.

*Laertes.* What part is that, my lord?
*King.* A very riband in the cap of youth,
Yet needful too; for youth no less becomes
The light and careless livery that it wears
Than settled age his sables and his weeds,
Importing health and graveness. Two months since,
Here was a gentleman of Normandy:—
I 've seen myself, and serv'd against, the French,
And they can well on horseback; but this gallant
Had witchcraft in 't: he grew into his seat,
And to such wondrous doing brought his horse,
As he had been incorps'd and demi-natur'd
With the brave beast. So far he topp'd my thought
That I, in forgery of shapes and tricks,
Come short of what he did.
*Laertes.* A Norman was 't?
*King.* A Norman.
*Laertes.* Upon my life, Lamond.
*King.* The very same.
*Laertes.* I know him well; he is the brooch indeed
And gem of all the nation.
*King.* He made confession of you,
And gave you such a masterly report
For art and exercise in your defence,
And for your rapier most especially,
That he cried out, 't would be a sight indeed,
If one could match you; the scrimers of their nation,
He swore, had neither motion, guard, nor eye,
If you oppos'd them. Sir, this report of his
Did Hamlet so envenom with his envy
That he could nothing do but wish and beg
Your sudden coming o'er, to play with him.
Now, out of this—
*Laertes.* What out of this, my lord?
*King.* Laertes, was your father dear to you?

Or are you like the painting of a sorrow,
A face without a heart?
*Laertes.* Why ask you this?
*King.* Not that I think you did not love your father;
But that I know love is begun by time,
And that I see, in passages of proof,
Time qualifies the spark and fire of it.
There lives within the very flame of love
A kind of wick or snuff that will abate it;
And nothing is at a like goodness still,
For goodness, growing to a plurisy,
Dies in his own too-much. That we would do,
We should do when we would; for this 'would' changes
And hath abatements and delays as many
As there are tongues, are hands, are accidents;
And then this 'should' is like a spendthrift sigh,
That hurts by easing. But, to the quick o' the ulcer:
Hamlet comes back; what would you undertake,
To show yourself your father's son in deed
More than in words?
*Laertes.* To cut his throat i' the church.
*King.* No place, indeed, should murther sanctuarize;
Revenge should have no bounds. But, good Laertes,
Will you do this, keep close within your chamber.
Hamlet return'd shall know you are come home:
We 'll put on those shall praise your excellence
And set a double varnish on the fame
The Frenchman gave you; bring you, in fine, together
And wager on your heads. He, being remiss,
Most generous and free from all contriving,
Will not peruse the foils; so that, with ease
Or with a little shuffling, you may choose
A sword unbated, and in a pass of practice
Requite him for your father.
*Laertes.* I will do 't;

And, for that purpose, I 'll anoint my sword.
I bought an unction of a mountebank,
So mortal that, but dip a knife in it,
Where it draws blood no cataplasm so rare,
Collected from all simples that have virtue
Under the moon, can save the thing from death
That is but scratch'd withal; I 'll touch my point
With this contagion, that, if I gall him slightly,
It may be death.

*King.* Let 's further think of this;
Weigh what convenience both of time and means
May fit us to our shape. If this should fail,
And that our drift look through our bad performance,
'T were better not assay'd; therefore this project
Should have a back or second, that might hold
If this should blast in proof. Soft!—let me see:—
We 'll make a solemn wager on your cunnings,—
I ha 't:
When in your motion you are hot and dry—
As make your bouts more violent to that end—
And that he calls for drink, I 'll have prepar'd him
A chalice for the nonce, whereon but sipping,
If he by chance escape your venom'd stuck,
Our purpose may hold there.—

*Enter* QUEEN.

How now, sweet queen!

*Queen.* One woe doth tread upon another's heel,
So fast they follow.—Your sister 's drown'd, Laertes.

*Laertes.* Drown'd! O, where?

*Queen.* There is a willow grows aslant a brook,
That shows his hoar leaves in the glassy stream;
There with fantastic garlands did she come
Of crow-flowers, nettles, daisies, and long purples,
That liberal shepherds give a grosser name,

But our cold maids do dead men's fingers call them:
There, on the pendent boughs her coronet weeds
Clambering to hang, an envious sliver broke,
When down her weedy trophies and herself
Fell in the weeping brook. Her clothes spread wide,
And, mermaid-like, a while they bore her up;
Which time she chanted snatches of old tunes,
As one incapable of her own distress,
Or like a creature native and indued
Unto that element: but long it could not be
Till that her garments, heavy with their drink,
Pull'd the poor wretch from her melodious lay
To muddy death.

*Laertes.* Alas, then, is she drown'd?

*Queen.* Drown'd, drown'd.

*Laertes.* Too much of water hast thou, poor Ophelia,
And therefore I forbid my tears. But yet
It is our trick; nature her custom holds,
Let shame say what it will: when these are gone,
The woman will be out.—Adieu, my lord;
I have a speech of fire, that fain would blaze,
But that this folly douts it. [*Exit.*

*King.* Let 's follow, Gertrude;
How much I had to do to calm his rage!
Now fear I this will give it start again;
Therefore let 's follow. [*Exeunt.*

CHURCH AT ELSINORE.

# ACT V.

## SCENE I. *A Churchyard.*

*Enter two* Clowns, *with spades, etc.*

1 *Clown.* Is she to be buried in Christian burial that wilfully seeks her own salvation?

2 *Clown.* I tell thee she is; and therefore make her grave straight: the crowner hath sat on her, and finds it Christian burial.

1 *Clown.* How can that be, unless she drowned herself in her own defence?

2 *Clown.* Why, 't is found so.

1 *Clown.* It must be *se offendendo;* it cannot be else. For

here lies the point: if I drown myself wittingly, it argues an act, and an act hath three branches; it is, to act, to do, and to perform: argal, she drowned herself wittingly.

2 *Clown.* Nay, but hear you, goodman delver,—

1 *Clown.* Give me leave. Here lies the water; good: here stands the man; good: if the man go to this water, and drown himself, it is, will he nill he, he goes,—mark you that; but if the water come to him and drown him, he drowns not himself: argal, he that is not guilty of his own death shortens not his own life.

2 *Clown.* But is this law?

1 *Clown.* Ay, marry, is 't; crowner's quest law.

2 *Clown.* Will you ha' the truth on 't? If this had not been a gentlewoman, she should have been buried out o' Christian burial.

1 *Clown.* Why, there thou say'st; and the more pity that great folk should have countenance in this world to drown or hang themselves, more than their even-Christian.—Come, my spade. There is no ancient gentlemen but gardeners, ditchers, and grave-makers; they hold up Adam's profession.

2 *Clown.* Was he a gentleman?

1 *Clown.* He was the first that ever bore arms.

2 *Clown.* Why, he had none.

1 *Clown.* What, art a heathen? How dost thou understand the Scripture? The Scripture says 'Adam digged;' could he dig without arms? I 'll put another question to thee; if thou answerest me not to the purpose, confess thyself—

2 *Clown.* Go to.

1 *Clown.* What is he that builds stronger than either the mason, the shipwright, or the carpenter?

2 *Clown.* The gallows-maker; for that frame outlives a thousand tenants.

1 *Clown.* I like thy wit well, in good faith: the gallows

does well; but how does it well? it does well to those that do ill; now thou dost ill to say the gallows is built stronger than the church: argal, the gallows may do well to thee. To 't again, come.

2 *Clown.* Who builds stronger than a mason, a shipwright, or a carpenter?

1 *Clown.* Ay, tell me that, and unyoke.

2 *Clown.* Marry, now I can tell.

1 *Clown.* To 't.

2 *Clown.* Mass, I cannot tell.

*Enter* HAMLET *and* HORATIO, *at a distance.*

1 *Clown.* Cudgel thy brains no more about it, for your dull ass will not mend his pace with beating; and when you are asked this question next, say 'a grave-maker:' the houses that he makes last till doomsday. Go, get thee to Yaughan; fetch me a stoup of liquor. [*Exit* 2 *Clown.*

[*He digs, and sings.*

*In youth, when I did love, did love,*
*Methought it was very sweet,*
*To contract*—O!—*the time, for*—ah!—*my behove,*
*O, methought, there was nothing meet.*

*Hamlet.* Has this fellow no feeling of his business, that he sings at grave-making?

*Horatio.* Custom hath made it in him a property of easiness.

*Hamlet.* 'T is e'en so; the hand of little employment hath the daintier sense.

1 *Clown.* [Sings]

*But age, with his stealing steps,*
*Hath claw'd me in his clutch,*
*And hath shipped me intil the land,*
*As if I had never been such.*

[*Throws up a skull.*

*Hamlet.* That skull had a tongue in it, and could sing

once; how the knave jowls it to the ground, as if it were Cain's jaw-bone, that did the first murther! It might be the pate of a politician, which this ass now o'er-reaches; one that would circumvent God, might it not?

*Horatio.* It might, my lord.

*Hamlet.* Or of a courtier, which could say 'Good morrow, sweet lord! How dost thou, good lord?' This might be my lord such-a-one, that praised my lord such-a-one's horse, when he meant to beg it, might it not?

*Horatio.* Ay, my lord.

*Hamlet.* Why, e'en so; and now my Lady Worm's, chapless, and knocked about the mazzard with a sexton's spade: here 's fine revolution, an we had the trick to see 't. Did these bones cost no more the breeding, but to play at loggats with 'em? mine ache to think on 't.

1 *Clown.* [Sings]

*A pick-axe, and a spade, a spade,*
*For and a shrouding sheet;*
*O, a pit of clay for to be made*
*For such a guest is meet.*

[*Throws up another skull.*

*Hamlet.* There 's another; why may not that be the skull of a lawyer? Where be his quiddits now, his quillets, his cases, his tenures, and his tricks? why does he suffer this rude knave now to knock him about the sconce with a dirty shovel, and will not tell him of his action of battery? Hum! This fellow might be in 's time a great buyer of land, with his statutes, his recognizances, his fines, his double vouchers, his recoveries; is this the fine of his fines, and the recovery of his recoveries, to have his fine pate full of fine dirt? will his vouchers vouch him no more of his purchases, and double ones too, than the length and breadth of a pair of indentures? The very conveyances of his lands will hardly lie in this box; and must the inheritor himself have no more, ha?

*Horatio.* Not a jot more, my lord.

*Hamlet.* Is not parchment made of sheep-skins?

*Horatio.* Ay, my lord, and of calf-skins too. 109

*Hamlet.* They are sheep and calves which seek out assurance in that. I will speak to this fellow.—Whose grave 's this, sirrah?

1 *Clown.* Mine, sir.—

[Sings] *O, a pit of clay for to be made*
*For such a guest is meet.*

*Hamlet.* I think it be thine, indeed, for thou liest in 't.

1 *Clown.* You lie out on 't, sir, and therefore it is not yours; for my part, I do not lie in 't, and yet it is mine.

*Hamlet.* Thou dost lie in 't, to be in 't and say it is thine; 't is for the dead, not for the quick: therefore thou liest.

1 *Clown.* 'T is a quick lie, sir; 't will away again, from
me to you. 122

*Hamlet.* What man dost thou dig it for?

1 *Clown.* For no man, sir.

*Hamlet.* What woman, then?

1 *Clown.* For none, neither.

*Hamlet.* Who is to be buried in 't?

1 *Clown.* One that was a woman, sir; but, rest her soul,
she 's dead. 129

*Hamlet.* How absolute the knave is! we must speak by the card, or equivocation will undo us. By the Lord, Horatio, these three years I have taken a note of it; the age is grown so picked that the toe of the peasant comes so near the heel of the courtier, he galls his kibe.—How long hast thou been a grave-maker?

1 *Clown.* Of all the days i' the year, I came to 't that day that our last king Hamlet overcame Fortinbras.

*Hamlet.* How long is that since?

1 *Clown.* Cannot you tell that? every fool can tell that: it was the very day that young Hamlet was born; he that
is mad, and sent into England. 141

*Hamlet.* Ay, marry, why was he sent into England?

1 *Clown.* Why, because he was mad: he shall recover his wits there; or, if he do not, it 's no great matter there.

*Hamlet.* Why?

1 *Clown.* 'T will not be seen in him there; there the men are as mad as he.

*Hamlet.* How came he mad?

1 *Clown.* Very strangely, they say.

*Hamlet.* How strangely?

1 *Clown.* Faith, e'en with losing his wits.

*Hamlet.* Upon what ground?

1 *Clown.* Why, here in Denmark; I have been sexton here, man and boy, thirty years.

*Hamlet.* How long will a man lie i' the earth ere he rot?

1 *Clown.* I' faith, if he be not rotten before he die—as we have many pocky corses now-a-days, that will scarce hold the laying in—he will last you some eight year or nine year; a tanner will last you nine year.

*Hamlet.* Why he more than another?

1 *Clown.* Why, sir, his hide is so tanned with his trade, that he will keep out water a great while; and your water is a sore decayer of your whoreson dead body. Here 's a skull now; this skull has lain in the earth three and twenty years.

*Hamlet.* Whose was it?

1 *Clown.* A whoreson mad fellow's it was; whose do you think it was?

*Hamlet.* Nay, I know not.

1 *Clown.* A pestilence on him for a mad rogue! a' poured a flagon of Rhenish on my head once. This same skull, sir, was Yorick's skull, the king's jester.

*Hamlet.* This?

1 *Clown.* E'en that.

*Hamlet.* Let me see.—[*Takes the skull.*] Alas, poor Yorick!—I knew him, Horatio; a fellow of infinite jest, of most excellent fancy: he hath borne me on his back a thousand times; and now, how abhorred in my imagination it is! my gorge rises at it. Here hung those lips that I have kissed I know not how oft.—Where be your gibes now? your gambols? your songs? your flashes of merriment, that were wont to set the table on a roar? Not one now, to mock your own grinning? quite chop-fallen? Now get you to my lady's chamber, and tell her, let her paint an inch thick, to this favour she must come; make her laugh at that.—Prithee, Horatio, tell me one thing.

*Horatio.* What 's that, my lord?

*Hamlet.* Dost thou think Alexander looked o' this fashion i' the earth?

*Horatio.* E'en so.

*Hamlet.* And smelt so? pah! [*Puts down the skull.*

*Horatio.* E'en so, my lord.

*Hamlet.* To what base uses we may return, Horatio! Why may not imagination trace the noble dust of Alexander, till he find it stopping a bung-hole?

*Horatio.* 'T were to consider too curiously, to consider so.

*Hamlet.* No, faith, not a jot; but to follow him thither with modesty enough, and likelihood to lead it; as thus: Alexander died, Alexander was buried, Alexander returneth into dust; the dust is earth; of earth we make loam; and why of that loam, whereto he was converted, might they not stop a beer-barrel?

Imperious Cæsar, dead and turn'd to clay,
Might stop a hole to keep the wind away;
O, that that earth, which kept the world in awe,
Should patch a wall to expel the winter's flaw!
But soft! but soft! aside! here comes the king,

*Enter* Priests, *etc., in procession; the Corpse of* OPHELIA, LAERTES *and* Mourners *following;* KING, QUEEN, *their trains, etc.*

The queen, the courtiers; who is that they follow?
And with such maimed rites? This doth betoken

The corse they follow did with desperate hand
Fordo it own life; 't was of some estate.
Couch we awhile, and mark. [*Retiring with Horatio.*

*Laertes.* What ceremony else?

*Hamlet.* That is Laertes, a very noble youth; mark.

*Laertes.* What ceremony else?

1 *Priest.* Her obsequies have been as far enlarg'd
As we have warrantise: her death was doubtful;
And, but that great command o'ersways the order,
She should in ground unsanctified have lodg'd
Till the last trumpet; for charitable prayers,
Shards, flints, and pebbles should be thrown on her:
Yet here she is allow'd her virgin crants,
Her maiden strewments, and the bringing home
Of bell and burial.

*Laertes.* Must there no more be done?

1 *Priest.* No more be done;
We should profane the service of the dead
To sing a requiem and such rest to her
As to peace-parted souls.

*Laertes.* Lay her i' the earth;—
And from her fair and unpolluted flesh
May violets spring!—I tell thee, churlish priest,
A ministering angel shall my sister be,
When thou liest howling.

*Hamlet.* What, the fair Ophelia!

*Queen.* Sweets to the sweet; farewell! [*Scattering flowers.*
I hop'd thou shouldst have been my Hamlet's wife;
I thought thy bride-bed to have deck'd, sweet maid,
And not t' have strew'd thy grave.

*Laertes.* O, treble woe
Fall ten times treble on that cursed head
Whose wicked deed thy most ingenious sense
Depriv'd thee of!—Hold off the earth awhile,
Till I have caught her once more in mine arms.
[*Leaps into the grave.*

Now pile your dust upon the quick and dead,
Till of this flat a mountain you have made
To o'ertop old Pelion or the skyish head
Of blue Olympus.

*Hamlet.* [*Advancing*] What is he whose grief
Bears such an emphasis? whose phrase of sorrow
Conjures the wandering stars, and makes them stand
Like wonder-wounded hearers? This is I,
Hamlet the Dane! [*Leaps into the grave.*

*Laertes.* The devil take thy soul! [*Grappling with him.*

*Hamlet.* Thou pray'st not well.
I prithee, take thy fingers from my throat;
For, though I am not splenitive and rash,
Yet have I something in me dangerous,
Which let thy wisdom fear. Hold off thy hand!

*King.* Pluck them asunder.

*Queen.* Hamlet, Hamlet!

*All.* Gentlemen,—

*Horatio.* Good my lord, be quiet.

[*The Attendants part them, and they come out of the grave.*

*Hamlet.* Why, I will fight with him upon this theme
Until my eyelids will no longer wag.

*Queen.* O my son, what theme?

*Hamlet.* I lov'd Ophelia; forty thousand brothers
Could not, with all their quantity of love,
Make up my sum.—What wilt thou do for her?

*King.* O, he is mad, Laertes.

*Queen.* For love of God, forbear him.

*Hamlet.* 'Swounds, show me what thou 'lt do:
Woo't weep? woo't fight? woo't fast? woo't tear thyself?
Woo't drink up eisel? eat a crocodile?
I 'll do 't. Dost thou come here to whine?
To outface me with leaping in her grave?
Be buried quick with her, and so will I;

And, if thou prate of mountains, let them throw
Millions of acres on us, till our ground,
Singeing his pate against the burning zone,
Make Ossa like a wart! Nay, an thou 'lt mouth,
I 'll rant as well as thou.

*Queen.* This is mere madness:
And thus awhile the fit will work on him;
Anon, as patient as the female dove,
When that her golden couplets are disclos'd,
His silence will sit drooping.

*Hamlet.* Hear you, sir;
What is the reason that you use me thus?
I lov'd you ever.—But it is no matter;
Let Hercules himself do what he may,
The cat will mew, and dog will have his day. [*Exit.*

*King.* I pray you, good Horatio, wait upon him.—
[*Exit Horatio.*
[*To Laertes*] Strengthen your patience in our last night's speech;
We 'll put the matter to the present push.—
Good Gertrude, set some watch over your son.
This grave shall have a living monument:
An hour of quiet shortly shall we see;
Till then, in patience our proceeding be. [*Exeunt.*

## SCENE II. *A Hall in the Castle.*

*Enter* HAMLET *and* HORATIO.

*Hamlet.* So much for this, sir; now let me see the other:
You do remember all the circumstance?

*Horatio.* Remember it, my lord!

*Hamlet.* Sir, in my heart there was a kind of fighting,
That would not let me sleep; methought I lay
Worse than the mutines in the bilboes. Rashly,—
And prais'd be rashness for it, let us know,

Our indiscretion sometimes serves us well,
When our deep plots do fail; and that should teach us
There 's a divinity that shapes our ends,
Rough-hew them how we will,—

*Horatio.* That is most certain.

*Hamlet.* Up from my cabin,
My sea-gown scarf'd about me, in the dark
Grop'd I to find out them; had my desire,
Finger'd their packet, and in fine withdrew
To mine own room again; making so bold,
My fears forgetting manners, to unseal
Their grand commission; where I found, Horatio,—
O royal knavery!—an exact command,
Larded with many several sorts of reasons
Importing Denmark's health and England's too,
With, ho! such bugs and goblins in my life,
That, on the supervise, no leisure bated,
No, not to stay the grinding of the axe,
My head should be struck off.

*Horatio.* Is 't possible?

*Hamlet.* Here 's the commission; read it at more leisure.
But wilt thou hear me how I did proceed?

*Horatio.* I beseech you.

*Hamlet.* Being thus be-netted round with villanies—
Ere I could make a prologue to my brains,
They had begun the play—I sat me down,
Devis'd a new commission, wrote it fair;
I once did hold it, as our statists do,
A baseness to write fair, and labour'd much
How to forget that learning, but, sir, now
It did me yeoman's service. Wilt thou know
The effect of what I wrote?

*Horatio.* Ay, good my lord.

*Hamlet.* An earnest conjuration from the king,
As England was his faithful tributary,

As love between them like the palm might flourish,
As peace should still her wheaten garland wear
And stand a comma 'tween their amities,
And many such-like as's of great charge,
That, on the view and knowing of these contents,
Without debatement further, more or less,
He should the bearers put to sudden death,
Not shriving-time allow'd.

*Horatio.* How was this seal'd?

*Hamlet.* Why, even in that was heaven ordinant.
I had my father's signet in my purse,
Which was the model of that Danish seal;
Folded the writ up in form of the other,
Subscrib'd it, gave 't the impression, plac'd it safely,
The changeling never known. Now, the next day
Was our sea-fight; and what to this was sequent
Thou know'st already.

*Horatio.* So Guildenstern and Rosencrantz go to 't.

*Hamlet.* Why, man, they did make love to this employment:
They are not near my conscience; their defeat
Does by their own insinuation grow.
'T is dangerous when the baser nature comes
Between the pass and fell incensed points
Of mighty opposites.

*Horatio.* Why, what a king is this!

*Hamlet.* Does it not, thinks 't thee, stand me now upon—
He that hath kill'd my king and whor'd my mother,
Popp'd in between the election and my hopes,
Thrown out his angle for my proper life,
And with such cozenage—is 't not perfect conscience,
To quit him with this arm? and is 't not to be damn'd,
To let this canker of our nature come
In further evil?

*Horatio.* It must be shortly known to him from England
What is the issue of the business there.

*Hamlet.* It will be short: the interim is mine;
And a man's life 's no more than to say 'One.'
But I am very sorry, good Horatio,
That to Laertes I forgot myself;
For, by the image of my cause, I see
The portraiture of his. I 'll court his favours;
But, sure, the bravery of his grief did put me
Into a towering passion.

*Horatio.* Peace! who comes here?

*Enter* OSRIC.

*Osric.* Your lordship is right welcome back to Denmark.

*Hamlet.* I humbly thank you, sir.—[*Aside to Horatio*] Dost know this water-fly?

*Horatio.* [*Aside to Hamlet*] No, my good lord.

*Hamlet.* [*Aside to Horatio*] Thy state is the more gracious; for 't is a vice to know him. He hath much land, and fertile; let a beast be lord of beasts, and his crib shall stand at the king's mess. 'T is a chough, but, as I say, spacious in the possession of dirt.

*Osric.* Sweet lord, if your lordship were at leisure, I should impart a thing to you from his majesty.

*Hamlet.* I will receive it, sir, with all diligence of spirit. Put your bonnet to his right use; 't is for the head.

*Osric.* I thank your lordship, it is very hot.

*Hamlet.* No, believe me, 't is very cold; the wind is northerly.

*Osric.* It is indifferent cold, my lord, indeed.

*Hamlet.* But yet methinks it is very sultry and hot for my complexion.

*Osric.* Exceedingly, my lord; it is very sultry,—as 't were,—I cannot tell how. But, my lord, his majesty bade me signify to you that he has laid a great wager on your head. Sir, this is the matter,—

*Hamlet.* I beseech you, remember—

[*Hamlet moves him to put on his hat*

*Osric.* Nay, in good faith; for mine ease, in good faith. Sir, here is newly come to court Laertes; believe me, an absolute gentleman, full of most excellent differences, of very soft society and great showing: indeed, to speak feelingly of him, he is the card or calendar of gentry, for you shall find in him the continent of what part a gentleman would see.

*Hamlet.* Sir, his definement suffers no perdition in you; though, I know, to divide him inventorially would dizzy the arithmetic of memory, and yet but yaw neither, in respect of his quick sail. But, in the verity of extolment, I take him to be a soul of great article, and his infusion of such dearth and rareness, as, to make true diction of him, his semblable is his mirror, and who else would trace him, his umbrage, nothing more.

*Osric.* Your lordship speaks most infallibly of him.

*Hamlet.* The concernancy, sir? why do we wrap the gentleman in our more rawer breath?

*Osric.* Sir?

*Horatio.* Is 't not possible to understand in another tongue? You will do 't, sir, really.

*Hamlet.* What imports the nomination of this gentleman?

*Osric.* Of Laertes?

*Horatio.* [*Aside to Hamlet*] His purse is empty already; all 's golden words are spent.

*Hamlet.* Of him, sir.

*Osric.* I know you are not ignorant—

*Hamlet.* I would you did, sir; yet, in faith, if you did, it would not much approve me. Well, sir?

*Osric.* You are not ignorant of what excellence Laertes is—

*Hamlet.* I dare not confess that, lest I should compare with him in excellence; but, to know a man well, were to know himself.

*Osric.* I mean, sir, for his weapon; but in the imputation laid on him by them, in his meed he 's unfellowed.

*Hamlet.* What 's his weapon?

*Osric.* Rapier and dagger.

*Hamlet.* That 's two of his weapons; but, well.

*Osric.* The king, sir, hath wagered with him six Barbary horses; against the which he has imponed, as I take it, six French rapiers and poniards, with their assigns, as girdle, hangers, and so. Three of the carriages, in faith, are very dear to fancy, very responsive to the hilts, most delicate carriages, and of very liberal conceit.

*Hamlet.* What call you the carriages?

*Horatio.* [*Aside to Hamlet*] I knew you must be edified by the margent ere you had done.

*Osric.* The carriages, sir, are the hangers.

*Hamlet.* The phrase would be more germane to the matter, if we could carry cannon by our sides; I would it might be hangers till then. But, on: six Barbary horses against six French swords, their assigns, and three liberal-conceited carriages; that 's the French bet against the Danish. Why is this 'imponed,' as you call it?

*Osric.* The king, sir, hath laid that in a dozen passes between yourself and him, he shall not exceed you three hits: he hath laid on twelve for nine; and it would come to immediate trial, if your lordship would vouchsafe the answer.

*Hamlet.* How if I answer no?

*Osric.* I mean, my lord, the opposition of your person in trial.

*Hamlet.* Sir, I will walk here in the hall: if it please his majesty, 't is the breathing time of day with me; let the foils be brought, the gentleman willing, and the king hold his purpose, I will win for him if I can; if not, I will gain nothing but my shame and the odd hits.

*Osric.* Shall I re-deliver you e'en so?

*Hamlet.* To this effect, sir, after what flourish your nature will.

*Osric.* I commend my duty to your lordship.

*Hamlet.* Yours, yours.—[*Exit Osric.*] He does well to commend it himself; there are no tongues else for 's turn.

*Horatio.* This lapwing runs away with the shell on his head.

*Hamlet.* He did comply with his dug, before he sucked it. Thus has he—and many more of the same bevy that I know the drossy age dotes on—only got the tune of the time and outward habit of encounter; a kind of yesty collection, which carries them through and through the most fond and winnowed opinions; and do but blow them to their trial, the bubbles are out. 185

*Enter a* Lord.

*Lord.* My lord, his majesty commended him to you by young Osric, who brings back to him, that you attend him in the hall; he sends to know if your pleasure hold to play with Laertes, or that you will take longer time.

*Hamlet.* I am constant to my purposes; they follow the king's pleasure: if his fitness speaks, mine is ready; now or whensoever, provided I be so able as now. 192

*Lord.* The king and queen and all are coming down.

*Hamlet.* In happy time.

*Lord.* The queen desires you to use some gentle entertainment to Laertes before you fall to play.

*Hamlet.* She well instructs me. [*Exit Lord.*

*Horatio.* You will lose this wager, my lord.

*Hamlet.* I do not think so: since he went into France, I have been in continual practice; I shall win at the odds. But thou wouldst not think how ill all 's here about my heart; but it is no matter. 202

*Horatio.* Nay, good my lord,—

*Hamlet.* It is but foolery; but it is such a kind of gain giving, as would perhaps trouble a woman.

*Horatio.* If your mind dislike any thing, obey it. I will forestall their repair hither, and say you are not fit.

*Hamlet.* Not a whit; we defy augury: there 's a special providence in the fall of a sparrow. If it be now, 't is not to come; if it be not to come, it will be now; if it be not now, yet it will come: the readiness is all. Since no man knows aught of what he leaves, what is 't to leave betimes? Let be.

*Enter* KING, QUEEN, LAERTES, Lords, OSRIC, *and* Attendants *with foils, etc.*

*King.* Come, Hamlet, come, and take this hand from me.
[*The King puts Laertes's hand into Hamlet's.*

*Hamlet.* Give me your pardon, sir: I 've done you wrong;
But pardon 't, as you are a gentleman.
This presence knows,
And you must needs have heard, how I am punish'd
With sore distraction. What I have done,
That might your nature, honour, and exception
Roughly awake, I here proclaim was madness.
Was 't Hamlet wrong'd Laertes? Never Hamlet:
If Hamlet from himself be ta'en away,
And when he 's not himself does wrong Laertes,
Then Hamlet does it not; Hamlet denies it.
Who does it, then? His madness: if 't be so,
Hamlet is of the faction that is wrong'd;
His madness is poor Hamlet's enemy.
Sir, in this audience,
Let my disclaiming from a purpos'd evil
Free me so far in your most generous thoughts,
That I have shot mine arrow o'er the house,
And hurt my brother.

*Laertes.* I am satisfied in nature,
Whose motive, in this case, should stir me most
To my revenge; but in my terms of honour
I stand aloof, and will no reconcilement
Till by some elder masters of known honour
I have a voice and precedent of peace,

To keep my name ungor'd. But till that time,
I do receive your offer'd love like love,
And will not wrong it.
*Hamlet.* I embrace it freely,
And will this brother's wager frankly play.—
Give us the foils.—Come on.
*Laertes.* Come, one for me.
*Hamlet.* I'll be your foil, Laertes; in mine ignorance
Your skill shall, like a star i' the darkest night,
Stick fiery off indeed.
*Laertes.* You mock me, sir.
*Hamlet.* No, by this hand.
*King.* Give them the foils, young Osric.—Cousin Hamlet,
You know the wager?
*Hamlet.* Very well, my lord;
Your grace hath laid the odds o' the weaker side.
*King.* I do not fear it; I have seen you both:
But since he is better'd, we have therefore odds.
*Laertes.* This is too heavy, let me see another.
*Hamlet.* This likes me well.—These foils have all a length?
*Osric.* Ay, my good lord. [*They prepare to play.*
*King.* Set me the stoups of wine upon that table.—
If Hamlet give the first or second hit,
Or quit in answer of the third exchange,
Let all the battlements their ordnance fire:
The king shall drink to Hamlet's better breath;
And in the cup an union shall he throw,
Richer than that which four successive kings
In Denmark's crown have worn. Give me the cups;
And let the kettle to the trumpet speak,
The trumpet to the cannoneer without,
The cannons to the heavens, the heavens to earth,
'Now the king drinks to Hamlet!'—Come, begin;—
And you, the judges, bear a wary eye.

*Hamlet.* Come on, sir.
*Laertes.* Come, my lord. [*They play.*
*Hamlet.* One.
*Laertes.* No.
*Hamlet.* Judgment.
*Osric.* A hit, a very palpable hit.
*Laertes.* Well; again.
*King.* Stay; give me drink.—Hamlet, this pearl is thine;
Here 's to thy health.—
[*Trumpets sound, and cannon shot off within.*
Give him the cup.
*Hamlet.* I 'll play this bout first; set it by awhile.—
Come. [*They play.*] Another hit; what say you?
*Laertes.* A touch, a touch, I do confess.
*King.* Our son shall win.
*Queen.* He 's fat and scant of breath.—
Here, Hamlet, take my napkin, rub thy brows;
The queen carouses to thy fortune, Hamlet.
*Hamlet.* Good madam,—
*King.* Gertrude, do not drink.
*Queen.* I will, my lord; I pray you, pardon me.
*King.* [*Aside*] It is the poison'd cup; it is too late.
*Hamlet.* I dare not drink yet, madam; by and by.
*Queen.* Come, let me wipe thy face.
*Laertes.* My lord, I 'll hit him now.
*King.* I do not think 't.
*Laertes.* [*Aside*] And yet 't is almost 'gainst my conscience.
*Hamlet.* Come, for the third, Laertes. You but dally;
I pray you, pass with your best violence;
I am afeard you make a wanton of me.
*Laertes.* Say you so? come on. [*They play.*
*Osric.* Nothing, neither way.
*Laertes.* Have at you now!
[*Laertes wounds Hamlet; then, in scuffling, they change rapiers, and Hamlet wounds Laertes.*

*King.* Part them; they are incens'd.
*Hamlet.* Nay, come, again. [*The Queen falls.*
*Osric.* Look to the queen there, ho!
*Horatio.* They bleed on both sides.—How is it, my lord?
*Osric.* How is 't, Laertes?
*Laertes.* Why, as a woodcock to mine own springe, Osric;
I am justly kill'd with mine own treachery.
*Hamlet.* How does the queen?
*King.* She swoons to see them bleed.
*Queen.* No, no, the drink, the drink,—O my dear Hamlet,—
The drink, the drink!—I am poison'd. [*Dies.*
*Hamlet.* O villany!—Ho! let the door be lock'd!
Treachery! Seek it out!
*Laertes.* It is here, Hamlet. Hamlet, thou art slain;
No medicine in the world can do thee good,
In thee there is not half an hour of life:
The treacherous instrument is in thy hand,
Unbated and envenom'd. The foul practice
Hath turn'd itself on me; lo, here I lie,
Never to rise again. Thy mother 's poison'd;
I can no more,—the king—the king 's to blame.
*Hamlet.* The point envenom'd too!—
Then, venom, to thy work! [*Stabs the King.*
*All.* Treason! treason!
*King.* O, yet defend me, friends; I am but hurt.
*Hamlet.* Here, thou incestuous, murtherous, damned Dane,
Drink off this potion! Is thy union here?
Follow my mother! [*King dies.*
*Laertes.* He is justly serv'd;
It is a poison temper'd by himself.—
Exchange forgiveness with me, noble Hamlet;
Mine and my father's death come not upon thee,
Nor thine on me! [*Dies.*
*Hamlet.* Heaven make thee free of it! I follow thee.—

I am dead, Horatio.—Wretched queen, adieu!—
You that look pale and tremble at this chance,
That are but mutes or audience to this act,
Had I but time—as this fell sergeant, death,
Is strict in his arrest—O, I could tell you—
But let it be.—Horatio, I am dead;
Thou livest; report me and my cause aright
To the unsatisfied.

*Horatio.* Never believe it;
I am more an antique Roman than a Dane:
Here 's yet some liquor left.

*Hamlet.* As thou 'rt a man,
Give me the cup: let go; by heaven, I 'll have 't.—
O God!—Horatio, what a wounded name,
Things standing thus unknown, shall live behind me!
If thou didst ever hold me in thy heart,
Absent thee from felicity awhile,
And in this harsh world draw thy breath in pain,
To tell my story.— [*March afar off, and shot within.*
What warlike noise is this?

*Osric.* Young Fortinbras, with conquest come from Poland,
To the ambassadors of England gives
This warlike volley.

*Hamlet.* O, I die, Horatio;
The potent poison quite o'er-crows my spirit.
I cannot live to hear the news from England;
But I do prophesy the election lights
On Fortinbras: he has my dying voice;
So tell him, with the occurrents, more and less,
Which have solicited—the rest is silence. [*Dies.*

*Horatio.* Now cracks a noble heart.—Good night, sweet prince,
And flights of angels sing thee to thy rest!
Why does the drum come hither? [*March within.*

*Enter* FORTINBRAS, *the* English Ambassadors, *and others.*

*Fortinbras.* Where is this sight?
*Horatio.* What is it ye would see?
If aught of woe or wonder, cease your search.
*Fortinbras.* This quarry cries on havoc.—O proud death,
What feast is toward in thine eternal cell,
That thou so many princes at a shot
So bloodily hast struck?
1 *Ambassador.* The sight is dismal;
And our affairs from England come too late:
The ears are senseless that should give us hearing,
To tell him his commandment is fulfill'd,
That Rosencrantz and Guildenstern are dead.
Where should we have our thanks?
*Horatio.* Not from his mouth,
Had it the ability of life to thank you;
He never gave commandment for their death.
But since, so jump upon this bloody question,
You from the Polack wars, and you from England,
Are here arriv'd, give order that these bodies
High on a stage be placed to the view;
And let me speak to the yet unknowing world
How these things came about: so shall you hear
Of carnal, bloody, and unnatural acts,
Of accidental judgments, casual slaughters,
Of deaths put on by cunning and forc'd cause,
And, in this upshot, purposes mistook
Fallen on the inventors' heads. All this can I
Truly deliver.
*Fortinbras.* Let us haste to hear it,
And call the noblest to the audience.
For me, with sorrow I embrace my fortune;
I have some rights of memory in this kingdom,
Which now to claim my vantage doth invite me.

*Horatio.* Of that I shall have also cause to speak,
And from his mouth whose voice will draw on more;
But let this same be presently perform'd,
Even while men's minds are wild, lest more mischance,
On plots and errors, happen.

*Fortinbras.* Let four captains
Bear Hamlet, like a soldier, to the stage;
For he was likely, had he been put on,
To have prov'd most royally: and, for his passage,
The soldiers' music and the rites of war
Speak loudly for him.—
Take up the bodies.—Such a sight as this
Becomes the field, but here shows much amiss.—
Go, bid the soldiers shoot.

[*A dead march. Exeunt, bearing off the dead bodies; after which a peal of ordnance is shot off.*

# NOTES.

## ABBREVIATIONS USED IN THE NOTES.

Abbott (or Gr.), Abbott's *Shakespearian Grammar* (third edition).
A. S., Anglo-Saxon.
A. V., Authorized Version of the Bible (1611).
A. Y. L. (followed by reference to *page*), Rolfe's edition of *As You Like It.*
B. and F., Beaumont and Fletcher.
B. J., Ben Jonson.
Caldecott, T. Caldecott's edition of *Hamlet* (London, 1819).
Camb. ed., "Cambridge edition" of *Shakespeare*, edited by Clark and Wright.
Cf. (*confer*), compare.
Coll., Collier (second edition).
Coll. MS., Manuscript Corrections of Second Folio, edited by Collier.
D., Dyce (second edition).
F., Furness's "New Variorum" edition of *Hamlet* (Philadelphia, 1877).
H., Hudson (first edition).
Hen. V. (followed by reference to *page*), Rolfe's edition of *Henry V.*
Hen. VIII. (followed by reference to *page*), Rolfe's edition of *Henry VIII.*
Id. (*idem*), the same.
J. C. (followed by reference to *page*), Rolfe's edition of *Julius Cæsar.*
J. H., John Hunter's edition of *Hamlet* (London, 1865).
K., Knight (second edition).
M., Rev. C. E. Moberly's "Rugby" edition of *Hamlet* (London, 1873).
Macb. (followed by reference to *page*), Rolfe's edition of *Macbeth.*
Mer., Rolfe's edition of *The Merchant of Venice.*
M. N. D. (followed by reference to *page*), Rolfe's edition of *A Midsummer-Night's Dream.*
Nares, *Glossary*, edited by Halliwell and Wright (London, 1859).
Prol., Prologue.
Rich. II. (followed by reference to *page*), Rolfe's edition of *Richard II.*
S., Shakespeare.
Schmidt, A. Schmidt's *Shakespeare-Lexicon* (Berlin, 1874).
Sr., Singer.
St., Staunton.
Temp. (followed by reference to *page*), Rolfe's edition of *The Tempest.*
Theo., Theobald.
V., Verplanck.
W., White
Walker, Wm. Sidney Walker's *Critical Examination of the Text of Shakespeare* (London, 1860).
Warb., Warburton.
Wb., Webster's Dictionary (revised quarto edition of 1864).
Worc., Worcester's Dictionary (quarto edition).
Wr., Clark and Wright's "Clarendon Press" edition of *Hamlet* (Oxford, 1872).

The abbreviations of the names of Shakespeare's Plays will be readily understood; as *T. N.* for *Twelfth Night*, *Cor.* for *Coriolanus*, 3 *Hen. VI.* for *The Third Part of King Henry the Sixth*, etc. *P. P.* refers to *The Passionate Pilgrim*; *V. and A.* to *Venus and Adonis*; *L. C.* to *Lover's Complaint*; and *Sonn.* to the *Sonnets.*

☞ The numbers of the lines (except for *Hamlet*) are those of the "Globe" edition.

# NOTES.

"He smote the sledded Polacks on the ice" (i. 1. 63).

## ACT I.

Scene I.—In the quartos the acts and scenes are not marked; in the folios they are indicated only as far as ii. 2.

*Elsinore.* "The scene is at the celebrated castle of Kronborg, commanding the entrance of the Sound. In its vaults the mythic Danish champion Holger was thought to be seated at the board, asleep for age after age, till the day of fate awakens him" (M.). The cut on p. 41 is taken from this castle.

1. *Who 's there?* For the "interjectional line," see Gr. 512.

Coleridge says: "That S. meant to put an effect in the actor's power in these very first words is evident from the impatience expressed by the startled Francisco in the line that follows. A brave man is never so peremptory as when he fears that he is afraid."

2. *Me.* Emphatic; as the measure shows.

3. *Long live the king!* Commonly explained as the watchword of the night; but, as Delius points out, Horatio and Marcellus in 15 below give a different response to the same challenge. Pye believes that it corresponds to the old French usage of replying *Vive le roi!* to the challenge *Qui vive?*

6. *Upon your hour.* Just at your hour. Wr. compares *Rich. III.* iii. 2. 5: "upon the stroke of four;" *M. for M.* iv. 1. 17: "much upon this time," etc. See also Gr. 191. Cf. the modern "on time."

7. *Now struck.* Steevens conjectured "new struck;" as in *R. and J.* i. 1. 167: "But new struck nine."

8. *Much thanks.* *Thanks* is a quasi-singular. Cf. *Luke,* xii. 19: "much goods," etc. For the old use of *much*=great, see Gr. 51; and for the adverbial use of *bitter,* Gr. 1.

9. *Sick at heart.* F. quotes Strachey: "The key-note of the tragedy is struck in the simple preludings of this common sentry's midnight guard, to sound afterwards in ever-spreading vibrations through the complicated though harmonious strains of Hamlet's own watch through a darker and colder night than the senses can feel."

10. *Not a mouse stirring.* Coleridge remarks: "The attention to minute sounds—naturally associated with the recollection of minute objects, and the more familiar and trifling, the more impressive from the unusualness of their producing any impression at all—gives a philosophic pertinency to this last image; but it has likewise its dramatic use and purpose. For its commonness in ordinary conversation tends to produce the sense of reality, and at once hides the poet, and yet approximates the reader or spectator to that state in which the highest poetry will appear, and in its component parts, though not in the whole composition, really is, the language of nature. If I should not speak it, I feel that I should be thinking it; the voice only is the poet's, the words are my own."

13. *Rivals.* Partners, companions. The 1st quarto has "partners." S. does not use the word again in this sense; unless, with Schmidt, we see it in *M. N. D.* iii. 2. 156: "And now both rivals to mock Helena." We find, however, *corrival*=companion in 2 *Hen. IV.* iv. 4. 31, and *rivality*=partnership in *A. and C.* iii. 5. 8. For the origin of the word, see Wb.

15. *Dane.* King of Denmark; as in i. 2. 44 below.

16. *Give you good night.* That is, *God* give, etc. For other contractions of like greetings, cf. *A. Y. L.* v. 1. 16: "God ye good even;" *R. and J.* i. 2. 58: "God gi' good-den;" *Hen. V.* iii. 2. 89: "God-den," etc. We have the full form in *L. L. L.* iv. 2. 84: "God give you good morrow," etc. Wr. quotes B. and F., *Knt. of Burning Pestle,* epil.: "God give you good night."

19. *A piece of him.* "As we say, 'something like him.' The phrase

has none of the deep meaning which some of the German editors find in it" (M.). For these German comments, see F.

21. *Has this thing*, etc. Coleridge remarks that "even the word *again* has its *credibilizing* effect;" and he points out how Marcellus from *this thing* rises to *this dreaded sight*, and then to *this apparition*, "an intelligent spirit, that is, to be spoken to."

23. *Fantasy*. Imagination; as in 54 below. Cf. 1 *Hen. IV.* v. 4. 138: "Or is it fantasy that plays upon our eyesight?" See also *M. N. D.* v. 1. 5, *M. W.* v. 5. 55, etc. For another sense see iv. 4. 62 below; and for another (=love), *M. N. D.* i. 1. 32, *A. Y. L.* ii. 4. 31, v. 2. 100, etc.

25. *Seen of us*. The 1st quarto has "seene by vs." *Of*=by is very common in S. Cf. iv. 2. 12 below; also *Macb.* iii. 6. 27, etc. Gr. 170.

27. *The minutes of this night*. "Through this night, minute by minute" (M.). Steevens quotes Ford, *Fancies Chaste and Noble*, v. 1: "Ere the minutes of the night warn us to rest."

29. *Approve*. Prove, confirm. Cf. *M. of V.* iii. 2. 79: "approve it with a text," etc.

33. *What*, etc. "*What* depends on a verb of speech, implied either in *assail your ears* or in *story;* that is, 'let us tell you *what* we have seen,' or 'our story describing *what* we have seen'" (Gr. 252).

*Sit we*. First person imperative; or, as Abbott calls it (Gr. 361), subjunctive=suppose we sit. Cf. 168 below: "Break we our watch up," etc.

35. *Last night*, etc. Coleridge observes: "In the deep feeling which Bernardo has of the solemn nature of what he is about to relate, he makes an effort to master his own imaginative terrors by an elevation of style—itself a continuation of the effort—by turning off from the apparition, as from something which would force him too deeply into himself, to the outward objects, the realities of nature, which had accompanied it."

36. *Yond*. See *J. C.* p. 134 or *Temp.* p. 121.

*Pole*. Pole-star; as in *Oth.* ii. 1. 15: "the ever-fixed pole."

Clarke remarks: "Nothing more natural than for a sentinel to watch the course of a particular star while on his lonely midnight watch; and what a radiance of poetry is shed on the passage by the casual allusion!"

37. *Illume*. Used nowhere else by S. He has *illuminate* twice, and *illumine* three times.

39. *Beating*. The 1st quarto has "towling," and the Coll. MS. "tolling."

40. *Thee*. Apparently=*thou*, as often after imperatives. See *Macb.* p. 170 (note on *Hie thee*), or Gr. 212.

Coleridge remarks: "Note the judgment displayed in having the two persons present, who, as having seen the Ghost before, are naturally eager in confirming their former opinions, whilst the skeptic is silent, and after having been twice addressed by his friends, answers with two hasty syllables—'Most like'—and a confession of horror—

'It harrows me with fear and wonder.'

O heaven! words are wasted on those who feel, and to those who do not feel the exquisite judgment of Shakspeare in this scene, what can be said?

—Hume himself could not but have had faith in this Ghost dramatically, let his anti-ghostism have been as strong as Samson against other ghosts less powerfully raised."

42. *Scholar.* Alluding to the use of Latin in exorcisms. Cf. *Much Ado*, ii. 1. 264: "I would to God some scholar would conjure her!" Reed quotes B. and F., *Night Walker*, ii. 1:

> "Let 's call the butler up, for he speaks Latin,
> And that will daunt the devil."

In like manner the honest butler in Addison's *Drummer* recommends the steward to speak Latin to the ghost.

44. *Harrows.* Steevens quotes Milton, *Comus*, 565: "Amaz'd I stood, harrow'd with grief and fear." Cf. i. 5. 16 below.

45. *It would be spoke to.* For *would*, see Gr. 329; and for *spoke*, Gr. 343. "There was, and is, a notion that a ghost cannot speak until it is spoken to" (Wr.).

46. *Usurp'st.* "Zeugma: the Ghost invades the night and assumes the form of the king" (M.).

49. *Sometimes.* Used by S. interchangeably with *sometime*=formerly. Cf. *Rich. II.* i. 2. 54, *Hen. VIII.* ii. 4. 181, etc.

55. *On 't.* Of it. See Gr. 181. M. thinks it is used here in its ordinary sense.

56. *Might.* Could. See Gr. 312.

57. *Sensible.* For adjectives used like this in both an active and a passive sense, see Gr. 3.

*Avouch* is not elsewhere made a noun by S. For other examples of verbs used as nouns (Gr. 451), see 73 ("cast"), iii. 1. 166 ("hatch" and "disclose"), iv. 5. 64 ("remove"), v. 2. 23 ("supervise"), v. 2. 207 ("repair"), etc.

60. *Armour.* F. asks: "Was this the very armour that he wore thirty years before, on the day Hamlet was born (see v. 1. 136–141)? How old is Horatio?"

61. *Norway.* The King of Norway. See *Macb.* p. 239, note on *England.*

62. *Parle.* Parley. See *Hen. V.* p. 164.

63. *Sledded Polacks.* Polanders on sleds, or sledges. The 1st quarto has "sleaded pollax," the 1st and 2d folios "sledded Pollax" (changed to "Polax" in the 3d and "Poleaxe" in the 4th folio). Rowe has "Pole-axe," and Pope (followed by Capell, Steevens, and Sr.) "Polack." The Germans, who have been much troubled by the passage, generally adopt "Pole-axe." Schmidt explains *sledded* as "probably=having a sled or sledge, that is, a heavy hammer to it, or similar to a heavy hammer." He adds, "Hamlet, provoked to anger in a conference with the king of Norway, struck the ice with his pole-axe as with a heavy hammer." F. gives nearly two pages of comical German comments on the passage, with some English ones equally amusing.

For *Polack*=Polander or Polish, cf. ii. 2. 63, 75, iv. 4. 23, and v. 2. 364 below; also Webster, *White Devil:* "Like a shav'd Polack." S. uses the word in no other play, and *sledded* only here.

65. *Jump.* The quarto reading; the folios have "just," which means

the same. Cf. v. 2. 363 below: "jump upon this bloody question." See also *Oth.* ii. 3. 392.

*Dead.* Cf. i. 2. 198 below: "the dead vast and middle of the night." See also *Sonn.* 43. 11, *Hen. V.* iii. chor. 19, *Rich. III.* v. 3. 180, etc.

67, 68. *In what,* etc. I know not what particular line of thought to follow, but in a general way my opinion is, etc.

70. *Good now.* For this "vocative use" of *good* (with or without *now*), cf. *Temp.* i. 1. 3, 16, 20, *C. of E.* iv. 4. 22, *T. and C.* iii. 1. 122, *A. and C.* i. 2. 25, etc. Johnson makes it here = "in good time, *à la bonne heure.*" See Gr. 13.

72. *Toils.* For the transitive use, cf. *M. N. D.* v. 1. 74: "have toiled their memories;" 2 *Hen. VI.* i. 1. 83: "toil his wits," etc. Abbott refers to Gr. 290 (verbs formed from nouns, etc.), but 291 (intransitive verbs used transitively) would be better.*

*Subject.* Used collectively (= people) as in i. 2. 33 below. Cf. *M. for M.* iii. 2. 145, v. 1. 14, *W. T.* i. 1. 43, etc.

74. *Mart.* Marketing, buying. The word is also used as a verb (= buy or sell); as in *W. T.* iv. 4. 363, *J. C.* iv. 3. 11, etc.

75. *Impress.* Impressment; as in *T. and C.* ii. 1. 107 and *A. and C.* iii. 7. 37. Lord Campbell remarks: "Such confidence has there been in Shakespeare's accuracy that this passage has been quoted both by text-writers and by judges on the bench as an authority upon the legality of the *press-gang*, and upon the debated question whether *shipwrights*, as well as *common seamen*, are liable to be pressed into the service of the royal navy."

77. *Toward.* At hand, forthcoming. Cf. *M. N. D.* iii. 1. 81: "a play toward," etc. See also v. 2. 353 below.

81. *Even but now.* See Gr. 130.

82. *Fortinbras.* According to Latham (quoted by F.), a corrupt French form, equivalent to *Fierumbras* or *Fierabras*, which is a derivative from *ferri brachium* (arm of iron).

83. *Emulate.* Emulous. Used by S. only here. Cf. *adulterate*, i. 5. 42 below. Gr. 342.

84. *The combat.* "That is, the combat that ends all dispute" (Gr. 92).

86. Wr. makes this line an Alexandrine; Abbott (Gr. 469) counts *this Fortinbras* as one foot. It might be scanned thus: "Did sláy | this Fórt | inbras, whó | by a seál'd | compáct." For *compáct*, see Gr. 490.

87. *Law and heraldry.* Wr. and Schmidt explain this as = "heraldic law," or "law of heraldry." M. says: "Law would be wanted to draw up accurately the contract, heraldry to give it a binding force in honour; as the court of chivalry 'has cognizance of contracts touching deeds of arms or of war out of the realm.'"

88. *Those his lands.* See *Macb.* p. 179 (note on *That their fitness*), and *Hen. V.* p. 169 (note on *This your air*). Gr. 239.

89. *Seiz'd of.* Possessed of; still a legal term.

---

* In quoting the passage he gives the preceding line, "Why this same *toil* and most observant watch," which would favour his explanation; but I do not know where he gets that reading. It is given neither in the collation of the Camb. ed. nor in that of F. S. has the intransitive *toil* nine times.

90. *Moiety.* Strictly a half (as in *A. W.* iii. 2. 69, *Hen. V.* v. 2. 229, etc.), but often used by S. for any portion (Schmidt). Cf. *M. of V.* iv. 1. 26, 1 *Hen. IV.* iii. 1. 96, etc.

91. *Had return'd.* Would haye returned. Gr. 361.

93. *Covenant.* The folio has "cou'nant," the quartos "comart." D. and Wr. think that S. may have coined the latter word (=joint bargain), and afterwards changed it to *covenant.*

94. *Carriage,* etc. "By the tenor of the article as drawn up" (M.).

96. *Unimproved.* "Not regulated or guided by knowledge or experience" (Johnson); "untutored" (Wr.); "undisciplined" (M.); "not yet turned to account, unemployed" (Schmidt). Nares and D., on the other hand, explain it as="unreproved, unimpeached," and St. as="ungovernable." The 1st quarto has "inapproved." On *mettle,* see *Macb.* p. 181 or *Rich. II.* p. 157.

97. *Skirts.* Cf. *A. Y. L.* iii. 2. 354: "here in the skirts of the forest, like fringe upon a petticoat."

98. *Shark'd up.* Picked up without distinction (Steevens) or illegally (Schmidt). *List*=muster-roll, as in i. 2. 32 below. On *resolutes,* see Gr. 433.

99. *For food and diet.* "For no pay but their keep. Being landless they have nothing to lose, and the war would at the worst feed them" (M.).

100. *Stomach.* Courage; with possibly a play on the other sense, as in *T. G. of V.* i. 2. 68 and *Hen. V.* iii. 7. 166. For some of the meanings of the word in S. see *Temp.* p. 115.

102. *But.* In the sense of *except,* where we should use *than* (Gr. 127). See also 108 below.

103. *Compulsative.* The folio reading; the quartos have "compulsatory." S. uses neither word elsewhere, but he has "compulsive" in iii. 4. 86 below and in *Oth.* iii. 3. 454.

107. *Romage.* "Bustle, turmoil" (Schmidt). S. uses the word only here. For its origin see Wb. Wedgwood gives a less probable derivation.

108. Lines 108–125 are omitted in the folio. K. suggests that S. probably suppressed the passage after he had written *J. C.*

*Be.* The word "expresses more doubt than *is* after a verb of thinking" (Gr. 299, where some striking examples are given).

109. *Sort.* Suit, accord. Schmidt wavers between this sense and "fall out, have an issue" (as in *Much Ado,* v. 4. 7, *M. N. D.* iii. 2. 352, etc.).

112. *Mote.* In three of the quartos it is spelt "moth," which probably had the same pronunciation. See *A. Y. L.* p. 179, note on *Goats.*

114. *Mightiest.* Used like the Latin superlative=very mighty (Gr. 8). On the passage, cf. *J. C.* ii. 2. 18 fol.

117. *As stars,* etc. There is some corruption here, and perhaps a line has dropped out. The attempts to mend the passage have not been satisfactory. As M. suggests, "if a line is supposed to be omitted, it would be better to borrow from *J. C.* ii. 2, and read

> '[Fierce fiery warriors fought upon the clouds,]
> As stars with trains of fire and dews of blood:
> Disaster hid the sun,' etc.,

rather than indulge the genius, as some editors have done, by coining a line."

*Disaster* (like *influence, aspect, retrograde*, etc.) was an astrological term. It is used as a verb in *A. and C.* ii. 7. 18.

118. *The moist star.* The moon. Cf. *W. T.* i. 2. 1: "the watery star;" and *M. N. D.* ii. 1. 162: "the watery moon." On the next line Wr. quotes *W. T.* i. 2. 427:

> "You may as well
> Forbid the sea for to obey the moon;"

and M. misquotes Coleridge, *Anc. Mariner*:

> "Still as a slave before his lord,
> The ocean hath no blast;
> His great bright eye most silently
> Up to the moon is cast,
> If he may know which way to go,
> For she guides him smooth or grim—
> See, brother, see, how graciously
> She looketh down on him!"

120. Voss refers to *Matt.* xxiv. 29.

121. *Precurse.* Used by S. only here; and *precursor* only in *Temp.* i. 2. 201. Wr. says that "precurser" occurs in *Phœnix and Turtle*, 6, but the eds. generally have "precurrer."

*Fierce.* Wild, terrible. It means "immoderate, excessive" (Schmidt) in *T. of A.* iv. 2. 30 and *Hen. VIII.* i. 1. 54; and Steevens would give it a similar sense ("conspicuous, glaring") here.

122. *Still.* Constantly, always; as often. Gr. 69. On *harbingers*, see *Macb.* p. 168.

123. *Omen.* The event portended by the omen. S. uses the word nowhere else. Upton cites Virgil, *Æn.* 1. 346, where *ominibus*, literally =the omens of the marriage rite, is put for the rite itself; and Farmer quotes Heywood, *Life of Merlin*:

> "Merlin, well vers'd in many a hidden spell,
> His countries omen did long since foretell."

124. *Demonstrated.* Accented on first syllable, as in *Hen. V.* iv. 2. 54; but on the second in *T. of A.* i. 1. 91, *Oth.* i. 1. 61, etc.

125. *Climatures.* Regions; used by S. only here. For *climate* in the same sense, see *Rich. II.* iv. 1. 130 and *J. C.* i. 3. 32.

127. *Cross it.* According to Blakeway, whoever crossed the spot on which a spectre was seen became subject to its malignant influence. Among the reasons for supposing the young Earl of Derby (who died in 1594) to have been bewitched, Lodge states that a figure of a tall man appeared in his chamber "who twice crossed him swiftly," and when the earl came to the place where he saw the apparition "he fell sick."

129. For the short line here and below, see Gr. 512.

130, 131. Alluding, as Simrock suggests, to the idea that a ghost may often be "laid" when a living person does for him what he himself ought to have done when alive.

134. *Happily.* According to Nares and Schmidt=*haply*, as often; but it may be=luckily, as some critics make it. H. points out that the

structure of this solemn appeal is almost identical with that of a very different strain in *A. Y. L.* ii. 4. 33–42.

136. *Or if thou hast*, etc. Steevens quotes Dekker, *Knight's Conjuring*: "If any of them had bound the spirit of gold by any charmes in caves, or in iron fetters under the ground, they should for their own soules quiet (which questionlesse else would whine up and down) if not for the good of their children, release it."

138. *They say.* Clarke notes the propriety of these words in the mouth of Horatio, "the scholar and the unbeliever in ghosts."

140. *Partisan.* A kind of halberd. Cf. *R. and J.* i. 1. 80, 101, *A. and C.* ii. 7. 14, etc.

143. *Majestical.* Used by S. oftener than *majestic.* Cf. *Hen. V.* iii. chor. 16, iv. 1. 284, etc.

145. *As the air, invulnerable.* Malone compares *Macb.* v. 8. 9 and *K. John*, ii. 1. 252.

149. *I have heard*, etc. Cf. *M. N. D.* iii. 2. 381 fol., and Milton, *Hymn on Nativ.* 229–234, etc. Farmer quotes Prudentius, *Ad Gallicinium*:

> "Ferunt, vagantes daemonas,
> Laetos tenebris noctium,
> *Gallo canente* exterritos
> Sparsim timere et cedere."

150. *The trumpet*, etc. For *trumpet*=trumpeter, cf. *Hen. V.* iv. 2. 61: "I will the banner from a trumpet take," etc. Malone quotes from *England's Parnassus*, 1600: "And now the cocke, the morning's trumpeter." Coleridge remarks that "how to elevate a thing almost mean by its familiarity, young poets may learn in this treatment of the cockcrow."

153. *Whether in sea*, etc. "According to the pneumatology of that time, every element was inhabited by its peculiar order of spirits" (Johnson). Cf. Milton, *Il Pens* 93:

> "And of those demons that are found
> In fire, air, flood, or under ground,
> Whose power hath a true consent
> With planet or with element."

154. *Extravagant.* In its etymological sense of *wandering beyond* its *confine*, or limit. Cf. *L. L. L.* iv. 2. 68: "a foolish extravagant spirit;" and *Oth.* i. 1. 137: "an extravagant and wheeling stranger." S. uses the word only in these passages, and *extravagancy* (=vagrancy) only in *T. N.* ii. 1. 12. So *erring* is used in its literal sense; as in *A. Y. L.* iii. 2. 138 and *Oth.* i. 3. 362. Cf. Gr. p. 13.

155. For the accent of *confine*, cf. *Temp.* iv. 1. 121, *Sonn.* 84. 3, etc.; for the other one, see *Rich. II.* i. 3. 137, *Rich. III.* iv. 4. 3, etc.

156. *Probation.* Proof; as in *Macb.* iii. 1. 80, *Cymb.* v. 5. 362, etc. The word is here a quadrisyllable. Gr. 479.

158. *'Gainst.* Used metaphorically of time (Gr. 142), as in *M. N. D.* iii. 2. 99: "against he do appear," etc. Cf. iii. 4. 50 below.

161. *Spirit.* Monosyllabic (=*sprite*), as often. Gr. 463.

*Can walk.* The folio reading; the 1st quarto has "dare walke," the later quartos "dare sturre."

162. *Strike.* Exert a malign influence. Cf. *T. A.* ii. 4. 14: "If I do wake, some planet strike me down." See also *Cor.* ii. 2. 117 and *W. T.* i. 2. 201. As Wr. remarks, we still have "moonstruck."

163. *Takes.* Bewitches, blasts. F. quotes Florio: "*Assiderare:* to blast or strike with a planet, to be taken." Cf. *M. W.* iv. 4. 32: "blasts the tree and takes the cattle;" *Lear*, ii. 4. 166: "taking airs;" *Id.* iii. 4. 61: "Bless thee from whirlwinds, star-blasting, and taking!" and *A. and C.* iv. 2. 37: "Now the witch take me, if I meant it thus!"

164. *Gracious.* Blessed, benign; "partaking of the nature of the epithet with which it is associated" (Caldecott).

165. *And do in part believe it.* "A happy expression of the half-sceptical, half-complying spirit of Shakespeare's time, when witchcraft was believed, antipodes doubted" (M.).

166, 167. As Hunter suggests, Milton must have had this beautiful personification in mind when he wrote *P. L.* v. 1:

> "Now morn, her rosy steps in th' eastern clime
> Advancing, sow'd the earth with orient pearls."

173. *Loves.* For the plural, see *Macb.* p. 209 or *Rich. II.* p. 206 (note on *Sights*).

175. *Conveniently.* The folio reading; the quartos have "convenient" (Gr. 1).

SCENE II.—1. "In the King's speech, observe the set and pedantically antithetic form of the sentences when touching that which galled the heels of conscience,—the strain of undignified rhetoric,—and yet in what follows concerning the public weal, a certain appropriate majesty. Indeed, was he not a royal brother?" (Coleridge).

2. *That.* See Gr. 284.

4. *Brow of woe.* "Mourning brow" (*L. L. L.* v. 2. 754). Wr. compares iv. 6. 19: "thieves of mercy;" *M. of V.* ii. 8. 42: "mind of love;" *Lear*, i. 4. 306: "brow of youth," etc.

6. *With wisest sorrow.* "With the due proportion of sorrow" (M.).

8. *Sometime.* The folio has "sometimes." S. uses both forms adjectively. Cf. *Rich. II.* i. 2. 54: "thy sometimes brother's wife;" *Id.* v. 1. 37: "good sometime queen," etc. See on i. 1. 49 above.

9. *Of.* The quartos have "to."

10. *Defeated.* Marred, disfigured. Cf. *Oth.* i. 3. 346: "defeat thy favour with an usurped beard." So *defeature*=disfigurement in *V. and A.* 736, *C. of E.* ii. 1. 98 and v. 1. 299.

11. *One ... one.* So in the folio; the quartos have "an ... a." Steevens quotes *W. T.* v. 2. 80: "She had one eye declined for the loss of her husband, another elevated that the oracle was fulfilled."

Malone explains *dropping* as "*depressed* or *cast downwards*," and W. substitutes "drooping."

14. *To wife.* Cf. *Temp.* ii. 1. 75: "Such a paragon to their queen," etc. Gr. 189.

*Barr'd.* Excluded, acted without the concurrence of. Cf. *Hen. V.* i. 2. 12, 92, *Lear*, v. 3. 85, etc.

15. *Wisdoms.* See on *loves*, i. 1. 173 above.

17. *That you know.* What you already know. See Gr. 244. Theo. points it thus: "Now follows that you know, young Fortinbras," etc. (so Walker, with colon instead of comma).

18. *Supposal.* Opinion; used by S. only here.

20. *Disjoint.* For the form cf. iii. 1. 155: "most deject." See also iii. 4. 180, 205, and iv. 5. 2. Gr. 342.

21. *Colleagued*, etc. With no ally but this imaginary advantage. The quartos have "this dream."

22. *Pester.* The word originally meant to crowd, as in Milton, *Comus*, 7: "Confin'd and pester'd in this pinfold here." Cf. *Cor.* iv. 6. 7: "Dissentious numbers pestering (that is, infesting) streets," etc. See also Webster, *Malcontent*, v. 2: "the hall will be so pestered anon."

23. *Importing.* Abbott (Gr. p. 16) thinks this is used for "importuning;" but cf. *T. of A.* v. 2. 11:

"With letters of entreaty, which imported
His fellowship i' the cause;"

*Oth.* ii. 2. 3: "tidings now arrived, importing the mere perdition of the Turkish fleet," etc. See also iv. 7. 80 and v. 2. 21 below.

24. *Bonds.* The folio reading; the quartos have "bands," which means the same.

27. *Writ.* For the past tense S. uses *writ* oftener than *wrote;* for the participle he has usually *writ* or *written*, sometimes *wrote.* Gr. 343.

31. *Gait.* "Used metaphorically for proceeding in a business" (Nares). *In that*=inasmuch as.

32. *Proportions.* Contingents, quotas; as in *Hen. V.* i. 2. 137, 304, etc.

33. *Subject.* See on i. 1. 72 above.

38. *Dilated.* "Detailed" (Schmidt). Cf. *A. W.* ii. 1. 59: "a more dilated farewell." The 1st quarto has "related," the later quartos "delated." Greene has the word in the sense of delayed, in *A Maiden's Dream:* "Nor might the pleas be over-long dilated."

For the "confusion of construction" in *allow*, see Gr. 412. On this point K. remarks: "We find in all the old dramatists many such lines as this in Marlowe: 'The *outside* of her garments *were* of lawn.' And too many such lines have been corrected by the editors of Shakespeare who have thus obliterated the traces of our tongue's history. It is remarkable that the very commentators who were always ready to fix the charge of ignorance of the rudiments of grammar upon Shakespeare, have admitted the following passage in a note to 2 *Hen. IV.* by that elegant modern scholar, T. Warton: 'Beaumont and Fletcher's play contains many satirical strokes against Heywood's comedy, the *force* of which *are* entirely lost to those who have not seen that comedy.'"

39. *Let your haste*, etc. "Let your haste show that you perform your duty well" (Wr.).

41. *Nothing.* Adverbially=not at all; as often in S. Cf. *M. of V.* i, 1. 165: "nothing undervalued to Cato's daughter," etc. Gr. 55.

42. *You.* For the change to *thou* in 45 fol., see Gr. 235.

45. *Lose your voice.* Waste your words. Cf. 118 below: "lose her prayers."

47. *Native.* Naturally related. Cf. *A. W.* i. 1. 238: "native things"

(that is, kindred things). Delius remarks that *native* expresses a connection that is congenital, *instrumental* one that is mechanical.

51. *Leave and favour.* "Kind permission" (Caldecott).

56. *Pardon.* "Almost=leave, permission" (Schmidt). Cf. *A. and C.* iii. 6. 60: "His pardon for return."

59. *Laboursome.* Cf. *Cymb.* iii. 4. 167: "laboursome (=elaborate) and dainty trims." S. uses the word only twice, *laborious* not at all.

Lines 58–60 are not in the folio.

63. *And thy best graces*, etc. "May the fairest graces that you are master of help you to spend the time at your will" (M.).

64. *Cousin.* Nephew. Elsewhere it means niece (as in *A. Y. L.* i. 2. 164, i. 3. 44, etc.), uncle (*T. N.* i. 5. 131, v. 1. 313), brother-in-law (1 *Hen. IV.* iii. 1. 51), and grandchild (*K. John*, iii. 3. 17, *Oth.* i. 1. 113, etc.). It is also used as a mere complimentary form of address between princes, etc. (*Hen. V.* v. 2. 4, *Rich. III.* iii. 4. 37, etc.).

65. *A little more than kin*, etc. If Hamlet refers to himself, the meaning seems to be: more than a mere kinsman (being step-son as well as nephew) and less than kind (because I hate you). If he applies them to the king, we may accept the paraphrase of W.: "In marrying my mother you have made yourself something more than my kinsman, and at the same time have shown yourself unworthy of our race, our kind." For sundry other explanations, see F. Coll. quotes Rowley, *Search for Money*, 1609: "I would he were not so near us in kindred, then sure he would be nearer in kindness." Steevens compares Lyly, *Mother Bombie*, 1594: "the nearer we are in blood, the further we must be from love; the greater the kindred is, the less the kindness must be;" and *Gorboduc*, 1561: "In kinde a father, but not kindelynesse."

67. *Too much i' the sun.* "More careless and idle than I ought to be" (Schmidt). Johnson, Caldecott, and others see here an allusion to the old proverb, "Out of heaven's blessing into the warm sun," that is, "out of house and home,"—in Hamlet's case, deprived of his right, or the succession to the throne. For a summary of other interpretations, see F.

68. *Nighted.* Black as night (Gr. 294). S. uses the word again in *Lear*, iv. 5. 13: "his nighted life."

Scarlet was the colour then worn by the kings, queens, and princes of Denmark. K. says: "It thus happens, curiously enough, that the objections of the queen and Claudius to the appearance of Hamlet in black are authorized, not only by the well-known custom of the early Danes never to mourn for their nearest and dearest relatives and friends, but also by the fact that, although black was at least their favourite, if not, indeed, their national colour, Hamlet, as a prince of the blood, should have been attired in the royal scarlet."

70. *Vailed lids.* Downcast eyes. Cf. *V. and A.* 956: "She vail'd her eyelids;" *M. of V.* i. 1. 28: "Vailing her high top lower than her ribs," etc. See *Mer.* p. 128. We have a play on the word in Marlowe's *Hero and Leander*: "Vail'd to the ground, veiling her eyelids close."

72. *Lives.* The 2d and later folios have "live," which is adopted by Coll., D., and H.

74. *Ay, madam*, etc. Coleridge says: "Here observe Hamlet's delicacy to his mother, and how the suppression prepares him for the overflow in the next speech, in which his character is more developed by bringing forward his aversion to externals, and which betrays his habit of brooding over the world within him, coupled with a prodigality of beautiful words, which are the half-embodyings of thought, and are more than thought, and have an outness, a reality *sui generis*, and yet contain their correspondence and shadowy affinity to the images and movements within. Note also Hamlet's silence to the long speech of the king which follows, and his respectful, but general, answer to his mother."

M. quotes Tennyson, *In Memoriam*, vi.:

> "That loss is common would not make
> My own less bitter; rather more:
> Too common! never morning wore
> To evening, but some heart did break."

77. *Inky*. Again used metaphorically in *A. Y. L.* iii. 5. 46: "your inky brows."

81. *Haviour*. Often printed "'haviour," but see *Rich. II.* p. 162.

82. *Shows*. The quartos have "chapes" or "shapes."

83. *Denote*. Indicate, mark. Cf. *Sonn.* 148. 7, *Oth.* iii. 3. 428, iv. 1. 290, etc.

85. *Passeth*. As Corson remarks, the older form suits the tone of the passage better, and avoids the concurrence of sibilants.

M. quotes *Rich. II.* iv. 1. 295–298: "'Tis very true, my grief lies all within," etc.

87. *Commendable*. Accented on the first syllable, as regularly in S. (cf. *Much Ado*, iii. 1. 71, 73, etc.), with the single exception (which Schmidt considers doubtful) of *M. of V.* i. 1. 111. Abbott (Gr. 490) would give the latter accent here.

90. *That father*, etc. That lost father lost his; or (Gr. 246) that father (who was) lost lost his.

*Bound*. Was bound. For the ellipsis, cf. iii. 3. 62 (Wr.). See Gr. 403.

92. *Obsequious*. Funereal; from *obsequies* (Johnson); as in *T. A.* v. 3. 152 and *Sonn.* 31. 5. Cf. the adverb *obsequiously* in *Rich. III.* i. 2. 3.

*Persever*. The regular spelling and accent in S. Cf. *A. W.* iv. 2. 36, 37, where it rhymes with *ever*. Gr. 492.

93. *Condolement*. Sorrow, mourning. Used by S. only here and (blunderingly) in *Per.* ii. 1. 156.

95. *Incorrect*. Contumacious, unsubmissive; used by S. only here, like *unfortified* (=weak) in the next line.

97. *Simple*. Foolish.

99. *Any the most*. Cf. *Cymb.* i. 4. 65: "any the rarest."

*To sense*. Depending on *vulgar*, and = "anything the most commonly perceived" (Gr. 419*a*).

104. *Who*. For *who* "personifying irrational antecedents," see Gr. 264.

105. *Till he*. See Gr. 184, 206.

107. *Unprevailing*. Unavailing. So *prevail*=avail in *R. and J.* iii. 3. 60: "It helps not, it prevails not." Cf. Peele, *Sir Clyomon*, 1599: "pursuit prevaileth nought;" Marlowe, *Dido*, v. 2: "What can my tears or

cries prevail me now?" Malone quotes Dryden, *Essay on Dramatic Poetry:* "He may often prevail himself of the same advantages;" and *Absalom and Achitophel*, 461 (1st ed.): "Prevail* yourself of what occasion gives."

109. *Immediate.* Cf. 2 *Hen. IV.* iv. 5. 42:

> "My due from thee is this imperial crown,
> Which, as immediate from thy place and blood,
> Derives itself to me."

110. *Nobility.* "Dignity, greatness" (Schmidt), or "eminence and distinction" (Heath).

112. *Impart.* As the verb has no object, various emendations, not worth mentioning, have been suggested. It is probably one of the many instances of "confusion of construction" in S. Cf. i. 3. 50 below, and see Gr. 415. As Delius suggests, the poet probably regarded *no less nobility of love* as the object of *impart*, and forgot, owing to the intermediate clause, that he had written *with no less.* On *for*=as for, as regards, see Gr. 149.

113. The university of Wittenberg was founded in 1502, and is mentioned in Marlowe's *Doctor Faustus* and other English books of the time. For *school*=university, cf. *A. Y. L.* i. 1. 6.

114. *Retrograde.* Contrary; an astrological term. Cf. *A. W.* i. 1. 212, where Parolles says he was born "under Mars," and Helena sarcastically remarks, "When he was retrograde, I think." See on i. 1. 117 above.

115. *Bend you.* Bend yourself (Gr. 223), be inclined. Cf. 1 *Hen. IV.* v. 5. 36: "bend you with your dearest speed."

120. *In all my best.* Cf. *Oth.* iii. 4. 127: "I have spoken for you all my best." In i. 5. 27 below we have "in the best" where we should say "at the best."

124. *Sits smiling to my heart.* The meaning is clear, but the expression is peculiar. Cf. *Cor.* iv. 2. 48:

> "it would unclog my heart
> Of what lies heavy to 't;"

*M. for. M.* v. 1. 394: "Your brother's death, I know, sits at your heart." Delius would connect *to* with *smiling.* Ritson proposed "on my heart."

*In grace.* In honour; as in *M. N. D.* iv. 1. 139: "in grace of our solemnity.".

125. *Denmark.* That is, the king of Denmark. Johnson says: "The king's intemperance is very strongly impressed; everything that happens to him gives him occasion to drink."

127. *Rouse.* Bumper; as in *Oth.* ii. 3. 66. The word is of Danish origin (see Wb.), and not connected with *carouse.* It is now used only in the sense of a drinking bout or carousal. Cf. i. 4. 8 and ii. 1. 58 below. See also Marlowe, *Dr. Faustus*, iii. 4: "He took his rouse with stoups

---

* The change to "Avail" in later eds. is due to Derrick, and not, as Malone states, to Dryden himself. There is another instance in the Introduction to the *Annus Mirabilis:* "I could not prevail myself of it in the English" (here also changed to "avail" by Derrick). It is an imitation of the French idiom, *se prévaloir de.*

of Rhenish wine;" Massinger, *Duke of Milan*, i. 1: "Stands bound to take his rouse;" *Bondman*, ii. 3: "another rouse!" etc.

The Danish court in the time of S. was known throughout Europe for its intemperance. Sir John Harrington in 1606 refers as follows to the visit of Christian IV. of Denmark (uncle of Anne, queen of James I.) to England: "From the day the Danish king came, until this hour, I have been well nigh overwhelmed with carousal, and sports of all kinds. . . . I think the Dane hath strangely wrought on our good English nobles; for those whom I could never get to taste good liquor, now follow the fashion, and wallow in beastly delights. The ladies abandon their sobriety, and are seen to roll about in intoxication. I do often say (but not aloud) that the Danes have again conquered the Britains; for I see no man, or woman either, that can now command himself or herself."

*Bruit.* Noise abroad. Cf. *Macb.* v. 7. 22, etc.

129. *Too, too.* A common reduplication. Cf. *R. of L.* 174, *T. G. of V.* ii. 4. 205, *M. W.* ii. 2. 260, *M. of V.* ii. 6. 42, etc. See *Mer.* p. 143.

On the passage Coleridge remarks: "This *tædium vitæ* is a common oppression on minds cast in the Hamlet mould, and is caused by disproportionate mental exertion, which necessitates exhaustion of bodily feeling. Where there is a just coincidence of external and internal action, pleasure is always the result; but where the former is deficient, and the mind's appetency of the ideal is unchecked, realities will seem cold and unmoving. In such cases, passion combines itself with the indefinite alone. In this mood of his mind the relation of the appearance of his father's spirit in arms is made all at once to Hamlet: it is—Horatio's speech, in particular—a perfect model of the true style of dramatic narrative; the purest poetry, and yet in the most natural language, equally remote from the ink-horn and the plough."

M. says: "The base affinities of our nature are ever present to Hamlet's mind. Here he thinks of the body as hiding from us the freshness, life, and nobleness of God's creation. If it were to pass away, silently and spontaneously, like the mist on a mountain-side, or if, curtain-like, we might tear it down by an act of violence, it may be that we should see quite another prospect; at any rate, the vile things now before us would be gone forever."

130. *Resolve.* Cf. *L. C.* 296: "resolv'd my reason into tears;" *T. of A.* iv. 3. 442:

> "The sea 's a thief, whose liquid surge resolves
> The moon into salt tears."

Nares quotes Lyly, *Euphues:* "I could be content to resolve myself into tears."

132. *Canon.* "Theo. first pointed out that this did not refer to a piece of artillery, but to a divine decree" (F.). Wordsworth (*Shakespeare's Knowledge and Use of the Bible*) says: "Unless it be the Sixth Commandment, the *canon* must be one of natural religion." Cf. *Cymb.* iii. 4. 77:

> "Against self-slaughter
> There is a prohibition so divine
> That cravens my weak hand."

137. *Merely.* Absolutely. See *Temp.* p. 111 or *J. C.* p. 129.

140. *Hyperion.* Apollo. Cf. *Hen. V.* iv. 1. 292, *T. and C.* ii. 3. 207, etc. The accent is properly on the penult, but the general usage of English poets has thrown it back. See Worc. Even an accomplished classical scholar like Gray could write: "Hyperion's march and glittering shafts of war."

*To* is often thus used in comparisons. Cf. *Temp.* i. 2. 480, *C. of E.* i. 2. 35, etc. See also i. 5. 52 and iii. 1. 52 below.

*A satyr.* Warb. says: "By the *satyr* is meant Pan, as by *Hyperion* Apollo. Pan and Apollo were brothers; and the allusion is to the contention between those gods for the preference in music." But more probably, as Steevens suggests, the beauty of Apollo is contrasted with the deformity of a satyr.

HEAD OF A SATYR.

141. *Might not beteem.* Could not allow. Gr. 312. S. uses *beteem* again in *M. N. D.* i. 1. 131. See note in our ed. p. 128.

142. *Visit.* For the omission of *to*, see Gr. 349.

147. *Or ere.* A reduplication, *or* being = before. See *Temp.* p. 112.

149. *Niobe.* Again alluded to in *T. and C.* v. 10. 19: "Make wells and Niobes of the maids and wives."

150. *Discourse of reason.* "The reasoning faculty" (Wr.). The phrase occurs again in *T. and C.* ii. 2. 116, and "discourse of thought" in *Oth.* iv. 2. 153. Cf. "reason and discourse" in *M. for M.* i. 2. 190, and "discourse" in iv. 4. 37 below.

153. *Hercules.* Cf. ii. 2. 353 below. Allusions to Hercules are very common in S.

155. *Left the flushing.* Ceased to produce redness. Cf. iii. 4. 34 below: "Leave wringing of your hands," etc. Schmidt suggests doubtfully,

NIOBE.

"ere her tears had had time to redden her eyes?" Wr. refers to the transitive use of *flush*=to fill with water; but the word here is probably used in the other sense. On *galled eyes*, cf. *Rich. III.* iv. 4. 53 and *T. and C.* v. 3. 55.

157. *Dexterity.* "Nimbleness" (Schmidt). Walker suspects that S. wrote "celerity;" but elsewhere the idea of adroitness in the word seems to have suggested to S. that of quickness. Cf. *R. of L.* 1389, *M. W.* iv. 5. 121 and 1 *Hen. IV.* ii. 4. 286.

158. *Nor it cannot.* Cf. iii. 2. 183 below: "nor 't is not strange," etc. Gr. 406.

159. *Break.* Subjunctive (Gr. 364) or 3d person imperative; not 2d person imperative, as many eds. make it by putting a comma after it.

163. *Change.* Exchange. Johnson explains the passage: "I 'll be

your servant, you shall be my friend;" but it may mean simply, "I 'll exchange the name of *friend* with you."

164. *What make you?* What are you doing? Cf. *Oth.* iii. 4. 169: "What make you from home?" The phrase is common in S. and is quibbled upon in *L. L. L.* iv. 3. 190 fol. and *Rich. III.* i. 3. 164 fol. See ii. 2. 266 below.

167. *Good even, sir.* Addressed to Bernardo, whom Hamlet does not recognize (W.).

170. *Hear.* The quarto reading; that of the folios is "have," adopted by K., Sr., and W.

171. *That.* Such. See Gr. 277, and cf. i. v. 48 below.

172. *Truster.* Cf. *T. of A.* iv. 1. 10: "And cut your trusters' throats." Gr. 443.

177. *I pray thee.* As Corson remarks, this reading of the folio is better than "I prithee," an earnest entreaty being meant.

179. *Upon.* For the adverbial use, see Gr. 192.

180. *Bak'd meats.* We have "bakemeats" in *Gen.* xl. 17 (printed with a hyphen in the ed. of 1611, as Wr. states) and "bake mete" in Chaucer, *C. T.* 343. It was an old custom to furnish a cold entertainment for the mourners at a funeral. Collins quotes the old romance of *Syr Degore:*

> "A great feaste would he holde
> Upon his quenes mornynge day,
> That was buryed in an abbay;"

and Malone adds from Hayward's *Life and Raigne of King Henrie the Fourth*, 1599: "Then hee [Richard II.] was . . . obscurely interred,—without the charge of a dinner for celebrating the funeral." For further information on the subject, see Brande's *Popular Antiquities* (Bohn's ed.) vol. ii. pp. 237–245. The custom did not continue long after the time of S., for Flecknoe, in his *Ænigmatical Characters*, 1665, says of "a curious glutton" that when he dies he "onely regrets that funeral feasts are quite left off, else he should have the pleasure of one feast more (in imagination at least) even after death."

182. *Dearest foe.* Cf. *A. Y. L.* i. 3. 34: "my father hated his father dearly," etc. See *Temp.* p. 124 (note on *The dear'st of th' loss*) or *Rich. II.* p. 151.

183. *Or ever I had.* The folio has "Ere I had ever," which some editors prefer. See on 147 above.

185. *O where.* The quartos omit the *O*.

*In my mind's eye.* Cf. *R. of L.* 1426: "unseen, save to the eye of mind;" Chaucer, *C. T.* 4972: "with eyen of his mynde. See also *Much Ado*, iv. 1. 231.

190. *Saw? who?* Some eds. print "Saw who?" and D. says that the Kembles, Kean, and Macready gave the words as a single question. For the *who=whom*, see Gr. 274.

192. *Season.* "Qualify, temper" (Schmidt), as in ii. 1. 28 below. Cf. *M. of V.* iv. 1. 197: "When mercy seasons justice."

193. *Attent.* Attentive; used again in *Per.* iii. prol. 11: "Be attent." Spenser uses it as a noun in *F. Q.* iii. 9. 52: "With vigilant regard and

dew attent;" and *Id.* vi. 9. 37: "And kept her sheepe with diligent attent."

*Deliver*=relate, as in 209 and v. 2. 374 below. Cf. *Temp.* ii. 1. 45, v. 1. 313, etc.

198. *Vast.* The reading of 1st quarto; the later quartos and the folio have "waste." Malone and Steevens read "waist"=middle. Marston, in his *Malecontent*, 1604, has "waist of night." *Vast*, like *waste*, =void, emptiness. Cf. *Temp.* i. 2. 327: "that vast of night."

200. *At point.* The folio has "at all points." Cf. *Rich. II.* i. 3. 2: "Yea, at all points;" Spenser, *F. Q.* i. 1. 16: "Armed to point;" *Id.* i. 2. 12: "all armde to point," etc. See also *Macb.* p. 241, note on *At a point.*

*Cap-a-pe.* Cap-à-pied, from head to foot; used again in *W. T.* iv. 4. 761: "I am courtier cap-a-pe." Cf. 228 below.

202. *Thrice.* In the folio joined to *by them.*

204. *Distill'd.* The folio has "bestil'd," and the Coll. MS. "bechill'd." Sr. quotes Sylvester, *Du Bartas:* "Melt thee, distill thee, turne to wax or snow."

205. *Act.* Action, operation. Cf. *Oth.* iii. 3. 328:

> "Dangerous conceits are in their natures poisons,
> Which at the first are scarce found to distaste,
> But with a little act upon the blood
> Burn like the mines of sulphur."

207. *Dreadful.* Filled with dread; as in *R. of L.* 450, *Rich. III.* i. 1. 8, etc. See on i. 1. 57 above.

216. *It head.* Cf. *Temp.* ii. 1. 163: "of it own kind;" *Hen. V.* v. 2. 40: "in it own fertility;" *Lear*, i. 4. 236: "it 's had it head bit off by it young," etc. See Gr. 228 or *Temp.* p. 120. This possessive *it* occurs fourteen times in the folio (not counting a doubtful case in *T. G. of V.* v. 2. 21), *it's* nine times, and *its* only once (*M. for M.* i. 2. 4). Milton has *its* three times (*P. L.* i. 254, iv. 813, and *Hymn on Nativ.* 106). *Its* does not occur in the *A. V.* of 1611, and the possessive *it* is found only in *Lev.* xxv. 5 ("its" in modern eds.).

217. *Like as.* Cf. *Sonn.* 60. 1: "Like as the waves make towards the pebbled shore;" *T. and C.* i. 2. 7: "like as there were husbandry in war," etc. Cf. Gr. 107 and 116.

218. *But even.* See on i. 1. 81 above.

222. *Writ.* See on 27 above.

226. *Arm'd, say you?* This refers to the ghost, not to Horatio and Marcellus as some have understood it.

230. *Beaver.* The movable front of the helmet. Cf. 2 *Hen. IV.* iv. 1. 120: "their beavers down," etc. It is sometimes put for the helmet, as in 1 *Hen. IV.* iv. 1. 104: "with his beaver on," etc. Hunter quotes Spenser, *F. Q.* iv. 6. 25: "they their bevers up did reare." For the derivation of the word, see Wb.

237. *Like.* Likely; as often. Cf. ii. 2. 341 below. See also *M. of V.* ii. 7. 49: "Is 't like that lead contains her?" etc.

238. *Tell.* Count. Cf. *Rich. III.* i. 4. 122: "while one would tell twenty," etc. The word is now obsolete in this sense, except in the

phrases "all told" and "telling one's beads." Cf. *teller*=one who counts money or votes.

240. *No?* As F. remarks, the anonymous suggestion that this belongs to Horatio, not to Hamlet, is very plausible. "It is eminently characteristic of the precise Horatio (e'en the justest man Hamlet had ever found) to draw a nice distinction between *grizzled* and *sable silvered*. He had been most exact in his estimate of the time the Ghost stayed, and he would be equally exact even as to the colour and texture of the beard."

248. *Tenable in your silence.* To be kept silent or secret. The folio has "treble," which Caldecott and K. (only in his 1st ed.) defend, making the passage = "impose a threefold obligation of silence."

251. *Loves.* See on i. 1. 173 above.

254. *Your loves.* Say rather your loves. Cf. 163 above.

256. *Doubt.* Suspect. Cf. *Cor.* iii. 1. 152, *Oth.* iii. 3. 19, etc.

258. *To men's eyes.* The folio omits the comma after *them;* and, as Corson says, it makes as good sense to connect *to men's eyes* with *o'erwhelm* as with *rise.*

SCENE III.—3. *Convoy is assistant.* Conveyance is ready. Cf. *A. W.* iv. 4. 10, *Hen. V.* iv. 3. 37, etc.

5. *For.* As for, as regards. See on i. 2. 112 above, and cf. i. 5. 139 below.

6. *Fashion.* Schmidt puts it under the head of *fashion*="that which good-breeding requires;" that is, a matter of form or courtesy. Wr. explains it as=that "which is changeable or temporary."

*A toy in blood.* A caprice, an impulsive fancy. Wr. quotes *Oth.* i. 3. 269: "Light-wing'd toys Of feather'd Cupid." For *blood,* cf. iii. 2. 64 below, and see *A. Y. L.* p. 197.

7. *Primy.* Early, vernal; perhaps peculiar to this passage (Nares).

8. *Forward.* Premature, and therefore liable to early decay. On the measure, see Gr. 484.

9. *Suppliance.* Gratification, pastime (Schmidt); used by S. only here.

10. *No more but so?* The early eds. have a period after *so;* the change is due to Rowe.

11. *Crescent.* Cf. *A. and C.* ii. 1. 10: "My powers are crescent."

12. *Thews.* Muscular powers; as in *J. C.* i. 3. 81 and 2 *Hen. IV.* iii. 2. 276. S. uses the word only three times. *Thews*=manners or mental qualities, used by Spenser, Chaucer, and earlier writers, has a different origin. Cf. Spenser, *F. Q.* i. 10. 4:

> "The mother of three daughters, well upbrought
> In goodly thewes, and godly exercise;"

*Id.* ii. 1. 33: "For well ye worthy bene for worth and gentle thewes," etc.

*Temple.* Only on grave occasions applied to the body (Caldecott). Cf. *R. of L.* 719, 1172, *Macb.* ii. 3. 73, *Cymb.* ii. 1. 69, iv. 2. 55, v. 5. 220, etc.

13. *The inward service,* etc. As the body grows, the duties of the indwelling soul increase.

15. *Cautel.* Craft, deceit. Used only here and in *L. C.* 303; but we have *cautelous* (=false, deceitful) in *Cor.* iv. 1. 33 and *J. C.* ii. 1. 129. Rushton suggests that S. had in mind Swinburn, *Treatise on Wills,* 1590: "There is no cautele under heaven, whereby the libertie of making or

revoking his testament can be utterly taken away." *Besmirch* is used literally in *Hen. V.* iv. 3. 110.

16. *The virtue of his will.* "His virtuous intentions" (Mason).

18. This line is not in the quartos.

19. *Unvalued.* Of low birth, mean. In the only other instance in S. (*Rich. III.* i. 4. 27) it means invaluable. Cf. Marlowe, *Tamburlane*, i. 2: "loss unvalued" (that is, inestimable). Here again Rushton cites Swinburn: "it is not lawful for legetaries to carve for themselves, taking their legacies at their own pleasure."

21. *Safety.* A trisyllable. Cf. Gr. 477 and 488. The folio has "sanctity," and Theo. substituted "sanity," which W. adopts and Abbott (Gr. 484) favours. D., H., and St. read "the health," which is perhaps the best emendation, if any be required.

26. *Particular act and place.* "The peculiar line of conduct prescribed to him by his rank" (Schmidt). The folio has "peculiar Sect and force." W. reads "peculiar sect and place;" making *sect*=class, rank.

28. *Withal.* An emphatic form of *with* (Gr. 196).

30. *Credent.* Credulous. Cf. *L. C.* 279:

> "Lending soft audience to my sweet design
> And credent soul to that strong-bonded oath
> That shall prefer and undertake my troth."

It means credible in *M. for M.* iv. 4. 29 and *W. T.* i. 2. 142.

32. *Unmaster'd.* "Uncontrolled, unbridled" (Schmidt).

36. *Chariest.* "Most scrupulous" (D.). So *chariness*=scrupulousness in *M. W.* ii. 1. 102.

38. *Scapes.* Not "'scapes," being used in prose by Bacon and others. See *Macb.* p. 214 or Wb. s. v.

39. *Canker.* Canker-worm. See *M. N. D.* p. 150.

40. *Buttons.* Buds (Fr. *bouton*).

42. *Blastments.* Blights; used by S. only here. Wr. quotes Coleridge, *Zapolya*: "Shall shoot his blastments on the land."

43. *Best safety*, etc. Cf. *Macb.* iii. 5. 32, and see note in our ed. p. 223.

44. *Youth*, etc. "In the absence of any tempter, youth rebels against itself, that is, the passions of youth revolt from the power of self-restraint; there is a traitor in the camp" (Wr.).

*None else near.* For the omission of *is*, see Gr. 403.

46. *Good my brother.* See Gr. 13.

47. *Ungracious.* "Graceless" (Wr.). Cf. *Rich. II.* ii. 3. 89, 1 *Hen. IV.* ii. 4. 490, etc.

49. *Whiles.* Used by S. interchangeably with *while* and *whilst*. The folio has "Whilst" here. *Puffed*=bloated.

50. *Primrose.* Cf. *Macb.* ii. 3. 21: "the primrose way to the everlasting bonfire."

51. *Recks not his own rede.* Cares not for his own counsel. Cf. Spenser, *F. Q.* vi. 2. 30: "To whose wise read she hearkning," etc. So the verb *rede* or *read*=advise; as in *F. Q.* i. 1. 13: "Therefore I read beware," etc.

*Fear me not.* Fear not for me. Cf. iii. 4. 7 and iv. 5. 105 below. See also *M. for M.* iv. 1. 70, *Much Ado*, iii. 1. 31, etc. Gr. 200.

52. *I stay too long.* "Laertes seems to think that Ophelia's spirited reply is giving the conversation a needless and inconvenient turn; for that for sisters to lecture brothers is an inversion of the natural order of things" (M.).

53. *Double.* Laertes had already taken leave of his father.

56. *Sits.* Often used of the wind. Cf. *M. of V.* i. 1. 18, *Rich. II.* ii. 1. 265, *Hen. V.* ii. 2. 12, etc.

59. *Character.* Write, inscribe. S. accents the verb either on the first or the second syllable; the noun on the first, except in *Rich. III.* iii. 1. 81 (Schmidt).

Dowden remarks on the passage: "The advice of Polonius is a cento of quotations from Lyly's *Euphues.** Its significance must be looked for less in the matter than in the sententious manner. Polonius has been wise with the little wisdom of worldly prudence. He has been a master of indirect means of getting at the truth, 'windlaces and assays of bias.' In the shallow lore of life he has been learned. Of true wisdom he has never had a gleam. And what Shakspere wishes to signify in this speech is that wisdom of Polonius' kind consists in a set of maxims; all such wisdom might be set down for the head-lines of copy-books. That is to say, his wisdom is not the outflow of a rich or deep nature, but the little, accumulated hoard of a long and superficial experience. This is what the sententious manner signifies. And very rightly Shakspere has put into Polonius' mouth the noble lines,

> 'To thine own self be true,
> And it must follow, as the night the day,
> Thou canst not then be false to any man.'

Yes; Polonius has got one great truth among his copy-book maxims, but it comes in as a little bit of hard, unvital wisdom like the rest. '*Dress well, don't lend or borrow money;* to thine own self be true.'"

60. *Unproportion'd.* "Disorderly, unsuitable" (Schmidt).

61. *Vulgar.* The word denotes the extreme of *familiar*, or "free-and-easy" with everybody. Cf. 1 *Hen. IV.* iii. 2. 41:

> "So common-hackney'd in the eyes of men,
> So stale and cheap to vulgar company."

62. *And their adoption.* "And whose adoption thou hast tried" (Wr.); or, perhaps, "their adoption having been tried," as Delius and others explain it (Gr. 376, 377).

63. *Grapple.* Cf. *Macb.* iii. 1. 106: "Grapples you to the heart and love of us." For *hoops* Pope substituted "hooks."

64. *Do not dull*, etc. "Do not make thy palm callous by shaking every man by the hand" (Johnson). Wr. quotes *Cymb.* i. 6. 106:

---

* Mr. W. L. Rushton, in his *Shakespeare's Euphuism*, pp. 44–47, places side by side the precepts of Polonius and Euphues. "*Pol.* Give thy thoughts no tongue. *Euph.* Be not lavish of thy tongue. *Pol.* Do not dull thy palm, etc. *Euph.* Every one that shaketh thee by the hand is not joined to thee in heart. *Pol.* Beware of entrance to a quarrel, etc. *Euph.* Be not quarrelous for every light occasion. *Pol.* Give every man thine ear, but few thy voice. *Euph.* It shall be thrice better to hear what they say, than to speak what thou thinkest." Both Polonius and Euphues speak of the advice given as "these few precepts."

"join gripes with hands
Made hard with hourly falsehood."

65. *Comrade.* Accented on the last syllable, as in 1 *Hen. IV.* iv. 1. 96; on the first in *Lear*, ii. 4. 213. S. uses the word only three times. The quartos have "courage" here.

69. *Censure.* Opinion; as often. Cf. *Macb.* v. 4. 14: "our just censures;" and see note in our ed. p. 251. See also i. 4. 35 and iii. 2. 24 below.

70. *Costly.* Tschischwitz makes the construction "costly thy habit buy as thy purse can;" but it is simpler to make it "as costly be thy habit as," etc. Cf. Gr. 276.

71. *Express'd in fancy.* "Marked or singular in device" (M.), or, in modern slang, "loud."

74. A corrupt line. The 1st quarto reads: "Are of a most select and generall chiefe in that;" the 2d and 3d: "Or of a most select and generous, chiefe in that," the "Or" being changed to "Ar" and "Are" in the 4th and 5th. The folio has "Are of a most select and generous cheff in that," which is followed (reading "chief") by K., V., M., and others; *chief* being explained as "eminence, superiority," or as "the upper part of a heraldic shield." The Coll. MS. changes *chief* to "choice." W. reads, very plausibly, "Are most select and generous in that." The reading in the text is due to Rowe, and is followed by D. (2d ed.). H., F., and others. *Chief*=chiefly, especially.

77. *Husbandry.* Thrift, economy. Cf. *Macb.* ii. 1. 4: "There 's husbandry in heaven; Their candles are all out," etc.

81. *Season.* "Mature, ripen" (Schmidt). Cf. iii. 3. 86 below.

83. *Tend.* Attend, are waiting; as in iv. 3. 44 below. Cf. the transitive use in *Temp.* i. 2. 47, *Lear*, ii. 4. 266, etc.

86. *And you*, etc. That is, I will remember it till you give me leave to forget it.

90. *Bethought.* Thought of. Cf. *Per.* v. 1. 44: "'T is well bethought." The verb is often used reflectively, as in *M. of V.* i. 1. 31, *M. N. D.* iv. 1. 155, etc. On *marry*, see *Mer.* p. 138.

94. *Put on me.* Told me (Schmidt); or possibly a little stronger than that, and=impressed upon me. Cf. *A. Y. L.* i. 2. 99, *M. for M.* ii. 2. 133, *T. N.* v. 1. 70, etc.

98. *Give me up the truth.* Cf. *Rich. III.* i. 4. 189: "have given their verdict up Unto the frowning judge."

101. *Green.* Still used colloquially in this sense=inexperienced, unsophisticated. Cf. *V. and A.* 806, *W. T.* iii. 2. 182, *K. John*, ii. 1. 472, iii. 4. 145, etc. See also "greenly," iv. 5. 66 below.

102. *Unsifted.* Untried; used by S. only here. Cf. *Luke*, xxii. 31. *Circumstance* is used collectively (Delius).

106. *Tenders.* That is, *promises* to pay. Cf. *M. N. D.* iii. 2. 87 and *Sonn.* 83. 4.

109. *Running.* The quartos have "Wrong," the folios "Roaming;" the emendation is due to Coll. "Wronging" and "Wringing" have also been suggested.

110. *Importun'd.* Accent on the second syllable, as regularly in S.

Cf. *A. and C.* iv. 15. 19: "I here importune death awhile, until;" *M. for M.* v. 1. 438: "Against all sense you do importune her," etc.

112. *Go to.* See *A. Y. L.* p. 186.

114. *Almost* and *holy* are not in the folio, and except for the measure might well be spared.

115. *Springes.* Snares. Cf. v. 2. 294 below and *W. T.* iv. 3. 36. *Woodcock* was proverbial for a simpleton (Nares). Cf. *T. of S.* i. 2. 161: "O this woodcock, what an ass it is!" *A. W.* iv. 1. 100: "We have caught the woodcock," etc. The bird was popularly supposed to have no brains. Cf. Ford, *Lover's Melancholy*, ii. 1: "A headpiece—of woodcock without brains in it."

116. *Prodigal.* Used adverbially. Gr. 1.

117. *Lends.* The folio has "Giues." To eke out the measure, Pope gave "oh my daughter," and Capell "gentle daughter." Coleridge suggested "go to; these vows" or "daughter, mark you." Walker would make *daughter* a trisyllable here and in some dozen other passages in S. and contemporary poets.

119. *A-making.* Cf. ii. 2. 573: "fall a-cursing;" also *T. and C.* i. 3. 159: "a-mending," etc. Gr. 24 (2).

120. *Fire.* A dissyllable. Gr. 478. The folio reads, "For this time daughter."

121. *Somewhat.* The quartos have "something."

122. *Your entreatments.* "The invitations you receive" (Schmidt). Johnson makes *entreatments*=company, conversation (Fr. *entretien*). S. uses the word nowhere else.

126. *In few.* In few words, in short. Cf. *Temp.* i. 2. 144, *Hen. V.* i. 2. 245, etc.

127. *Brokers.* "Procurer, go-between" (Schmidt). Cf. *K. John*, ii. 1. 568, *T. and C.* v. 10. 33, *L. C.* 173, etc.

128. *That dye.* The folio has "the eye," which means the same. Cf. *Temp.* ii. 1. 55: "With an eye of green in it" (=tinge of green).

*Investments.* Vesture, dress; used by S. only here and in 2 *Hen. IV.* iv. 1. 45: "white investments."

129. *Implorators.* Changed by Pope to "implorers," for the sake of the measure; not found elsewhere in S.

130. *Bawds.* Substituted by Theo. for the "bonds" of the early eds. and generally adopted. K., St., and M. retain "bonds"=vows, or, as M. explains it, "law papers headed with religious formulæ."

133. *Slander.* Disgrace (Johnson, Schmidt), or misuse (M.).

*Moment's.* The 2d and 3d quartos and the folios have "moment," the later quartos "moments." Abbott (Gr. 430) gives "any-moment-leisure" as a compound (cf. Gr. 22).

135. *Come your ways.* Used by S. oftener than *Come your way.* Cf. *A. Y. L.* i. 2. 221, ii. 3. 66, etc. So with *go your ways* (iii. 1. 129 below, *M. W.* i. 2. 1, iv. 1. 81, etc.).

Scene IV.—Coleridge remarks: "The unimportant conversation with which this scene opens is a proof of Shakspeare's minute knowledge of human nature. It is a well-established fact, that on the brink of any serious enterprise, or event of moment, men almost invariably endeavour to elude the pressure of their own thoughts by turning aside to trivial objects and familiar circumstances: thus this dialogue on the platform begins with remarks on the coldness of the air, and inquiries, obliquely connected, indeed, with the expected hour of the visitation, but thrown out in a seeming vacuity of topics, as to the striking of the clock and so forth. The same desire to escape from the impending thought is carried on in Hamlet's account of, and moralizing on, the Danish custom of wassailing: he runs off from the particular to the universal, and in his repugnance to personal and individual concerns, escapes, as it were, from himself in generalizations, and smothers the impatience and uneasy feelings of the moment in abstract reasoning. Besides this, another purpose is answered; for by thus entangling the attention of the audience in the nice distinctions and parenthetical sentences of this speech of Hamlet's, Shakspeare takes them completely by surprise on the appearance of the Ghost, which comes upon them in all the suddenness of its visionary character. Indeed, no modern writer would have dared, like Shakspeare, to have preceded this last visitation by two distinct appearances, —or could have contrived that the third should rise upon the former two in impressiveness and solemnity of interest."

1. *Shrewdly.* Sharply, keenly. See *Hen. V.* p. 170, and cf. *J. C.* p. 145. The folio reads, "is it very cold?"

2. *Eager.* Sharp, biting (Fr. *aigre*). Cf. i. 5. 69 below.

5. *It then.* The folio reads "then it."

8. *Rouse.* See on i. 2. 127.

9. *Wassail.* Drinking-bout, carousal. Cf. *L. L. L.* v. 2. 318: "At wakes and wassails," etc. See *Macb.* p. 180.

*Upspring.* Probably a wild German dance. Steevens quotes Chapman's *Alphonsus, Emperor of Germany:*

> "We Germans have no changes in our dances,
> An Almain and an up-spring, that is all."

According to Elze, the word is a translation of the German *Hüpfauf*, the last and wildest dance at the old German merry-makings; but Schmidt says that "*Hüpfauf* is an apochryphal dance and may as well be translated from *upspring.*" Pope substituted "upstart," and some make *upspring*=upstart.

*Reels* is a verb with *upspring* for its object, as Schmidt and F. explain it; not a noun, as St. makes it.

10. *Rhenish.* Cf. *M. of V.* i. 2. 104: "a deep glass of Rhenish wine;" *Id.* iii. 1. 44: "red wine and Rhenish." See also v. 1. 170 below.

11. *Kettle-drums.* Douce quotes Cleaveland, *Fuscara:* "As Danes carowse by kettle-drums."

12. *The triumph*, etc. "The universal acceptance of his pledge" (M.); or the expression may be "bitterest irony" (Delius).

15. *Manner.* Custom, fashion; with perhaps a reference to *manor.* Cf. the play on the words in *L. L. L.* i. 1. 207 fol.

16. D. quotes from an old play: "He keeps his promise best that breaks with hell."

17. *This heavy-headed revel*, etc. Lines 17–38 are omitted in the folios.

*East and west.* As Johnson points out, these words modify *traduc'd*, not *revel*.

18. *Tax'd.* Censured. Cf. *A. Y. L.* ii. 7. 71:

> "Why, who cries out on pride,
> That can therein tax any private party," etc.

See also *A. Y. L.* p. 142, note on *Taxation;* and cf. Webster, *Cure for a Cuckold*, i. 1: "She is without taxation."

19. *Clepe.* Call. Cf. *Macb.* iii. 1. 94, and see note in our ed. p. 209.

*Drunkards.* Steevens says that in Queen Elizabeth's time there was a Dane in London who is referred to in Rowland's *Looke to It* as follows:

> "You that will drinke Reynaldo vnto death:
> The Dane, that would carowse out of his Boote."

Cf. *Oth.* ii. 2. 84: "Why, he drinks you, with facility, your Dane dead drunk."

*With swinish phrase*, etc. Stain our name by calling us swine. *Addition*=title, as in *Macb.* i. 3. 106, etc. Hunter thinks there may be an allusion to "some parody on the style of the kings of Denmark," and Wr. suggests the possibility of a pun on *Sweyn*, a common name of those kings.

21. *At height.* "To the utmost" (Caldecott). Cf. *Sonn.* 15. 9: "at height decrease," etc.

22. *The pith*, etc. "The best and most valuable part of the praise that would otherwise be attributed to us" (Johnson); or, more concisely, the best part of our reputation. For *attribute*=reputation, Schmidt compares *T. and C.* ii. 3. 125 and *Per.* iv. 3. 18.

24. *Mole of nature.* Natural blemish.

25. Malone quotes *R. of L.* 538:

> "For marks descried in men's nativity
> Are nature's faults, not their own infamy."

On *as*=namely, see Gr. 113.

26. *His.* Its. Gr. 228.

27. *Complexion.* "Temperament, natural disposition" (Schmidt). Cf. *M. of V.* iii. 1. 32 and v. 2. 99 below.

30. *Plausive.* Plausible, pleasing. Cf. *A. W.* i. 2. 53 and iv. 1. 29.

32. *Nature's livery*, etc. A defect either natural (cf. "mole of nature" above) or accidental. *Star*=a mark like a star. Cf. *Cymb.* v. 5. 364: "Upon his neck a mole, a sanguine star." Ritson says it is a term in farriery. Theo. substituted "scar."

33. *Their.* The quartos have "His," which S. may have written. Cf. the change from singular to plural in iii. 2. 173, 174 below, and see Gr. 415.

34. *Undergo.* Experience, enjoy (Schmidt). Cf. *M. for M.* i. 1. 24: "To undergo such ample grace and honour."

35. *Censure.* Opinion, judgment. See on i. 3. 69 above.

36, 37. A corrupt passage, not satisfactorily mended by any of the countless attempts to do it. F. fills six closely printed pages with a summary of these, and they are more amusing than edifying. Some of the changes proposed are comparatively simple and plausible, while others are of the wildest and most preposterous sort. The general meaning of the passage is obvious from the preceding statement, of which it is evidently a figurative repetition. The idea is that of a little leaven of evil leavening the whole lump of "noble substance;" and it seems probable that "evil," or some word of the same sense ("ill," "vile," "base," etc., have been suggested) is disguised in *eale*. D. says that *eale* itself is used in the western counties of England in the sense of "reproach;" and "*eale*, to reproach," is given in Halliwell and Wright's *Archaic Dict.* as a Devonshire word. *Of a doubt* has been changed to "often dout" (=do out, efface), "ever dout," "oft corrupt," etc. These are samples of the better sort of emendations; for such absurdities as "dram of ale," "dram of eel," "bran of meal," "often daub," "over-clout," etc., we must refer the reader to F.

38. *His.* Its; as in 26 above.

40. *A spirit of health.* "A healed or saved spirit" (Wr.).

42. *Intents.* The folio has "events," which Nichols and Corson defend.

43. *Questionable.* "Inviting question" (Theo.). Cf. *unquestionable*= averse to conversation, in *A. Y. L.* iii. 2. 393. S. uses the word only here.

45. *Royal Dane.* We follow F. in adopting the punctuation proposed anonymously in a London journal in 1761. The modern eds. generally, with the folio, join *Royal Dane* to *Father*, but the climax naturally ends with the latter word. F. says: "Mr. Edwin Booth has informed me that his father always spoke the line thus, and that he himself has always so spoken it."

47. *Canoniz'd.* The regular accent in S. Cf. *K. John*, iii. 1. 177, iii. 4. 52, *T. and C.* ii. 2. 202, etc.

*Hearsed.* Coffined. Cf. *M. of V.* iii. 1. 93: "Would she were hearsed at my foot."

49. *Inurn'd.* The quartos have "interr'd."

52. *Complete.* Accented by S. on either syllable, as suits the measure. Schmidt says that "*cómplete* always precedes a noun accented on the first syllable, *complète* is always in the predicate." Cf. *M. for M.* i. 3. 3, *L. L. L.* i. 1. 137, *Rich. III.* iv. 4. 189, etc., with *T. G. of V.* ii. 4. 73, *K. John*, ii. 1. 433, *Hen. VIII.* iii. 2. 49, etc.

53. *Glimpses.* That is, glimmering through the clouds or through the openings among the battlements (Hunter).

54. *We.* See Gr. 216.

*Fools of nature.* Of whom nature makes fools. Cf. *R. and J.* iii. 1. 141: "O I am fortune's fool!" See also *Lear*, iv. 6. 195, *Macb.* ii. 1. 44, etc.

55. *Disposition.* Constitution, nature. See *Macb.* p. 220.

56. *Reaches.* "The plural is here used as in i. 1. 173" (Wr.).

57. *Why.* For the use of the word, see Gr. 75.

59. *Impartment.* Communication; used by S. nowhere else.

61. *Waves.* The folio has "wafts," which S. uses in the same sense. Cf. *C. of E.* ii. 2. 111: "who wafts us yonder?" See also *M. of V.* v. 1. 11, *T. of A.* i. 1. 70, etc.

*Removed.* Remote. See *A. Y. L.* p. 177.

64. *Should.* See Gr. 328.

73. *Deprive.* Take away; as in *R. of L.* 1186 and 1752 (Schmidt).

*Your sovereignty of reason.* The sovereignty of your reason, the command of your reason. Gr. 423.

75. *Toys.* Freaks. Cf. *R. and J.* iv. 1. 119: "no inconstant toy," etc. Lines 75–78 are omitted in the folio.

83. *The Nemean lion's.* We have this mythic beast again in *L. L. L.* iv. 1. 90, where *Nemean* is accented as here.

*Nerve.* Sinew; the only meaning that Schmidt recognizes. Cf. *Sonn.* 120. 4, *Temp.* i. 2. 484, *Macb.* iii. 4. 102, etc.

85. *Lets.* Hinders. Cf. *T. N.* v. 1. 256: "If nothing lets to make us happy," etc. So the noun=hindrance, as in *Hen. V.* v. 2. 65, etc.

89. *Have after.* Let 's after him! Cf. *have with you*=I 'll go with you; as in *A. Y. L.* i. 2. 268, *Oth.* i. 2. 53, etc. So *have at it* (*W. T.* iv. 4. 302), *have at you* (v. 2. 290 below), *have to it* (*T. of S.* i. 1. 143), etc.

91. *It.* Referring to *issue.*

*Nay.* "That is, let us not leave it to heaven, but do something ourselves" (Wr.).

SCENE V.—6. *Bound.* The adjective=ready (Schmidt). The Ghost uses it as the participle of *bind.*

11. *To fast.* Cf. Chaucer, *Persones Tale:* "And moreover the misese of helle shall be in defaute of mete and drink."

19. *An end.* The 1st quarto and most modern eds. have "on end." See Gr. 24.

20. *Porpentine.* Porcupine; the only name by which S. knows the animal. Cf. Ascham, *Toxophilus:* "nature geve example of shootinge first by the porpentine," etc. Topsell, in his *Hist. of Beasts*, 1607, has "porcuspine."

21. *Eternal blazon.* "This promulgation of the mysteries of eternity" (M.). Abbott (Gr. p. 16) thinks it is=*infernal* here; also in *J. C.* i. 2. 160 and *Oth.* iv. 2. 130. In these passages Schmidt defines it as "used to express extreme abhorrence." Cf. the use of *eternal* in the provincial dialects of the east of England, and in Yankee slang ("'tarnal").

29. *Haste.* For the transitive use, cf. *M. of V.* ii. 2. 121, *T. and C.* iv. 3. 5, *Cor.* v. 1. 74, etc.

32. *Shouldst.* Wouldst. Gr. 322.

33. *Roots.* The folio has "rots," which is preferred by many editors.

*Lethe wharf.* Lethe's bank. See Gr. 22. Cf. *A. and C.* ii. 2. 218: "the adjacent wharfs" (that is, banks). For the allusion to *Lethe*, cf. *T. N.* iv. 1. 66, 2 *Hen. IV.* v. 2. 72, *Rich. III.* iv. 4. 250, and *A. and C.* ii. 7. 114.

37. *Forged process.* A false account of the manner. Wr. thinks that *process* may mean "an official narrative."

40. *O my prophetic soul!* "My very soul abhorred the murderer even when I knew not his crime" (M.). Cf. i. 2. 255–258 above.

42. *Adulterate.* Used by S. oftener than *adulterous.* Cf. *R. of L.* 1645, *C. of E.* ii. 2. 142, *Rich. III.* iv. 4. 79, etc.

46. *Seeming-virtuous.* See Gr. 2.

48. *That.* Such. Gr. 277. Cf. i. 2. 171 above.

50. *Decline upon.* Sink down to. Cf. *T. and C.* iv. 5. 189: "Not letting it decline on the declin'd," etc. Wr. quotes Tennyson, *Locksley Hall:*

> "Having known me, to decline
> On a range of lower feelings and a narrower heart than mine."

52. *To.* Compared to. See on i. 2. 140 above.

53. *Virtue.* For the "absolute" or pleonastic construction, see Gr. 417.

56. *Sate.* The 1st quarto has "fate," the other quartos "sort."

58. *Soft.* "Hold, stop" (Schmidt). See *M. N. D.* p. 176.

60. *In.* The quartos have "of" (cf. *M. N. D.* ii. 1. 253, etc.).

61. *Secure.* Careless, unsuspicious (Latin *securus*). Cf. *Rich. II.* v. 3. 43, *Hen. V.* iv. chor. 17, *T. and C.* ii. 2. 15, etc. S. accents the word on either syllable. Cf. 52 above. Cf. *complete* in i. 4. 52 above.

62. *Hebenon.* The folio reading; the quartos have "Hebona." Probably henbane is meant, but Schmidt and some others think it may be *ebony*, the juice of which was supposed to be poisonous.

63. *Ears.* It was a belief even among medical men in that day that poison might be thus introduced into the system. The eminent surgeon, Ambroise Paré, the contemporary of S., was suspected of having infused poison into the ear of Francis II. while dressing it (Caldecott).

68. *Vigour.* Power, activity. St. reads "rigour."

*Posset.* Coagulate, curdle. See *Macb.* p. 189.

69. *Eager.* Sour (Fr. *aigre*). See on i. 4. 2 above.

71. *Instant.* Instantaneous. Cf. ii. 2. 501 below. It is used adverbially in 94 below.

72. *Lazar-like.* Like a leper. Cf. *Hen. V.* i. 1. 15, *T. and C.* ii. 3. 36, v. 1. 72, etc.

75. *Dispatch'd.* "Deprived by death" (Schmidt). The 1st quarto has "depriued," and the Coll. MS. "despoil'd."

76. *Blossoms.* W. reads "blossom;" perhaps a misprint. Cf. *W. T.* v. 2. 135: "in the blossoms of their fortune."

77. *Unhousel'd.* Not having received the eucharist (Old English *housel* or *husel*). Cf. Chaucer, *Persones Tale:* "And certes ones a yere at the lest way it is lawful to be houseled;" *Romaunt of the Rose*, 6386: "Ere any wight his housel tooke," etc. Spenser (*F. Q.* i. 12. 37) has "The housling fire" (sacramental or sacrificial fire).

*Disappointed.* "Unappointed" (which Theo. substituted), unprepared; used by S. only here.

*Unanel'd.* Not having received extreme unction. Nares quotes Sir Thomas More: "The extreme vnccion or anelynge."

80. *O horrible*, etc. This line is given to Hamlet by Rann, V., H., and some others; and W., St., and D. think that it probably belongs to him, as perhaps it does.

81. *Nature.* Natural feeling. Cf. *Temp.* v. 1. 76: "Expell'd remorse and nature," etc.

83. *Luxury.* Lust; its only meaning in S. Cf. *Hen. V.* iii. 5. 6, *M. W.* v. 5. 98, etc.

88. *Fare thee well.* On *thee=thou*, see Gr. 212. Cf. i. 1. 40 above.

89. *Matin.* Matin hour, morning; used by S. only here. Elze is in-

clined to change it to "matins;" but the noun is used in the singular by Milton, *L'All.* 114: "Ere the first cock his matin rings."

90. *Gins.* Not "'gins," as usually printed. See *Macb.* p. 153.

*Uneffectual.* Either "shining without heat" (Warb.), or lost in the light of the morning (Steevens, Schmidt). For the use of *un-* and *in-*, see Gr. 442.

91. *Adieu*, etc. The quartos have "Adiew, adiew, adiew;" the folio, "Adue, adue, *Hamlet:* remember me."

97. *This distracted globe.* "Here Hamlet puts his hand upon his head" (Wr.); but Schmidt thinks that *globe* "perhaps = world."

98. *Table.* Tablet. Cf. *T. G. of V.* ii. 7. 3:

> "Who art the table wherein all my thoughts
> Are visibly character'd and engrav'd."

99. *Fond.* Foolish. See *M. N. D.* p. 163, or *M. of V.* p. 152.

*Records.* Walker (quoted by F.) says that the accent of the *noun* is on the last syllable in S.; but cf. *Rich. II.* i. 1. 29: "First,—heaven be the record to my speech;" *A. and C.* v. 2. 117: "The record of what injuries you did us," etc. In *recorder* it is on the first syllable in the only passage in which S. uses the word in verse (*Rich. III.* iii. 7. 30).

100. *Saws.* Maxims, sayings. Cf. *A. Y. L.* ii. 7. 156: "wise saws;" *Id.* iii. 5. 82: "now I find thy saw of might;" *Lear*, ii. 2. 167: "the common saw," etc.

*Pressures.* Impressions. S. uses the word only here and in iii. 2. 22 below. He has *impressure* in the same sense in *A. Y. L.* iii. 5. 23, *T. N.* ii. 5. 103 (=seal), and *T. and C.* iv. 5. 131.

107. *Tables.* Memorandum-book. Cf. 2 *Hen. IV.* ii. 4. 289: "his master's old tables, his note-book," etc. Cf. *table-book* in ii. 2. 136 below and *W. T.* iv. 4. 610.

110. *Word.* Watchword. Cf. *Rich. III.* v. 3. 349: "Our ancient word of courage, fair Saint George," etc.

115. *Hillo*, etc. "A falconer's cry to recall his hawk" (M.). Hence the *come, bird, come.*

121. *Once.* Ever. Cf. *Macb.* iv. 3. 167, *Rich. II.* ii. 3. 91, etc.

125. *Come.* For the omitted *to*, see Gr. 349.

127. *Circumstance.* Ceremony (Schmidt), or circumlocution (Wr.). Cf. *M. of V.* i. 1. 154, 2 *Hen. VI.* i. 1. 105, etc.

129. *You.* "To go," or something of the sort, is understood.

132. *Go pray.* A very common ellipsis with *go.* Cf. ii. 1. 101 below, etc. Gr. 349.

136. *Saint Patrick.* "The patron saint of all blunders and confusions" (M.).

*Horatio.* The folio has "my lord," which Corson takes to be a retort to the same words in Horatio's speech.

141. *Soldiers.* A trisyllable; as in *J. C.* iv. 1. 28: "But he's a tried and valiant soldier;" and *Lear*, iv. 5. 3: "Your sister is the better soldier." Gr. 479.

147. *Upon my sword.* The sword was often used in oaths because the hilt was in the form of a cross (and, as Halliwell shows, sometimes had a cross inscribed upon it); and this swearing by the sword was, more-

over, an old Scandinavian custom. Cf. *W. T.* ii. 3. 168, iii. 2. 125, *Rich. II.* i. 3. 179, *Hen. V.* ii. 1. 105, etc.

*Already.* Referring to *in faith* above (H.).

150. *Truepenny.* "Honest fellow" (Johnson, Schmidt). Forby gives it in his *Vocabulary of East Anglia* as="hearty old fellow; stanch and trusty; true to his purpose or pledge."

161. In the quartos the ghost says "Sweare by his sword."

163. *Pioner.* Pioneer. Cf. *Hen. V.* iii. 2. 92 and *Oth.* iii. 3. 146. In *R. of L.* 1380 it rhymes with "appear." Gr. 492.

165. *As a stranger*, etc. "Receive it without doubt or question" (Wr.). Mason makes it="seem not to know it;" but this is not so much in keeping with what follows.

167. *Your.* The folio has "our," which is preferred by Walker, K., W., and D. *Your* is probably used colloquially as in iii. 2. 3, 108, iv. 3. 21 fol., etc. Gr. 221.

172. *Antic.* "Disguised" (Wr.); "fantastic, foolish" (Schmidt). Cf. *R. and J.* i. 5. 58: "cover'd with an antic face;" *Id.* ii. 4. 29: "antic fantasticoes," etc. See *Macb.* p. 130.

174. *Encumber'd.* "Folded thus in sign of wisdom" (M.).

*This head-shake.* The quartos have "this head shake," the folio "thus, head shake." Theo. inserted the hyphen.

175. *Of.* See Gr. 178.

176, 177. *An if.* The folio has "and if." Gr. 101, 103. For *there be*, cf. iii. 2. 26, and see Gr. 300.

178. *Giving out.* Indication, intimation. Cf. *M. for M.* i. 4. 54, *Oth.* iv. 1. 131, etc.

*To note.* Caldecott points out the grammatical irregularity in *never shall . . . to note.* Cf. *A. Y. L.* v. 4. 21:

> "Keep your word, Phebe, that you 'll marry me,
> Or else, refusing me, to wed this shepherd."

See Gr. 416.

180. *Most.* Greatest. Gr. 17.

186. *Friending.* Friendliness; used by S. only here. *Friend* is found as a verb in *M. for M.* iv. 2. 116, *Hen. V.* iv. 5. 17, *Hen. VIII.* i. 2. 140, etc.

187. *Lack.* Be wanting; as in *T. A.* iv. 2. 44. Cf. i. 4. 3 above.

189. *O cursed spite!* Cf. *C. of E.* ii. 2. 191: "O spite of spites!" *M. N. D.* i. 1. 138: "O spite!" *Id.* iii. 2. 145: "O spite! O hell!" 3 *Hen. VI.* v. 1. 18: "O unbid spite!" etc.

---

## ACT II.

SCENE I.—3. *Shall.* Will. Gr. 315.

4. *Inquire.* The folio has "inquiry," which some editors prefer. Cf. *Per.* iii. prol. 22.

5. *Of.* About, concerning (Gr. 174). Cf. *Rich. II.* iii. 2. 186: "Inquire of him," etc.

7. *Danskers.* Danes; used by S. only here. Cf. Webster, *White Devil:* "Like a Dansk drummer." *Danske,* for Denmark, occurs often in Warner's *Albion's England.* On *me,* see Gr. 220.

8. *Keep.* Live, dwell. Cf. *M. for M.* iii. 1. 10: "this habitation where thou keep'st," etc.

10. *Encompassment and drift.* "Winding and circuitous course" (Caldecott).

11. *More nearer.* For the double comparative, cf. iii. 2. 283, iii. 4. 155, and v. 2. 121 below. Gr. 11.

The meaning is, "By these natural and circuitous inquiries you will get nearer to the point than you possibly could by a direct question" (M.).

12. *It.* For the indefinite use of *it,* see Gr. 226.

13. *Take you,* etc. Assume the appearance of having, etc.

22. *Slips.* Offences. Cf. *T. A.* ii. 3. 86: "these slips have made him noted long;" *Oth.* iv. 1. 9: "a venial slip," etc.

28. *Season.* See on i. 2. 192.

29. *Another scandal.* "A deeper kind of scandal; much as ἄλλως means particularly, and ἄλλος ὁδίτης, in the *Odyssey,* an out-of-the-way (or foreign) traveller" (M.).

31. *Breathe.* Utter, speak; as in 44 below. *Quaintly*=artfully, ingeniously. Cf. *T. G. of V.* iii. i. 117: "a ladder quaintly made with cords," etc.

32. *Taints.* Cf. *Macb.* iv. 3. 124: "The taints and blames I laid upon myself," etc.

34. *Unreclaimed.* Untamed (Schmidt). So *reclaim*=tame, in *R. and J.* iv. 2. 47, etc.

The passage means "A wildness in untamed blood to which all young men are liable" (D.).

36. *Ay.* Metrically a dissyllable. Gr. 482.

38. *Fetch of warrant.* A warranted or justifiable artifice. The quartos have "fetch of wit"=cunning device. Cf. *Lear,* ii. 4. 90: "Mere fetches."

40. *As 't were,* etc. "Just as you might speak of an article slightly soiled" (M.).

42. *Converse.* Conversation. Cf. *L. L. L.* v. 2. 745 and *Oth.* iii. 1. 40. S. uses the noun only three times, and with the accent as here.

For *him*=*he,* see *A. Y. L.* p. 136 or Gr. 208.

43. *Prenominate.* Aforesaid. Cf. *T. and C.* iv. 5. 250: "to prenominate in nice conjecture." For the form of the participle here, see Gr. 342, and cf. *deject* in iii. 1. 155 below.

45. *In this consequence.* "In thus following up your remark" (Schmidt).

47. *Addition.* Title. See on i. 4. 20 above.

50. *By the mass.* Omitted in the folios, because it is an oath (Coll.).

51. *Leave.* Leave off. Cf. *V. and A.* 715: "Where did I leave?" *T. of S.* iii. 1. 26: "Where left we last?" etc.

58. *O'ertook.* For the form, cf. *Macb.* iv. 1. 145: "never is o'ertook." For *rouse,* see on i. 2. 127 above.

64. *Of wisdom and of reach.* Schmidt takes *of* to be "used to denote a quality," as in "thieves of mercy," iv. 6. 18 below. The expression

would then be=wise and shrewd. Abbott (Gr. 168) makes *of*=by means of. Wr. compares *L. L. L.* iv. 2. 30: "we of taste and feeling."

65. *Windlasses.* Windings, roundabout ways; used nowhere else by S. Cf. Golding, *Cæsar:* "bidding them fetche a windlasse a great waye about."

*Assays of bias.* "Indirect ways" (Schmidt); a figure taken from the game of bowls, in which the player sends the ball in a curved line instead of a straight one.

66. *Indirections.* Cf. *K. John,* iii. 1. 276: "Yet indirection thereby grows direct."

71. *In yourself.* Perhaps=in your own person, for yourself, as Johnson and Capell explain it. Caldecott says, "The temptations you feel, suspect in him." Wr. thinks it may mean "Conform your own conduct to his inclinations."

73. *Ply his music.* It is doubtful whether this is to be taken figuratively ("Let him go on, to what tune he pleases," as Clarke explains it) or literally (=attend to his music-lessons), as Schmidt supposes.

76. *God.* Changed in the folio to "Heaven," probably on account of the act of parliament in the time of James I. forbidding the use of the name of God on the stage.

77. *Closet.* Chamber. Cf. iii. 2. 307 below.

78. *Doublet.* See *A. Y. L.* p. 158. For *unbrac'd*=unfastened, cf. *J. C.* i. 3. 48 and ii. 1. 262.

80. *Ungarter'd.* Cf. the description of a lover in *A. Y. L.* iii. 2. 398: "then your hose should be ungartered;" and see also *T. G. of V.* ii. 1. 78.

*Down-gyved.* Hanging like gyves or fetters. The 4th and 5th quartos have "downe gyred," which Theo. adopts ("down-gyred"), explaining it as "rolled down." The 1st folio has "downe giued," changed in the 2d to "downe-gyved."

82. *Purport.* Accented on the last syllable; used by S. nowhere else, either as noun or as verb.

*On so . . . as,* see Gr. 275; and for the repetition of *he*, Gr. 242.

84. *Horrors.* Abbott (Gr. 478) makes the word a trisyllable; but, as F. suggests, "why not let Ophelia's strong emotion shudderingly fill the gap?"

90. *Perusal.* Study. Cf. iv. 7. 135: "peruse (that is, carefully examine) the foils." See also *Rich. II.* p. 194, note on *Perus'd.*

91. *As.* As if. Cf. i. 2. 217 above. Gr. 107. On the measure, see Gr. 507.

92. *Shaking of.* See Gr. 178. Tschischwitz thinks that "is made" is understood.

95. *As.* The quarto reading; the folio has "That."

*Bulk.* Explained by some as=breast. Sr. quotes Baret, *Alvearie:* "The Bulke or breast of a man;" and Malone cites *R. of L.* 467: "her heart . . . Beating her bulk."

99. *Help.* The folio has "helpe;" the later quartos "helps" or "helpes."

100. *Bended.* S. uses *bended* and *bent* interchangeably, both as past tense and as participle.

F. here quotes Miles, *Review of Hamlet:* "We are not permitted to see Hamlet in this ecstasy of love, but what a picture! How he must have loved her, that love should bring him to such a pass!—his knees knocking each other!—knees that had firmly followed a beckoning ghost! There is more than the love of forty thousand brothers in that hard grasp of the wrist,—in that long gaze at arm's length,—in the force that *might*, but *will* not, draw her nearer! And never a word from this king of words! His *first* great silence,—the *second* is death!"

102. *Ecstasy.* Madness. Cf. iii. 1. 160, iii. 4. 74, 136, 137, below. See *Macb.* p. 211.

103. *Fordoes.* Undoes, destroys. Cf. v. 1. 210 below. See *M. N. D.* p. 188, note on *Fordone.*

112. *Quoted.* Noted, marked; formerly pronounced and often written "coted," which is the quarto reading here. Cf. *R. and J.* i. 4. 31, *T. and C.* iv. 5. 233, etc.

113. *Wrack.* Wreck, ruin. The word was spelt and pronounced *wrack* in the time of S. It rhymes with *alack* in *Per.* iv. prol. 12, and with *back* in *V. and A.* 558, *R. of L.* 841, 965, *Sonn.* 126. 5, and *Macb.* v. 5. 51.

*Beshrew.* A mild form of imprecation (Schmidt). See *M. N. D.* p. 152.

114. *Proper.* Appropriate. Cf. *J. C.* i. 2. 41: "Conceptions only proper to myself," etc.

115. *Cast.* Schmidt puts this passage under *cast*=compute, calculate (a common meaning in S.) and explains it as="to be mistaken." M. takes it to mean, "to forecast more than we ought for our own interests." Wr. makes *cast*=contrive, design, plan. Johnson says: "The vice of age is too much suspicion. Men long accustomed to the wiles of life *cast* commonly *beyond themselves*, let their cunning go farther than reason can attend it."

118. *Which, being kept close*, etc. "The king may be angry at my telling of Hamlet's love; but more grief would come from hiding it" (M.).

SCENE II.—2. *Moreover that.* Over and above that. On the other hand, *more above* in 126 below=moreover (M.).

5. *So I call it.* The quartos omit *I.*

6. *Sith.* The quarto reading=*since*, which is derived from it (see Wb.). The folio has "Since not."

8. *Put him . . . from*, etc. Cf. iii. 1. 174 below: "puts him thus From fashion of himself." See also *R. and J.* iii. 5. 109, *T. of A.* iii. 4. 104, *Lear*, ii. 4. 293, etc.

10. *Dream of.* The folio has "deeme of," which some editors prefer.

11. *Of.* From. We still say "of late" (Gr. 167). Cf. *Acts*, viii. 11.

12. *Sith.* The folio has "since," as in 6 above.

*Neighbour'd to.* Associated or intimate with. Cf. *Lear*, i. 1. 121, *Hen. V.* i. 1. 62, etc.

*Humour.* Disposition. The quartos have "hauior," and some modern eds. give "haviour."

13. *That.* Redundant, as Delius points out.

*Vouchsafe your rest.* "Please to reside" (Caldecott).

14. *Companies.* See on *loves*, i. 1. 173 above.

17. *Whether.* Monosyllabic, as often (Gr. 466). This line is not in the folio.

18. *Open'd.* Disclosed. Cf. *W. T.* iv. 4. 764, *Hen. V.* i. 1. 78, etc.

22. *Gentry.* Courtesy; as in v. 2. 109 below (Schmidt). It is=gentle birth in *R. of L.* 569, *Cor.* iii. 1. 144, etc.

23. *Expend your time.* Cf. *Oth.* i. 3. 391: "If I would time expend with such a snipe."

24. *Supply and profit.* "Aid and furtherance" (Caldecott).

27. *Of.* Over. See Gr. 174.

29. *But.* Omitted in the folio.

30. *Bent.* Endeavour, straining; a metaphor from the bending of a bow (Johnson, Schmidt). Cf. iii. 2. 359 below; also *Much Ado*, ii. 3. 232 and *T. N.* ii. 4. 38.

38. *Heavens.* The plural is often thus used by S. Cf. *Temp.* i. 2. 175: "Heavens thank you for 't!" *Id.* ii. 1. 324: "Heavens keep him from these beasts!" (see also iii. 1. 75 and iii. 3. 20); *M. N. D.* iii. 2. 447: "Heavens shield Lysander," etc.

42. *Still.* Ever. See on i. 1. 122 above.

43. *Assure you.* Be assured. Cf. *Lear*, ii. 1. 106: "Nor I, assure thee, Regan;" *Oth.* iii. 3. 20: "assure thee, If I do vow a friendship," etc. The quartos have "I assure you."

45. *And.* The folio has "one," which K. and Coll. retain.

52. *Fruit.* The dessert. The folio has "newes."

54. *My sweet queen.* The folio reading; the 2d and 3d quartos have "my deere *Gertrard*," which, as W. remarks, "smacks less of the honey-moon."

56. *Doubt.* Suspect. See on i. 2. 256 above, and cf. iii. 1 166 below: "I do doubt the hatch," etc.

*No other but.* See on i. 1. 102 above.

*The main.* The main point or cause; as in 2 *Hen. VI.* i. 1. 208: "look unto the main" (Schmidt).

60. *Desires.* Good wishes.

61. *First.* That is, first audience or opening of our business (Caldecott).

64. *Truly.* Modifying *was*, not *found* (Wr.). For similar transpositions, see Gr. 420.

67. *Borne in hand.* Deceived, deluded. See *Mach.* p. 208.

*Sends.* For ellipsis of subject, see Gr. 399, and cf. iii. 1. 8 below.

71. *Assay.* Proof, trial. Cf. iii. 3. 69 below.

73. *Three.* The quartos have "threescore."

79. *Such regards*, etc. Such conditions as are safe and allowable.

80. *Likes.* Pleases. Cf. *Hen. V.* iii. prol. 32: "The offer likes not;" *Id.* iv. 3. 77: "Which likes me better," etc. Gr. 297.

81. *Our more consider'd time.* "When we have more time for considering" (Caldecott). See Gr. 374.

83. *Well-took.* For the form of the participle, see Gr. 343. S. also uses *taken* (i. 2. 14 above) and *ta'en* (i. 3. 106 above).

84. *Feast.* "The king's intemperance is never suffered to be forgotten" (Johnson).

86. *Expostulate.* Discuss. Hunter quotes Capt. John Smith's book on *Virginia:* "How these isles came by the name of the Bermudas . . . I will not expostulate."

90. *Wit.* Wisdom; as often in S. See *Mer.* p. 137.

95. *More matter*, etc. More matter with less mannerism. See *A. Y. L.* p. 155, note on *Matter.*

96. *Art.* "The Queen uses *art* in reference to Polonius's stilted style; he uses it as opposed to truth and nature" (Delius).

98. *Figure.* "A figure in rhetoric," as Touchstone says (*A. Y. L.* v. i. 45). Cf. *L. L. L.* i. 2. 58.

100. *Remains.* For the ellipsis of *it*, see Gr. 404.

105. *Perpend.* Ponder, consider; "a word used only by Pistol, Polonius, and the clowns" (Schmidt). Cf. *M. W.* i. 1. 119, *A. Y. L.* iii. 2. 69, etc.

109. *Beautified.* Theo. substituted "beatified" on the ground that S. would not call *beautified* "a vile phrase" when he had used it in *T. G. of V.* iv. 1. 55: "seeing you are beautified With goodly shape;" but it is not there used adjectively.

113. *In.* Into. Gr. 159. Wr. quotes *T. G. of V.* iii. 1. 250–252.

116–119. *Doubt.* In the first three lines *doubt*=have a misgiving, have a half-belief; in the fourth line=disbelieve (Clarke).

121. *Reckon.* Count, number (Schmidt); or perhaps=express in numbers or verse, as Delius explains it.

124. *Whilst this machine is to him.* Whilst this body is his; "the affected language of euphuism" (Wr.). S. uses *machine* nowhere else.

126. *More above.* Moreover. See on 2 above.

127. *By.* See Gr. 145.

133. *As I perceived it.* "There is much humour in the old man's inveterate foible for omniscience. He absurdly imagines that he had discerned for himself all the steps of Hamlet's love and madness; while of the former he had been unaware till warned by some friends, and the latter did not exist at all" (M.).

136. *If I had play'd*, etc. "If I had just minuted the matter down in my own mind" (M.); or, as Warb. and Wr. explain it, "if I had been the agent of their correspondence," or their confidant. See on *tables*, i. 5. 107 above.

137. *Or given*, etc. Or had connived at it. For *winking* the quartos have "working."

139. *Round.* Directly, without ceremony. See *Hen. V.* p. 175, and cf. iii. 1. 183 and iii. 4. 5 below. As Caldecott remarks, it has "the reverse of its literal meaning, that is, *without* circuity." For the adverbial use, see Gr. 60.

140. *Bespeak.* Speak to. Cf. *Rich. II.* v. 2. 20, etc.

141. *Out of thy star.* "Out of thy sphere" (2d folio); "above thee in fortune" (Schmidt). Sr. quotes *T. N.* ii. 5. 156: "In my stars I am above thee."

142. *Precepts.* The folio reading; the quartos have "prescripts" (cf. *A. and C.* iii. 8. 5).

145. *Took the fruits*, etc. "Profited by my advice" (Schmidt). "She

took the *fruits* of advice when she obeyed advice; the advice was then made *fruitful*" (Johnson).

148. *Watch.* "A sleepless state" (Caldecott). Cf. *Cymb.* iii. 4. 43: "To lie in watch there and to think on him." For the measure, see Gr. 483.

149. *Lightness.* Lightheadedness. Schmidt compares *C. of E.* v. 1. 72 and *Oth.* iv. 1. 280.

151. *All we.* We all (Gr. 240). The object of *for* is implied in *wherein.*

159. *The centre.* That is, of the earth. Cf. *M. N. D.* iii. 2. 54:

> "I 'll believe as soon
> The whole earth may be bor'd, and that the moon
> May through the centre creep," etc.

In *W. T.* ii. 1. 102 and *T. and C.* i. 3. 85 *centre*=the earth, the centre of the Ptolemaic universe.

160. *Four.* Hanmer substituted "for," as does the Coll. MS.; but, as Malone notes, "four hours together," "two hours together," etc., were common phrases. Cf. *Lear*, i. 2. 170, *W. T.* v. 2. 148, etc. So in Webster, *Duchess of Malfi:* "She will muse four hours together."

162. *Loose.* He had forbidden her to have any intercourse with Hamlet.

163. *Arras.* Tapestry hangings; so called from Arras, where they were largely made.

168. *Wretch.* Sometimes used as a term of endearment, mingled with pity. Cf. *R. and J.* i. 3. 44: "The pretty wretch left crying;" *Oth.* iii. 3. 90: "Excellent wretch!" etc.

170. *Board.* Accost, address; as often. Cf. *T. N.* i. 3. 60, *M. W.* ii. 1. 92, *L. L. L.* ii. 1. 218, etc.

*Presently*=immediately; its usual meaning in S. Cf. 578 below; also iii. 2. 43, 350, v. 2. 381, etc.

172. *God-a-mercy.* God have mercy. Cf. iv. 5. 179 below.

182. *A good kissing carrion.* The reading of all the early eds., as of Pope, Theo., K., Coll., F., and others. *Good kissing*, as Caldecott and Corson have explained, is=good *for* kissing, or *to be* kissed, by the sun. See *J. C.* p. 126, note on *A labouring day.* Warb. substituted "God" for *good*, and has been followed by many editors. He compares *M. for M.* ii. 2. 163–168 and *Cymb.* iii. 4. 164. Malone adds 1 *Hen. IV.* ii. 4. 113 and *King Edward III.*, 1596:

> "The freshest summer's day doth soonest taint
> The loathed carrion, that it seems to kiss."

184. *Conception*, etc. "Understanding is a blessing; but if you leave your daughter unrestrained, she will understand what you will not like" (M.). There is probably a play on *conception*, as in *Lear*, i. 1. 12.

187. *How say you by that?* Cf. *M. of V.* i. 2. 58: "How say you by the French lord?" and see note in our ed. p. 132. Gr. 145.

190. *I suffered*, etc. "It *may* have been so; but one rather suspects that Polonius's love-reminiscences are like those of Touchstone in *A. Y. L.* ii. 4" (M.).

193. *Matter.* Subject-matter. Cf. 95 above. "Hamlet purposely misunderstands the word to mean 'cause of dispute,' as in *T. N.* iii. 4. 172" (Wr.).

194. *Who.* Whom. Cf. *Macb.* iii. 4. 42, *Oth.* i. 2. 52, etc. Gr. 274.

196. *Rogue.* The folio has "slave." Warb. sees here a reference to Juvenal, *Sat.* x. 188.

202. *For you yourself*, etc. "The natural reason would have been 'For some time I shall be as old as you are now' (and therefore I take such remarks as proleptically personal); but Hamlet turns it to the opposite" (M.). For *should*=would, see Gr. 322.

204. *There is method in 't.* Cf. *M. for M.* v. 1. 60:

> "If she be mad—as I believe no other—
> Her madness hath the oddest frame of sense,
> Such a dependency of thing on thing,
> As e'er I heard in madness."

208. *Pregnant.* Ready, apt, clever. Cf. iii. 2. 56 below. So *pregnancy* =cleverness in 2 *Hen. IV.* i. 2. 192.

215. *Withal.* The emphatic form of *with* (Gr. 196).

226. *Indifferent.* Middling, average. Cf. *T. G. of V.* iii. 2. 44, etc.

236–265. *Let me . . . attended.* All this is omitted in the quartos.

242. *Confines.* Places of confinement. See on i. 1. 155 above.

246. *Thinking makes it so.* M. quotes Lovelace:

> "Stone walls do not a prison make,
> Nor iron bars a cage;
> Minds innocent and quiet take
> These for a hermitage."

259. *Then are our beggars*, etc. "If ambition is the shadow of pomp, and pomp the shadow of a man, then the only true substantial men are beggars, who are stript of all pomp and all ambition" (M.).

*Outstretch'd*=strained, exaggerated; "strutting stage heroes" (Delius).

261. *Fay.* "Faith" (Schmidt). Cf. *T. of S.* ind. 2. 83, etc.

265. *Beaten.* Familiar, unceremonius. For *make*, see on i. 2. 164 above.

269. *Dear a halfpenny.* "Dear *of*" and "dear *at*" have been proposed, but no change is called for. Cf. *A. Y. L.* ii. 3. 74: "too late a week." Wr. quotes Chaucer, *C. T.* 8875: "dere y-nough a jane" (a small coin of Genoa); and *Id.* 12723: "deere y-nough a leeke."

276. *Modesties.* See on *loves*, i. 1. 173.

280. *Consonancy*, etc. Cf. 11 above.

282. *A better proposer.* A more eloquent speaker. Cf. *propose*=speak, in *Much Ado*, iii. 1. 3, *Oth.* i. 1. 25, etc.

283. *Even.* Plain, honest. Cf. *Hen. V.* iv. 8. 114.

286. *Of you.* Upon you (Caldecott). Cf. *Lear*, i. 5. 22, and see Gr. 174, 175.

289. *Prevent your discovery.* Anticipate your disclosure. Gr. 439. Cf. *J. C.* v. 1. 105: "to prevent The time of life," etc.

294. *A sterile promontory.* "Thrust out into the dread ocean of the unknown, and as barren as the waves themselves" (M.).

295. *Brave.* Beautiful, grand. Cf. *Sonn.* 12. 2: "And see the brave day sunk in hideous night," etc. For *majestical*, see on i. 1. 143.

296. *Fretted.* Embossed, adorned. Cf. *Cymb.* ii. 4. 88:

> "The roof o' the chamber
> With golden cherubins is fretted;"

Milton, *P. L.* i. 717: "The roof was fretted gold," etc.

298. *A congregation of vapours.* "Veiling the true sunlight. Cf. *Sonn.* 33. 1–8" (M.).

*Man.* The early eds. have "a man," which is followed by the modern editors except D. and F. As Walker suggests, the *a* is probably an accidental interpolation.

299. *Faculty.* The folio reading; the quartos have "faculties."

300. *Express.* "Expressive" (Schmidt); or, perhaps, "exact, fitted to its purpose" (Wr.). Cf. *Heb.* i. 3.

303. *Quintessence.* The fifth or highest essence of the alchemists. S. uses the word only here and in *A. Y. L.* iii. 2. 147.

310. *Lenten.* Meagre, poor. Cf. *T. N.* i. 5. 9: "A good lenten answer."

311. *Coted.* Passed by, outstripped, "o'er-raught" (iii. 1. 17 below). Steevens quotes *The Return from Parnassus*, 1606: "we presently coted and outstript them;" Golding, *Ovid:* "With that Hippomenes coted [Latin, praeterit] her;" Warner, *Albion's England:* "Gods and goddesses for wantonness out-coted," etc. See also Greene, *Friar Bacon:* "Cote him, and court her to control the clown." It was a term in hunting. Turbervile says: "A Cote is when a Greyhound goeth endwayes by his fellow and giveth the Hare a turn," etc. It is not simply to come up with (as Wr. explains it), but to go beyond. Thus, in this case, Rosencrantz and Guildenstern, having "coted" the players, reach the palace first and tell Hamlet that they are coming.

316. *Humorous.* Capricious. See *A. Y. L.* p. 146.

317. *The clown . . . sere.* Omitted in the quartos.

*Tickle o' the sere.* This expression, long a stumbling-block to the critics, appears to have been correctly explained by Mr. Nicholson in *Notes and Queries*, July 22, 1871: "The *sere*, or, as it is now spelt, *sear* (or *scear*) of a gun-lock is the bar or balance-lever interposed between the trigger on the one side, and the tumbler and other mechanism on the other, and is so called from its acting the part of a *serre*, or talon, in gripping the mechanism and preventing its action. . . . Now if the lock be so made on purpose, or be worn, or be faulty in construction, this *sear*, or grip, may be so *tickle* or ticklish in its adjustment that a slight touch or even jar may displace it, and then of course the gun goes off. Hence 'light' or 'tickle of the sear' (equivalent to, like a hair-trigger), applied metaphorically, means that which can be started into action at a mere touch, or on the slightest provocation, or on what ought to be no provocation at all." *Lungs tickle o' the sere*, then, are lungs easily moved to laughter. For *tickle*=ticklish, cf. *M. for M.* i. 2. 177: "thy head stands so tickle on thy shoulders that a milk-maid, if she be in love, may sigh it off;" and 2 *Hen. VI.* i. 1. 216:

> "the state of Normandy
> Stands on a tickle point."

On the passage, cf. *Temp.* ii. 1. 174: "who are of such sensible [that is, sensitive] and nimble lungs that they always use to laugh at nothing."

319. *The lady*, etc. The lady shall mar the measure rather than not express herself freely (Henderson); or, if through delicacy she omit anything, the lameness of the metre will show it (Seymour).

322. *Their residence.* Their remaining in the city.

324. *Inhibition.* Prohibition. Coll. thinks this probably refers to the limiting of public theatrical performances to two theatres, the Globe and the Fortune, in 1600 and 1601. The players, by a *late innovation*, were *inhibited*, or forbidden to act in or near *the city*, and therefore *travelled*, or *strolled*, into the country. Wr. is disposed to think that the *innovation* was the license given Jan. 30, 1603–4, to the Children of the Queen's Revels to play at the Blackfriars Theatre and other convenient places. The popularity of the children may well have driven the older actors into the country, and so have operated as an *inhibition*, though no formal inhibition was issued. For other explanations of the passage, see F. vol. i. pp. 162–164.

331. *Aery.* A brood of nestlings (literally, an eagle's or hawk's nest). Cf. *K. John*, v. 2. 149, *Rich. III.* i. 3. 264, 270.

*Eyases.* Unfledged hawks, nestlings.

332. *Top of question.* At the top of their voices. Cf. *question*=speech, talk; as in *Macb.* iii. 4. 118, *A. Y. L.* iii. 4. 39, v. 4. 167, etc. See also iii. 1. 13 below.

M. paraphrases the whole passage thus: "What brings down the professional actors is the competition of a nest of young hawks (the boys of the Chapel Royal, etc.) who carry on the whole dialogue without modulation at the top of their voices, get absurdly applauded for it, and make such a noise on the common stage, that true dramatists, whose wit is as strong and keen as a rapier, are afraid to encounter these chits, who fight, as it were, with a goose-quill."

*Tyranically.* Vehemently, extravagantly; probably alluding to what Bottom calls "a tyrant's vein," or "a part to make all split." See *M. N. D.* p. 133.

338. *Escoted.* Paid; used by S. nowhere else. D. quotes Cotgrave, *Fr. Dict.*: "*Escotter.* Euery one to pay his shot," etc.

*Will they pursue*, etc. "Will they follow the profession of players no longer than they can keep the voices of boys?" (Johnson). For *quality*= profession, cf. 418 below; also *Hen. V.* iii. 6. 146: "What is thy name? I know thy quality?"

342. *Succession.* Futurity (Schmidt). Cf. *C. of E.* iii. 1. 105: "For slander lives upon succession" (that is, feeds on futurity, makes all that is to come its prey).

344. *To-do.* Equivalent to *ado* (Schmidt).

345. *Tarre.* Set on (to fight); used literally of dogs. Cf. *K. John*, iv. 1. 117:

> "And like a dog that is compell'd to fight,
> Snatch at his master that doth tarre him on;"

and *T. and C.* i. 3. 392:

> "pride alone
> Must tarre the mastiffs on, as 't were their bone."

346. *Argument.* The plot of the play. Cf. 1 *Hen. IV.* ii. 4. 310: "the argument shall be thy running away," etc.

*Unless the poet*, etc. Schmidt calls this an "obscure passage," and so it is. It probably does *not* mean, as Delius makes it, "unless the dialogue (the *question*) is well seasoned with warfare (*cuffs*)." M. says: "See iii. 2 [35–41], where the same contest between actor and dramatist is spoken of."

352. *Carry it away.* Carry off the palm, gain the day.

353. *Hercules.* Perhaps, as Steevens suggests, an allusion to the Globe Theatre, the sign of which was Hercules carrying the globe.

355. *It is not very strange,* etc. "I do not wonder that the new players have so suddenly risen to reputation; my uncle supplies another example of the facility with which honour is conferred on new claimants" (Johnson).

356. *Mows.* Grimaces. The folio reading; the quartos have "mouths." Cf. *Temp.* iv. 1. 47: "with mop and mow;" *Cymb.* i. 6. 41: "Contemn with mows." We have the word as a verb in *Temp.* ii. 2. 9 and *Lear,* iv. 1. 64.

358. *In little.* In miniature. Cf. *A. Y. L.* iii. 2. 148: "Heaven would in little show;" and *L. C.* 90: "in little drawn."

*'Sblood.* An abbreviation of "God's blood," a mode of swearing by the eucharist. Cf. iii. 2. 345 below. In the folio it is generally omitted (as here) or replaced by other words (as "I' faith" in 1 *Hen. IV.* ii. 4. 488).

362. *Appurtenance.* "Proper accompaniment" (Wr.); used by S. only here.

363. *Comply with you,* etc. "Use ceremony with you in this fashion" (Wr.). Cf. v. 2. 179 below.

*Extent.* "Behaviour, deportment" (Schmidt). Cf. *T. N.* iv. 1. 57: "this uncivil and unjust extent."

369. *North-north-west.* For a genuine German gloss, take that of Francke (*apud* F.): "Perhaps the meaning is: Great powerful tempests in the moral world, apparitions from the mysterious Hereafter, can make me mad, can crush my reason; but such people as you are, who come around me with sweet phrases and mock friendship, I have yet wit enough to elude." "A Daniel come to judgment, yea, a Daniel!"

370. *Handsaw.* The word in this proverb is probably a corruption of *hernshaw,* a heron; but the old "saw" is always found in this form, and, as Schmidt says, "S. undoubtedly thought of a real *saw.*" A writer in *Notes and Queries,* with evident "fellow-feeling," suggests "*anser,* the generic name for our domestic water-fowl"—which in the vulgar, as Touchstone would say, is *goose.* F. thinks he has heard "*handschuh,* the German for *glove,*" proposed as an emendation, but let us hope that he is mistaken. W., on the other hand, suspects that *hawk* is "the tool called a hawk." For more of this admirable fooling of the commentators, see F.

371. *Well be with you.* Cf. *A. W.* i. 1. 190: "God send him well!" See also 2 *Hen. IV.* iv. 4. 19. Wr. quotes *Psa.* cxxviii. 2 [Prayer-book version]: "Well is thee;" and Chaucer, *C. T.* 16362: "He loved hir so that well him was therwith."

375. *Happily.* Haply. See on i. 1. 134 above. Gr. 42.

378. *You are right,* etc. This is said merely that Polonius may not suspect what they have been talking about.

382. *Buz, buz!* Blackstone says that *buz* was an interjection used at Oxford when one began a story already well known. See *Macb.* p. 243.

384. *Then came*, etc. Probably a line from an old ballad (Johnson).

388. *Individable.* Delius thinks this refers to dramas in which the unity of place was observed, *poem unlimited* to those that disregarded such restrictions. Schmidt (better, we think) makes it="not to be distinguished by a particular appellation (that is, not to be called tragedy, comedy, etc.)," and *unlimited*=undefined.

The plays of Seneca and Plautus were often acted at the Universities, and had been partially translated into English.

389. *The law of writ and liberty.* "For adhering to the text or extemporizing when need requires" (M.). Coll. and Wr. explain it essentially in the same way. Caldecott says: "For the observance of the rules of the drama, while they take such liberties as are allowable, they are the only men." The quarto of 1676 has "wit," which Rowe, Pope, Theo., and Warb. adopt.

390. *O Jephthah*, etc. The old song from which Hamlet quotes may be found in Percy's *Reliques*. The old copies of it vary somewhat. Halliwell gives a fac-simile of one form, beginning

> "I read that many years agoe,
> When Jepha Judge of Jsrael,
> Had one fair Daughter and no more,
> whom he loved so passing well.
> And as by lot God wot,
> It came to passe most like it was,
> Great warrs there thould be,
> and who should be the chiefe, but he, but he."

393. *What treasure.* The early eds. and most modern ones have "What a treasure;" but as Walker (followed by D., H., and F.) suggests, the *a* is probably an interpolation.

407. *Row.* Properly=line, but perhaps here=stanza.

*Pious chanson* is the quarto reading; the folio has "Pons Chanson," which Hunter defended as="chanson du Pont-Neuf." As K. remarks, this would not justify such a form as "pons chansons;" and we may add that it is doubtful if the French expression dates back to the time of S. The Pont-Neuf in Paris was not finished until 1624, though begun in 1578.

408. *Abridgments come.* The folio reading; the quartos give "abridgement comes." In either case, the meaning seems to be that the players by coming shorten his talk. Schmidt explains *abridgment* by "that which is my pastime and makes me be brief." Wr. says that "technically *abridgment* means a dramatic performance," and refers to *M. N. D.* v. 1. 39: "what abridgment have you for this evening?" But there it probably means simply pastime; here it may be explained by 509 below.

411. *Valanced.* Fringed with a beard. The folio has "valiant," which Rowe, K., and St. retain. We find the noun *valance* in *T. of S.* ii. 1. 356.

412. *My young lady.* In the time of S. female parts were played by boys or young men. See *A. Y. L.* p. 201, note on *If I were a woman.*

414. *Chopine.* A kind of high shoe. Coryat, in his *Crudities*, 1611, describes it as "a thing made of wood and covered with leather of sundry colours, some with white, some redde, some yellow." He adds, "It is called a chapiney, which they wear under their shoes... There are many

of these chapineys of a great height, even half a yard high." F. says: "At a Jewish wedding in Jerusalem at which I was present, in 1856, the young bride, aged twelve, wore chopines at least ten inches high."

415. *Cracked within the ring.* "There was a ring on the coin within which the sovereign's head was placed; if the crack extended from the edge beyond this ring, the coin was rendered unfit for currency" (Douce).

416. *Like French falconers.* According to some critics this is meant to be contemptuous; but Tollet quotes Sir Thomas Browne, who says that "the French seem to have been the first and noblest falconers in the western part of Europe."

418. *Straight.* Straightway; as in iii. 4. 1 below, etc.

*Quality.* See on 338 above.

421. *Me.* "Ethical dative." See Gr. 220.

423. *Caviare.* A Russian condiment made from the roe of the sturgeon; at that time a new and fashionable delicacy, not obtained nor relished by the vulgar, and therefore used by S. to signify anything above their comprehension (Nares). Steevens cites many references to it in contemporaneous writers.

For *the general*=people in general, the public, cf. *J. C.* ii. 1. 12: "But for the general;" and see note in our ed. p. 142.

425. *Cried in the top of mine.* "Were higher than mine" (Johnson and Schmidt). In hunting, a dog is said to *over-top* "when he gives more tongue than the rest" (Henley), and to this Hamlet probably refers here. The phrase is then=proclaimed with a tone of authority that my voice could not give.

427. *No sallets*, etc. "Nothing that gave a relish to the lines as salads do to meat" (Schmidt). Cf. *A. W.* iv. 5. 18: "She was the sweet marjoram of the salad" ("sallet" in the folio). See also 2 *Hen. VI.* iv. 10. 9 fol. where there is a play upon *sallet*=salad and *sallet*=a kind of helmet. Pope substituted "salts" and later "salt" here. The Coll. MS. also has "salt," which Sr. approves.

429. *Indict.* Accuse; as in *Oth.* iii. 4. 154, the only other instance of the word in S.

*Affectation.* The folio reading; the quartos have "affection," which S. uses in the same sense in *L. L. L.* v. 1. 4 (where the later folios have "affectation"). So *affectioned*=affected in *T. N.* ii. 3. 160.

431. *Handsome* denotes genuine, natural beauty; *fine*, artificial, laboured beauty (Delius).

432. *Thereabout.* Possibly a noun, as Wr. makes it; but *thereabout of it* seems to be merely=there. We might now say colloquially: "I liked that speech—there especially where," etc.

436. *The rugged Pyrrhus*, etc. Whether this speech was meant to be admired or to be laughed at has been much disputed. See F. vol. i. pp. 180–185. Pope thought it "purely ironical;" Warb., Ritson, Caldecott, Coleridge, and others have taken the opposite ground. What Hamlet has said just before shows that the latter are right. Coleridge says: "The fancy that a burlesque was intended sinks below criticism; the lines, as epic narrative, are superb."

*The Hyrcanian beast* is the tiger. Cf. *Macb.* iii. 4. 101: "the Hyrcan tiger;" and see note in our ed. p. 219.

443. *Gules.* Red; an heraldic term. S. uses it again in *T. of A.* iv. 3. 59: "With man's blood paint the ground, gules, gules." Cf. Keats, *St. Agnes' Eve:*

> "Full on this casement shone the wintry moon,
> And threw warm gules on Madeline's fair breast."

*Trick'd.* Adorned. Cf. *Hen. V.* iii. 6. 80: "which they trick up with new-tuned oaths;" Milton, *Il Pens.* 123: "Not trick'd and frounc'd as she was wont," etc. In heraldry, a *trick* is "a delineation of arms in which the colours are distinguished by their technical marks, without any colour being laid on" (D.).

445. *Impasted.* Made into a paste; a word used by S. nowhere else.

448. *O'ersized.* Covered as with "size," or glue. For the form of *coagulate* cf. *adulterate*, i. 5. 42 above.

449. *Eyes like carbuncles.* Wr. quotes Milton, *P. L.* ix. 500: "and carbuncle his eyes."

452. *Fore.* See *Hen. V.* p. 155.

455. *Striking too short*, etc. Cf. Virgil, *Æn.* ii. 544 fol.

458. *Drives.* Followed by *upon* in *T. A.* ii. 3. 64:

> "and the hounds
> Should drive upon thy new-transformed limbs."

459. *But.* According to Delius, here = merely.

464. *Declining.* Cf. *T. and C.* iv. 5. 189:

> "When thou hast hung thy advanc'd sword i' the air,
> Not letting it decline on the declin'd."

*Milky.* Probably = white, but Schmidt makes it = "weak," as in *T. of A.* iii. 1. 57 and *Lear*, i. 4. 364. S. has *milk-white* six times.

466. *A painted tyrant.* Malone thinks that S. had in mind "the tremendous personages often represented in old tapestry, whose uplifted swords stick in the air, and do nothing." Delius cites *Macb.* v. 8. 25–27.

467. *Neutral.* "Taking no part in the contest" (Schmidt). *Matter* = that on which his will is to be exercised (M.).

469. *Against.* Cf. i. 1. 158 above, and iii. 4. 50 below. Gr. 142.

470. *Rack.* Mass of cloud, especially in motion. Cf. *Sonn.* 33. 6:

> "Anon permit the basest clouds to ride
> With ugly rack on his celestial face," etc.

See also *Temp.* p. 137.

472. *Hush.* Not elsewhere used as an adjective by S. Gr. 22.

473. *Region.* Originally a division of the sky marked out by the Roman augurs (Wr.). S. uses it several times for the air. Cf. 565 below: "the region kites." See also *Sonn.* 33. 12 and *R. and J.* ii. 2. 21. Wr. quotes Milton, *P. L.* vii. 425: "wing the region."

474. *A-work.* Cf. *R. of L.* 1496: "So Lucrece, set a-work." See also *T. and C.* v. 10. 38, *Lear*, iii. 5. 8, etc. Gr. 24.

476. *Mars's.* The quartos have "Marses," the folio "Mars his." On *proof*, see *Rich. II.* p. 162; and for *eterne*, cf. *Macb.* iii. 2. 38.

477. *Remorse.* Pity. See *Macb.* p. 171.

479. *Fortune.* See *A. Y. L.* p. 141.

480. *Synod.* For the use of the word in S. see *A. Y. L.* p. 173.

486. *Jig.* The word sometimes meant a facetious ballad (Schmidt). Cf. *jig-maker*, iii. 2. 108 below.

488. *Mobled.* The reading of the 2d folio; the 1st has "inobled," evidently a misprint. The word means veiled or *muffled*, of which it may be a corruption. Farmer quotes Shirley, *Gent. of Venice:* "The moon does mobble up herself;" and Holt White adds from Ogilby's *Fables:* "Mobbled nine days in my considering cap." *Mabled* (which Malone substitutes) is another form of the word. Nares cites Sandys, *Travels:* "Their heads and faces are mabled in fine linen, that no more is seen of them than their eyes."

490. *That 's good.* "Polonius praises the epithet to make up for his blunder in objecting to the length" (M.); or, perhaps, because it is a "quaint and fantastical word" (Warb.).

492. *Bisson rheum.* "Blinding tears" (Schmidt). We find *bisson*= purblind, in *Cor.* ii. 1. 70, and some modern eds. give it in *Cor.* iii. 1. 131. For *rheum*=tears, cf. *Much Ado*, v. 2. 85, *K. John*, iii. 1. 22, iv. 1. 33, iv. 3. 108, etc.

494. *O'erteemed.* "Exhausted by child-bearing" (Wr.).

500. *Mincing.* Cutting in pieces. Cf. *T. of A.* iv. 3. 122: "And mince it [the babe] sans remorse."

501. *Instant.* See on i. 5. 71 above.

503. *Milch.* Milk-giving; a metaphor for tearful. For the literal use of the word, see *M. W.* iv. 4. 33, *T. of S.* ii. 1. 359, etc. Steevens quotes Drayton, *Polyolbion*, xiii.: "Exhaling the milch dew."

504. *Passion.* Sorrow (Schmidt), or compassion (Sr.). Cf. 536 and 545 below. See also *L. L. L.* v. 2. 118, *M. N. D.* v. 1. 293, 321, etc. For *passion in* the Coll. MS. gives "passionate."

505. *Whether.* The early eds. have "where," and some modern ones print "whe'r" or "whêr." See *J. C.* p. 128 or Gr. 466. For *in 's*, see Gr. 461.

508. *Bestowed.* Lodged, taken care of. Cf. iii. 4. 174 and iv. 3. 12 below. It is used reflexively (=hide) in iii. 1. 33 and 44 below.

509. *Abstract.* The folio has "abstracts."

510. *You were better.* See *A. Y. L.* p. 180 (note on *But I were better*), or Gr. 230, 352.

514. *Bodykins.* A diminutive of *body*. "The reference was originally to the sacramental bread" (Wr.). Cf. *M. W.* ii. 3. 46; and see on 358 above.

515. *Scape.* See on i. 3. 38 above.

525. *Some dozen or sixteen lines.* Many attempts have been made to find these added lines in the play (iii. 2 below), but we are disposed to agree with Dr. Ingleby in the view that Hamlet writes no speech at all. The poet simply *represents* him as doing so in order to adapt the old play to his purpose. As F. remarks, "it would tax the credulity of an audience too severely to represent the possibility of Hamlet's finding an old play exactly fitted to Claudius's crime, not only in the plot, but in all the accessories, even to a single speech which should tent the criminal to the

very quick . . . The discussion, therefore, that has arisen over these 'dozen or sixteen lines' is a tribute to Shakespeare's consummate art."

533. *Alone.* "The eagerness shown by Hamlet to be left in peace by himself appears to be a main evidence of his merely acting a part and *assuming* madness; he longs to get rid of the presence of persons before whom he has resolved to wear a show of insanity. Alone, he is collected, coherent, full of introspection. That he is neither dispassionate nor cool appears to be the result of his unhappy source of thought, not the result of derangement; he is morally afflicted, not mentally affected" (Clarke).

534. *Peasant slave.* Mr. Furnivall has shown (*Notes and Queries* for Apr. 12 and May 3, 1873) that S. might possibly have seen in the flesh some of the bondmen or *peasant slaves* of England.

538. *Her working.* Wr. says: "*Soul* when personified is feminine in S." Cf., however, *Rich. II.* v. 5. 6:

> "My brain I 'll prove the female to my soul,
> My soul the father."

Milton also personifies the soul as feminine. See *Il Pens.* 92, *Comus*, 454 fol., *P. L.* v. 486, etc.

*Wann'd.* The quartos have "wand," the folio "warm'd," which Rowe, Pope, Theo., and some others retain. S. does not elsewhere use *wan* as a verb.

539. *Aspect.* Always accented on the last syllable by S. Gr. 40.

540. *Function.* Action; "the whole energies of soul and body" (Caldecott).

541. *Conceit.* Conception (that is, of the character). See *A. Y. L.* p. 162 and cf. p. 194.

545. *Cue.* Still used as a stage term. For its literal use, cf. *M. W.* iii. 3. 39, *M. N. D.* iii. 1. 78, 102, etc.; and for the figurative, as here, *Hen. V.* iii. 6. 130, *Oth.* i. 2. 83, etc.

548. *Free.* Free from guilt, innocent. Cf. iii. 2. 224 below, and see *A. Y. L.* p. 165.

549. *Amaze.* Confuse, confound. See *A. Y. L.* p. 143.

552. *Muddy-mettled.* "Heavy, irresolute" (Schmidt). For the literal meaning of *rascal* see *A. Y. L.* p. 179.

*Peak.* Literally=grow lean, pine, as in *Macb.* i. 3. 23; figuratively= "sneak, play a contemptible part" (Schmidt), as here and in *M. W.* iii. 5. 71.

553. *John-a-Dreams.* That is, *John of Dreams*, or *John the Dreamer* =a dreamy, idle fellow. Cf. *Jack-a-lent* (a puppet thrown at during Lent) in *M. W.* iii. 3. 27, v. 5. 134, *Jack-a-lanthorn* (the ignis fatuus), and similar forms. Coll. quotes Armin, *Nest of Ninnies*, 1608: "His name is John, indeede. saies the cinnick; but neither John a nods nor John a dreames, yet either as you take it."

*Unpregnant of.* Not quickened by, not inspired with. Cf. *M. for M.* iv. 4. 23: "unpregnant And dull to all proceedings."

555. *Property.* Wr. thinks this may be="own person" or perhaps "kingly right," and doubts whether it can have its ordinary modern sense. Schmidt, however, gives it the latter meaning here; and F. says: "I suppose it refers to his crown, his wife, everything, in short, which he

might be said to be possessed of, except his life." He compares *M. W.* iii. 4. 10, to which may be added *J. C.* iv. 1. 40.

556. *Defeat.* Ruin, destruction; as in v. 2. 58 below. See also *Hen. V.* i. 2. 107: "Making defeat on the full power of France." Steevens quotes Chapman, *Revenge for Honour:*

"That he might meantime make a sure defeat
On our good aged father's life."

559. *The lie*, etc. Cf. *Rich. II.* i. 1. 124:

"as low as to thy heart
Through the false passage of thy throat, thou liest."

560. *Me.* For me. See Gr. 220.

562. *'Swounds.* A contraction of "God's wounds;" used again in v. 1. 264 below. Here the folio substitutes "Why," there "Come." *Zounds* is a corruption of the same oath, and is either omitted or changed in the folio. See on ii. 1. 76 and on 358 above.

563. *Pigeon-liver'd.* "It was supposed that pigeons and doves owed their gentleness of disposition to the absence of gall" (W.). Cf. Drayton, *Eclogue* ix.:

"A Milk-white Doue upon her hand shee brought,
So tame 't would goe returning at her call,
About whose Necke was in a Choller wrought
'Only like me my Mistress hath no gall.'"

564. *To make*, etc. To make me feel the bitterness of oppression (D.).

565. *Region.* See on 473 above.

567. *Kindless.* Unnatural (Johnson). So *kindly*=natural; as in *A. Y. L.* ii. 3. 53, *Much Ado*, iv. 1. 75, etc.

570. *A dear father murther'd.* The reading of the 4th and 5th quartos. The earlier quartos have "a deere murthered," and the folio "the Deere murthered," which K. and W. prefer.

573. *A-cursing.* See on i. 3. 119 above. Gr. 24.

574. *Scullion.* The 1st quarto has "scalion," the later quartos have "stallyon" or "stallion." Theo. substituted "cullion" (cf. *Lear*, ii. 2. 3, etc.).

576. *About.* "To your work!" (Johnson). Steevens quotes Heywood, *Iron Age:*

"My brain about again! for thou hast found
New projects now to work on."

577–580. *Guilty creatures*, etc. Todd quotes *A Warning for Faire Women*, 1599:

"Ile tell you, sir, one more to quite your tale.
A woman that had made away her husband,
And sitting to behold a tragedy
At Linne a towne in Norffolke,
Acted by players trauelling that way,
Wherein a woman that had murtherd hers
Was euer haunted with her husbands ghost:
The passion written by a feeling pen,
And acted by a good tragedian,
She was so mooued with the sight thereof,
As she cryed out, the play was made by her,
And openly confesst her husbands murder."

Cf. Massinger, *Roman Actor*, ii. 1:

> "I once observed,
> In a tragedy of ours, in which a murder
> Was acted to the life, a guilty hearer,
> Forc'd by the terror of a wounded conscience,
> To make discovery of that which torture
> Could not wring from him."

578. *Presently.* Immediately. Cf. 170 above.

580. *For murther*, etc. Cf. *Macb.* iii. 4. 122–126 and *Rich. II.* i. 1. 104. M. quotes Wordsworth:

> "Beliefs coiled serpent-like about
> The adage on all tongues, 'Murder will out.'"

584. *Tent.* Probe; as in *Cymb.* iii. 4. 118: "tent to bottom." We have the noun in *T. and C.* ii. 2. 16:

> "the tent that searches
> To the bottom of the worst;"

and again, with a play on the word, in *Id.* v. 1. 11.

*Blench.* Flinch, start. Cf. *T. and C.* i. 1. 28:

> "Patience herself, what goddess e'er she be,
> Doth lesser blench at sufferance than I do."

Steevens quotes Fletcher, *Night-Walker*: "Blench at no danger, though it be a gallows."

586. *The devil hath power*, etc. Cf. 2 *Cor.* xi. 14.

Sir Thomas Browne (quoted by M.) says: "I believe that these apparitions and ghosts of departed persons are not the wandering souls of men, but the unquiet walks of devils, prompting and insinuating to us... that the blessed spirits are not at rest in their graves, but wander solicitous of the affairs of the world."

590. *Abuses.* Deceives. Cf. *Much Ado*, v. 2. 100: "Hero hath been falsely accused, the prince and Claudio mightily abused," etc.

591. *Relative.* "To the purpose, conclusive" (Schmidt). S. uses the word nowhere else.

"Shall we," says Dr. Bucknill, "think the less nobly of him because his hand is not ready to shed kindred blood; because, gifted with godlike discourse of reason, he does look before and after; because he does not take the law in his own hands upon his oppressor, until he has obtained conclusive evidence of his guilt; that he seeks to make sure he is the natural justiciar of his murdered father, and not an assassin instigated by hatred and selfish revenge?"

---

## ACT III.

SCENE I.—1. *Drift of circumstance.* "Roundabout method" (Wr.). Cf. ii. 1. 10: "By this encompassment and drift of question;" also i. 5. 127: "without more circumstance at all." *Drift*=scheme in *T. G. of V.* ii. 6. 43, iii. 1. 18, iv. 2. 83, etc. The quartos have "conference" for *circumstance.*

3. *Grating.* Vexing. Cf. *A. and C.* i. 1. 18: "Grates me." So with *on* in 2 *Hen. IV.* iv. 1. 90: "suborn'd to grate on you," etc.

7. *Forward.* Disposed, inclined.

8. *Keeps.* For the ellipsis of the subject, see Gr. 399. Cf. ii. 2. 67 above and iv. 1. 10 below.

On *crafty madness*, cf. iii. 4. 186: "mad in craft."

12. *With much forcing*, etc. With apparent unwillingness (M.).

13. *Niggard of question*, etc. Warb. transposed *Niggard* and *Most free.* Malone (so also Schmidt) makes *question*=talk, and explains the passage thus: "Slow to begin conversation, but free enough in his answers to our demands." Wr. says: "Rosencrantz and Guildenstern were completely baffled, and Hamlet had the talk almost to himself. Perhaps they did not intend to give a correct account of the interview."

*Of our demands.* The Coll. MS. has "to" for *of.* See Gr. 173.

14. *Assay him to.* "Try his disposition towards" (Caldecott).

17. *O'er-raught.* "Over-reached, that is, overtook" (Johnson). Cf. *C. of E.* i. 2. 96: "o'er-raught of all my money." We find *raught* both as the past tense and participle of *reach.* See *Hen. V.* p. 180.

20. *Order.* S. regularly uses the singular in this sense. Cf. v. 2. 365 below.

22. *Beseech'd.* The only instance of the past tense in S.; and the only one of the participle is in *L. C.* 207, where he also has "beseech'd." In *Hen. V.* iii. 2. 115 "beseeched"=besieged.

24. *Content.* Gratify, please; as often in S. Cf. *T. G. of V.* iii. 1. 93: "A woman sometimes scorns what best contents her," etc.

26. *Edge.* Incitement, setting-on. It is a slight modification of *edge* =desire, appetite, as in *Sonn.* 56. 2, *M. for M.* i. 4. 60, *T. of S.* i. 2. 73, etc.

29. *Closely.* Secretly; as in *K. John*, iv. 1. 133, etc.

31. *Affront.* Meet directly, encounter. Cf. *W. T.* v. 1. 75: "Affront his eye." See also *T. and C.* iii. 2. 174 and *Cymb.* iv. 3. 29. J. H. quotes Cook, *Green's Tu Quoque*, 1614: "This I must caution you of, in your affront or salute, never to move your hat."

32. *Lawful espials.* "Spies justifiably inquisitive" (Caldecott). We find *espials* in the same sense in 1 *Hen. VI.* i. 4. 8 and iv. 3. 6. Sr. quotes Baret, *Alvearie:* "An espiall in warres, a scoutwatch."

33. *Bestow ourselves.* See on ii. 2. 508 above.

39. *Beauties.* F. adopts Walker's suggestion of "beauty;" also "virtue" in next line.

40. *Wildness.* Distraction, madness; as in *Cymb.* iii. 4. 9 (Schmidt).

43. *Gracious.* Addressed to the king. Cf. "High and mighty," iv. 7. 43 below.

47. *Too much prov'd.* Found by too frequent experience (Johnson).

51. *Beautied.* Not elsewhere used by S. as a verb.

52. *To.* Compared to. See on i. 2. 140 above.

53. *Painted.* Falsely coloured, unreal. Cf. *K. John*, iii. 1. 105: "painted peace;" *T. A.* ii. 3. 126: "painted hope," etc.

56. *To be*, etc. "In ii. 2. Hamlet has spoken of suicide as being against the 'canon of the Everlasting.' Here he considers it as viewed by philosophy... 'Doubtless it might be more entirely desirable to turn the flank

of all sorrows by self-slaughter; and this might be the course which a man of quick decision would take. But reflection, if allowed, must needs make us think that if death is a sleep, it still may have dreams; while conscience warns us what we have deserved that these dreams should be. Thus, instead of condensing into strong purpose, thought melts into mere dreaming meditation; the will is puzzled, the moment of action passes, and we end by inertly bearing our present evils rather than daring to fly to others of whose nature we are ignorant; giving up our deliverance as we should, from the same weakness, give up any other enterprise of pith and moment'" (M.).

59. *Take arms against a sea*, etc. For *a sea of* Pope suggested "a siege of," Theo. "th' assay of," Warb. "assail of," etc.; but no change is called for. There are worse cases of "mixed metaphor" in S. than this, which, as Wr. remarks, is "rather two metaphors blended into one." The expression is="take arms against a host of troubles which break in upon us like a sea." Cf. 156 below: "That suck'd the honey of his music vows," which, if a "mixed metaphor," is a very beautiful one—better than many of the "faultily faultless" figures of inferior poets. Keightley, who favours Pope's conjecture, says that this is "almost a solitary instance of the figurative use of *sea* by S." On the contrary, it is a common metaphor with him. See *R. of L.* 1100, *T. G. of V.* iii. 1. 224, 1 *Hen. VI.* iv. 7. 14, 3 *Hen. VI.* ii. 5. 106, *Hen. VIII.* ii. 4. 200, iii. 2. 360, *T. and C.* iii. 2. 84. *T. of A.* i. 1. 47, iv. 2. 22, *Per.* v. 1. 194, etc.

61. *No more.* Nothing more.

65. *Rub.* A metaphor taken from the game of bowls. See *Rich. II.* p. 197 or *Hen. V.* p. 157.

67. *Coil.* Turmoil. Cf. *Temp.* i. 2. 207, *C. of E.* iii. 1. 48, *M. N. D.* iii. 2. 339, etc. S. never uses the word in the familiar modern sense.

68. *Give us pause.* That is, for reflection. Cf. iii. 3. 42 and iv. 3. 9 below. *Respect*=consideration, motive; as in *Sonn.* 49. 4, *Much Ado*, ii. 3. 176, *A. W.* ii. 5. 71, etc. See also iii. 2. 166 below.

70. *Of time.* Of the times, of the world. Warb. wished to read "of th' time;" but cf. *K. John*, v. 2. 12: "such a sore of time;" 1 *Hen. IV.* iv. 1. 25: "the state of time," etc. S. generally uses the article, as in i. 5. 189 above.

72. *Dispriz'd.* Misprized, undervalued; the folio reading. The 2d and 3d quartos have "despiz'd," which most modern eds. adopt. As F. remarks, "a love that is disprized falls more frequently to the lot of man, and is perhaps more hopeless in its misery, than a love that is despised." *Disprize* occurs again in *T. and C.* iv. 5. 74.

75. *Quietus.* The law term for the final settlement of an account. Cf. *Sonn.* 126. 12: "And her quietus is to render thee." Steevens quotes Webster, *Duchess of Malfi*, i. 1: "I sign your *quietus est*."

76. *Bare.* Mere, as Schmidt explains it, not "unsheathed," as Malone says; though S. may have had the latter meaning also in mind.

A *bodkin* was a small dagger. Cf. *L. L. L.* v. 2. 615 and *W. T.* iii. 3. 87. Steevens quotes B. and F., *Custom of the Country*, ii. 3:

> "Out with your bodkin,
> Your pocket-dagger, your stiletto."

See also Chaucer, *C. T.* 3958: "with knyf or boydekyn;" and *Id.* 16193: "stiked him with boydekyns anoon."

*Fardels.* Burdens; literally, packs, bundles. Cf. *W. T.* iv. 4. 728, 739, 781, 783, etc. The folio reads "these Fardles," which is preferred by K., W., H., and others.

77. *Grunt.* Groan. Steevens quotes many contemporaneous examples; as from Stanyhurst's *Virgil*, 1582: "sighing it grunts" (*congemuit*); Turbervile's *Ovid:* "greefe forst me grunt;" and again: "Of dying men the grunts," etc. The quarto of 1676 has "groan," which is adopted by Pope, Capell, and others. Cf. *J. C.* iv. 1. 22: "To groan and sweat under the business." Armin (*Nest of Ninnies*) has "gronte and sweat under this massie burden."

79. *Bourn.* Limit, boundary. Cf. *Temp.* ii. 1. 152: "Bourn, bound of land;" *A. and C.* i. 1. 16: "I 'll set a bourn," etc.

80. *No traveller returns.* This has been foolishly criticised, because the Ghost was such a returned traveller; and as foolishly defended by Theo. (on the ground that the Ghost came only from the intermediate state of Purgatory) and others. A child ought to see, and probably would see—having no critical spectacles to dim its vision—that the meaning is, does not come back to *live* here, as he returns from a visit to a foreign land; or, as Coleridge puts it, "no traveller returns to this world as to his home or abiding-place."

83. *Thus conscience*, etc. Blakeway compares *Rich. III.* i. 4. 138 fol.

84. *Native hue.* Natural colour. Wr. quotes *L. L. L.* iv. 3. 263: "For native blood is counted painting now."

85. *Thought.* Anxiety. See *J. C.* p. 146, and cf. iv. 5. 168 below.

86. *Pith.* The folio reading; the quartos have "pitch," which the Camb. editors prefer. In either case, as Wr. notes, there is a change of metaphor in *currents.* See on 59 above.

88. *Soft you now.* "Hold, stop" (Schmidt). Cf. *Oth.* v. 2. 338: "Soft you; a word before you go." See also *M. N. D.* p. 176.

89. *Orisons.* Prayers. Cf. *Hen. V.* ii. 2. 53, 3 *Hen. VI.* i. 4. 110, *R. and J.* iv. 3. 3, etc.

Johnson remarks: "This is a touch of nature. Hamlet, at the sight of Ophelia, does not immediately recollect that he is to personate madness, but makes her an address grave and solemn, such as the foregoing meditation excited in his thoughts."

97. *I know.* So in the folio; the quartos have "you know." Ophelia means, they may have been trifles to *you* and you forgot that you gave them, but *I* did not, for they were most precious to *me.*

103. *Honest.* Virtuous. See *A. Y. L.* p. 141. So *honesty*=virtue in 107 below.

107. *Should admit*, etc. Your honesty should be so chary of your beauty as not to suffer it to entertain discourse, or to be parleyed with (Caldecott).

109. *Commerce.* Intercourse. Cf. *T. N.* iii. 4. 191, *T. and C.* iii. 3. 205, etc.

114. *Sometime.* See on i. 2. 8 above.

116. *Indeed*, etc. See p. 27 above.

118. *Relish of it.* Have a flavour of it, retain a trace of it.

121. *Get thee.* A common reflexive use of *get* in S., but never with the full form of the pronouns, *thyself*, etc. (Schmidt). Cf. *Hen. V.* iv. 1. 287: "gets him to rest;" *J. C.* ii. 4. 37: "I 'll get me to a place more void," etc.

122. *Indifferent.* "Fairly, ordinarily" (Wr.). Cf. v. 2. 97 below; also *T. of S.* i. 2. 181, *T. N.* i. 3. 143, i. 5. 265, etc. Gr. 1.

125. *At my beck.* "Always ready to come about me" (Steevens). The Coll. MS. has "back" for *beck.*

129. *Go thy ways.* See on i. 3. 135 above.

134. *O, help him,* etc. This speech and that in 141 below were first marked *aside* by F.

136. *Chaste as ice.* Cf. *A. Y. L.* iii. 4. 18: "the very ice of chastity."

139. *Monsters.* Delius compares *Oth.* iv. 1. 63.

142. *Your paintings.* The *your* refers to women generally, as the plural *yourselves* shows. The folio has "your pratlings," and "pace" for *face.*

144. *Jig.* Walk as if dancing a jig. In *L. L. L.* iii. 1. 11 it means to *sing* a jig or in the manner of a jig. See on ii. 2. 486 above. For the contemptuous use of *amble*, cf. 1 *Hen. IV.* iii. 2. 60, *Rich. III.* i. 1. 17, and *R. and J.* i. 4. 11.

*Nickname.* Misname, miscall. Cf. *L. L. L.* v. 2. 349: "You nickname virtue; vice you should have spoke."

145. *Make your wantonness,* etc. You mistake wantonly, and pretend that you do it through ignorance (Johnson); or, perhaps, affect an innocent ignorance as a mask for wantonness (W.).

151. *Scholar's, soldier's.* The early eds. have "soldier's, scholar's," except the 1st quarto in which the passage reads:

> "The Courtier, Scholler, Souldier, all in him,
> All dasht and splintered thence, O woe is me," etc.

The correction is Hanmer's, and is generally adopted. Farmer thinks that the early text is what S. wrote, and points out a similar oversight in *R. and L.* 615, 616:

> "For princes are the glass, the school, the book,
> Where subjects' eyes do learn, do read, do look."

152. *Fair.* That is, because Hamlet adorns it as the *rose.* For the prolepsis, cf. *Macb.* i. 3. 84: "the insane root;" and see also *Id.* i. 6. 3 and iii. 4. 76.

153. *The glass of fashion.* Cf. 2 *Hen. IV.* ii. 3. 21:

> "he was indeed the glass
> Wherein the noble youth did dress themselves;"

and B. J., *Cynthia's Revels*, dedic.: "in thee the whole kingdom dresseth itself, and is ambitious to use thee as her glass."

*The mould of form.* "The model by whom all endeavoured to form themselves" (Johnson).

155. *Deject.* See on i. 2. 20. Gr. 342.

156. *Music vows.* See on 59 above. F. prints "music-vows." Gr. 22. The quartos have "musickt."

158. *Jangled out of tune.* Most modern eds. print "jangled, out of tune," but the comma is not in the folio. "The two ideas attached to *bells* are: 1. *jangled out of tune;* 2. *harsh*, which expresses to what extent jangled out of tune" (Corson).

159. *Feature.* Figure, form. Cf. *Sonn.* 113. 12, *K. John*, iv. 2. 264, 1 *Hen. VI.* v. 5. 68, etc. See also iii. 2. 21 below.

*Blown*="in its bloom" (Capell). Cf. iii. 3. 81 below.

160. *Ecstasy.* Madness; as in ii. 1. 102 above.

162. *Affections.* Feelings, inclinations.

163. *Nor . . . not.* See on i. 2. 158.

165. *On brood.* Brooding. Gr. 24, 180.

166. *Doubt.* Suspect. See on i. 2. 256 above. For *disclose*, see on i. 1. 57. The word was regularly used of the hatching of birds. Cf. v. 1. 277 below. Malone quotes Massinger, *Maid of Honour*, i. 2:

> "One aerie with proportion ne'er discloses
> The eagle and the wren."

167. *For to.* Cf. v. 1. 92 below, and see Gr. 152.

169. *Shall.* For *shall*=will, see Gr. 315 (cf. 176 below); and for the ellipsis of the verb of motion, see Gr. 405. Cf. ii. 2. 485 above.

173. *Something-settled.* See Gr. 68, and cf. 2.

174. *Puts.* M. says that *brains* is singular; but S. elsewhere makes it plural. Cf. *A. W.* iv. 3. 216: "his brains are forfeit," etc. The real subject is "the beating of his brains on this" (Gr. 337).

175. *Fashion of himself.* His usual bearing or behaviour. For *on't*, see on i. 1. 55 above.

183. *Round.* See on ii. 2. 139 above.

184. *So please you.*. If it so please you. See *A. Y. L.* p. 138 or *Mer.* pp. 134, 136. Gr. 133.

*In the ear*="within hearing" (Schmidt).

185. *Find.* "Detect, unmask" (Schmidt). Cf. *A. W.* ii. 3. 216, ii. 4. 32, v. 2. 46, 1 *Hen. IV.* i. 3. 3, etc.

SCENE II.—3. *Your.* See on i. 5. 167 above, or Gr. 221; and for *had as lief*, *A. Y. L.* p. 139.

8. *Hear.* The folio has "see." *Robustious* occurs again in *Hen. V.* iii. 7. 159.

*Periwig-pated.* In the time of S. wigs were worn only by actors; they did not come into general use until the time of Charles II. (Steevens). Cf. *T. G. of V.* iv. 4. 196 and *C. of E.* ii. 2. 76. In *Every Woman in her Humour*, 1609, it is said that "none wear hoods but monks and ladies, . . . none periwigs but players and pictures."

10. *Groundlings.* The rabble in the pit, which in the theatres of that day had neither floor nor benches. Steevens quotes Ben Jonson, *Bartholomew Fair:* "the understanding gentlemen of the ground;" also *Lady Alimony:* "Be your stage-curtains artificially drawn, and so covertly shrowded that the squint-eyed groundling may not peep in." According to Nares, these gentry paid only a penny for admission.

11. *Inexplicable.* "Unintelligible" (Schmidt). Johnson explains it as "without words to explain them."

12. *Termagant.* An imaginary god of the Saracens, often introduced into the old mystery-plays, and represented as a most violent character (Nares). Cf. Spenser, *F. Q.* vi. 7. 47: "And oftentimes by Turmagant and Mahound swore;" Chaucer, *C. T.* 15221: "He swar, 'Child, by Termagaunt,'" etc. S. uses the word only here and in 1 *Hen. IV.* v. 4. 114, where it is an adjective.

*Herod* was also a common character in the old mysteries, and always a violent one. Steevens quotes Chaucer, *C. T.* 3384: "He pleyeth Herod on a scaffold hye." Douce gives a long extract from a pageant performed at Canterbury in 1534, in which this stage-direction occurs: "Here Erode ragis in thys pagond, and in the strete also."

18. *From the purpose.* That is, away from, or contrary to it. Gr. 158.

22. *His.* Its. Gr. 228.

*Pressure.* Imprint, character. Cf. i. 5. 100 above.

23. *Come tardy off.* The reading of the early eds. The quarto of 1676 has "of" for *off*, and is followed by Theo., Warb., F., and others. The emendation is plausible (cf. *came short of*, iv. 7. 89 below); but no change seems really required. Cf. *T. G. of V.* ii. 1. 115: "it came hardly off," etc.; and for *come*=having come, *R. of L.* 1784: "Weak words, so thick come in his poor heart's aid." See Gr. 165.

24. *Censure.* Judgment. See on i. 3. 69 above. *Of the which one*= of which one class of persons (Caldecott); or, possibly, as Delius and Wr. explain it, "of the judicious man singly." Hanmer substituted "of one of which."

26. *There be.* For this use of *be*, see Gr. 300.

27. *Profanely.* "The profanity consists in alluding to Christians" (F.).

29. *Nor man.* Nor even man (Wr.). The 1st quarto has "Nor Turke," the folio "or Norman." Farmer conjectured "nor Mussulman." W. and H. read "or Turk." The Coll. MS. has "nor man."

31. *Had made men.* The reading of the early eds. Theo. suggested "made them," which F. adopts. Farmer (followed by H.) conjectured "the men." These emendations are plausible, but S. may have written *had made men*; that is, had been making men, had tried their hand at making men (instead of sticking to their regular work on inferior creatures). This seems in keeping with "*imitated* humanity."

33. *Indifferently.* Tolerably well. Cf. *indifferent*, iii. 1. 122 above.

36. *Your clowns*, etc. The clowns were given to this extemporizing. Stowe (quoted by Steevens) informs us that among the twelve players who were sworn the queen's servants in 1583 "were two rare men, viz. Thomas Wilson, for a quick delicate refined extemporall witte; and Richard Tarleton, for a wondrous plentifull, pleasant extemporall witt," etc. Cf. *Tarleton's Newes out of Purgatory*: "that merrye Roscius of plaiers that famosed all comedies so with his pleasant and extemporall invention;" and, even earlier, *The Contention Betwyxte Churchyard and Camell*, 1560:

"But Vices in stage plaies,
When theyr matter is gon,
They laugh out the reste
To the lookers on," etc.

In the 1st quarto this passage reads as follows:

"*Ham.* And doe you heare? let not your Clowne speake
More then is set downe, there be of them I can tell you
That will laugh themselues, to set on some
Quantitie of barren spectators to laugh with them,
Albeit there is some necessary point in the Play
Then to be obserued: O t'is vile, and shewes
A pittiful ambition in the foole that vseth it.
And then you haue some agen, that keepes one sute
Of ieasts, as a man is knowne by one sute of
Apparell, and Gentlemen quotes his ieasts downe
In their tables, before they come to the play, as thus:
Cannot you stay till I eate my porrige? and, you owe me
A quarters wages: and, my coate wants a cullison:*
And, your beere is sowre: and, blabbering with his lips,
And thus keeping in his cinkapase† of ieasts,
When, God knows, the warme Clowne cannot make a iest
Vnlesse by chance, as the blinde man catcheth a hare:
Maisters tell him of it.
*players* We will my Lord.
*Ham.* Well, goe make you ready. *exeunt players.*"

Hunter and Halliwell are inclined to think that this should be retained; but, as W. remarks, "it was probably an extemporaneous addition to the text by the actor."

37. *There be of them.* Cf. Gr. 399 fol.

38. *Barren.* Barren of wit, dull. Cf. *M. N. D.* iii. 2. 13: "that barren sort;" *T. N.* i. 5. 90: "a barren rascal," etc.

42. *Piece of work.* In *M. N. D.* i. 2. 14, Bottom calls the play "a very good piece of work." Cf. *T. of S.* i. 1. 258.

43. *Presently.* See on ii. 2. 170 above.

50. *Coped withal.* Met with, encountered. Cf. *A. Y. L.* ii. 1. 67: "I love to cope him in these sullen fits;" *W. T.* iv. 4. 435: "The royal fool thou copest with," etc.

53. *Revenue.* Accented by S. either on the first or on the second syllable, as suits the measure. Cf. *M. N. D.* i. 1. 7: "Long withering out a young man's revenue;" and 158 in the same scene: "Of great revenue, and she hath no child." Gr. 490.

55. *Candied.* Sugared, flattering (D.). Elsewhere it means congealed. See *Temp.* ii. 1. 279 and *T. of A.* iv. 3. 226.

*Absurd.* The only instance of this accent in S. Gr. 490.

56. *Crook.* The subject of this verb is *tongue*, unless with Tschischwitz we consider it a 3d person imperative. It is probably an instance of "construction according to sense," the real subject being the person implied in *tongue.* Cf. Gr. 415.

*Pregnant.* Quick, ready (Johnson and Schmidt); or "because untold thrift is born from a cunning use of the knee" (F.).

On *hinges of the knee*, cf. *T. of A.* iv. 3. 211: "hinge thy knee."

* A corruption of *cognizance*, or badge of arms (Nares). Cf. *The Owles Almanack*, 1618: "A blew coat without a cullizan." P. Hentzner, in his *Travels*, 1598, says that in England servants "wear their masters' arms in silver, fastened to their left arms."

† That is, *cinque-pace*, a kind of dance. Cf. *Much Ado*, ii. 1. 77: "falls into the cinque-pace faster and faster," etc.

57. *Fawning.* The folio has "faining."

58. *Dear.* See on i. 2. 182.

59. *Of men distinguish.* Cf. 2 *Hen. VI.* ii. 1. 130: "distinguish of colours." The 2d and 3d quartos have

> "distinguish her election,
> S' hath [=she hath] seal'd," etc.,

and some editors have preferred this reading.

64. *Blood and judgment.* "Passions and reason" (Caldecott). Cf. *Much Ado*, ii. 3. 70: "wisdom and blood combating," etc.

For *commingled* the quartos have "comedled," which means the same. For *meddle*=mingle, cf. *Temp.* i. 2. 22, and see note in our ed. p. 112.

On the passage cf. *J. C.* v. 5. 73:

> "His life was gentle, and the elements
> So mix'd in him that Nature might stand up
> And say to all the world 'This was a man!'"

and see note in our ed. p. 185.

69. *Something too much*, etc. "The genuine manliness of this little sentence, where Hamlet checks himself when conscious that he has been carried away by fervour of affectionate friendship into stronger protestation than mayhap becomes the truth and simplicity of sentiment between man and man, is precisely one of Shakespeare's exquisite touches of innate propriety in questions of feeling. Let any one who doubts for a moment whether Shakespeare intended that Hamlet should merely *feign* madness, read carefully over the present speech, marking its sobriety of expression even amid all its ardour, its singleness and purity of sentiment amid its most forcible utterance, and then decide whether it could be possible that he should mean Hamlet's wits to be touched. That his heart is shaken to its core, that he is even afflicted with melancholia and hypochondria, we admit; but that his intellects are in the very slightest degree disordered, we cannot for one instant believe" (Clarke).

73. *Afoot.* Being performed. Cf. *M. for M.* iv. 5. 3: "The matter being afoot," etc.

74. *With the very comment of thy soul.* "With all thy powers of observation" (Wr.). The folio has "my soul," which K. and Corson defend.

75. *Occulted.* Hidden; used by S. nowhere else.

76. *One speech.* The one prepared by Hamlet (ii. 2. 525). For the metaphor in *unkennel*, cf. *M. W.* iii. 3. 174.

77. *Damned ghost.* A "goblin damned" (i. 4. 40), and therefore not to be believed. Cf. ii. 2. 585 fol. Douce quotes Spenser, *F. Q.* i. 2. 32:

> "What voice of damned Ghost from Limbo lake,
> Or guilefull spright wandring in empty aire,
> Both which fraile men doe oftentimes mistake," etc.

79. *Stithy.* Smithy, forge. The 1st folio has "Stythe," the later folios "styth." *Stith* was properly the anvil; as in *C. T.* 2028: "That forgeth scharpe swerdes on his stith." The two words seem, however, to have been sometimes confounded. S. has *stithy* again in *T. and C.* iv. 5. 255, where it is a verb.

*Note*=attention; as in *A. W.* iii. 5. 104: "Worthy the note," etc.

82. *In censure of his seeming.* In forming an opinion of his appearance. See on i. 3. 69 above, and cf. *W. T.* iv. 4. 667, *Cymb.* v. 5. 65, etc.

83. *If he steal*, etc. Caldecott understands this to refer directly to possible manifestation of guilt on the part of the King; but of course all that Horatio means is, I 'll watch him so closely that if he were trying to steal something I would pledge myself to detect him or else to pay for the stolen property.

On *the whilst*, cf. *K. John*, iv. 2. 194: "The whilst his iron did on the anvil cool," etc.

84. On *theft*=the thing stolen, cf. *Exod.* xxii. 4 (Wr.).

85. *Idle.* Delius, St., Wr., and Schmidt make this refer to his feigned madness. Cf. iii. 4. 11 below and *Lear*, i. 3. 16. But though *idle* is often used in this sense, we are inclined here to agree with M., who explains the passage "I must appear to have nothing to do with the matter."

87. *Fares.* In his reply Hamlet plays upon the word; as Sly does in *T. of S.* ind. 2. 102: "Marry, I fare well; for here is cheer enough." Cf. *P. P.* 186:

> "'Farewell,' quoth she, 'and come again to-morrow.'
> Fare well I could not, for I supp'd with sorrow."

88. *Of the chameleon's dish.* For another allusion to the popular belief that the chameleon fed on air, see *T. G. of V.* ii. 1. 178; and for references to its supposed changes of colour, *Id.* ii. 4. 26 and 3 *Hen. VI.* iii. 2. 191. For *of*, see Gr. 177.

90. *I have nothing*, etc. I have nothing to do with it. Cf. *Cor.* ii. 3. 81: "I have no further with you."

93. *The university.* "The practice of acting Latin plays in the universities of Oxford and Cambridge is very ancient, and continued to near the middle of the last century. They were performed occasionally for the entertainment of princes and other great personages; and regularly at Christmas, at which time a *Lord of Misrule* was appointed at Oxford to regulate the exhibitions, and a similar officer with the title of *Imperator* at Cambridge" (Malone). English plays were also sometimes performed; this very one of *Hamlet* among the number. See the title-page of 1st quarto on p. 9 above.

96. *Enact.* Act, play. Cf. *Temp.* iv. 1. 121:

> "Spirits, which by mine art
> I have from their confines call'd to enact
> My present fancies," etc.

97. *Cæsar.* A Latin play on the subject of Cæsar's death was performed at Oxford in 1582 (Malone).

On the erroneous notion that Cæsar was killed "i' the Capitol," see *J. C.* p. 155. Cf. *A. and C.* ii. 6. 18.

99. *A brute part.* Steevens quotes Sir John Harrington, *Metamorphosis of Ajax*, 1596: "O brave-minded Brutus! but this I must truly say, they were two brutish parts both of him and you; one to kill his sons for treason, the other to kill his father in treason."

101. *Stay upon.* Await. Cf. "stay upon your leisure" (*A. W.* iii. 5. 48, *Macb.* i. 3. 148), "stays upon your will" (*A. and C.* i. 2. 119), etc.

*Patience*=permission; as in "by your patience" (*Temp.* iii. 3. 3, *A. Y.*

*L.* v. 4. 186, *Hen. V.* iii. 6. 31, etc.), "with your patience" (1 *Hen. VI.* ii. 3. 78), etc.

108. *Jig-maker.* See on ii. 2. 486 above.

110. *Within 's.* Within this (Delius). Cf. *R. and J.* v. 2. 25: "Within this three hours," etc.

113. *For I 'll have a suit of sables.* Warb. (followed by W. and H.) changed *for* to "'fore." Capell and others take *sables* to mean the fur of the sable, which was used only in rich and splendid apparel. Malone says that by a statute of Henry VIII. no one under the rank of an earl could wear sables. Wr. sees here "an intended contrast combined with a play upon words," and Schmidt takes the same view of the passage. Cf. iv. 7. 79 below, where "sables" are mentioned, not as badges of mourning, but as "importing health and graveness"—the dignified apparel of age as opposed to "the light and careless livery" of youth.

117. *Not thinking on.* That is, being forgotten (K.).

118. *The hobby-horse.* A figure in the rural May-games and morris-dances, probably referred to in ballads of the time as "forgot," either because it came to be omitted from the games or because of the attempts of the Puritans to put down these sports. Cf. *L. L. L.* iii. 1. 30. Steevens quotes B. and F., *Women Pleased,* iv. 1: "Shall the hobby-horse be forgot then?" also Ben Jonson, *Entertainment at Althorpe:* "But see the hobby-horse is forgot," etc.

*The dumb-show.* This stage-direction is as Steevens gives it, and agrees substantially with that in the folio. Why the "dumb-show" should have been introduced is a question that has been much discussed but not satisfactorily settled. See Furness, vol. i. pp. 241–243.

120. *Miching mallecho.* "Probably=secret and insidious mischief" (Schmidt). Florio, in his *Ital. Dict.*, 1598, defines *acciapinare* as "To miche, to shrug or sneake in some corner." *Micher*=truant, occurs in 1 *Hen. IV.* ii. 4. 450. Minsheu gives "To Miche, or secretly to hide himselfe out of the way, as Truants doe from schoole." *Mallecho* is the Spanish *malhecho* (literally, ill-done). D. quotes Connelly's *Spanish Dict.:* "*Malhecho* . . . An evil action, an indecent and indecorous behaviour; malefaction." Cf. Shirley, *Gent. of Venice:* "Be humble, Thou man of mallecho, or thou diest."

122. *Belike.* "As it seems, I suppose" (Schmidt). Cf. *M. N. D.* i. 1. 130, *Hen. V.* iii. 7. 55, etc. It is followed by *that* in *T. G. of V.* ii. 4. 90.

*Argument*=plot; as in ii. 2. 346 above.

135. *Posy.* Motto. See *Mer.* p. 164. Hamlet refers to the brevity of the prologue, as Ophelia evidently understands.

138. *Cart.* Chariot; but obsolete in that sense in the time of S. Wr. quotes Chaucer, *C. T.* 2043: "The statue of Mars upon a carte stood."

139. *Wash.* The sea. In *K. John,* v. 6. 41 and v. 7. 63, it means the "flats," or land overflowed by the tide.

140. *Sheen.* Shine, light. Used by S. only here and in *M. N. D.* ii. 1. 29, where also it is a rhyming word.

143. *Commutual.* "An intensified form of *mutual*" (Wr.).

146. *Woe is me.* The old form was "woe is to me"=is mine. See Gr. 230.

147. *Cheer.* Cheerfulness. For its original meaning, see *Mer.* p. 152 or *M. N. D.* p. 163.

148. *Distrust you.* "Am solicitous about you" (Schmidt).

150. *For women's*, etc. The quartos have an extra line here:

> "For women feare too much, euen as they love,
> And womens," etc.

Some editors believe that a line, rhyming with *love*, has been lost; others, that the extra line was superseded by 150, but accidentally retained at first in printing. The latter is the more probable explanation.

*Holds quantity* = are proportioned to each other. Cf. *M. N. D.* i. 1. 232: "Things base and vile, holding no quantity," etc. For *holds*, see Gr. 336.

151. *In neither*, etc. "They either contain nothing, or what they contain is in extremes" (Gr. 388*a*).

153. *Sized.* Used by S. only here; but we find *great-sized* (*large-sized*, *small-sized*, etc. are still in colloquial use) in *T. and C.* iii. 3. 147 and v. 10. 26. Theo. quotes *A. and C.* iv. 15. 4.

154. *Littlest.* Walker quotes B. and F., *Queen of Corinth*, iv. 1: "The poorest littlest page." He also gives examples of *gooder* and *goodest*, *badder* and *baddest*, from writers of the time. Chaucer has *badder* in *C. T.* 10538.

157. *Operant.* Active; used by S. only here and in *T. of A.* iv. 3. 25: "most operant poison." For *leave*, see on i. 2. 155; and for the infinitive in *to do*, Gr. 355.

164. *Wormwood.* For the figure, cf. *R. of L.* 893 and *L. L. L.* v. 2. 857.

165. *Instances.* Inducements, motives. Cf. *A. W.* iv. 1. 44: "What's the instance?" *Rich. III.* 3. 2. 25: "wanting instance," etc.

166. *Respects.* Considerations. Cf. iii. 1. 68 above.

167. *Kill . . . dead.* Elze compares *T. A.* iii. 1. 92: "he kill'd me dead." He might have added *M. N. D.* iii. 2. 269: "kill her dead?"

171–196. Mr. and Mrs. Cowden Clarke believe that these are the "dozen or sixteen lines" of ii. 2. 525, because the diction is different from the rest of the dialogue and is signally like Hamlet's own argumentative mood. Sievers, who was the first to try to point out the supposed insertion, had fixed upon 234–239. See on ii. 2. 525 above.

171. *Purpose*, etc. "Purposes last only so long as they are remembered" (M.).

172. *Validity.* Value, efficacy. Cf. *A. W.* v. 3. 192, *T. N.* i. 1. 12, etc.

174. *Fall.* For the "confusion of construction," see Gr. 415. Cf. *destroy* in 180 just below.

176. *Most necessary*, etc. "The performance of a resolution in which only the *resolver* is interested is a debt only to himself, which he may therefore remit at pleasure" (Johnson).

180. *Enactures.* Action (Schmidt); or, perhaps, resolutions (Johnson).

181. *Where joy*, etc. "The very temper that is most cast down with grief is also most capable of joy, and passes from one to the other with slenderest cause" (M.).

184. *Our loves.* The love which others feel for us.

186. *Whether.* See on ii. 2. 17 above, or Gr. 466.

187. *Favourites flies.* The quartos have "favourite," a reading which, as Abbott says (Gr. 333), "completely misses the intention to describe the *crowd* of favourites *scattering in flight* from the fallen patron." Cf. *V. and A.* 1128:

> "She lifts the coffer-lids that close his eyes
> Where, lo! two lamps burnt out in darkness lies."

There, as here, the form seems to be due to the rhyme. See also *Sonn.* 41. 3.

190. *Not needs.* Cf. *Temp.* v. 1. 38: "Whereof the ewe not bites," etc. Gr. 305.

192. *Seasons.* Matures, ripens (Schmidt). Cf. i. 3. 81 above.

194. *Contrary.* The accent on the penult, as in "Mary, Mary, quite contrary," etc. Cf. *K. John*, iv. 2. 198, and *T. of A.* iv. 3. 144. Schmidt adds *W. T.* v. 1. 45: "My lord should to the heavens be contrary;" but there it seems to have the other accent, as in *R. and J.* iii. 2. 64: "What storm is this that blows so contrary?" etc.

198. *Die.* The 3d person imperative, or "subjunctive used imperatively" (Gr. 364). See other examples in the speech that follows, and in 210, 211, etc.

202. *An anchor's cheer.* An anchorite's fare. Steevens quotes the old *Romance of Robert the Devil*, printed by Wynkyn de Worde: "We have robbed and killed nonnes, holy aunkers, preestes;" and again: "the foxe will be an aunker, for he begynneth to preche;" and *The Vision of Piers Plowman:* "As ancres and heremites," etc.

203. *Opposite.* Contrary thing; as in *A. and C.* i. 2. 130. Oftener in S. it is=opponent, adversary; as in v. 2. 62 below. Cf. *Lear*, v. 3. 42:

> "you have the captives
> That were the opposites of this day's strife;"

and *Id.* v. 3. 153: "An unknown opposite."

*Blanks.* Blanches, makes pale; the only instance of the verb in S.

208. *Deeply sworn.* Cf. *Rich. III.* iii. 1. 158: "Thou art sworn as deeply to effect," etc. Wr. quotes *K. John*, iii. 1. 231: "deep-sworn faith."

215. *Argument.* See on 122 above.

The king could hardly be in doubt as to the plot of the play after seeing the "dumb-show." Halliwell asks: "Is it allowable to direct that the king and queen should be whispering confidentially to each other during the dumb-show, and so escape a sight of it?" If the dumb-show is to be introduced on the stage, that would not be a bad way out of the difficulty (see on 118 above). If S. is responsible for the dumb-show, we may consider it a piece of carelessness like making Philostrate in *M. N. D.* speak of shedding "merry tears" at the rehearsal of the clowns' play when he certainly could not have been present at the rehearsal—to say nothing of the fact that the play as rehearsed in iii. 1. is entirely different from the play as acted in v. 1. (see *M. N. D.* p. 122).

220. *Tropically.* By a trope, or "a figure in rhetoric" (*A. Y. L.* v. 1. 45); used by S. nowhere else.

221. *Image.* Representation; as in *Macb.* ii. 3. 83, *Lear*, v. 3. 264, etc.

Cf. 21 above. For *Vienna* the 1st quarto has "Guiana," perhaps due to the short-hand writer's mishearing the name (Coll.).

222. *Duke's.* Elsewhere he is a *king.* Walker shows that *king*, *duke*, and *count* were often confounded in sense. In the mouths of Dull, Armado, and Dogberry, *duke* may have been intended as a blunder, but hardly so in the case of the princess in *L. L. L.* ii. 1. 38. Cf. Viola's use of *count* in *T. N.* v. 1. 263 with *Id.* i. 2. 25.

*Baptista.* Properly a man's name, as in *T. of S.* Hunter says that he has known it to be a female name in England; and it is sometimes so used even in Italy.

224. *Free.* See on ii. 2. 548 above.

225. *Let the gall'd jade.* Apparently a proverb. Steevens quotes Edwards, *Damon and Pythias*, 1582: "I know the gall'd horse will soonest wince;" and Wr. adds from Lyly's *Euphues:* "For well I know none will winch except she bee gawlded." On *jade*, see *Hen. V.* p. 170.

227. *Chorus.* Explaining the action of the play, as in *W. T.*, *R. and J.*, and *Hen. V.* (Delius).

228. *I could interpret*, etc. Alluding to the interpreter who used to sit on the stage at puppet-shows and explain them to the audience. Cf. *T. G. of V.* ii. 1. 101 and *T. of A.* i. 1. 34. Steevens quotes Greene, *Groatsworth of Wit:* "It was I that . . . for seven years' space was absolute interpreter of the puppets." In the present passage some of the critics see an indirect meaning; but, as Schmidt remarks, it is more probable that the allusion is simply "to a puppet-show in which Ophelia and her lover were to play a part."

232. *The croaking raven*, etc. Mr. Simpson (in the London *Academy*, Dec. 19, 1874) says: "Hamlet rolls into one two lines of an old familiar play, *The True Tragedie of Richard the Third:*

> "The screeking raven sits croking for revenge,
> Whole herds of beasts comes bellowing for revenge."

235. *Confederate.* Conspiring, favouring, assisting.

236. *Midnight weeds.* Steevens compares *Macb.* iv. 1. 25: "Root of hemlock digg'd i' the dark."

237. *Hecate.* For the pronunciation, see *Macb.* p. 187.

239. *On wholesome life usurp.* Wr. compares *Per.* iii. 2. 82: "Death may usurp on nature many hours." Add *T. A.* iii. 1. 269.

250. *Strucken.* The folio reading; the quartos have "strooken" or "stroken." See *J. C.* p. 146 or Gr. 344.

The stanza is probably a quotation from some ballad (D.).

254. *Feathers.* Much worn on the stage in the time of S. (Malone).

255. *Turn Turk.* Proverbially = to undergo a complete change for the worse (Schmidt). Cf. *Much Ado*, iii. 4. 57. Steevens quotes Cook, *Green's Tu Quoque:* "This it is to turn Turk, from an absolute and most compleat gentleman, to a most absurd, ridiculous, and fond lover."

*Provincial.* Some make this refer to Provence, others to Provins near Paris. Both were famous for their roses. The reference is to rosettes of ribbon worn on shoes. Fairholt quotes *Friar Bacon's Prophecy*, 1604:

"When roses in the gardens grew,
And not in ribbons on a shoe;
Now ribbon-roses take such place,
That garden-roses want their grace."

Tschischwitz (who is much given to these fantastic tricks of emendation —God save the mark!) is sure that S. wrote "provisional roses!"

256. *Razed.* Slashed; that is, with cuts or openings in them (Steevens). Stubbes, in his *Anatomie of Abuses*, 1585, has a chapter on corked shoes, which, he says, are "some of black veluet, some of white, some of red, some of greene, razed, carued, cut, and stitched all ouer with Silke." Theo. conjectured "rais'd," that is, with high heels. Schmidt wavers between these two explanations.

*Cry.* Company; literally, a pack of hounds. Cf. *Cor.* iii. 3. 120: "You common cry of curs!" (see also iv. 6. 148); *Oth.* ii. 3. 370: "not like a hound that hunts, but one that fills up the cry," etc.

258. *Share.* "The actors in our author's time had not annual salaries as at present. The whole receipts of each theatre were divided into *shares*, of which the proprietors of the theatre, or *house-keepers*, as they were called, had some; and each actor had one or more shares, or part of a share, according to his merit" (Malone).

259. *A whole one, I.* Malone's conjecture of "ay" for *I* has been adopted by Sr., W., and H. The meaning, as it stands, is "A whole one, say I" (Caldecott). *Ay* is always printed "I" in the old eds.

263. *Pajock.* Peacock; which is substituted by Pope, Warb., Coll., Sr., H., and others. The quartos have "paiock," the 1st folio "Paiocke," the 2d "Pajocke," etc. D. says: "I have often heard the lower classes in the north of Scotland call the peacock the 'pea-jock;' and their almost invariable name for the turkey-cock is 'bubbly-jock.'" Among the changes suggested, where none is needed, are "paddock," "hedjocke" (=hedgehog), "patchock" (=a clown), "Polack," etc.

264. *Rhymed.* "The natural rhyme, of course, is easily discerned, and expresses his contempt for his uncle, who has shown, as he intimates, consummate weakness in allowing himself to be so easily unmasked" (M.).

266. *Pound.* Cf. *Rich. II.* ii. 2. 91: "a thousand pound;" and see note in our ed. p. 182.

270. *Recorders.* A kind of flageolet. See *M. N. D.* p. 183.

273. *Perdy.* A corruption of *par Dieu.* Cf. *Hen. V.* ii. 1. 52, etc.

280. *Marvellous.* For the adverbial use, cf. ii. 1. 3 above.

*Distempered.* Discomposed, disturbed. Cf. *Temp.* iv. 1. 145: "touch'd with anger so distemper'd," etc. The word was also used of bodily disorder (as in 2 *Hen. IV.* iii. 1. 41), and so Hamlet pretends to understand it (Wr.).

283. *Should.* Would. See on ii. 2. 202 above; and for *more richer* on ii. 1. 11.

284. *Put him to his purgation.* "A play upon the legal and medical senses of the word" (Wr.). Cf. *A. Y. L.* v. 4. 45, *Hen. VIII.* v. 3. 152, etc.

286. *Into some frame.* That is, "frame of sense" (*M. for M.* v. 1. 61). Cf. *L. L. L.* iii. 1. 193: "out of frame" (that is, disordered).

288. *Pronounce.* Speak out, say on. Cf. *Temp.* iii. 3. 76, *Macb.* iii. 4. 7, etc.

295. *Pardon.* Leave to go. See on i. 2. 56 above.

298. *Wholesome.* Reasonable (Schmidt); or sane, sensible (Wr.). Cf. *Cor.* ii. 3. 66:

> "Speak to 'em, I pray you,
> In wholesome manner."

303. *Admiration.* Wonder; as in i. 2. 192 above.

307. *Closet.* Chamber; as in ii. 1. 77, iii. 3. 27, etc. Cf. *Matt.* vi. 6.

310. *Trade.* Business. Cf. *T. N.* iii. 1. 83: "if your trade be to her," etc.

312. *Pickers and stealers.* Hands; which the church catechism admonishes us to keep from "picking and stealing" (Whalley).

313. *Your cause of distemper.* The cause of your distemper. Cf. i. 4. 73: "your sovereignty of reason;" and see Gr. 423 for other examples.

317. *The voice,* etc. Cf. i. 2. 109 (Malone).

319. *While the grass grows.* Malone quotes the whole proverb from Whetstone's *Promos and Cassandra,* 1578: "Whylst grass doth growe, oft sterves the seely steede;" and again in the *Paradise of Daintie Devises,* 1578: "While grass doth growe, the silly horse he starves."

321. *To withdraw with you.* "A much-vexed passage, probably = to speak a word in private with you" (Schmidt). M. Mason proposed "So, withdraw you" or "So withdraw, will you?" St. takes it to be addressed to the players, and would read "So, (*taking a recorder*) withdraw with you." Tschischwitz conjectures "Go, withdraw with you."

322. *Go about.* Undertake, attempt. See *M. N. D.* p. 177 or *Hen. V.* p. 174.

*To recover the wind of me.* A hunting term, meaning to get to windward of the game, so that it may not scent the toil or its pursuers (Sr.). Cf. *Gentleman's Recreation:* "Observe how the wind is, that you may set the net so as the hare and wind may come together; if the wind be sideways it may do well enough, but never if it blow over the net into the hare's face, for he will scent both it and you at a distance;" also Churchyard, *Worthiness of Wales:*

> "Their cunning can with craft so cloke a troeth
> That hardly we shall have them in the winde,
> To smell them forth or yet their fineness finde."

324. *If my duty,* etc. If my sense of duty makes me too bold, it is my *love* for you that causes it. *Bold* and *unmannerly* have essentially the same meaning. Tyrwhitt wanted to read "not unmannerly."

333. *Ventages.* Vents, holes.

345. *'Sblood.* See on ii. 2. 358 above. These oaths were extremely common in that day, and indeed much earlier. Chaucer (*C. T.* 13886) makes the Pardoner say:

> "Her othes been so greet and so dampnable,
> That it is grisly for to hiere hem swere.
> Our blisful Lordes body thay to-tere;
> Hem thoughte Jewes rent him nought y-nough."

347. *Fret.* Douce notes the play upon the word: "though you can

vex me, you cannot impose upon me; though you can stop the instrument, you cannot play on it." *Frets* are stops, or "small lengths of wire on which the fingers press the strings in playing the guitar" (Busby's *Dict. of Musical Terms*). Cf. North, *Plutarch* (*Pericles*): "Rhetoric and eloquence (as Plato saith) is an art which quickeneth men's spirits at her pleasure; and her chiefest skill is to know how to move passions and affections thoroughly, which are as stops and sounds of the soul, that would be played upon with a fine-fingered hand of a cunning master."

358. *By and by.* Presently, soon; as often in S. See *Hen. V.* p. 155.

359. *To the top of my bent.* To the utmost, as much as I could wish. For *bent*, see on ii. 2. 30 above.

363. *'Tis now*, etc. Cf. *Macb.* ii. 1. 49 fol.

366. *Bitter business.* The folio reading; the quartos have "such business as the bitter day."

369. *Nero.* For another allusion to his murder of his mother, see *K. John*, v. 2. 152.

371. *Speak daggers.* Cf. iii. 4. 93: "These words like daggers enter in mine ears;" and *Much Ado*, ii. 1. 255: "She speaks poniards, and every word stabs." See also *Prov.* xii. 18 (Wr.).

*Use none.* Hunter says: "To be sure not; and strange it is that the Poet should have thought it necessary to put such a remark into the mouth of Hamlet," etc. It is not necessary to suppose that Hamlet had seriously thought of killing his mother. He may be recalling the injunction of the Ghost: Revenge my murder, but only on your uncle, not on your mother. And yet he must *speak* daggers to her, though he is to use none against her.

373. *How . . . soever.* For the tmesis, cf. i. 5. 170 above; also *M. W.* iv. 2. 25, etc. *How* is sometimes = however; as in *Much Ado*, iii. 1. 60:

> "I never yet saw man,
> How wise, how noble, young, how rarely featur'd,
> But she would spell him backward," etc.

*Shent.* "Put to the blush, shamed, reproached" (Schmidt). Cf. *M. W.* i. 4. 38: "We shall all be shent;" *Cor.* v. 2. 104: "Do you hear how we are shent?" etc. It is the participle of *shend*, which is found (= destroy) in Fairfax's *Tasso*, vi. 4: "But we must yield whom hunger soon will shend." Cf. Spenser, *F. Q.* ii. 8. 12:

> "Thou dotard vile,
> That with thy brutenesse shendst thy comely age," etc.

374. *Give them seals.* Confirm them by action. Cf. *Cor.* ii. 3. 115: "I will not seal your knowledge with showing them;" 2 *Hen. IV.* iv. 5. 104: "Thou hast seal'd up my expectation," etc.

Scene III.—3. *Your commission.* "Rosencrantz and Guildenstern are therefore privy to the traitorous scheme for killing Hamlet in England" (M.).

4. *Shall along.* For the omission of the verb, see Gr. 30 and cf. 405.

6. *So near us.* The quarto reading; the folio has "so dangerous," which does not suit the context so well.

7. *Lunacies.* The folio reading; that of the quartos is "browes," which Theo. took to be a misprint of "lunes" = lunacies.

9. *Many many.* Cf. *K. John*, i. 1. 183: "many a many foot." Wr. compares *Hen. V.* iv. 2. 33: "A very little little let us do." The Coll. MS. reads "very many."

11. *The single and peculiar life.* That is, the private individual (Wr.).

13. *Noyance.* Injury; not to be printed "'noyance," as it often is. Cf. Spenser, *F. Q.* iii. 12. 2:

> "A direfull stench of smoke and sulphure mixt
> Ensewd, whose noyaunce fild the feareful sted
> From the fourth howre of night untill the sixt."

14. *Depends and rests.* For the singular form, see Gr. 335.

15. *Cease.* Decease. The only other instance of *cease* as a noun noted by Schmidt is in *Lear*, v. 3. 264, where he thinks it may be a verb.

16. *Gulf.* Whirlpool; as often. Cf. *R. of L.* 557, *Hen. V.* ii. 4. 10, iv. 3. 82, etc.

17. *Massy.* S. uses the word five times (cf. *Temp.* iii. 3. 67, *Much Ado*, iii. 3. 147, *T. and C.* prol. 17, ii. 3. 18), *massive* not at all. See quotation in note on iii. 1. 77 above.

21. *Annexment.* A word not found elsewhere (Wr.). *Annexion* occurs in *L. C.* 208.

24. *Arm you.* Prepare yourselves. Cf. *M. N. D.* i. 1. 117:

> "For you, fair Hermia, look you arm yourself
> To fit your fancies to your father's will."

25. *Fear.* Object of fear; as in *M. N. D.* v. 1. 21:

> "Or in the night, imagining some fear,
> How easy is a bush suppos'd a bear!"

26. *We will haste us.* See Gr. 212.

Elze gives this speech to Rosencrantz alone, on the ground that he is regularly the spokesman, while Guildenstern seems to be a subordinate attendant; but the king and queen treat them both alike as "gentlemen" (see ii. 2. 1–26, 33, 34, etc.), and so does Hamlet (ii. 2. 224, etc.). Elze cites iv. 3. 16, which is sufficiently explained by the context.

29. *Tax him home.* Reprove him soundly. See on i. 4. 18 above. Cf. iii. 4. 1 below; also *M. for M.* iv. 3. 148: "Accuse him home and home," etc.

30. *As you said.* "Polonius's own suggestion, which, courtier-like, he ascribes to the king" (M.).

32. *Them.* That is, mothers.

33. *Of vantage.* By some opportunity of secret observation (Warb.). Cf. Gr. 165.

37. *Eldest.* Used now only in the sense of eldest-born. Cf. *Temp.* v. 1. 186: "your eld'st acquaintance cannot be three hours."

39. *Will.* Hanmer substituted "'t will" and Warb. "th' ill;" but *inclination* and *will* are not identical. As Boswell says, "I may *will* to do a thing because my understanding points it out to me as right, though I am not *inclined* to it."

42. *In pause.* In doubt or consideration. Cf. iii. 1. 68 above.

47. *Confront.* To face, or rather outface.

49. *To be forestalled*, etc. "What is the very meaning of prayer, except that we pray first not to be led into temptation, and then to be delivered from evil?" (M.). On *forestall*=prevent, cf. v. 2. 207 below.

55. *Ambition.* The realization of my ambition; the cause for the effect, like *offence* in the next line (Delius). Cf. *theft* in iii. 2. 84.

57. *Currents.* Courses (Schmidt). D. and F. adopt Walker's conjecture of "'currents"="occurrents" (see v. 2. 345 below); but the mixing or blending of metaphors is no worse than in the use of the very same word in iii. 1. 87 above; and though, as F. pleads, it is easily avoided here by the apostrophe, we prefer to stick to the old text.

59. *Prize.* The Coll. MS. has "purse;" but the meaning obviously is that the guilty gain itself (or a part of it) is used to bribe the officers of the law; as has often happened in these latter days.

61. *Lies.* Used in the legal sense (Wr.).

62. *His.* Its. See Gr. 228; and for the ellipsis of the auxiliary with *compell'd*, Gr. 403 (cf. 95).

64. *Rests.* Remains. See *A. Y. L.* p. 146.

65. *Can.* Can do. Cf. *Temp.* iv. 1. 27: "Our worser genius can," etc. Gr. 307.

68. *Limed.* Caught (as with bird-lime). Cf. *R. of L.* 88: "Birds never lim'd no secret bushes fear." See also 3 *Hen. VI.* v. 6. 13, 17, *Macb.* iv. 2. 34, etc.

69. *Engaged.* Entangled. It is curious that neither Worc. nor Wb. recognizes this meaning, though both give "disentangle" as one of the meanings of *disengage*. Cf. Milton, *Comus*, 193: "They had engag'd their wandering steps too far;" and *P. R.* iii. 347 (where Satan is trying to ensnare Christ):

> "That thou mayst know I seek not to engage
> Thy virtue," etc.

In architecture, *engaged* columns are probably so called because they are caught or entangled, as it were, in the wall.

*Make assay.* According to Brae (quoted by F.), *assay* here=charge, onset, and *make assay*="throng to the rescue." Cf. *Hen. V.* i. 2. 151: "Galling the gleaned land with hot assays;" and ii. 2. 71 above: "the assay of arms." This meaning is not recognized by Worc. or Wb., but Schmidt gives it for the two passages just quoted. Here he makes *assay* =trial; but the other meaning would be at once more forcible and more poetical. J. H. thinks that *make assay* is addressed to himself, not to the angels.

73. *Pat, now.* The quartos have "but now." For *pat*, cf. *M. N. D.* iii. 1. 2, v. 1. 188, and *Lear*, i. 2. 146.

This speech has been considered inhuman and unworthy of Hamlet. According to Coleridge, it is rather his way of excusing himself for putting off the act of vengeance. It seems better, however, with M., to regard this notion of killing soul and body at once as the natural impulse of his mind. It does not strike us as unnatural that the sight of the king at prayer should suggest the idea that killing him then and there would be sending him straight to heaven, and that for the moment Hamlet should shrink from doing this. His first thought is not so much of sending him to hell as of *not* sending him to heaven; but he dwells upon it in his usual meditative fashion until it leads him logically to that "damn'd and black" conclusion.

Caldecott says: "Shakespeare had a full justification in the practice of the age in which he lived . . . With our ruder Northern ancestors, revenge, in general, was handed down in families as a duty, and the more refined and exquisite, the more honourable it was." He also refers to iv. 7. 127 below, where the king says "Revenge should have no bounds;" and adds that "even the philosophizing and moralizing Squire of Kent, in his beloved retirement from the turmoils of the world, exclaims on killing Cade (2 *Hen. VI.* iv. 10. 83):

> 'Die, damned wretch, the curse of her that bare thee;
> And as I thrust thy body in with my sword,
> So wish I, I might thrust thy soul to hell.'"

Wordsworth (*Shakespeare's Knowledge of the Bible*) excuses Hamlet in much the same way. See also p. 30 above.

75. *That would be scann'd.* That should be carefully considered. Gr. 329.

77. *Sole.* The folio has "foule." Warb. conjectured "fal'n" (=disinherited), and Capell "fool." Cf. *A. W.* i. 1. 44: "His sole child," etc.

79. *Hire and salary.* The quartos have "base and silly."

80. *Grossly.* The word refers to *father*, not to *took*. *Full of bread*, as Malone notes, is suggested by *Ezekiel*, xvi. 49: "pride, fulness of bread," etc.

81. *Broad blown.* Cf. i. 5. 76: "in the blossoms of my sin." *Flush*= in its prime, in full vigour (Schmidt). Cf. *A. and C.* i. 4. 52: "flush youth." The folio has "fresh."

82. *And how*, etc. Warb. says that the Ghost had told him how his audit stood; but Ritson replies that, the Ghost being in purgatory, it was doubtful how long he might have to stay there.

83. *In our circumstance and course of thought.* From our human point of view and according to our line of thought; or "according to human relations and thoughts" (Delius). For *circumstance*=condition, state of things, cf. *T. G. of V.* i. 1. 37: "So, by your circumstance, I fear you 'll prove." See also i. 3. 102 above.

84. *'T is heavy with him.* It goes hard with him, or he "hath a heavy reckoning to make" (*Hen. V.* iv. 1. 141).

85. *To take.* For the "indefinite" use of the infinitive, see Gr. 356. On *purging*, cf. i. 5. 13 above; and on *season'd*, iii. 2. 192.

88. *Hent.* Hold, seizure (Johnson and Schmidt). No other example of the noun has been found, but the verb (=take) occurs in *W. T.* iv. 3. 133 and *M. for M.* iv. 6. 14. Cf. Chaucer, *C. T.* 700: "till Jhesu Crist him hente," etc. *A more horrid hent*="a more fell grasp on the villain" (M.), or "a more terrible occasion to be grasped" (Wr.).

95. *Stays.* Is waiting for me. Cf. *T. G. of V.* i. 2. 131: "Dinner is ready, and your father stays," etc.

96. *This physic.* That is, this temporary forbearance of mine is like a medicine that merely delays the fatal end of the disease.

SCENE IV.—1. *Straight.* See on ii. 2. 418 above; and for *home*, on iii. 3. 29.

2. *Broad.* Free, unrestrained. Cf. *Macb.* iii. 4. 23 and iii. 6. 21.

4. *Silence.* The reading of the early eds. Sr., Coll., D., H., and Wr. adopt Hanmer's emendation, "Sconce me even here," which is plausible, but not really called for. *I 'll silence me e'en here*=I 'll say no more.

5. *Round.* See on ii. 2. 139 above.

7. *Fear me not.* See on i. 3. 51 above.

12. *Wicked.* The folio has "idle," probably repeated by accident from the preceding line.

14. *Rood.* Cross, crucifix. Cf. 2 *Hen. IV.* iii. 2. 3, *Rich. III.* iii. 2. 77, iv. 4. 165, etc. We have it in the name of *Holyrood Palace*, Edinburgh. See also 1 *Hen. IV.* i. 1. 52.

19. *Set you up a glass.* Cf. iii. 2. 20 above: "hold, as 't were, the mirror up to nature."

29. *Kill a king?* According to the *Hystorie of Hamblet* (see p. 13 above) the queen was not privy to the murder of her husband. Cf. the 1st quarto:

> "But as I haue a soule, I sweare by heauen,
> I neuer knew of this most horride murder."

34. *Wringing of.* Cf. i. 5. 175: "pronouncing of," etc. Gr. 178.

38. *Proof.* Cf. *W. T.* iv. 4. 872: "I am proof against that title," etc. But the word in this sense was also a noun, as in *Rich. II.* i. 3. 73: "Add proof unto mine armour," etc. Cf. ii. 2. 476 above: "forg'd for proof eterne." Schmidt makes it an adjective here, but its association with *bulwark* suggests that it may be a noun. Cf. *V. and A.* 626:

> "His brawny sides, with hairy bristles arm'd,
> Are better proof than thy spear's point can enter."

This seems better than to say that *bulwark* is "used for an adjective," as Wr. does.

*Sense.* "Feeling," as Caldecott explains it, rather than "reason," as Schmidt makes it.

39. *Wag thy tongue.* Wr. quotes *Hen. VIII.* i. 1. 33: "Durst wag his tongue in censure." He might have added *Id.* v. 3. 127: "And think with wagging of your tongue to win me." In the same speech (131), we have "wag his finger at thee."

41. *That.* For *such . . . that*, see Gr. 279. Just below we have *such . . . as.* Cf. *Sonn.* 73. 5. 9.

43. *The rose.* "The *ornament*, the *grace*, of an innocent love" (Boswell). Cf. iii. 1. 152 above.

44. *Sets a blister there.* Wr. explains this, "brands as a harlot," and refers to *C. of E.* ii. 2. 138. Cf. iv. 5. 101 below.

46. *Contraction.* The marriage contract (Warb. and Schmidt). S. uses the word nowhere else.

48. *Rhapsody.* Wr. well illustrates the meaning of the word here by quoting Florio, *Montaigne*: "This concerneth not those mingle-mangles of many kindes of stuffe, or as the Grecians call them *Rapsodies.*"

49. *This solidity*, etc. The earth (K.).

50. *Tristful.* Sorrowful (Fr. *triste*). Cf. 1 *Hen. IV.* ii. 4. 434: "My tristful queen" ("trustful" in the early eds.).

*As against the doom.* As if doomsday were coming. For *against*, see on i. 1. 158.

51. *Thought-sick.* Cf. iii. 1. 85: "Sicklied o'er with the pale cast of thought." Tschischwitz ("O dear discretion! how his words are suited!") omits the hyphen, and explains the passage, "Is thought to be sick!"

52. *Index.* Prologue. The index was formerly placed at the beginning of a book (Edwards). Cf. *Rich. III.* ii. 2. 149, iv. 4. 85, *T. and C.* i. 3. 343, and *Oth.* ii. 1. 263.

53. *Look here*, etc. The original practice of the stage seems to have been to have the two pictures hanging in the queen's closet. They are so represented in a print prefixed to Rowe's *Hamlet*, published in 1709. Afterwards it became the fashion for Hamlet to take two miniatures from his pocket; but as Hamlet would not be likely to carry his uncle's picture in that way, a Bath actor suggested snatching it from his mother's neck. Another arrangement was to have the new king's portrait hanging on the wall, while Hamlet took his father's from his bosom. Fitzgerald, in his *Life of Garrick*, suggested that the pictures be seen with the mind's eye only; and this is followed by Irving and Salvini. Fechter tears the miniature from the queen's neck and throws it away. Edwin Booth makes use of two miniatures, taking one from his own neck and the other from the queen's (F.).

54. *Counterfeit.* Cf. the use of the noun in *Sonn.* 16. 8: "your painted counterfeit;" and see also *M. of V.* iii. 2. 116 and *T. of A.* v. 1. 83.

*Presentment.* Representation. In the only other instance of the word in S. (*T. of A.* i. 1. 27) it means presentation. Wr. quotes Milton, *Comus*, 156:

> "Of power to cheat the eye with blear illusion,
> And give it false presentments."

55. *This brow.* The 4th and 5th quarto and the folios have "his."

56. *Hyperion's.* See on i. 2. 140 above.

*The front of Jove.* That is, the forehead; as in *Rich. III.* i. 1. 9: "his wrinkled front," etc. See cut on p. 166.

58. *Station.* Attitude in standing (Theo.). Cf. *Macb.* v. 8. 42 and *A. and C.* iii. 3. 22.

59. *New-lighted.* Cf. 1 *Hen. IV.* i. 1. 63: "new-lighted from his horse." S. is fond of compounds with *new*; as "new-added" (*J. C.* iv. 3. 109), "new-apparelled" (*C. of E.* iv. 3. 14), "new-built" (*T. of S.* v. 2. 118, *Cymb.* i. 5. 59), "new-crowned" (*M. of V.* iii. 2. 50, *K. John*, iv. 2. 35), "new-fallen" (*V. and A.* 354, *A. Y. L.* v. 4. 182, 1 *Hen. IV.* v. 1. 44), and so on.

*Heaven-kissing.* Cf. *R. of L.* 1370: "cloud-kissing Ilion."

66. *Leave.* See on i. 2. 155 above.

67. *Batten.* Fatten. Cf. *Cor.* iv. 5. 35: "batten on cold bits;" Milton, *Lycidas*, 29: "battening our flocks," etc.

69. *Hey-day.* "Frolicsome wildness" (Schmidt). Steevens quotes Ford, '*T is Pity*, etc.: "The hey-day of your luxury." S. does not use

it elsewhere as a noun. We have it as an exclamation in *Temp.* ii. 2. 190 ("highday" in the old eds.), *Rich. III.* iv. 4. 460, *T. and C.* v. 1. 73, and *T. of A.* i. 2. 137 (in these last three passages "hoyday" in most of the early eds.). *Highday* in *M. of V.* ii. 9. 98 is another word=holiday.

71–76. *Sense . . . difference.* This passage is omitted in the folio. *Sense*=sensibility, sensation; and *motion*=impulse, desire (as in *M. for M.* i. 4. 59: "The wanton stings and motions of the sense," etc.). "You must have perception, else how could you still have desire?" (M.).

73. *Apoplex'd.* Affected as with apoplexy.

*Would not err.* That is, err so (Wr.).

74. *Ecstasy.* Insanity; as in ii. 1. 102 and iii. 1. 160 above.

75. *Quantity.* Measure, degree. "Sense was never so dominated by the delusions of insanity but that it retained some power of choice" (H.). *Quantity* is sometimes used contemptuously (=an insignificant portion), as in *C. of E.* iv. 3. 112, *K. John*, v. 4. 23, and 2 *Hen. IV.* v. 1. 70.

76. *To serve*, etc. "To help your decision where the difference is so complete" (M.).

77. *Hoodman-blind.* Blind-man's-buff. Cf. *A. W.* iv. 3. 136: "Hoodman comes!" Sr. quotes Baret, *Alvearie:* "The Hoodwinke play, or hoodmanblinde, in some places called the blindmanbuf."

79. *Sans.* See *A. Y. L.* p. 163 or *Temp.* p. 114.

81. *So mope.* Be so stupid. Cf. *Temp.* v. 1. 239: "And were brought moping hither" (that is, bewildered); and *Hen. V.* iii. 7. 143: "to mope with his fat-brained followers."

83. *Mutine.* The same as *mutiny* (=rebel), which S. elsewhere uses. We find *mutine* as a noun (=a rebel) in v. 2. 6 below, and also in *K. John*, ii. 1. 378. *Mutineer* occurs once (*Temp.* iii. 2. 40), and so does *mutiner* (*Cor.* i. 1. 254).

86. *Compulsive.* Cf. *compulsative*, i. 1. 103 above. *Compulsive* occurs again in *Oth.* iii. 3. 454. On *gives the charge*, cf. *R. of L.* 434.

88. *Panders will.* Panders to appetite.

90. *Grained.* Dyed in grain. Marsh (*Lect. on Eng. Lang.*) shows that *grain* originally meant the dye *kermes*, obtained from the coccus insect; but as this sense grew less familiar, and the word came to be used chiefly as expressive of *fastness* of colour, an idea which was associated with dyeing *in the wool* or other raw material, *dyed in grain* got this latter meaning. Wr. quotes Cotgrave, *Fr. Dict.:* "Graine: . . . graine wherewith cloth is dyed in graine; Scarlet dye, Scarlet in graine."

91. *Leave their tinct.* Part with or give up their dye. On *leave*, cf. *M. of V.* v. 1. 172, 196, *Cor.* ii. 3. 180, etc.; and on *tinct*, cf. *Cymb.* ii. 2. 23. The latter word=tincture in *A. W.* v. 3. 102 and *A. and C.* i. 5. 37.

94. *In.* Into. See Gr. 159.

97. *Precedent.* Former; used also in *T. of A.* i. 1. 133 and *A. and C.* v. 14. 83, and with the same accent as here. The *noun* is always accented on the first syllable. See v. 2. 237 below; also *M. of V.* iv. 1. 220, etc.

*A vice of kings.* A clown of a king; alluding to the *Vice* in the old moralities or moral-plays. Cf. *T. N.* iv. 2. 134:

> "Like to the old Vice,
> . . . . .
> Who, with dagger of lath,
> In his rage and his wrath,
> Cries, ah, ha! to the devil," etc.

The Vice was equipped with a wooden sword or dagger, with which he used to beat the devil and sometimes tried to pare his nails. Cf. 2 *Hen. IV.* iii. 2. 343 and *Hen. V.* iv. 4. 76.

98. *Cutpurse.* "Purses were usually worn outside attached to the girdle" (Wr.).

101. *A king of shreds and patches.* Referring to the motley dress worn by the professional fool (see *A. Y. L.* p. 162) and generally by the Vice.

102. The stage-direction in the 1st quarto is "*Enter the Ghost in his night gowne;*" that is, in his dressing-gown. See *Macb.* p. 194. The Coll. MS. has "*Enter Ghost unarmed.*"

*Save me*, etc. M. remarks here: "Just when Hamlet's rage is on the verge of becoming impotent and verbose, it is restored to overpowering grandeur by the ghost's reappearance, . . . who with divine compassion interferes to save his erring wife from distraction. Cf. the splendid passage in Tennyson's *Guinevere*, where Arthur says to his false queen:

> 'I did not come to curse thee, Guinevere,
> I whose vast pity almost makes me die
> To see thee laying there thy golden head . . .
> Lo, I forgive thee, as Eternal God
> Forgives; do thou for thine own soul the rest . . .
> Let no man dream but that I love thee still—
> Perchance, and so thou purify thy soul,
> And so thou lean on our fair father Christ,
> Hereafter, in that world where all are pure,
> We too may meet before high God, and thou
> Wilt spring to me, and claim me thine, and know
> I am thine husband.'"

105. *Laps'd in time and passion.* The meaning seems to be, having let time slip by while indulging in mere passion. Johnson says: "having suffered time to slip and passion to cool;" and Schmidt: "who, surprised by you in a time and passion fit for the execution of your command, lets them go by."

106. *Important.* Momentous; or, perhaps, urgent (as in *C. of E.* v. 1. 138, *Much Ado*, ii. 1. 74, etc.).

112. *Conceit.* Imagination. Cf. *W. T.* iii. 2. 145: "with mere conceit and fear;" *Rich. II.* ii. 2. 33: "'T is nothing but conceit," etc.

116. *Incorporal.* Immaterial. Cf. *corporal* in *J. C.* iv. 1. 33, *Macb.* i. 3. 81, etc. S. uses neither *corporeal* nor *incorporeal.*

119. *Bedded.* Lying flat (Schmidt). Wr. explains it as "matted."

*Hair.* The quartos and 1st and 2d folios have "haire," and are followed by most of the modern eds. The Camb. and W. give "hairs." S. uses the plural very often in this way. Cf. *M. of V.* iii. 2. 120, *J. C.* ii. 1. 144, *A. and C.* ii. 7. 123, etc.

*Excrements.* Excrescences, outgrowths (as if from *excrescere*, like *increment* from *increscere*). Cf. *C. of E.* ii. 2. 79, *L. L. L.* v. 1. 109, *M. of V.*

iii. 2. 87, and *W. T.* iv. 4. 734. See *Mer.* p. 149. S. uses the word only once in its modern sense (*T. of A.* iv. 3. 445).

120. *Start . . . stand.* The reading of the early quartos and the folio. For *an end*, see on i. 5. 19 above.

121. *Distemper.* Cf. ii. 2. 55 and iii. 2. 280 above.

125. *Capable.* Capable of feeling, susceptible. Cf. *A. Y. L.* iii. 5. 23: "the capable impressure." See also iii. 2. 10 above, and cf. *incapable*= insensible, in iv. 7. 177 below.

127. *Effects.* Action (Schmidt). Cf. *V. and A.* 605, *Lear*, i. 1. 188, etc. *Convert my stern effects*=change my stern action, or the execution of my stern purpose.

128. *Will want true colour.* Will lose its proper character. Caldecott compares "leave their tinct" in 91 above.

133. *In his habit*, etc. In his dress as when alive. See on 102 above.

136. *Ecstasy.* See on 74 above. The meaning here is evident from Hamlet's reply.

141. *Re-word.* Repeat in the same words. Cf. *L. C.* 1, where it is applied to the echo.

142. *For love.* For the omission of *the*, see Gr. 89.

148. *What is to come.* Seymour would read "what else will come," as what *is to come* cannot be *avoided;* but this is to change rhetoric to logic, poetry to prose. Of course Hamlet means what is to come if the future is to be like the past, but it was not necessary to state it in that precise way.

150. *Forgive*, etc. Possibly St. is right in taking this to be addressed to his own *virtue*, and marking it "aside." Clarke says: "Surely the context shows that Hamlet asks his mother to pardon the candour of his virtuous reproof, emphasizing it by line 151."

151. *Pursy.* "Swelled with pampering" (Schmidt). Cf. *T. of A.* v. 4. 12: "pursy insolence."

153. *Curb and woo.* "Bend and truckle" (Steevens); "bow and beg" (Wr.). *Curb* is the Fr. *courber*, and is printed "courb" in the folio. Perhaps it is as well to retain that spelling, as Theo., Warb., F., and some others do. Cf. *Piers Plowman:*

> "Thanne I courbed on my knees,
> And cried hire of grace."

Schmidt makes *curb* here="keep back, refrain."

154. "Note the use of the more affectionate *thou*" (F.). See Gr. 231.

155. *Worser.* Often used by S. See *R. of L.* 249, 294, 453, *M. N. D.* ii. 1. 208, *Rich. III.* i. 3. 102, etc.

M. remarks here: "The manly compassion of a pure heart to the weak and fallen could not express itself with more happy persuasiveness than in this reply, which takes the unhappy queen's mere wail of sorrow and transmutes it to a soul-strengthening resolve."

159–163. *That monster . . . put on.* This is omitted in the folio. Many attempts have been made to emend it, but without really amending it. As it stands, the meaning seems to be: That monster, custom, who destroys all sensibility (or sensitiveness), the evil genius of our habits (that is, bad ones), is yet an angel in this respect, that it tends to give to our good actions also the ease and readiness of habit. M. paraphrases the latter part of the passage thus: "Just as a new dress or uniform becomes familiar to us by habit, so custom enables us readily to execute the outward and practical part of the good and fair actions which we inwardly desire to do." No doubt, as Wr. remarks, the double meaning of *habits* suggested the *frock or livery.*

165–168. *The next more . . . potency.* Omitted in the folio.

167. *And either master the*, etc. The 2d and 3d quartos have "And either the;" the 4th, "And Maister the;" the 5th, "And master the." The gap in the earlier text has been filled by "curb," "quell," "mate," "lay," "house," "aid," "mask," "shame," etc. *Master* may have been a mere conjecture of the editor of the 4th quarto, but it has at least that much of authority in its favour, and completes the sense as well as any other word. It has been objected that it mars the metre; but if we read it "master th' devil," it is like a hundred other lines in S. This reading is adopted by Walker, D. (2d ed.), and F. "Curb" is preferred by Sr., W., and H. Furnivall suggests "tame."

169. *To be blest.* By God; that is, when you are repentant.

170. *For.* As for. Cf. i. 5. 139 above. Gr. 149.

172. *To punish me*, etc. "To punish me by making me the instrument of this man's death, and to punish this man by my hand" (Malone).

173. *Their.* For other examples of the plural use of *heaven*, see *Rich. II.* p. 157. Cf. *heavens*, ii. 2. 38 above.

174. *Bestow him.* Dispose of him, put him out of the way. Cf. *M. W.* iv. 2. 48: "Which way should he go? how should I bestow him? Shall I put him into the basket again?" See also on ii. 2. 508 above.

*Answer.* Account for. Cf. *T. N.* iii. 3. 28: "were I ta'en here it would scarce be answer'd;" *W. T.* i. 2. 83: "The offences we have made you do we 'll answer," etc.

180. *Bloat.* Bloated. See on i. 2. 20 above, or Gr. 342.

181. *Mouse.* For its use as a term of endearment, cf. *L. L. L.* v. 2. 19 and *T. N.* i. 5. 69. Steevens quotes Warner, *Albion's England:* "God bless thee, mouse, the bridegroom said;" and Burton, *Anat. of Melancholy:* "pleasant names may be invented, bird, mouse, lamb, pus, pigeon, etc."

182. *Reechy.* Dirty. Cf. *Much Ado*, iii. 3. 143: "the reechy painting;" and *Cor.* ii. 1. 225: "her reechy neck." The word is only another form of *reeky*, soiled with smoke or *reek* (cf. *M. W.* iii. 3. 86).

183. *Paddling.* Cf. *W. T.* i. 2. 115 and *Oth.* ii. 1. 259.

184. *Ravel out.* Unravel, disentangle. Cf. *Rich. II.* iv. 1. 228: "Must I ravel out My weav'd-up folly?" *Ravel*=tangle in *T. G. of V.* iii. 2. 52 and *Macb.* ii. 2. 37.

185. *Essentially am not.* Am not essentially or really. Cf. Gr. 420, 421.

187. *For who*, etc. Spoken ironically.

188. *Paddock.* Toad. See *Macb.* p. 152.

*Gib.* A male cat. Nares says: "An expression exactly analogous to that of a *Jack-ass*, the one being formerly called *Gib*, or *Gilbert*, as commonly as the other *Jack*. *Tom-cat* is now the usual term, and for a similar reason. Coles has '*Gib*, a contraction for *Gilbert*,' and 'a Gib-cat, *catus, felis mas*.'" The female cat was called *Graymalkin* or *Grimalkin*; *Malkin* being originally a diminutive of *Mall* (Moll) or *Mary*. We find *gib-cat* in 1 *Hen. IV.* i. 2. 83.

189. *Concernings*. Concerns; as in *M. for M.* i. 1. 57.

191–193. The reference is to some old story that has not come down to us; perhaps, as Warner suggests, also alluded to by Sir John Suckling in one of his letters: "It is the story of the jackanapes and the partridges; thou starest after a beauty till it be lost to thee, and then let'st out another, and starest after that till it is gone too."

193. *Conclusions*. Experiments. Cf. *R. of L.* 1160:

> "That mother tries a merciless conclusion
> Who, having two sweet babes, when death takes one,
> Will slay the other and be nurse to none."

See also *A. and C.* v. 2. 358, *Cymb.* i. 5. 18, etc.

195. *Be thou assur'd*, etc. "The queen keeps her word, and is rewarded by the atoning punishment which befalls her in this world. Rue is herb of grace to her, as poor Ophelia says" (M.).

198. *I must to England*. We are not told how Hamlet came to know this. Miles says that on his way to his mother he *must* have overheard the interview between the king and Rosencrantz and Guildenstern. S. does not always take the trouble to make these little matters clear in the play.

199. For *forgot*, see Gr. 343; and for *There's* in next line, Gr. 335.

200–208. Omitted in the folio.

201. *Fang'd*. Johnson and Schmidt understand this to mean *with* their fangs, Seymour and Caldecott *without* them. It may be noted that S. expresses the latter idea by *fangless* in 2 *Hen. IV.* iv. 1. 218.

204. *Enginer*. The folio has the word also in *T. and C.* ii. 3. 8 and *Oth.* ii. 1. 65; *engineer* not at all. Cf. *pioner* in i. 5. 163 above, *mutiner* (see on 83 above), etc. See Gr. 443; and for the accent, 492.

205. *Hoist*. Schmidt makes this the participle of *hoise*, which occurs in 2 *Hen. VI.* i. 1. 169: "We 'll quickly hoise Duke Humphrey from his seat;" and in *Rich. III.* iv. 4. 529: "Hoised sail." S. also uses the verb *hoist*; as in *Sonn.* 117. 7: "I have hoisted sail;" *A. and C.* iii. 10. 15: "Hoists sails," etc. Cf. Gr. 342.

*Petar*. The same as *petard*. Wr. quotes Cotgrave, *Fr. Dict.*: "Petart: A Petard, or Petarre; an Engine (made like a Bell, or Morter) wherewith strong gates are burst open."

For *'t shall go hard*, cf. *M. of V.* iii. 1. 75, 2 *Hen. IV.* iii. 2. 354, etc.

207. *At*. See Gr. 143.

209. *Packing*. Schmidt makes this=going off in a hurry. Cf. *send packing* in 1 *Hen. IV.* ii. 4. 328, *Rich. III.* iii. 2. 63, etc. Wr. explains it as "contriving, plotting" (with a play on the other sense); as in *T. of S.* v. 1. 121, etc.

210. *Guts*. Steevens gives examples to show that anciently this word was not so offensive to delicacy as at present. It is used by Lyly, "who made the first attempt to polish our language;" also by Stonyhurst in his translation of Virgil, and by Chapman in his *Iliad*. Halliwell says:

"I have seen a letter, written about a century ago, in which a lady of rank, addressing a gentleman, speaks of her *guts* with the same nonchalance with which we should now write *stomach*." St. remarks that here "it really signifies no more than *lack-brain* or *shallow-pate*."

On the adjective use of *neighbour*, cf. *L. L. L.* v. 2. 94, *A. Y. L.* iv. 3. 79, etc.

St. considers that this line was introduced merely to afford the player an excuse for removing the body. In the time of S. an actor was obliged not only to play two or more parts in the same drama, but to perform such servile offices as are now done by attendants of the stage. This explains Falstaff's clumsy and unseemly exploit of carrying off Harry Percy's body on his back. See also *R. and J.* iii. 1. 201, *Rich. II.* v. 5. 118, 119, 1 *Hen. IV.* v. 4. 160, *Rich. III.* i. 4. 287, 288, *Lear*, iv. 6, 280–282, *J. C.* iii. 2. 261, etc.

214. *To draw.* See Gr. 356, and cf. iii. 2. 321 above.

---

## ACT IV.

Scene I.—1. *Profound.* The king uses *profound* equivocally, as it may mean *deep* literally and *deep* in significance, and upon the latter meaning *translate* bears (Corson).

7. *Mad.* "The queen both follows her son's injunction in keeping up the belief in his madness, and, with maternal ingenuity, makes it the excuse for his rash deed" (Clarke).

10. *Whips.* For the omission of the subject, cf. iii. 1. 8 above. The folio reads: "He whips his Rapier out, and cries," etc.

11. *Brainish.* "Brainsick" (Schmidt); used by S. nowhere else.

16. *Answer'd.* Explained, accounted for. Cf. iii. 4. 174 above.

18. *Kept short.* "Kept, as it were, tethered, under control" (Wr.).

*Out of haunt.* "Out of company" (Steevens). Cf. *A. Y. L.* ii. 1. 15 and *A. and C.* iv. 14. 54.

22. *Divulging.* Being divulged, becoming known.

24. *Apart.* Aside. Cf. *Oth.* ii. 3. 391: "to draw the Moor apart," etc. See also iv. 5. 183 below.

25. *Ore.* Apparently used by S. only of gold. Cf. *A. W.* iii. 6. 40: "this counterfeit lump of ore." In *R. of L.* 56, some eds. read "ore," but "o'er" is better. In the English-French appendix to Cotgrave's *Dict. ore* is confined to gold (Wr.).

26. *Mineral.* Mine (Steevens and Schmidt). Cf. Hall, *Satires*, vi. 148: "fired brimstone in a minerall." St. says it is "rather a *metallic vein* in a mine." Elsewhere in S. it means a poisonous mineral. See *Oth.* i. 2. 74, ii. 1. 306, and *Cymb.* v. 5. 50.

27. *Weeps.* "Either this is an entire invention of the queen, or Hamlet's mockeries had been succeeded by sorrow" (M.).

36. *Speak fair.* Speak gently or kindly. Cf. *C. of E.* iii. 2. 11, *Rich. II.* iii. 3. 128, etc. So also "speak *him* fair," "speak *you* fair," etc.; as in *C. of E.* iv. 2. 16, *M. N. D.* ii. 1. 199, etc.

40. *Untimely.* Often used adverbially; as in *Macb.* v. 8. 16, *R. and J.* iii. 1. 123, v. 3. 258, etc.

*So, haply, slander.* The text of both quartos and folios is defective here. Theo. inserted "For, haply, slander," and Capell changed "For" to "So." The emendation has been generally adopted. The remainder of the passage, *Whose whisper . . . woundless air*, is found in the quartos, but not in the folios.

41. *O'er the world's diameter.* M. explains this, "Slander can pass in direct line from hence to the antipodes without going round by the semi-circumference of the earth;" but we doubt whether S. thought of it in that mathematical way. *O'er the world's diameter* probably meant to him "to the ends of the earth."

42. *Blank.* "The *white* mark at which shot or arrows were aimed" (Steevens). Cf. *W. T.* ii. 3. 5, *Lear*, i. 1. 161, etc.

44. *Woundless air.* Cf. i. 1. 145 above: "as the air invulnerable."

SCENE II.—3. The early quartos and some modern eds. have "But soft, what noise?"

7. *Compounded it*, etc. Cf. *Sonn.* 71. 10: "When I perhaps compounded am with clay." See also 2 *Hen. IV.* iv. 5. 116.

12. *Demanded of.* Questioned by. Cf. *Temp.* i. 2. 139: "Well demanded;" *Oth.* v. 2. 301: "Will you, I pray, demand that demi-devil, Why," etc. For *of*, see Gr. 170.

13. *Replication.* Reply. Cf. *L. L. L.* iv. 2. 15, *J. C.* i. 1. 51, and *L. C.* 122.

15. *Countenance.* Patronage, favour. Cf. 2 *Hen. IV.* iv. 2. 13:

> "The man that sits within a monarch's heart,
> And ripens in the sunshine of his favour,
> Would he abuse the countenance of the king," etc.

*Authorities.* Attributes or offices of authority. Cf. *M. for M.* iv. 4. 6, *Lear*, i. 3. 17, etc.

17. *As an ape doth nuts.* The reading of the 1st quarto; adopted by Sr., St., and H. The other quartos have "like an apple;" the folio, "like an Ape," which is followed by most of the modern eds. F. has "like an ape doth apples," a construction found only in *Per.* i. 1. 163 (where the folios have "as") and ii. 4. 36.

19. *Squeezing you*, etc. Steevens quotes Marston, *Sat.* vii.:

> "He 's but a spunge, and shortly needs must ieese
> His wrong-got juice, when greatnes' fist shall squeese
> His liquor out."

Caldecott adds from *Apology for Herodotus*, 1608: "When princes (as the toy takes them in the head) have used courtiers as sponges to drinke what juice they can from the poore people, they take pleasure afterwards to wring them out into their owne cisternes."

22. *A knavish speech*, etc. A proverb since the time of S., but not known to have been such earlier (Steevens).

26. *The body*, etc. If this is not meant to be nonsense, the commentators have made nothing else of it.

29. *Of nothing.* Steevens gives several examples of the phrase "a

thing of nothing;" and Whalley adds *Ps.* cxliv. 4 (Prayer-book version): "Man is like a thing of nought." Cf. *M. N. D.* iv. 2. 14: "A thing of naught," and see note in our ed. p. 178.

*Hide fox*, etc. "There is a play among children thus called" (Hanmer). M. says: "Hamlet sheathes his sword, and, as if he were playing hide-and-seek, cries, 'now the fox is hid: let all go after him.'" For *fox*=sword, see *Hen. V.* p. 179.

SCENE III.—4. *Of.* See on iv. 2. 12 above.

6. *Scourge.* Punishment; as in *Rich. III.* i. 4. 50, etc.

9. *Deliberate pause.* "A matter of deliberate arrangement" (M.). Cf. iii. 3. 42 above.

*Diseases desperate*, etc. Rushton quotes Lyly, *Euphues:* "But I feare me wher so straunge a sicknesse is to be recured of so vnskilfull a Phisition, that either thou wilt be to bold to practise, or my body too weake to purge. But seeing a desperate disease is to be committed to a desperate Doctor, I wil follow thy counsel, and become thy cure."

21. *Convocation of politic worms.* "Holding congress over the great politician" (M.); perhaps alluding, as Sr. suggests, to the Imperial Diets held at Worms.

*Your.* See on i. 5. 167, and cf. iii. 2. 108 above. See also v. 1. 161 below: "your water," etc.

27. *Eat.* For the form of the participle, see *Rich. II.* p. 104 or *A. Y. L.* p. 165. Gr. 343.

31. *Progress.* A royal journey of state was always so called (Steevens). Cf. 2 *Hen. VI.* i. 4. 76: "The king is now in progress towards Saint Alban's."

33. *Send thither to see.* For you cannot go yourself, as you can to "the other place."

40. *Tender.* Regard, cherish. Cf. i. 3. 107 above. According to Delius *dearly* is to be understood: "as dearly tender as we grieve."

42. *With fiery quickness.* "In hot haste" (Wr.).

43. *At.* Abbott (Gr. 143) explains this as used instead of the obsolescent *a* (as in "a-cursing," ii. 2. 573 above) governing a noun, and compares *W. T.* v. 1. 140: "at friend," etc. Cf. i. 3. 2 above: "as the winds give benefit."

44. *Tend.* Attend, wait. Cf. i. 3. 83 above. For *is bent* the folio has "at bent."

47. *A cherub*, etc. "The cherubs are angels of love; they therefore of course know of such true affection as the king's for Hamlet" (M.).

53. *At foot.* At his heels (Gr. 143). Schmidt compares *A. and C.* i. 5. 44 and ii. 2. 160.

56. *Leans on.* Depends on; as in 2 *Hen. IV.* i. 1. 164, *T. and C.* iii. 3. 85, etc. There is a play upon the expression in *M. for M.* ii. 1. 49.

57. *Hold'st at aught.* Dost value at all. Gr. 143.

58. *As.* For so (Gr. 110). Cf. iv. 7. 157 and v. 2. 324 below.

60. *Free.* Willing, ready (Schmidt); no longer enforced by the Danish sword. Or we may say that *free awe pays homage*=awe pays free

homage. Cf. the examples of the "transposition of epithets" in Schmidt, *Appendix*, p. 1423.

61. *Coldly set.* "Regard with indifference" (Schmidt). Cf. "set me light" = esteem me lightly, in *Sonn.* 88. 1 and "sets it light" in *Rich. II.* i. 3. 293.

63. *Conjuring.* The folio reading; the quartos have "congruing," which Wr. prefers. On the accent of *conjure* in S. see *M. N. D.* p. 164.

64. *Present.* Instant. Cf. *R. of L.* 1263, 1307, *M. for M.* ii. 4. 152, iv. 2. 171, 223, etc. See on *presently*, ii. 2. 170 above.

65. *Hectic.* Wr. quotes Cotgrave, *Fr. Dict.*: "Hectique: Sicke of an Hectick, or continuall Feauer." S. uses the word only here.

67. *Haps.* Cf. *Much Ado*, iii. 1. 105: "loving goes by haps;" *T. A.* v. 3. 202: "our heavy haps," etc. The Coll. MS. has "hopes," which was also a conjecture of Johnson's.

*Begun.* "Tschischwitz, having found that *gin* is used for *begin*, suggests, reads, and defends 'my joys will ne'er be *gun*'" (F.).

Scene IV.—3. *Claims.* The folio reading; the quartos have "Craues" (Craves) which some editors prefer.

5. *If that.* For *that* as a "conjunctional affix," see Gr. 287.

6. *In his eye.* In his presence; especially used of the royal presence (Steevens). Cf. *A and C.* ii. 2. 212: "tended her i' the eyes," etc. Steevens quotes *The Establishment of the Household of Prince Henry*, 1610: "all such as doe service in the Prince's eye;" and *The Regulations for the Queen's Household*, 1627: "Such as doe service in the Queen's eye." F. refers to iv. 7. 45 below.

8. *Softly.* Slowly, gently; probably addressed to his soldiers. Cf. *J. C.* v. 1. 16: "Octavius, lead your battle softly on," etc. The folio has "safely."

The remainder of this scene (9–66) is omitted in the folio.

9. *Powers.* Troops. Both the singular and the plural are used in this sense (cf. *force* and *forces*). See *J. C.* p. 168, note on *Are levying powers.*

11. *How purpos'd?* Having what purpose or destination? Cf. *Lear*, ii. 4. 296: "So am I purpos'd," etc.

14. *Norway.* The King of Norway. See on i. 2. 125 above.

15. *The main.* "The chief power" (Wr.); or the country as a whole (Schmidt). Cf. *T. and C.* ii. 3. 273: "all our main of power," etc.

17. To mend the metre Pope read "speak it" and Capell "speak, sir." "Speak on 't" and "no more addition" have also been suggested.

20. *Five ducats, five.* "A rent of five ducats, only five" (Wr.).

*Farm.* Take on lease. S. uses the verb only here and in *Rich. II.* i. 4. 45: "to farm our royal realm."

22. *Ranker.* Greater. See *A. Y. L.* p. 186.

25, 26. It has been plausibly suggested that these lines belong to the Captain, not to Hamlet. *Debate the question* = decide the question.

27. *Imposthume.* Inward sore or abscess. Cf. *V. and A.* 743 and *T. and C.* v. 1. 24. Caldecott quotes 1 *Hen. IV.* iv. 2. 32: "the cankers of a calm world and long peace." For the origin of the word, see Wb.

34. *Market of his time.* "That for which he sells his time" (Johnson).

36. *Such large discourse*, etc. "Such latitude of comprehension, such power of reviewing the past and anticipating the future" (Johnson). Theo. remarks that *looking before and after* is "an expression purely Homeric," and refers to *Iliad*, iii. 109 and xviii. 250.

39. *Fust.* To grow mouldy or "fusty" (*T. and C.* i. 3. 161, ii. 1. 111, and *Cor.* i. 9. 7). S. uses the verb nowhere else.

41. *Of.* In consequence of. Gr. 168.

"Hamlet envies every one who has quick and determined resolution, and whose energy does not, like his own, evaporate in meditation, and pass by opportunity after opportunity for action" (M.).

*Event*=issue; as in 50 below.

44. *To do.* For this use of the active infinitive, see Gr. 359.

45. *Sith.* See on ii. 2. 6. Gr. 132.

46. *Gross.* Palpable, obvious. Cf. 1 *Hen. IV.* ii. 4. 250: "gross as a mountain, open, palpable."

47. *Charge.* Cost, expense. Cf. *K. John*, i. 1. 49: "This expedition's charge," etc.

49. *Puff'd.* Inspired.

50. *Makes mouths*, etc. "Utterly scorns the dire uncertainties of the war" (M.). For *makes mouths*, cf. *M. N. D.* iii. 2. 238 and *Lear*, iii. 2. 36.

54. *Is not*, etc. The *not* modifies *is*, as F. notes: "To stir without great argument, upon every trifling occasion, is not an attribute of greatness; . . . but it *is* the attribute of greatness to stir instantly and at a trifle when the heart is touched."

For *argument*=matter in dispute, see *Hen. V.* p. 163.

58. *My reason and my blood.* Cf. iii. 2. 64: "blood and judgment," and see note.

61. *Trick of fame.* "Point of honour" (Caldecott). Cf. *Cor.* iv. 4. 21: "Some trick [that is, trifle] not worth an egg." Delius considers that *of fame* belongs to *fantasy* also: "an illusion and a whim that promise fame." On the passage, cf. *A. Y. L.* ii. 7. 152:

> "Seeking the bubble reputation
> Even in the cannon's mouth."

63. *Whereon*, etc. That is, not large enough to hold the armies that fight for it.

64. *Continent.* Receptacle, that which *contains*. Cf. *M. N. D.* ii. 1. 92:

> "Have every pelting river made so proud
> That they have overborne their continents;"

*A. and C.* iv. 14. 40: "Heart, once be stronger than thy continent," etc. Reed quotes Bacon, *Adv. of L.*: "and if there be no fullness, then is the continent greater than the content."

SCENE V.—The stage-direction in the quartos is "*Enter Horatio, Gertrard, and a Gentleman;*" in the folio, "*Enter Queene and Horatio.*" The latter gives to Horatio the speeches of the Gentleman. "Lines 11–13, so cautiously obscure, seem better suited to an ordinary courtier than to Horatio" (Wr.).

2. *Distract.* See on *deject*, iii. 1. 155, or Gr. 342.

3. *Will.* See Gr. 319.

5. *There's.* See on iii. 4. 199 above.

6. *Spurns.* Kicks (Schmidt). Cf. *C. of E.* ii. 1. 83: "That like a football you do spurn me thus," etc.

*Enviously*=angrily, spitefully (Nares). So *envious* often=spiteful, and *envy*=malice, spite. See *Rich. II.* p. 172.

8. *Unshaped.* Formless, confused. Cf. *M. for M.* iv. 4. 23: "This deed unshapes me quite;" that is, deranges or confuses me.

9. *To collection.* "To endeavour to collect some meaning from it" (Mason).

For *aim* the quartos have "yawne." *Aim*=guess; as in *T. G. of V.* iii. 1. 45, *T. of S.* ii. 1. 237, 2 *Hen. VI.* ii. 4. 58, etc.

11–13. "The general sense of this ill-expressed sentence is more easily understood than paraphrased. The speaker is afraid of committing himself to any definite statement. If he had spoken out he would have said, 'Her words and gestures lead one to infer that some great misfortune has happened to her'" (Wr.).

14–16. The quartos give all three lines to Horatio; the folio to the queen. The arrangement in the text was suggested by Blackstone, and is adopted by Coll., St., the Camb. editors, M., and F.

On the measure of 14, see Gr. 461.

*Ill-breeding*="hatching mischief" (Schmidt).

18. *Toy.* Trifle. Cf. 1 *Hen. VI.* iv. 1. 145: "a toy, a thing of no regard," etc.

*Amiss.* Misfortune, disaster. Also used as a noun in *Sonn.* 35. 7 and 151. 3. Steevens quotes *The Arraignment of Paris*, 1584: "Gracious forbearers of this world's amiss;" and Lyly, *Woman in the Moon:* "to witness my amiss."

19. *Jealousy.* Suspicion; as in ii. 1. 113 above. The meaning is, "Guilt is so full of suspicion that it unskilfully betrays itself in fearing to be betrayed" (Wr.).

21. Sir Joshua Reynolds says: "There is no part of the play in its representation on the stage more pathetic than this scene; which, I suppose, proceeds from the utter insensibility Ophelia has to her own misfortunes. A great sensibility, or none at all, seems to produce the same effect. In the latter the audience supply what she wants, and with the former they sympathize." See also p. 28 above.

25. *Cockle-hat.* The cockle-shell in the hat was the badge of a pilgrim.

26. *Shoon.* As Delius remarks, this plural was archaic in the time of S. He puts it also into the mouth of Cade, 2 *Hen. VI.* iv. 2. 195.

37. *Larded.* Garnished (Caldecott). Cf. v. 2. 20 below. See also *M. W.* iv. 6. 14, *T. and C.* v. 1. 63, etc.

38. *Did go.* All the early eds. have "did not go;" corrected by Pope.

41. *God 'ield you!* God yield or reward you. See *Macb.* p. 175, or *A. Y. L.* p. 180.

*The owl*, etc. According to Douce, there is a story current in Gloucestershire that our Saviour went into a baker's shop to ask for bread. The mistress of the shop would have given him all he wanted, but was reprimanded by her daughter, who for her lack of charity was transformed into an owl.

44. *Conceit.* Imagination; as in iii. 4. 112 above.

45. *Of.* About. Gr. 174.

49. *And I*, etc. The first girl seen by a man on the morning of this day was considered his Valentine or true-love. The custom continued until the last century, and is graphically alluded to by Gay (Halliwell).

59. *This is.* Metrically equivalent to one syllable. Gr. 461.

60. *O Gertrude, Gertrude.* The quartos read "death, and now behold, o," etc. Stratmann suggests that S. first wrote "And now behold," and then substituted "O Gertrude, Gertrude."

61. *When sorrows come*, etc. That is, "misfortunes never come single."

*Spies.* Scouts sent in advance of the main army.

64. *Remove.* See on *avouch*, i. 1. 57; and cf. *Lear*, ii. 4. 4, *A. and C.* i. 2. 203, etc.

*Muddied . . . unwholesome.* These refer primarily to the blood, and then to the mood of the people (Delius).

66. *Greenly.* Foolishly. Cf. *Hen. V.* v. 2. 149: "look greenly." See also i. 3. 101 above.

67. *In hugger-mugger.* Secretly and hurriedly. Steevens quotes North's *Plutarch*: "Antonius thinking good . . . that his bodie should be honorably buried, and not in hugger-mugger." Malone cites Florio, *Ital. Dict.*: "Dinascoso, secretly, hiddenly, in hugger-mugger." Cf. also Spenser, *Mother Hubberds Tale*, 139:

> "Of all the patrimonie, which a few
> Now hold in hugger mugger in their hand."

68. *Divided*, etc. Cf. v. 2. 112 below.

72. *Feeds on his wonder.* The quartos read "Feeds on this wonder;" the folio, "Keepes on his wonder." The reading in the text is Johnson's. "The mysterious death of Polonius filled his son with doubt and amazement" (Wr.).

*Keeps himself in clouds.* Is reserved and mysterious in his conduct (Theo.).

73. *Buzzers.* Whisperers, tale-bearers (Schmidt); used by S. only here. Cf. the verb *buzz*=whisper, in *Rich. II.* ii. 1. 26, 3 *Hen. VI.* v. 6. 86, *Hen. VIII.* ii. 1. 148, etc.

75. *Wherein*, etc. "Wherein (that is, in which pestilent speeches) necessity, or the obligation of an accuser to support his charge, will nothing stick," etc. (Johnson).

76. *Person.* The quarto reading; the folio has "persons." The king is speaking of himself only (D.).

78. *A murthering-piece.* A cannon loaded with case-shot. Steevens quotes Smith's *Sea Grammar*, 1627: "A case shot is any kinde of small bullets, nailes, old iron, or the like, to put into the case, to shoot out of the ordinances [see *Hen. V.* p. 161] or murderers." M. defines it as "a rude *mitrailleuse* of the day, the *pévier* or *perrier*, which discharged stones so that they shattered into many fragments."

80. *Switzers.* "Swiss guards such as served in France, Spain, and Naples—the men whose fidelity to Louis XVI. on the terrible 10th of August is commemorated by the Lucerne lion" (M.). Reed says: "In

many of our old plays the guards attendant on kings are called *Switzers*, and that without any regard to the country where the scene lies." Malone quotes Nash, *Christ's Teares over Jerusalem*, 1594: "Law, logicke, and the Switzers, may be hired to fight for any body."

82. *Overpeering of his list.* Rising above (literally, looking over) its boundary. Cf. *M. of V.* i. 1. 12: "Do overpeer the petty traffickers;" 3 *Hen. VI.* v. 2. 14: "Whose top-branch overpeer'd Jove's spreading tree," etc. For *list*, cf. *Hen. V.* v. 2. 295: "confined within the weak list of a country's fashion;" *Oth.* iv. 1. 76: "Confine yourself but in a patient list," etc.

83. *Eats not*, etc. Cf. 2 *Hen. IV.* i. 1. 47: "He seem'd in running to devour the way."

84. *Head.* Armed force (Schmidt); as in 1 *Hen. IV.* i. 3. 284: "To save our heads by raising of a head;" *Id.* iv. 4. 25: "a head Of gallant warriors," etc.

86. *As.* As if. Cf. iii. 4. 133 above.

87. *Forgot.* For the form, see Gr. 343; and for the construction, Gr. 376.

88. *Of every word.* "Of everything that is to serve as a watchword and shibboleth to the multitude" (Schmidt). "Ward," "weal," "work," etc., have been proposed as emendations, but none is necessary.

93. *Counter.* Hounds *run counter* when they trace the scent backwards. Turbervile, in his *Book of Hunting*, says: "When a hound hunteth backwards the same way that the chase is come, then we say he hunteth counter." Cf. *C. of E.* iv. 2. 39 and 2 *Hen. IV.* i. 2. 102.

99. *Calmly*, etc. Johnson inserts here the stage-direction, "*Laying hold on him.*" Cf. 105 below.

102. *Unsmirched.* Unstained, unsullied. Cf. *besmirch*, i. 3. 15 above; and *smirched* in *Hen. V.* iii. 3. 17, etc. The early eds. have "brow" or "browe."

105. *Fear.* Fear for. See on i. 3. 51 above. M. remarks: "The king is truly royal where conscience does not stand in his way."

106. *There 's such divinity*, etc. Boswell quotes from Chettle's *Englandes Mourning Garment* the following anecdote of Queen Elizabeth: While her majesty was on the river near Greenwich, a shot was fired by accident which struck the royal barge, and hurt a waterman near her. "The French ambassador being amazed, and all crying Treason, Treason! yet she, with an undaunted spirit, came to the open place of the barge, and bad them never feare, for if the shot were made at her, they durst not shoote againe: such majestie had her presence, and such boldnesse her heart, that she despised all feare, and was, as all princes are or should be, so full of divine fullnesse, that guiltie mortalitie durst not beholde her but with dazeled eyes."

*Hedge.* Caldecott refers to *Job*, i. 10 and iii. 21.

117. *Both the worlds.* This world and the next. Cf. *Macb.* iii. 2. 16, where the expression means heaven and earth.

119. *Throughly.* Thoroughly. See *Mer.* p. 144, note on *Throughfares.*

120. *My will.* That is, only my own will (Wr.). The quartos have "worlds," and Pope "world's."

124. *Is 't writ*, etc. Wr. compares i. 2. 222 above.

125. *Swoopstake.* "Are you going to vent your rage on both friend and foe; like a gambler who insists on sweeping the stakes whether the point is in his favour or not?" (M.).

128. *Thus wide.* With appropriate gesture. Cf. *T. and C.* iii. 3. 167 (Wr.).

129. *Pelican.* The folio has "Politician." Caldecott quotes Dr. Sherwen: "By the pelican's dropping upon its breast its lower bill to enable its young to take from its capacious pouch, lined with a fine flesh-coloured skin, this appearance is, on feeding them, given." Rushton cites Lyly, *Euphues:* "the Pelicane, who stricketh bloud out of hir owne bodye to do others good." For other allusions to the same fable, see *Rich. II.* ii. 1. 126 and *Lear*, iii. 4. 77.

130. *Repast.* The verb is used by S. nowhere else.

133. *Sensibly.* The reading of the earlier quartos; the folio has "sensible," which some prefer. *Sensibly*=feelingly, as in *L. L. L.* iii. 1. 114.

135. *Let her come in.* Given by the quartos to Laertes. The folio gives, as a stage-direction in the margin, "*A noise within. Let her come in.*" As Theo. notes, Laertes could not know that it was his sister who caused the noise; nor would he command the guards to let her in, and then ask what the noise meant.

137. *Virtue.* Power. Cf. *V. and A.* 1131: "Their virtue lost" (referring to eyes); and *L. L. L.* v. 2. 348: "The virtue of your eye."

139. *By weight.* The folio reading; "with weight" in the quartos.

144–146. Omitted in the quartos. M. paraphrases the passage thus: "Nature is so spiritualized by love that it sends its most precious functions one by one after dear ones lost, as instances or samples of itself, till none remain."

149. *Rains.* The quartos have "rain'd."

154. *Wheel.* Malone explains this as the spinning-wheel, at which the singer is supposed to be occupied. Cf. *T. N.* ii. 4. 45. Steevens makes the word=burden, or chorus, and quotes "from memory" a passage (but he cannot recollect where he saw it) in which it is thus used; but, as F. remarks, "when Steevens does not adduce line, page, and title, his illustrations are to be received with caution." No satisfactory example of the word in this sense has been found by anybody else.

The story of *the false steward* to which Ophelia alludes has not come down to our day.

156. *Matter.* Sense, meaning. Cf. ii. 2. 95 above.

157. *Rosemary.* The symbol of remembrance, particularly used at weddings and funerals (Schmidt). Cf. *W. T.* iv. 3. 74 and *R. and J.* iv. 5. 79. Sir Thomas More says of it: "I lett it run alle over my garden walls, not onlie because my bees love it, but because tis the herb sacred to remembrance, and therefore to friendship; whence a sprig of it hath a dumb language that maketh it the chosen emblem at our funeral wakes and in our buriall grounds." Cf. Herrick, *The Rosemarie Branch:*

> "Grow for two ends, it matters not at all,
> Be 't for my bridall or my buriall;"

and Dekker, *Wonderful Year*: "The rosemary that was washed in sweet water to set out the bridal, is now wet in tears to furnish her burial."

158. *For thoughts.* Because the name is from the Fr. *pensée*, thought. The flower is the *love-in-idleness* of *M. N. D.* ii. 1. 168 and *T. of S.* i. 1. 156. Spenser calls it by the old name *paunce*. Cf. *F. Q.* iii. 1. 36:

> "Sweet Rosemaryes
> And fragrant violets, and Paunces trim;"

*Id.* iii. 11. 37: "The one a Paunce, the other a Sweet-breare;" and *Shep. Kal. Apr.*:

> "The pretie Pawnce,
> And the Chevisaunce."

Milton (*Lycidas*, 144) speaks of it as "the pansy freak'd with jet." Cf. *P. L.* ix. 1040 and *Comus*, 851.

159. *Document.* Lesson, precept; used by S. nowhere else. Cf. Spenser, *F. Q.* i. 10. 19: "And heavenly documents thereout did preach."

161. *Fennel.* Malone says: "Ophelia gives her fennel and columbines to the king. In *A Handfull of Pleasant Delites*, 1584, the former is thus mentioned: 'Fennel is for flatterers,' etc. See also Florio, *Ital. Dict.* 1598: 'Dare finocchio, to give fennel, . . . to flatter, to dissemble.'" The plant was supposed to have many virtues, which are well stated by Longfellow in *The Goblet of Life*:

> "Above the lowly plants it towers,
> The fennel, with its yellow flowers,
> And in an earlier age than ours
> Was gifted with the wondrous powers,
>     Lost vision to restore.
> It gave new strength and fearless mood;
> And gladiators, fierce and rude,
> Mingled it in their daily food;
> And he who battled and subdued
>     A wreath of fennel wore."

Cf. 2 *Hen. IV.* ii. 4. 267: "and a' plays at quoits well, and eats conger and fennel." *

*Columbines.* Cf. *L. L. L.* v. 2. 661: "That columbine." Steevens quotes Chapman, *All Fools*, 1605:

> "What 's that?—a columbine?
> No: that thankless flower grows not in my garden."

It was the emblem of cuckoldom on account of the horns of its nectaria. The *Caltha Poetarum*, 1599, speaks of it as "the blue cornuted columbine." It was also emblematic of forsaken lovers. Holt White quotes Browne, *Brit. Past.* i. 2:

> "The columbine in tawny often taken
> Is then ascribed to such as are forsaken."

162. *Rue.* This she gives to the queen. It was "the symbol of sorry remembrance" (Schmidt). Cf. *W. T.* iv. 4. 74 and *Rich. II.* iii. 4. 105. It was also called *herb of grace*, a name appropriate on Sunday, as Ophelia

---

* Our younger readers may be interested in the fact that *ferule* is derived from the Latin *ferula*, the name of the giant fennel, the stalks of which were used as "birches" by the Roman schoolmaster.

says. Cf. *A. W.* iv. 5. 18. It was specially in repute as an eye-salve. Cf. Milton, *P. L.* xi. 414:

> "then purg'd with euphrasy and rue
> The visual nerve, for he had much to see."

Ellacombe quotes the old lines of the *Schola Salerni*: "Nobilis est ruta quia lumina reddit acuta," etc.

163. *With a difference.* "The difference between the ruth and wretchedness of guilt, and the ruth and sorrows of misfortune" (Caldecott). Skeat explains the passage thus: "I offer you rue, which has two meanings: it is sometimes called *herb of grace*, and in that sense I take some for myself; but with a slight difference of spelling it means *ruth*, and in that respect it will do for you." He adds that the explanation is Shakespeare's own, and refers to *Rich. II.* iii. 4. 105. For a different explanation, see Schmidt, s. v.

164. *Daisy.* Cf. iv. 7. 168 below; also *L. L. L.* v. 2. 904 and *R. of L.* 395. *Daisied* occurs in Cymb. iv. 2. 398. It was the favourite flower of Chaucer. Cf. *Legende of Goode Women*, 40:

> "Now have I thanne suche a condicion,
> That of al the floures in the mede,
> Thanne love I most these floures white and rede,
> Suche as men callen daysyes in our toune."

It does not appear to whom Ophelia gives the daisy; probably either to the king or queen (Wr.). Henley quotes Greene, who calls it "the dessembling daisie."

*Violets.* Malone quotes a sonnet printed in 1584: "Violet is for faithfulnesse." Cf. i. 3. 7 above and v. 1. 229 below.

167. The song of *Bonny Sweet Robin* is found in Anthony Holborne's *Cittharn Schoole*, 1597, in William Ballet's *Lute Book*, and in many other books and manuscripts of the time. In Fletcher's *Two Noble Kinsmen*, ii. 1, the jailer's daughter, when mad, says: "I can sing *The Broom* and *Bonny Robin*" (Chappell).

168. *Thought.* Anxiety, trouble. Cf. iii. 1. 85 above. *Passion* = "violent sorrow" (Schmidt); as in *T. A.* i. 1. 106: "A mother's tears in passion for her son," etc. Cf. ii. 2. 504 above.

169. *Favour.* Attractiveness. Cf. *Oth.* iv. 3. 21: "even his stubbornness, his checks, his frowns . . . have grace and favour in them." See p. 28 above.

179. *God ha' mercy.* The folio has "Gramercy;" perhaps to avoid the introduction of the name of God. See on ii. 1. 76 above.

180. *Of all.* On all. See Gr. 181.

182. *Commune.* Accented on the first syllable by S., except, perhaps, in *W. T.* ii. 1. 162 (Schmidt). The folio has "common."

184. *Of whom*, etc. That is, "of your wisest friends, whom you will" (Wr.). Cf. Gr. 426.

187. *Touch'd.* That is, accessary to the deed (Schmidt).

193. *His means of death.* The means of his death (Gr. 423).

*Obscure.* The usual accent in S., but we have the modern one in *V. and A.* 237 and 2 *Hen. VI.* iv. 1. 50 (Schmidt). The verb is always *obscúre.* See Gr. 490 and 492.

*Burial.* The quartos and some modern eds. have "funeral."

194. *Hatchment.* An armorial escutcheon used at funerals.

195. *Ostentation.* Also used of funeral pomp in *Much Ado*, iv. 1. 207: "a mourning ostentation."

197. *That.* For the omission of *so*, see Gr. 283, and cf. iv. 7. 146 below.

SCENE VI.—1. *What.* Equivalent, as often, to *who*, but only in the predicate (Schmidt). Cf. *Temp.* v. 1. 85, *M. for M.* ii. 1. 62, iv. 2. 132, iv. 3. 27, v. 1. 472, etc.

10. *Let to know.* Caused or made to know (Schmidt). For the *to*, see Gr. 349.

12. *Overlooked.* Looked over, perused. Cf. *Hen. V.* ii. 4. 90: "Willing you overlook this pedigree."

13. *Means.* Means of access, introduction (Caldecott).

14. *Two days old at sea.* Cf. *M. for M.* iv. 2. 135: "one that is a prisoner nine years old;" *C. of E.* i. 1. 45: "my absence was not six months old;" *Id.* ii. 2. 150: "In Ephesus I am but two hours old," etc.

15. *Appointment.* Equipment; as in *K. John*, ii. 1. 296, etc.

16. *Compelled.* Enforced, involuntary. Cf. *R. of L.* 1708: "this compelled stain;" *M. for M.* ii. 4. 57: "our compell'd sins," etc.

18. *Thieves of mercy.* Merciful thieves. Cf. i. 2. 4 above: "brow of woe," etc.

19. *But they knew what they did.* This has been thought to prove that the capture of Hamlet was not accidental, but a prearranged plan of his own. Clearly, however, it does not refer to the capture, but to the "mercy" shown him afterwards, and it is explained by what follows: "I am to do a good turn for *them*." Hamlet saw how he could turn the accident to account, and had persuaded the pirates to assist him in the plan. What Hamlet says in iii. 4. 202–207 has been quoted in proof of this supposed counterplot; but all that he meant there was that he would find some way to circumvent his enemies. He had no plan formed, but felt that he was a match for them in craft. "Let it work," he says, "for it shall go hard but I will manage to countermine them." As Snider has said, his own account (in v. 2) of the adventure with the pirates refutes the notion that it was a device of his own.

21. *As thou wouldst fly death.* That is, wouldst fly death *with.* For similar ellipses with *as*, see Gr. 384.

22. *Will make.* For the omission of the relative, see Gr. 244.

23. *For the bore*, etc. "For the calibre of the facts" (M.).

27. *Make.* The reading of the 4th quarto, the word being omitted in the earlier quartos; the folio has "give."

SCENE VII.—3. *Sith.* See on ii. 2. 6 above.

4. *Which.* See Gr. 265.

7. *Crimeful.* The quartos have "criminall." Wr. says that S. does not use *crimeful* elsewhere; but cf. *R. of L.* 970: "To make him curse this cursed crimeful night."

8. *Safety.* Some modern eds. follow the quartos in reading "safety, greatness."

10. *Unsinew'd.* Weak. Cf. *sinewed* (=strengthened) in *K. John*, v. 7. 88, and *insinewed* (=joined in sinews, allied) in 2 *Hen. IV.* iv. 1. 172.

11. *But.* The quarto reading; the folio has "And."

13. *Be it either which.* Whichever it be. See Gr. 273.

14. *Conjunctive.* Conjoined, closely united; as in *Oth.* i. 3. 374: "conjunctive in our revenge."

15. *Sphere.* Alluding to the old Ptolemaic theory that the heavenly bodies were set in crystal spheres, by the revolution of which they were carried round. Cf. *Temp.* ii. 1. 183, *M. N. D.* ii. 1. 7, 153, iii. 2. 61, *K. John*, v. 7. 74, *T. and C.* i. 3. 90, etc. See also Milton, *Hymn on Nativ.* 125 fol.: "Ring out, ye crystal spheres," etc.

17. *Count.* Account, trial. It is the same as *compt.* Cf. *Oth.* v. 2. 273: "when we shall meet at compt" ("count" in the 1st quarto); that is, at the judgment-day. Abbott (Gr. 460) gives it as a contraction of *account*, but we find both *compt* and *count* in this sense in prose. See on *scape*, i. 3. 38 above.

18. *General gender.* "The *common race* of the people" (Johnson). S. uses the word also in *Oth.* i. 3. 326: "one gender of herbs;" and in *The Phœnix and the Turtle*, 18: "thy sable gender." Cf. "the general," ii. 2. 423 above.

20. *The spring*, etc. Reed says that the allusion is to the dropping-well at Knaresborough in Yorkshire, which is described by Camden in his *Britannia*, 1590. Wr. quotes Lyly, *Euphues*: "Would I had sipped of that ryuer in Caria, which turneth those that drinke of it to stones."

21. *Convert his gyves*, etc. "Were I to put him in fetters, the bonds would only give him more general favour" (M.). Schmidt calls this "an obscure passage not yet satisfactorily explained or amended," but perhaps having the meaning just given.

22. *Loud a wind.* The quartos have "loued Arm'd" or "loued armes." Steevens quotes Ascham, *Toxophilus*: "Weake bowes, and lyghte shaftes can not stande in a rough wynde."

24. *And not where.* For the ellipsis, cf. Gr. 382.

25. *Have.* Here used in its original sense = find, as the next line shows (Gr. 425).

27. *If praises*, etc. "If I may praise what has been, but is now to be found no more" (Johnson).

28. *Stood challenger*, etc. "Challenged all the age to deny her perfection" (F.). M. thinks there is an allusion to the coronation of the Emperor of Austria as King of Hungary, "when on the Mount of Defiance at Presburg, he unsheathes the ancient sword of state, and shaking it towards north, south, east, and west, challenges the four corners of the world to dispute his rights."

30. *Sleeps.* See on *loves*, i. 1. 173.

32. *Shook.* S. generally has *shook* for both past tense and participle, but sometimes *shaked* (cf. *Temp.* ii. 1. 319, *Hen. V.* ii. 1. 124, etc.). *Shaken* occurs five times. Gr. 343. For *with*=by, see Gr. 193.

45. *Your kingly eyes.* See on iv. 4. 6 above.

46. *Sudden*, etc. "Sudden, and even more strange than sudden" (Gr. 6).

48. *Should.* See Gr. 325.

49. *Abuse.* Deception, delusion. Cf. *M. for M.* v. 1. 205: "a strange abuse;" also the use of the verb in ii. 2. 590 above.

50. *Character.* Handwriting. Cf. *W. T.* v. 2. 38: "the letters of Antigonus found with it which they know to be his character," etc. For the accent, see on i. 3. 59 above.

56. *Didest.* The folio has "diddest," the quartos "didst." The 1st quarto, in the corresponding passage, reads: "That I shall liue to tell him, thus he dies." *Didest* is not found elsewhere in S.

57. *As how,* etc. We should expect "How should it *not* be so?" but S. is elsewhere inexact in repeating and omitting the negative (Delius). See *A. Y. L.* p. 156, note on *No more do yours.* Perhaps, as Wr. suggests, the first clause refers to Hamlet's return, the second to Laertes's feelings.

58. *Rul'd.* So in the folio, which makes one line of *how otherwise . . . by me?* and omits *Ay, my lord.* Walker, to fill out the measure, suggests "my *good* lord." Abbott (Gr. 482) makes *Ay* a dissyllable, as in ii. 1. 36 above. Cf. *T. of S.* iv. 4. 2, *Cor.* v. 3. 125, and *Lear,* ii. 1. 111.

59. *So.* Provided that. Gr. 133.

61. *Checking at.* The earlier quartos have "the King at," the later ones "liking not." To *check at* was a term in falconry, applied to a hawk when she forsakes her proper game and follows some other (D.). Cf. *T. N.* ii. 5. 124 and iii. 1. 71.

66. *Uncharge.* "Acquit of blame, not accuse" (Schmidt). So *unbless* =not bless, neglect to bless, in *Sonn.* 3. 4.

*Practice*=artifice, plot; as in 137 and v. 2. 305 below. Cf. *M. for M.* v. 1. 123: "This needs must be a practice," etc.

67–80. *My lord . . . graveness.* Omitted in the folio.

69. *Falls.* Happens. Cf. *M. N. D.* v. 1. 188: "it will fall pat as I told you," etc.

72. *Your sum of parts.* All your "qualities" or gifts. Cf. v. 2. 110 below: "the continent of what part a gentleman would see."

73. *Pluck.* A favourite word with S. For *pluck from*=draw from, cf. *Sonn.* 14. 1, *M. of V.* iv. 1. 30, *Hen. V.* iv. chor. 42, *Cor.* ii. 3. 200, etc.

75. *Siege.* Rank; literally, seat (*M. for M.* iv. 2. 101). Cf. *Oth.* i. 2. 22: "From men of royal siege."

79. *Sables.* See on iii. 2. 113 above; and for *weeds*=robes, dress, see *M. N. D.* p. 149. Cf. Milton, *L'All.* 120: "In weeds of peace," etc.

80. *Health.* Malone, Wr., and others explain this as=care for health, such as characterizes elderly men; but it seems better, with Schmidt, to make it=prosperity. Cf. i. 3. 21 above and v. 2. 21 below; also *L. L. L.* ii. 1. 178, etc. F. thinks that *health* may refer to *careless livery,* and *graveness* to *sables* and *weeds.* Cf. iii. 1. 151 above and *Macb.* i. 3. 60. Warb. proposed "wealth."

83. *Can.* The folio has "ran," an obvious misprint, but followed by Rowe and Caldecott. For this absolute use of *can,* cf. v. 2. 308 below: "I can no more." See Gr. 307.

84. *Into.* The quartos and many modern eds. have "unto."

86. *As he had.* The early eds., except the quarto of 1676, have "As had he." For *as,* see Gr. 109.

*Incorps'd.* Made one body, "incorporate" (*C. of E.* ii. 2. 124, *M.N.D.* iii. 2. 208, etc.). Steevens quotes Sidney, *Arcadia:* "As if, Centaur-like, he had been one peece with the horse."

87. *Topp'd.* Overtopped, surpassed; as in *Macb.* iv. 3. 57: "to top Macbeth," etc.

88. *Forgery.* Invention (Schmidt). "I could not contrive so many proofs of dexterity as he could perform" (Johnson).

91. *Lamond.* The quartos have "Lamord," the folio "Lamound." Mr. C. E. Brown (quoted by F.) thinks there may be an allusion to Pietro Monte (whose name is given in English of the time as "Peter Mount"), a famous cavalier and swordsman, the instructor of Louis the Seventh's Master of Horse.

92. *Brooch.* An ornamental buckle for the hat. See *Rich. II.* p. 219.

94. *Confession.* Implying that Lamond would not willingly acknowledge the superiority of Laertes (Delius).

95. *Such a masterly report.* "Such a report of mastership, an account of your consummate skill" (Schmidt).

96. *Defence.* That is, the *science* of defence (Johnson).

99. *Scrimers.* Fencers (Fr. *escrimeur*); a word not found elsewhere. W. prints "th' escrimeurs."

101. *Sir*, etc. "Note how the king first awakens Laertes's vanity by praising the reporter, and then gratifies it by the report itself, and finally points it by these lines" (Coleridge).

110. *Love is begun*, etc. "As love begins at some given point of time, so I see by passages of experience that time also abates it" (M.); in other words, love is not innate, and experience shows that it is not immutable.

On *proof*, cf. *J. C.* ii. 1. 21: "'t is a common proof," etc. See also iii. 2. 152 above.

113–122. *There lives . . . the ulcer.* Omitted in the folio.

115. *A like.* A uniform, the same. *Still*=always, constantly; as in ii. 2. 42 above.

116. *Plurisy.* Plethora. "The dramatic writers of that time frequently call a fulness of blood a *plurisy*, as if it came, not from πλευρά, but from *plus, pluris*" (Warb.). Cf. Massinger, *The Picture*, iv. 2: "A plurisy of ill blood you must let out;" and *Unnatural Combat*, iv. 1: "Thy plurisy of goodness is thy ill," etc.

117. *Too-much.* Schmidt compares *Lear*, v. 3. 206: "To amplify too-much would make much more." On compounds in S. see Gr. 429 fol.

118. On *should* and *would*, see Gr. 323, 329.

121. *Spendthrift sigh.* The reading of the quarto of 1676; the earlier quartos have "spend thirfts sigh" and "spend-thrifts sigh." It probably means a wasting sigh, alluding to the old notion that every sigh caused the loss of a drop of blood from the heart. Cf. *M.N.D.* iii. 2. 97: "With sighs of love that costs the fresh blood dear;" and see note in our ed. p. 163. M. explains the passage thus: "he who vainly acknowledges that he 'should' have done a thing is like a spendthrift sighing for his squandered estate."

122. *To the quick.* Cf. ii. 2. 584 above.

126. *Sanctuarize.* Be a sanctuary to, or protect from punishment (Schmidt). Cf. *C. of E.* v. 1. 94:

> "he took this place for sanctuary,
> And it shall privilege him from your hands."

For similar allusions, see 3 *Hen. VI.* iv. 4. 31, *Rich. III.* ii. 4. 66, iii. 1. 28, 42, iv. 1. 94, etc.

130. *Put on those shall,* etc. For *put on*=instigate, cf. v. 2. 371 below: "deaths put on by cunning," etc.; and for the omission of the relative, Gr. 244.

133. *Remiss.* Careless. As Wr. notes, the word is "seldom if ever used now except with reference to some particular act of negligence." Cf. 1 *Hen. VI.* iv. 3. 29: "while remiss traitors sleep."

134. *Contriving.* In a bad sense=plotting; as in *J. C.* ii. 3. 16, *Rich. II.* i. 3. 189, *Hen. V.* iv. 1. 171, etc.

135. *Peruse.* Examine closely. Cf. *perusal,* ii. 1. 90 above.

137. *Unbated.* Not blunted, as foils are by a button fixed to the end (Malone). In *M. of V.* ii. 6. 11, it means unabated. For *bate*=to blunt, see *L. L. L.* i. 1. 6; and for *bateless*=not to be blunted, *R. of L.* 9. Steevens quotes North's *Plutarch:* "the cruel fight of fencers at unrebated swords." Cf. *M. for M.* i. 4. 60: "rebate and blunt his natural edge." So *abate*=blunt, in 2 *Hen. IV.* i. 1. 117 and *Rich. III.* v. 5. 35.

*A pass of practice.* A treacherous thrust; or, possibly, a pass in which you are well practised. For *practice* in the former sense, cf. 66 above.

138. *I will do 't,* etc. "Laertes shows by his horrid suggestion of the poison how little need there was for the king to prepare the temptation as carefully as he had done" (M.).

140. *Mountebank.* Quack (Schmidt). Cf. *Oth.* i. 3. 61: "medicines bought of mountebanks," etc. Wr. quotes Bacon, *Adv. of L.* ii. 10. 2: "Nay, we see the weakness and credulity of men is such, as they will often prefer a mountebank or witch before a learned physician;" and Cotgrave, *Fr. Dict.* (under *charlatan*): "A Mountebanke, a cousening drug-seller, a pratling quack-saluer."

141. *Mortal.* Deadly; as often. See *Rich. II.* p. 189 or *Macb.* p. 171.

143. *Simples.* Herbs (as the ingredients of a compound). Cf. *R. of L.* 530, *A. Y. L.* iv. 1. 16, *R. and J.* v. 1. 40, etc.

144. *Under the moon.* Probably = on the earth. Cf. *Lear,* iv. 6. 26, *A. and C.* iv. 15. 68, etc. J. H. explains it: "plants that have magic virtue when gathered by moonlight."

146. *Contagion.* Poison; the abstract for the concrete, like *unction*= ointment (Wr.). *That=so* that, as in iv. 5. 197 above.

149. *May fit us,* etc. May enable us to act our part (Johnson).

150. *And that.* And if. Gr. 285. So *and that*=and when, in 158 below. *Look through*=show itself through, appear through.

152. *A back.* "A support in reserve" (Schmidt).

153. *If this,* etc. "A metaphor taken from the trying or proving of fire-arms or cannon, which blast or burst in the proof" (Steevens).

154. *Your cunnings.* Your respective skill. Cf. ii. 2. 427, 577 above. The folio has "commings," which Caldecott (followed by K.) explains

as=bouts at fence. Cotgrave has "Venuë, f. A comming; also, a vennie in fencing."

157. *As.* For so. See on iv. 3. 58 above.

158. *Prepar'd.* The quartos have "prefard" or "preferd."

159. *For the nonce.* For the occasion; a corruption of *for then once* (Wb.). Cf. 1 *Hen. IV.* i. 2. 201: "cases of buckram for the nonce," etc.

160. *Stuck.* Thrust; "more properly *stock*, an abbreviation of *stoccata*" (D.). Cf. *T. N.* iii. 4. 303: "he gives me the stuck."

162. *One woe*, etc. Cf. iv. 5. 61 above: "When sorrows come," etc. Wr. quotes *Per.* i. 4. 63; and Ritson cites *Locrine* (one of the plays that have been ascribed to S.), v. 5, where Sabren drowns herself and Queen Gwendoline exclaims: "One mischief follows [on] another's neck."

165. *There is*, etc. Wr. considers this speech, with its enumeration of flowers, "unworthy of its author and the occasion." F. quotes Campbell (see p. 21, foot-note), *Blackwood's Mag.*: "The queen was affected after a fashion by the picturesque mode of Ophelia's death, and takes more pleasure in describing it than any one would who really had a heart. Gertrude was a gossip,—and she is gross even in her grief."

*Aslant.* Beisley says: "This willow, the *Salix alba*, grows on the banks of most of our small streams, particularly the Avon, near Stratford, and from the looseness of the soil the trees partly lose their hold, and bend 'aslant' the stream."

166. *Hoar.* "Willow leaves are green on the upper side, but silvery-grey, or *hoary*, on the under side, which it shows in the glassy stream" (Clarke). Cf. Lowell, *Among My Books*, p. 185 (though he misquotes the passage).

167. *Come.* The quartos have "make," and the 2d and 3d quartos "Therewith."

168. *Crow-flowers.* According to Beisley, the crowfoot (*Ranunculus bulbosus* and *acris*); but Ellacombe says that in the time of S. the name was applied to the "Ragged Robin" (*Lychnis floscuculi*).

*Long purples.* "The *early purple orchis* (*Orchis mascula*) which blossoms in April and May" (Beisley). According to the same authority, the name *dead-men's-fingers* was given to other species having palmated roots (*Orchis maculata* and *latifolia*).

169. *Liberal.* Free-spoken; as in *Rich. II.* ii. 1. 229: "a liberal tongue;" and *Oth.* v. 2. 220: "No, I will speak as liberal as the north." Elsewhere, it means wanton, licentious; as in *Much Ado*, iv. 1. 93, *M. of V.* ii. 2. 194, etc. It may have that sense here. The old *Herbals* give more than one "grosser name" for the flower.

170. *Cold.* Chaste; as in *Temp.* iv. 1. 66: "To make cold nymphs chaste crowns," etc.

172. *Sliver.* Here = a small branch. See *Macb.* p. 229.

176. *Which time.* For the omission of the preposition, see Gr. 202. For *tunes* the quartos have "laudes" or "lauds" (=psalms).

177. *Incapable.* Insensible. See on iii. 4. 125 above.

178. *Native.* Cf. i. 2. 47 above. *Induced*=fitted, suited. Cf. *Oth.* iii. 4. 146:

> "For let our finger ache, and it indues
> Our other healthful members even to that sense
> Of pain;"

that is, imparts to them the feeling of the same pain. In *Hen. V.* ii. 2. 139, "best indued"=best endowed.

181. *Poor wretch.* Cf. ii. 2. 168 above.

186. *Trick.* Habit. Cf. *A. and C.* v. 2. 75: "Is 't not your trick?" 2 *Hen. IV.* i. 2. 240: "the trick of our English nation," etc.

188. *The woman.* Steevens quotes *Hen. V.* iv. 6. 31:

> "But I had not so much of man in me,
> And all the mother came into mine eyes,
> And gave me up to tears."

Wr. adds *T.N.* ii. 1. 41. Cf. *Hen. VIII.* iii. 2. 431: "to play the woman."

190. *Douts.* That is, *does out*, extinguishes. The quartos and later folios have "drownes" or "drowns;" the 1st folio "doubts," as in the only other passage in which S. uses the word, *Hen. V.* iv. 2. 11: "And dout them with superfluous courage." Cf. note on i. 4. 36, 37 above.

---

## ACT V.

SCENE I.—4. *Straight.* Probably=immediately; as in ii. 2. 418 above. Johnson says: "Make her grave from east to west, in a direct line, parallel with the church; not from north to south, athwart the regular line;" and M.: "Not the mere hole in which a person should be buried on whom a *felo de se* verdict has been found."

9. *Offendendo.* The clown's blunder for *defendendo;* as *argal* in 12 is his corruption of *ergo.* J. H. thinks he uses it intentionally: "by offending herself; that is, it cannot be in defence of herself, but by offence to herself."

13. *Delver.* "Hence it would appear that the Second Clown is not a grave-digger" (Walker).

16. *Nill.* Will not. Cf. *P. P.* 188: "In scorn or friendship, nill I construe whether;" and *Per.* iii. prol. 55: "I nill relate." J. H. quotes Latimer, *Sermons:* "Such men should be witnesses—will they nill they;" and Edwards, *Damon and Pythias:* "Will I or nill I, it must be done."

21. *Crowner's quest law.* Sir John Hawkins suspects that S. here meant to ridicule a case reported by Plowden. Sir James Hales had drowned himself in a fit of insanity, and the legal question was whether his lease was thereby forfeited to the Crown. Much subtlety was expended in finding out whether Sir James was the *agent* or the *patient,* that is, whether *he went to the water* or *the water came to him.* The following is part of the argument: "Sir James Hales was dead, and how came he to his death? It may be answered, by drowning; and who drowned him? Sir James Hales; and when did he drown him? In his lifetime. So that Sir James Hales being alive caused Sir James Hales to die, and the act of the living man was the death of the dead man. And then for this offence it is reasonable to punish the living man who

committed the offence, and not the dead man. But how can he be said to be punished alive when the punishment comes after death?" etc., etc.

25. *Say'st.* That is, well, or to the purpose (Schmidt). Cf. *T. G. of V.* ii. 4. 29: "You have said, sir." See also *T. N.* iii. 1. 12, *Oth.* iv. 2. 204, and *A. and C.* ii. 6. 113.

27. *Even-Christian.* Fellow-Christian. The quartos have "theyr euen Christen;" and Capell and F. read "their even-Christen." Steevens quotes Chaucer, *Persones Tale:* "his neighebour, that is to say, of his even Christen" (Morris prints "evencristen"). Nares cites Sir Thomas More: "to fighte against their even Christen." Caldecott and Wr. add other examples of this and similar expressions; as "euen-seruant" (fellow-servant), "euene-caytif" (fellow-prisoner), etc.

29. *Hold up.* Follow up, continue (Schmidt). Cf. *M. N. D.* iii. 2. 239: "hold the sweet jest up;" 2 *Hen. IV.* iv. 2. 48: "And heir from heir shall hold this quarrel up," etc.

30. *A gentleman.* Douce says that Gerard Leigh, one of the oldest writers on heraldry, speaks of "Jesus Christ, a gentleman of great lineage, and King of the Jews;" and again: "the second man that was born was a gentleman, whose name was Abell. I say a gentleman both of vertue and lignage, with whose sacrifice God was much pleased. His brother Cain was ungentle, for he offered God the worst of his fruites." Adam's spade is mentioned in some of the books of heraldry as the most ancient form of escutcheon.

39. *Go to.* Come! a common phrase of exhortation or reproof. Cf. *Temp.* v. 1. 297, etc.

40. *What.* Who. See on iv. 6. 1 above.

51. *Unyoke.* That is, your day's work is done (Caldecott). J. H. sees an allusion to *Judges*, xiv. 18.

54. *Mass.* "By the mass" (ii. 1. 50 above).

58. *Yaughan.* The folio reading (in italics, as if a proper name); the quartos have "get thee in." The word is apparently meant as the name of an alehouse-keeper, and has been suspected to be a corruption of *Johan*, the Danish *John*. Mr. C. E. Browne (quoted by F.) says that it is a common Welsh name, and may have been that of some Welsh tavern-keeper near the theatre.

59. *Stoup.* A drinking-cup. Cf. v. 2. 255 below; also *T. N.* ii. 3. 14, 129, and *Oth.* ii. 3. 30.

60. *In youth*, etc. The clown sings some disjointed lines of a song by Lord Vaux, entitled "The aged lover renounceth love." It was printed in a collection of "Songes and Sonnettes," published by Tottel in 1557. The following are the stanzas that are of interest here:

"I lothe that I did loue,
In youth that I thought swete:
As time requires for my behoue
Me thinkes they are not mete.

. . . . . . . .

For age with stelyng steppes,
Hath clawed me with his cowche [crowch],
And lusty life away she leapes,
As there had bene none such.

. . . . . . . .

> A pikeax and a spade
> And eke a shrowdyng shete,
> A house of claye for to be made,
> For such a gest most mete.
>
> . . . . . . .
>
> For beauty with her bande
> These croked cares hath wrought:
> And shipped me into the lande,
> From whence I first was brought."

62. The *O!* and *ah!* form no part of the song, but are "only the breath forced out by the strokes of the mattock" (Jennens).

66. *Easiness.* "Freedom from emotion, unconcernedness" (Schmidt). Perhaps *property of easiness* is simply=an easy property, an easy thing for him. Cf. iv. 6. 19 above: "thieves of mercy."

69. *Daintier.* Nicer, more delicate. Cf. *L. L. L.* iv. 3. 339, etc.

72. *Intil.* Into. Wr. quotes Chaucer, *C. T.* 2064: "Ther saugh I Dyane turned intil a tree."

75. *Jowls.* Knocks. Cf. *A. W.* i. 3. 58: "They may jowl horns together." Clarke remarks here: "If proof were wanted of the exquisite propriety and force of effect with which S. uses words, and words of even homely fashion, there could hardly be a more pointed instance than the verb *jowls* here. What strength it gives to the impression of the head and cheek-bone smiting against the earth! and how it makes the imagination feel the bruise in sympathy!"

77. *Politician.* "A plotter, a schemer for his own advantage; as in 1 *Hen. IV.* i. 3. 241, and *T. N.* iii. 2. 34" (St.).

*O'er-reaches.* Apparently=has the better of. The folio has "o're Offices," and some modern eds. read "o'er-offices"=is higher in office.

82. *That praised,* etc. Steevens compares *T. of A.* i. 2. 216 fol.

86. *Mazzard.* The head (contemptuous). Cf. *Oth.* ii. 3. 155: "I 'll knock you over the mazzard."

87. *Revolution.* Change of fortune. Cf. *A. and C.* i. 2. 129:

> "the present pleasure,
> By revolution lowering, does become
> The opposite of itself."

*Trick*="knack, faculty" (Caldecott).

88. *Loggats.* A game in which *loggats*, or small logs, are thrown at a mark. We have seen a similar game played in some parts of New England under the name of "loggerheads." Wr. quotes B. J., *Tale of a Tub,* iv. 6:

> "Now are they tossing of his legs and arms
> Like loggats at a pear-tree."

Halliwell gives the following from a poem of 1611:

> "To wrastle, play at stooleball, or to runne,
> To pich the Barre, or to shoote off a Gunne,
> To play at Loggets, Nine-holes, or Ten-pinnes;
> To try it out at Foot-ball by the shinnes."

91. *For and.* Equivalent to "And eke" in the song as given above. D. quotes B. and F., *Knt. of Burning Pestle,* ii. 3:

> "and with him comes the lady
> For and the Squire of Damsels," etc.

92. *For to.* See on iii. 1. 167 above.

95. *Quiddits.* The folio reading; the quartos have "quiddities," of which *quiddits* is a contraction. It was applied to the subtleties or nice distinctions of logic and law. Overbury, in his *Characters*, speaks of the pettifogger who "makes his will in form of a law-case, full of quiddits." *Quillets* means much the same. Cf. *L. L. L.* iv. 3. 288: "Some tricks, some quillets, how to cheat the devil;" 1 *Hen. VI.* ii. 4. 17: "these nice sharp quillets of the law," etc.

On the law terms which follow, Lord Campbell remarks that they are "all used seemingly with a full knowledge of their import; and it would puzzle some practising barristers . . . to go over the whole *seriatim*, and to define each of them satisfactorily."

101. *The fine of his fines.* The end of all his fines; a play upon the word. We have *fine*=end in ii. 2. 69 and iv. 7. 132 above.

104. *A pair of indentures.* "Indentures were agreements made out in duplicate, of which each party kept one. Both were written on the same sheet, which was cut in two in a crooked or *indented* line, in order that the fitting of the two parts might prove the genuineness of both in case of dispute" (Wr.).

106. *Box.* Alluding to the boxes in which attorneys keep their deeds (Rushton).

*Inheritor* here=owner, possessor; as in *L. L. L.* ii. 1. 5 and *Rich. III.* iv. 3. 34 (Schmidt).

110. *Assurance.* Safety, security; with a play on the legal sense of "conveyance of lands by deed."

116. *Thine.* "Note that throughout this dialogue Hamlet addresses the Clown in the second person singular, while the Clown replies in the second person plural" (F.). See Gr. 231, 232.

120. *Quick.* Opposed to *dead*, as in 240 below. Cf. *Acts*, x. 42, etc. See *Hen. V.* p. 156.

130. *Absolute.* Positive, certain; as in *Macb.* iii. 6. 40, *Cor.* iii. 1. 90, iii. 2. 39, etc.

*Speak by the card.* That is, with the utmost precision. The *card* is probably the *chart* of the navigator, though some take it to be the *compass-card.* St. thinks the allusion is to the *card* and *calendar* of etiquette, or *book of manners.* See *A. Y. L.* p. 198, and cf. v. 2. 109 below.

133. *Picked.* "Refined" (Schmidt); "smart, sharp" (Hanmer). Cf. *L. L. L.* v. 1. 14: "He is too picked, too spruce, too affected, too odd;" and *K. John*, i. 1. 193: "My picked man of countries."

134. *Kibe.* Chilblain. Cf. *Temp.* ii. 1. 276, *M. W.* i. 3. 35, and *Lear*, i. 5. 9.

136. *Of all the days*, etc. Wr. quotes *R. and J.* i. 3. 16:

> "Even or odd, of all days in the year,
> Come Lammas-eve at night shall she be fourteen."

140. *Hamlet was born.* This, in connection with what follows, makes Hamlet thirty years old, which Blackstone thought to be inconsistent with his going back to Wittenberg (i. 2. 113). Tschischwitz replies that this is now no unusual age for a student at a German university; but, according to Minto and others, it would have been unusual in the time

of S., when young men generally left the university at the age of seventeen or eighteen. Besides, many other things in the early part of the play seem to show that Hamlet was "nearer twenty than thirty." Dowden, on the other hand, argues that these allusions to youth are not inconsistent with the theory that Hamlet was thirty. The age at which S. conceives "that boyhood is blooming into adult strength and beauty" is "from twenty-one to twenty-five." Henry V. when he ascended the throne was twenty-six, yet the Bishop of Ely speaks of him as "in the very May-morn of his youth." "The stolen sons of Cymbeline, boys just ready to be men, are aged twenty-three and twenty-two," etc. Cf. *Much Ado*, iii. 3. 141: "all the hot bloods between fourteen and five-and-thirty." The grave-digger himself speaks of "young Hamlet." On the whole, we may make Hamlet at least twenty-five, even if we hesitate to call him thirty. Perhaps, as Furnivall suggests, "when S. began the play he conceived Hamlet as quite a young man; but as the play grew, as greater weight of reflection, of insight into character, of knowledge of life, etc. were wanted, he necessarily and naturally made Hamlet a formed man; and by the time that he got to the grave-diggers' scene, told us the Prince was thirty—the right age for him then." For a *résumé* of the interesting discussion on this subject, see F. vol. i. pp. 391–394, and cf. preface, pp. xiv.–xvii.

146. *There the men*, etc. Wr. quotes Marston, *Malcontent*, iii. 1: "Your lordship shall ever finde . . . amongst a hundred Englishmen fourscore and ten madmen."

158. *You*. See on *me*, ii. 2. 421 above, or Gr. 220.

*Eight year*. See on *a thousand pound*, iii. 2. 266 above.

171. *Yorick*. Perhaps the Danish *Jörg* (George). F. notes that "Jerick" is the name of a "Dutch Bowr" in Chapman's *Alphonsus*.

178. *It is*. That is, this skull which is all that is left of him. W. says: "What he abhors, what his gorge rises at, is *his imagination that here hung the lips that he has kissed*." *Gorge* = throat, swallow, stomach (Schmidt). Cf. *V. and A.* 58, *W. T.* ii. 1. 44, *Oth.* ii. 1. 236, etc.

181. *On a roar*. For *on*, see Gr. 180.

184. *Favour*. Look, appearance; as often. Cf. *M. for M.* iv. 2. 34: "Pray, sir, by your good favour,—for surely, sir, a good favour you have, but that you have a hanging look," etc. See also *M. N. D.* p. 130.

195. *Curiously*. Fancifully, ingeniously. Cf. *T. of S.* iv. 3. 144: "the sleeves curiously cut." Horatio anticipates some fanciful or far-fetched reasoning here, to which Hamlet replies that he will "follow him thither with *modesty* enough and *likelihood*," that is, not overstepping "the modesty of nature" (iii. 2. 18) and probability—naturally, not sophistically.

199. *Loam*. The word seems to mean *clay*, or something more tenacious than what we call *loam*; and so in the three other instances in which S. uses the word: *M. N. D.* iii. 1. 70, v. 1. 162, and *Rich. II.* i. 1. 179.

202–205. These lines are marked in the Coll. MS. as a quotation; but probably, as Clarke remarks, "Hamlet is merely putting into rhyming form the fancy that for the moment passes through his mind." On this "tendency to doggerelize when he is speaking lightly or excitedly," cf. iii. 2. 272, etc.

*Imperious* is the quarto reading; the folio has "Imperiall." Cf. *T. and C.* iv. 5. 172: "most imperious Agamemnon;" *T. A.* iv. 4. 81: "be thy thoughts imperious, like thy name" (cf. *Id.* v. 1. 6), etc.

*Flaw.* Gust. D. quotes Smith's *Sea Grammar*, 1627: "A flaw of wind is a gust, which is very violent upon a sudden, but quickly endeth." It is still used by sailors in the same sense; and so *flawy*=gusty. Cf. *V. and A.* 456, *Cor.* v. 3. 74, etc.

M. remarks that "the passage of the living body into the state of inanimate beings has often been seriously illustrated in a somewhat similar way;" and he quotes Wordsworth:

> "No motion has she now, no force—
> She neither hears nor sees,
> Rolled round in earth's diurnal course
> With rocks, and stones, and trees."

Still more similar is *In Memoriam*, lv. "Shall man," the poet asks,

> "Who loved, who suffered countless ills,
> Who battled for the true, the just,
> Be blown about the desert dust.
> Or sealed within the iron hills?"

208. *Maimed.* Imperfect, defective; as in *Oth.* i. 3. 99, etc. By the English law, a suicide was formerly buried at the meeting of cross-roads with a stake driven through his body and without any form of burial service (Wr.).

210. *Fordo.* See on ii. 1. 103 above; and for *it*=its, on i. 2. 216.

*Estate.* Rank. Cf. *R. of L.* 92, *M. of V.* ii. 9. 41, etc.

211. *Couch.* Hide; perhaps, literally, lie down. Cf. *M. W.* v. 2. 1, etc.

216. *Warrantise.* The folio has "warrantis," the quartos "warrantie." For *warrantise*, cf. *Sonn.* 150. 7 and 1 *Hen. VI.* i. 3. 13.

*Doubtful.* "Only so far as that she was a lunatic, and had died by her own act; the presumption in such a case being held to be that the act was wilful, and there being always a *doubt* whether Christian burial could then be demanded; although, as Burn's *Ecclesiastical Law* states, there is no record of its having been actually refused in any instance" (M.). The queen has said that the death was accidental (iv. 7. 171 fol.). The context implies that a kind of "maimed" burial-service had been secured for Ophelia by the "great command" of the king.

217. *Order.* That is, the course which ecclesiastical rules prescribe (Caldecott).

219. *For.* Instead of. See Gr. 148.

220. *Shards.* Potsherds, fragments of pottery. In the only other instance of the word in S. it means the wing-cases of beetles. See *A. and C.* iii. 2. 20, and cf. *Macb.* iii. 2. 42 and *Cymb.* iii. 3. 20.

221. *Crants.* The quarto reading; the folio has "rites," which Rowe, K., W., H., and some others prefer. D. and Schmidt define *crants* as "garland" (German *Kranz*). According to Jamieson's *Scottish Dict.*, *crance* is used in Lowland Scotch in the same sense. Nares says that no other example of *crants* has been found in English; but Elze has discovered *corance*, which is evidently the same word, in a stage-direction of Chapman's *Alphonsus:* "with Corances on their heads;" and again

in a line of the same play: "When thou hast stolen her dainty rose-corance." Johnson suggests that S. wrote *crants*, and then finding that the word was provincial, and perhaps not understood, changed it to *rites*, "a term more intelligible, but less proper."

222. *Strewments.* Not used elsewhere by S., but we have *strewings* in the same sense in *Cymb.* iv. 2. 285: "strewings fitt'st for graves." For the custom, Wr. refers to *R. and J.* iv. 5. 79, 89, v. 3. 281, *W. T.* iv. 4. 128, and *Cymb.* iv. 2. 218.

*Bringing home.* "As the bride was brought home to her husband's house with bell and festivity, so the dead maiden is brought to her last home *with bell and burial*" (Wr.).

223. *Of.* With. Gr. 193.

227. *Peace-parted.* Having parted in peace. For *part*=depart or die, cf. *Hen. V.* ii. 3. 12, *Macb.* v. 8. 52, etc. So *timely-parted*=having died in time, or by a natural death, in 2 *Hen. VI.* iii. 2. 161.

229. *May violets spring.* Steevens quotes Persius, *Sat.* 1:

> "e tumulo fortunataque favilla
> Nascentur violae?"

and M. compares Tennyson, *In Memoriam*, xviii.:

> "'T is well; 't is something; we may stand
> Where he in English earth is laid,
> And from his ashes may be made
> The violet of his native land."

233, 234. For *shouldst have been* and *to have deck'd*, now commonly considered ungrammatical when used as here, see Gr. 360.

237. *Ingenious sense.* Keen intellect. Wr. compares *Lear*, iv. 6. 287.

242. *Skyish.* "Sky-aspiring" (*Rich. II.* i. 3. 130).

245. *Wandering stars.* Wr. explains this as=planets, but it may mean simply the stars moving through the heavens.

246. *Wonder-wounded.* Wonderstruck.

249. *Thou pray'st not well.* "A litotes marking the perfect self-possession of Hamlet at first, and his real love for Laertes" (M.).

251. *Splenitive.* Passionate. Cf. *spleeny* in *Hen. VIII.* iii. 2. 99, and *spleenful* in 2 *Hen. VI.* iii. 2. 128 and *T. A.* ii. 3. 191. So *spleen* often= passion, impetuosity; as in *K. John*, ii. 1. 68, 448, iv. 3. 97, v. 7. 50, *Rich. III.* v. 3. 50, etc. See also *M. N. D.* p. 129, note on *Spleen*.

253. *Wisdom.* The folio has "wisenesse," and is followed by K., St., M., and others.

257. *Wag.* Move. Cf. iii. 4. 39 above; also *M. of V.* iv. 1. 76, *Cymb.* iv. 2. 173, etc. As Wr. remarks, the word had not then the grotesque signification which it now has.

260. *Quantity.* See on iii. 4. 75 above.

264. *'Swounds.* See on ii. 2. 562 above.

265. *Woo't.* A provincial contraction for *wouldst thou* or *wilt thou*, perhaps used here contemptuously. Cf. *A. and C.* iv. 2. 7 and iv. 15. 59, where it "denotes affectionate familiarity" (Wr.).

266. *Eisel.* "With the exception of the *dram of eale*, no word or phrase in this tragedy has occasioned more discussion than this *Esill* [in the quartos] or *Esile* [in the folio], which, as it stands, represents nothing

in the heavens above, or the earth beneath, or the waters under the earth" (F.). Theo. suggested that the word either represents the name of a river (as the *Yssel*) or is an old word meaning vinegar. The latter is the more probable, as the A. S. *aisil*=vinegar. Cf. also *Sonn.* III. 10:

> "I will drink
> Potions of eisel 'gainst my strong infection;"

vinegar being esteemed a protection against contagion. Wr. finds "vynegre or aysel" in a MS. in the Library of Trinity College, Cambridge. There is, however, something to be said in favour of the river, for which, as well as for other explanations, see F. vol. i. pp. 405–409.

*Eat a crocodile.* Referring, as some suppose, to the dried or pickled crocodile of the apothecary (cf. *R. and J.* v. 1. 43); or more probably, as others believe, to the toughness of the creature's hide.

268. *In.* Equivalent to *into*, as often. See Gr. 159.

273. *Mouth.* Brag, rant. Cf. iii. 2. 2 above.

277. *When that.* See Gr. 287, and cf. iv. 4. 5 above.

*Golden couplets.* The pigeon generally sits on two eggs, and her young when first *disclosed*, or hatched (see on iii. 1. 166 above), are covered with a yellow down.

282. *The cat will mew*, etc. That is, things have their appointed course, nor have we power to divert it (Caldecott). "Bay" has been proposed instead of *day*, but the expression was a common one. The Princess Elizabeth, in a letter to her sister, Queen Mary, says: "As a doge hathe a day, so may I." Mr. Daniel quotes *New Custom*, 1573: "Well if it chaunce that a dogge hath a day;" and B. J. *Tale of a Tub*, ii. 1: "A man hath his hour, and a dog his day."

284. *Strengthen your patience.* Cf. *J. C.* ii. 1. 248: "Fearing to strengthen that impatience," etc. *In*=in the thought of (Gr. 162).

285. *We 'll put*, etc. "Let us push on the matter immediately" (Schmidt); we will go to work at once. For *present*, see on iv. 3. 64 above; and for *push*, cf. *W. T.* v. 3. 129.

287. *A living monument.* A lasting one (Schmidt). M. makes it="a statue like life itself." Wr. suggests that the expression may be used in a double sense: that of enduring, as the queen would understand; and the deeper meaning, which Laertes would see, by which the life of Hamlet is menaced.

288. *Shortly.* The folio reading; the 2d quarto has "thirtie," the later ones "thereby."

SCENE II.—6. *Mutines.* See on iii. 4. 83 above.

*Bilboes.* A kind of fetters by which mutinous sailors were linked together; so called from Bilboa, in Spain, which was famous from Roman times for manufactures of iron and steel. The sword known as the *bilbo* (see *M. W.* i. 1. 165 and iii. 5. 112) gets its name from the same place. As the prisoners in the bilboes were fastened close together, every motion of the one must disturb the sleep of the other.

*Rashly.* Hastily; as in *Rich. III.* iii. 5. 43 (Schmidt). Hamlet begins the account of his escape, "and then is carried into a reflection upon the weakness of human wisdom. I rashly—praised be rashness for it—let us not think these events casual, but let us know, that is, take notice and remember, that we sometimes succeed by indiscretion when we fail by deep plots, and infer the perpetual superintendence and agency of the Divinity" (Johnson).

9. *Deep.* The folio has "deare," and is followed by Rowe, K., St., and others. *Fail* is Pope's emendation for the "fall" of the later quartos. The folio has "paule" and the 2d quarto "pall." For *teach* the quartos have "learne," which S. uses in the same sense; as in *Temp.* i. 2. 365, etc.

10. *Shapes our ends*, etc. Steevens says: "Dr. Farmer informed me that these words are merely technical. A wool-man, butcher, and dealer in *skewers*, lately observed to him that his nephew (an idle lad) could only *assist* him in making them:—'he could *rough-hew* them, but I was obliged to *shape their ends*.' Whoever recollects the profession of Shakespeare's father [see *Mer.* p. 9] will admit that his son might be no stranger to such terms. I have frequently seen packages of wool pinned up with *skewers*." *Rough-hew*, however, is not limited to skewer-making, but is a general word in carpentry (and metaphorically in other connections) for such work as the word naturally suggests—the first rough hewing-cut of the material, which a common workman can do, as distinguished from the subsequent shaping and finishing, which require a master hand. Hunter quotes Palsgrave, *Table of Verbs*, 1530: "I rough-hewe a pece of tymber to make an ymage of;" and Florio, *Ital. Dict.* 1598: "Abbozzare, to rough hew any first draught, to bungle ill-favouredly."

11. *That is most certain.* "Horatio for once expresses a slight impatience, which cuts short Hamlet's generalization" (M.).

13. *Sea-gown.* Sr. quotes Cotgrave, *Fr. Dict.*: "Esclavine, . . . a sea-gowne; or a course high-collered, and short-sleeued gowne, reaching downe to the mid-leg, and vsed most by sea-men, and Saylors." *Scarf'd* = "put on loosely like a scarf" (Schmidt).

14. *Find out them.* Cf. *J. C.* i. 3. 134: "To find out you;" and see Gr. 240.

15. *Finger'd.* Cf. 3 *Hen. VI.* v. 1. 44: "The king was slily finger'd from the deck."

17. *To unseal.* For the omission of *as*, see Gr. 281. Cf. *Macb.* ii. 3. 55, etc.

20. *Larded.* See on iv. 5. 37 above.

*Several.* Separate, different. Cf. *L. C.* 206: "I have received from many a several fair," etc. For *reasons* the folio has "reason."

21. *Importing.* Concerning. Cf. *L. L. L.* iv. 1. 57: "This letter is mistook, it importeth none here;" and *Oth.* i. 3. 284: "As doth import you" (where the quarto has "concern"). For other meanings of *import*, see i. 2. 23, iv. 3. 62, and iv. 7. 80 above.

22. *Bugs.* Bugbears. Cf. *T. of S.* i. 2. 211: "Tush! tush! fear boys with bugs;" 3 *Hen. VI.* v. 2. 2: "For Warwick was a bug that fear'd us all," etc. In both passages *fear* = frighten. Wr. quotes Coverdale's translation of the *Psalms* (xci. 5): "thou shalt not nede to be afrayed for eny bugges by night ner for arowe that flyeth by daye."

23. *On the supervise.* That is, at sight, on the *looking-over* or reading

of the document. So the verb=look over, inspect, in *L. L. L.* iv. 2. 124; Gr. 451. *Bated*=excepted, allowed.

24. *Stay.* Stay for, wait for; as in *A. Y. L.* iii. 2. 221, etc. Cf. the intransitive use in iii. 3. 95 above.

29. *Be-netted.* For verbs compounded with *be-*, see Gr. 438.

*Villanies.* The quartos have "villaines," the folio "Villaines;" but the sense and the measure both require *villanies*, and Walker shows that the two words have been several times confounded in the folio.

30. *Ere I could make*, etc. "Before I formed my real plan, my brains had done the work. This line should be carefully remarked. Hamlet writes the commission under a strong impulse rather of imagination than will, the ingenuity of the trick captivating him. Then the encounter with the pirate puts an end to the chance of undoing it; and thus he is driven, somewhat uneasily, to justify his action to Horatio. As the latter receives his narrative with something like surprise, and even with a touch of compassion, we may conclude with safety that Hamlet's kindly nature would have cancelled the letters but for the accident which hindered his doing so" (M.).

31. *Sat me down.* For the reflexive use, cf. iii. 4. 18 above; also 2 *Hen. IV.* iii. 1. 56, 3 *Hen. VI.* ii. 5. 14, etc. We find it sometimes in modern writers; as in Goldsmith, *Traveller*, 32: "I sit me down a pensive hour to spend;" Tennyson, *Lotos-Eaters:* "They sat them down upon the yellow sand," etc.

33. *Statists.* Statesmen; as in *Cymb.* ii. 4. 16: "Statist though I am none." Wr. quotes Milton, *P. R.* iv. 354: "statists indeed, And lovers of their country." Blackstone says: "Most of the great men of Shakespeare's time, whose autographs have been preserved, wrote very bad hands; their secretaries very neat ones."

36. *Yeoman's service.* The ancient yeomen were famous for their military valour (Steevens). Cf. *Hen. V.* iii. 1. 25 and *Rich. III.* v. 3. 338.

42. *A comma.* "So as to separate them as little as possible" (M.). Schmidt says, "keep their amities from falling together by the ears." Hanmer, followed by W. and H., reads "cement." For the many other attempts at emendation, see F.

43. *As's.* A quibble is intended between *as* and *ass* (Johnson). Malone remarks that in the midland counties the *s* in *as* is usually pronounced as in *us*. *Charge*=load, weight; as in *W. T.* iv. 4. 261, *R. and J.* v. 2. 18, etc.

44. *Knowing.* The folio has "know," which many eds. follow. Cf. Gr. 451. For *knowing* as a noun, cf. *T. of A.* iii. 2. 74, *Macb.* ii. 4. 4, *Cymb.* i. 4. 30 and ii. 3. 102.

45. *Debatement.* Debate, consideration; as in *M. for M.* v. 1. 99: "after much debatement."

47. *Shriving-time.* "A term in common use for any short period" (Hunter).

48. *Ordinant.* Ordaining, ruling. The folio has "ordinate."

50. *Model.* Copy, counterpart. Cf. *Rich. II.* i. 2. 28, iii. 2. 153, etc.

51. *Writ.* Commission, mandate. Cf. *Cymb.* iii. 7. 1: "the emperor's writ."

53. *Changeling.* Alluding to fairy changelings. See *M. N. D.* p. 138.

54. *Sequent.* Cf. *A. W.* ii. 2. 56: "Indeed your 'O Lord, sir!' is very sequent to your whipping," etc. The folio misprints "sement."

57. *Make love to.* Court, seek. Cf. *Macb.* iii. 1. 124: "I to your assistance do make love," etc.

58. *Near my conscience.* Cf. *A. Y. L.* v. 2. 68: "near the heart;" *Hen. VIII.* iii. 1. 71: "so near mine honour," etc. For *defeat* the folio misprints "debate." See on ii. 2. 556 above.

59. *Insinuation.* Meddling; *insinuating* themselves into the business. So *insinuate*=intermeddle in *W. T.* iv. 4. 760, etc.

61. *Pass.* Thrust; as in 159 below. Cf. the stage-direction at iii. 4. 23 above.

62. *Opposites.* Opponents. See on iii. 2. 203 above.

63. *Thinks 't thee.* That is, *thinks it thee*=seems it to thee. In *Rich. III.* iii. 1. 63, the folio has "Where it think'st best vnto your Royall selfe;" the 1st and 2d quartos "seems best." This *think* is the same verb that we have in *methinks* (=it seems to me), from the A. S. *thincan*, to seem, not from *thencan*, to think. See Gr. 297 (cf. 212). The folio has "meethink'st" in *L. L. L.* ii. 3. 269.

*Stand me now upon.* Be incumbent on me. Cf. *Rich. II.* ii. 3. 138: "It stands your grace upon to do him right;" and *A. and C.* ii. 1. 50:

"It only stands
Our lives upon to use our strongest hands."

See Gr. 204.

66. *Angle.* Angling-line; used literally in *A. and C.* ii. 5. 10; and again figuratively, as here, in *W. T.* iv. 2. 52. On *proper*, cf. *Temp.* iii. 3. 60: "their proper selves," etc.

67. *Is 't not perfect conscience.* That is, perfectly consistent with a good conscience. We should not use such an expression now, nor "Made it no conscience to destroy a prince" (*K. John*, iv. 2. 229). Cf. *Hen. VIII.* v. 3. 67.

68. *Quit.* Requite; as in 257 below. See *Rich. II.* p. 208. Lines 68–80 are omitted in the quartos.

70. *In.* Into; as in v. 1. 268 above. *Come in further evil*=commit further crimes (M.).

73. *It will be short*, etc. "You never suspect the errand Hamlet is on until you happen to hear that little word, '*the interim is mine!*' It means more mischief than all the monologues! No threats, no imprecations, no more mention of smiling, damned villain; no more self-accusal; but solely and briefly, '*It will be short;* the interim is mine!' Then, for the first time, we recognize the extent of the change that has been wrought in Hamlet; then, for the first time, we perfectly comprehend his quiet jesting with the Clown, his tranquil musings with Horatio. The man is transformed by a great resolve; *his mind is made up!* The return of the vessel from England will be the signal for his own execution, and therefore the moral problem is solved: the only chance of saving his life from a lawless murderer is to slay him; it has become an act of self-defence; he can do it with perfect conscience. He has calculated the return voyage; he has allowed the longest duration to his own existence and the

king's. At the very moment he encounters the Clown in the churchyard he is on his death-march to the palace at Elsinore" (Miles).

78. *Court.* The folio has "count;" corrected by Rowe. "Count" has, however, been defended as=make account of, reckon up, value.

79. *Bravery.* Bravado (D.). Cf. *J. C.* v. 1. 10: "With fearful bravery;" and see note in our ed. p. 175.

83. *Water-fly.* "A water-fly skips up and down upon the surface of the water without any apparent purpose or reason, and is thence the proper emblem of a busy trifler" (Johnson). Cf. *T. and C.* v. 1. 38: "how the poor world is pestered with such water-flies, diminutives of nature!"

85. *Gracious.* Cf. i. 1. 164 above.

88. *Chough.* See *Macb.* p. 221, or *Temp.* p. 127. F. favours Caldecott's suggestion that the word here is=*chuff*, a wealthy boor or clown. Cf. Cotgrave, *Fr. Dict.*: "Franc-gontier. A substantiall yonker, wealthie chuffe;" and again: "Maschefouyn. A chuffe, boore, lobcocke, lozell; one that is fitter to feed with cattell, then to conuerse with men." See also Massinger, *Duke of Milan*, iii. 1:

"To see these chuffs, that every day may spend
A soldier's entertainment for a year,
Yet make a third meal of a bunch of raisins."

90. *Sweet.* A common form of address in the Elizabethan court language (Mommsen *apud* F.). Cf. iii. 2. 48 above.

91. *Bonnet.* Cap. See *Rich. II.* p. 169.

94. *Lordship.* The folio has "friendship," which K. adopts.

97. *Indifferent.* See on iii. 1. 122 above. On the dialogue here, cf. iii. 2. 351 fol.

98. *For my*, etc. The quartos have "or my complection." (or "complexion."), and some modern eds. read "or my complexion—" Cf. i. 4. 27 above.

104. *I beseech you, remember—.* The full expression is found in *L. L. L.* v. 1. 103: "I do beseech thee, remember thy courtesy; I beseech thee, apparel thy head." Malone thought it should read "remember *not* thy courtesy;" but St. shows that the old text is right. He cites *Lusty Juventus*: "I pray you be remembred, and cover your head;" and *Every Man in His Humour*, i. 1: "Pray you, remember your courts'y . . . Nay, pray you be cover'd." No one has explained the phrase; but probably, as W. suggests, *remember* is used in some peculiar and perhaps elliptical way. It is curious that "*leave* your courtesy" is used in the same sense in *M. N. D.* iv. 1. 21.

105. *For mine ease.* Farmer quotes Marston, *Malcontent*, ind.:

"*Cun.* I beseech you, sir, be coverd.
*Sly.* No, in good faith, for mine ease."

Malone adds from Massinger, *New Way to Pay Old Debts*, ii. 3:

"Is 't for your ease
You keep your hat off?"

and from Florio, *Second Frutes*:

"Why do you stand barehedded? . . .
Pardon me, good sir, I doe it for mine ease."

106–139. *Sir, here . . . unfellowed.* This is omitted in the folio, which has only "Sir, you are not ignorant of what excellence *Laertes* is at his weapon."

106. *Absolute.* Complete, perfect. See *Hen. V.* p. 170.

107. *Excellent differences.* "Different excellencies," as Schmidt explains it (p. 1416), adding many similar examples; as "murderous shame" (*Sonn.* 9. 14) = shameful murder; "aged honour" (*A. W.* i. 3. 216) = honourable age; "expert allowance" (*Oth.* ii. 1. 49) = allowed or acknowledged expertness; "negligent danger" (*A. and C.* iii. 6. 81) = dangerous negligence, etc. Caldecott makes it = "every nice punctilio of good breeding;" and Wr., "distinctions marking him out from the rest of men."

108. *Feelingly.* So as to hit it exactly (Schmidt). Cf. *M. for M.* i. 2. 36: "Do I speak feelingly now?" See also *T. N.* ii. 3. 172.

109. *Card or calendar of gentry.* "The general preceptor of elegance; the card [see on v. 1. 131 above] by which a gentleman is to direct his course; the calendar by which he is to choose his time, that what he does may be both excellent and seasonable" (Johnson). *Gentry* = courtesy, gentlemanliness. Cf. ii. 2. 22 above.

110. *The continent*, etc. The sum total of all gentlemanly qualities. See on iv. 4. 64 and iv. 7. 72 above.

111. *Definement.* Definition, description. The sense of this affected jargon seems to be: You describe him justly; though to do it minutely and thoroughly would overtask one's memory and yet not come up to his deserts. Verily, he is a man of manifold virtues, and of so rare a nature that none but himself can be his parallel, while those who would imitate him are at best only his shadow.

113. *Yaw.* A vessel *yaws* when she falls off for the moment from her true course. The term is still in use among sailors; we have heard it often. D. quotes Coles, *Dict.*: "To yaw (as a ship), huc illuc vacillare, capite nutare." The noun occurs in Massinger, *Very Woman*, iii. 5: "O, the yaws that she will make!" where Gifford remarks: "A *yaw* is that unsteady motion which a ship makes in a great swell, when, in steering, she inclines to the right or left of her course."

115. *Of great article.* That is, of many items.

*Infusion.* Endowments, qualities (Schmidt). *Dearth* = high value (Johnson and Schmidt).

116. *Semblable.* Cf. *T. of A.* iv. 3. 22: "His semblable, yea, himself, Timon disdains," etc.

117. *Trace.* Follow. Cf. *Macb.* iv. 1. 153: "That trace him in his line," etc.

*Umbrage.* Shadow; used by S. only here.

120. *The concernancy, sir?* The meaning, sir? What does this mean?

121. *More rawer.* See on ii. 1. 11 above.

123. *Is 't not possible*, etc. "The meaning may be, 'Can't you understand your own absurd language on another man's tongue? Use your wits, sir, and you 'll soon be at the bottom of it'" (M.).

125. *Nomination.* Naming, mentioning by name. Cf. *L. L. L.* iv. 2. 138.

132. *Approve.* Make approved, commend (Schmidt).

135. *Compare with.* Assume to rival.

138. *Imputation.* Reputation, opinion. Cf. *M. of V.* i. 3. 13, *T. and C.* i. 3. 339, etc.

139. *Meed.* Merit. Cf. 3 *Hen. VI.* iv. 8. 38: "my meed hath got me fame," etc.

144. *Imponed.* Staked (Schmidt). The quartos have "hee has impaund;" the folio has "he impon'd." The text is due to Theo.

145. *Assigns.* Appendages; an "affected expression" (Schmidt).

146. *Hangers.* The straps by which the sword was hung to the belt. Steevens quotes Chapman, *Iliad*, xi. 27: "The scaberd was of silver-plate, with golden hangers grac'd."

148. *Liberal conceit.* Tasteful design. Cf. *R. of L.* 1423:

> "For much imaginary work was there;
> Conceit deceitful, so compact, so kind," etc.

150. *Edified by the margent.* Instructed by the explanation in the margin; a very common thing in old books. See *M.N.D.* p. 142. This speech of Horatio is omitted in the folio.

153. *Germane.* Akin, pertinent. Cf. *W. T.* iv. 4. 802 and *T. of A.* iv. 3. 344.

161. *Twelve for nine.* Johnson says: "This wager I do not understand. In a dozen passes one must exceed the other more or less than three hits. Nor can I comprehend how in a dozen there can be twelve for nine." Various attempts have been made to "figure it out," but they are not very satisfactory. We venture to suggest that S. wrote the "three hits" at random, and added the "twelve for nine" without stopping to think whether subtracting the three from twelve made the arithmetic all right. Cf. *Hen. V.* i. 2. 57 fol., where he subtracts 426 from 805 and gets a remainder of 421. The error is copied from Holinshed, but the fact that S. did not see and correct it shows his carelessness in regard to such matters.

162. *Answer.* Acceptance of the challenge. Cf. *T. and C.* i. 3. 332: "And wake him to the answer" (referring to the challenge of Hector).

167. *Breathing time.* Time for exercise (Schmidt). Cf. *A. W.* i. 2. 17: "For breathing and exploit;" *Id.* ii. 3. 271: "thou wast created for men to breathe themselves upon thee;" *Per.* ii. 1. 101: "Here is a lady that wants breathing too" (where the exercise is dancing), etc.

168. *Hold.* Changed by Capell to "holding." For similar "confusion of two constructions," see Gr. 411 fol.

169. *Will gain.* For the *will*, see Gr. 319.

171. *Re-deliver.* Report (Schmidt). Cf. iii. 1. 94, where it is used in a less affected way.

177. *This lapwing*, etc. Steevens quotes Greene, *Never too Late*: "Are you no sooner hatched, with the lapwing, but you will run away with the shell on your head?" Malone adds from Meres, *Wit's Treasury*: "As the lapwing runneth away with the shell on her head as soon as she is hatched." So Webster, *White Devil*, ii.: "Forward lapwing, he flies with the shell on 's head." Hence the bird was the symbol of a forward fellow; and also of insincerity, from its habit of alluring intruders from

its nest by crying far away from it (Wr.). Cf. *M. for M.* i. 4. 32 and *C. of E.* iv. 2. 27.

179. *Comply.* Use compliment, play the courtier. Cf. ii. 2. 363 above.

*Bevy.* The folio has "Beauy," the quartos "breede" or "breed."

181. *Outward habit*, etc. "Exterior politeness of address" (Henley).

*Yesty.* Frothy. The quartos have "histy" or "misty." Cf. *Macb.* iv. 1. 53: "the yesty waves."

183. *Fond and winnowed.* The folio reading; the quartos have "prophane (or "profane") and trennowed" (or "trennowned"). "Fanned" and "profound" have been suggested in place of *fond.* If any change is called for, the former is very plausible; but *fond and winnowed* may be= foolish and over-refined (cf. *picked* in v. 1. 133 above).

185–197. *Enter a Lord . . . instructs me.* Omitted in the folio.

186. *Commended him.* Cf. *T. and C.* iii. 1. 73: "Commends himself most affectionately to you;" *M. of V.* iii. 2. 235: "Antonio commends him to you," etc.

189. *Or that.* Or if. Cf. iv. 7. 61, 150, and 158 above. Gr. 285.

191. *Fitness.* Convenience (Schmidt).

194. *In happy time.* Just in time; "like the Fr. *à la bonne heure*" (Wr.). Cf. *T. of S.* ind. 1. 90, *A. W.* v. 1. 6, *J. C.* ii. 2. 60, etc.

195. *Gentle entertainment.* "Conciliating behaviour" (Caldecott).

200. *At the odds.* "With the advantage that I am allowed" (Malone).

201. *But thou wouldst not think*, etc. Coleridge remarks: "Shakespeare seems to mean all Hamlet's character to be brought together before his final disappearance from the scene: his meditative excess in the grave-digging, his yielding to passion with Laertes, his love for Ophelia blazing out, his tendency to generalize on all occasions in the dialogue with Horatio, his fine gentlemanly manners with Osric, and his and Shakespeare's own fondness for presentiment."

204. *Gain-giving.* Misgiving. Cf. *gainsay* (*gain*=against, A. S. *geán*). So *gainstand*=withstand, *gainstrive*=strive against (Spenser, *F. Q.* ii. 4. 14: "Who him gainstriving nought at all prevaild"), etc.

207. *Repair.* Cf. *M. for M.* iv. 1. 43, *L. L. L.* ii. 1. 240, and 3 *Hen. VI.* v. 1. 20. *Fit*=ready; as in *Cor.* i. 3. 47: "We are fit to bid her welcome," etc.

211. *Since no man*, etc. The quartos have "since no man of ought he leaues, knowes what ist to leaue betimes, let be;" the folio, "since no man ha's ought of what he leaues. What is 't to leaue betimes?" Warb., followed by Coll., Sr., Halliwell, H., and others, reads, "Since no man, of aught he leaves, knows, what is 't to leave betimes?" Rowe, Pope, Theo., K., D., St., W., and others, have "Since no man has aught of what he leaves, what is 't," etc. The reading in the text was suggested by Johnson, who assumed that the "knows" of the quartos was right, but was misprinted "ha's" in the revised form of the passage in the folio. Johnson paraphrases the passage thus: "Since *no man knows aught of* the state of life which *he leaves*, since he cannot judge what other years may produce, why should he be afraid of *leaving* life betimes? Why should he dread an early death, of which he cannot tell whether it is an exclusion of happiness or an interception of calamity? I despise the

superstition of augury and omens, which has no ground in reason or piety; my comfort is, that I cannot fall but by the direction of Providence." Caldecott explains the re-pointed folio reading as follows: "Since no man has (that is, has any secure hold, or can properly be denominated the possessor, of) any portion of that which he leaves, or must leave, behind him, of what moment is it that this leave-taking, or parting with a possession so frail, should be made thus early?" Clarke and F. prefer the quarto reading, as we do, on the ground that "it is more characteristic of Hamlet to think little of leaving life, because he cannot solve its many mysteries, than because he cannot carry with him life's goods."

214. *Give me your pardon*, etc. Johnson says: "I wish Hamlet had made some other defence; it is unsuitable to the character of a brave or a good man to shelter himself in falsehood." Seymour believes that the passage from *This presence* to *enemy* in 227 below is an interpolation, as "the falsehood contained in it is too ignoble."

216. *This presence.* The abstract for the concrete (Wr.). Cf. *L. L. L.* v. 2. 102, *K. John*, ii. 1. 196, *Rich. II.* i. 1. 34, etc.

219. *Exception.* Disapprobation, objection. Cf. *Hen. V.* ii. 4. 34: "modest in exception," etc.

228. *Sir, in this audience.* Omitted in the quartos.

232. *Brother.* The folio has "Mother."

*In nature.* "A piece of satire on fantastical honour. Though *nature* is satisfied, yet he will ask advice of older men of the sword whether artificial honour ought to be contented with Hamlet's submission" (Steevens).

238. *Ungor'd.* Unwounded, unhurt. The folio has "ungorg'd." Wr. quotes *T. and C.* iii. 3. 228: "My fame is shrewdly gor'd."

245. *Stick fiery off.* Be brilliantly set off, "stand in brilliant relief" (Wr.).

249. *Your grace*, etc. "I understand that your grace has taken care that points shall be given me; but for all that I fear that I shall be the weaker. No, replies the king, I have seen you both, and the points given will counterbalance his Paris improvement" (M.). According to Jennens, the *odds* are those that were laid in the wager, namely, the greater value of the king's stake as compared with that of Laertes (Ritson computes the values as twenty to one), and not to the number of hits, which is what the king refers to in his reply.

251. *Since he is better'd.* "Since he has perfected himself in his art" (Schmidt). The quartos have "better."

253. *Likes.* Pleases, suits. See on ii. 2. 80 above. *A* = one (Gr. 81).

257. *Quit*, etc. Pay him off in meeting him at the third encounter (Wr.). Cf. 68 above.

258. *Ordnance.* The folio has "Ordinance." See *Hen. V.* p. 161.

260. *Union.* A fine pearl. Malone quotes Florio, *Ital. Dict.*: "Vnione, . . . a faire, great, orient pearle." Steevens cites Holland's *Pliny*: "our dainties and delicates here at Rome, haue deuised this name for them, and call them Vnions; as a man would say, Singular, and by themselues alone."

263. *Kettle.* That is, kettle-drum. Cf. i. 4. 11 above.

270. *This pearl*, etc. "Under pretence of throwing a pearl into the cup, the king may be supposed to drop some poisonous drug into the wine. Hamlet seems to suspect this, when he afterwards discovers the effects of the poison, and tauntingly asks him, 'Is thy union here?'" (Steevens).

275. *He 's fat*, etc. Coll. has shown that Richard Burbadge was the original Hamlet, and that these words were inserted because he was corpulent. This is evident from an elegy upon the actor, which says:

> "No more young Hamlet, though but scant of breath,
> Shall cry 'Revenge!' for his dear father's death."

276. *Napkin.* Handkerchief; the only meaning of the word in S. See *A. Y. L.* p. 190; or cf. *L. C.* 15, *Oth.* iii. 3. 290, 306, etc.

277. *Carouses.* Drinks a health. Cf. *Oth.* ii. 3. 55:

> "Now my sick fool Roderigo,
> Whom love hath turn'd almost the wrong side out,
> To Desdemona hath to-night carous'd
> Potations pottle-deep," etc.

284. *And yet*, etc. "This symptom of relenting is not only a redeeming touch in the character of Laertes (and Shakespeare, in his large tolerance and true knowledge of human nature, is fond of giving these redeeming touches even to his worst characters), but it forms a judiciously interposed link between the young man's previous determination to take the Prince's life treacherously and his subsequent revealment of the treachery. From the deliberate malice of becoming the agent in such a plot, to the remorseful candour which confesses it, would have been too violent and too abrupt a moral change, had not the dramatist, with his usual skill, introduced this connecting point of half compunction" (Clarke).

287. *Afeard.* Used by S. interchangeably with *afraid.* See *M. N. D.* p. 156 or *Macb.* p. 163.

*Make a wanton of me.* "Trifle with me as if you were playing with a child" (Ritson). Cf. *Rich. II.* iii. 3. 164. Schmidt makes it=treat me like an effeminate boy. Cf. *K. John*, v. 1. 70 and *Rich. II.* v. 3. 10. H. remarks here: "This is a quiet but very significant stroke of delineation. Laertes is not playing his best, and it is the conscience of what is at the point of his foil that keeps him from doing so; and the effects are perceptible to Hamlet, though he dreams not of the reason."

290. Much has been written on the *change of rapiers* in the stage-direction, for an abstract of which, and also for the practice of celebrated actors, see F.

294. *As a woodcock.* F. quotes a writer in *Notes and Queries* (Aug. 8, 1874) who says: "This bird is trained to decoy other birds, and sometimes, while strutting incautiously too near the springe, it becomes itself entangled." Cf. i. 3. 115 above.

296. *How does the queen?* That is, what is the matter with the queen?

*Swoons.* The quartos and 1st and 2d folios have "sounds," the later folios "swounds" (=swoons), a pet word with Mrs. Browning.

305. *Unbated.* See on iv. 7. 137 above; and for *practice*, iv. 7. 66, 137.

309. *Envenom'd too.* That is, envenomed as well as unbated.

314. *Is thy union here?* See on 270 above.

316. *Temper'd.* Mixed, compounded (Schmidt). Cf. *R. and J.* iii. 5. 98 and *Cymb.* v. 5. 250.

319. Laertes, who was not wounded till after Hamlet, dies first of the poison; but possibly, as F. suggests, Hamlet gave Laertes a mortal thrust in return for the "scratch," which was all that Laertes was aiming at,—so that Laertes dies of the wound, Hamlet of the poison.

323. *Mutes.* "That are either auditors of this catastrophe, or at most only mute performers, that fill the stage without any part in the action" (Johnson).

324. *As.* See Gr. 110, and cf. iv. 3. 58 above.

*Sergeant.* Ritson, Schmidt, and others explain this as = "bailiff, or sheriff's officer;" but Mr. J. F. Marsh, in *Notes and Queries* (March 16, 1878), says that a sheriff's officer was *not* called a sergeant, and that the allusion is probably to the sergeants-at-arms, the executive officers of the two Houses of Parliament and the High Court of Chancery. Malone quotes Silvester's *Du Bartas:* "And Death, drad Seriant of th' eternall Iudge." Cf. *C. of E.* iv. 2. 56, 61, iv. 3. 30, 40, and *Hen. VIII.* i. 1. 198.

329. *Antique.* For the accent, cf. ii. 2. 455 above, and see *Macb.* p. 234. Wr. quotes here *A. and C.* iv. 15. 87.

332. *O God!* The quartos have "O god *Horatio*," or "O God *Horatio!*" The folio has "Oh good *Horatio*," which is followed by many modern eds.

333. *Live behind.* St. quotes *Much Ado,* iii. 1. 110: "No glory lives behind the back of such." For *live* the quartos have "I leave;" and W. reads "leave."

335. *Felicity.* The joys of heaven (Delius).

341. *O'er-crows.* "As a victorious cock crows over his defeated antagonist" (Jennens). Steevens quotes Chapman, *Odyssey:*

"and told his foe
It was not fair nor equal t' overcrow
The poorest guest;"

and Malone adds from the epistle prefixed to Nash's *Pierce Pennilesse,* 1593: "and overcrowe me with comparative terms."

345. *Occurrents.* Occurrences, incidents. Steevens quotes Drayton, *Barons' Wars,* i. 12: "As our occurrents happen in degree;" and Wr. adds from Holland's *Pliny,* xxv. 2: "This occurrent fell out in Lacetania."

346. *Which have solicited.* "Which have induced me to act as I have done" (M.). Cf. *Rich. II.* i. 2. 2.

*The rest is silence.* "To Hamlet silence would come as the most welcome and most gracious of friends, as relief to the action-wearied soul, freedom from conflicting motives, leisure for searching out all problems, release from the toil of finding words for thought; as the one sole language of immortality, the only true utterance of the infinite" (M.).

347. *Cracks.* Breaks. Cf. *M. W.* ii. 2. 301: "My heart is ready to crack;" *K. John,* v. 7. 52: "The tackle of my heart is crack'd;" *Cor.* v. 3. 9: "with a crack'd heart," etc.

352. *This quarry cries on havoc.* "This heap of dead proclaims an indiscriminate slaughter" (W.). *Quarry*=the game killed; as in *Macb.*

iv. 3. 206, etc. Johnson makes *cries on*=exclaims against; but it is rather, as Schmidt gives it,=cries out. Cf. *Oth.* v. 1. 48: "whose noise is this that cries on murther?" For *havoc*, see *J. C.* p. 160.

353. *Toward.* See on i. 1. 77 above, and cf. *A. and C.* ii. 6. 75: "Four feasts are toward." For *eternal*, see on i. 5. 21 above.

360. *His mouth.* That is, the king's (Warb.). Theo. strangely referred it to Hamlet.

363. *Jump.* See on i. 1. 65 above.

369. *Carnal.* Sensual (Schmidt); as in *Oth.* i. 3. 335. The allusion is to the murder of the elder Hamlet by Claudius previous to his incestuous union with Gertrude (Malone).

370. This line refers to Polonius, and the next to Rosencrantz and Guildenstern, whose deaths were *forced* on Hamlet (Delius).

371. *Put on.* See on iv. 7. 130 above.

372. *Upshot.* Conclusion, final issue. Cf. *T. N.* iv. 2. 76. "In archery the *upshot* was the final shot, which decided the match" (Wr.). For *mistook*, see Gr. 343.

374. *Deliver.* Report, relate. See on i. 2. 193 above.

377. *Rights of memory.* Rights which are remembered (Malone).

380. *Will draw on more.* Will be seconded by others (Theo.).

383. *On.* In consequence of (Gr. 180).

385. *Put on.* Put to the proof, tried (Caldecott).

386. *Passage.* Departure, death; as in iii. 3. 86 above.

391. "Hamlet has gained the haven for which he longed so often; yet without bringing guilt on himself by his death: no fear that his sleep should have bad dreams in it *now.* Those whom he loved, his mother, Laertes, Ophelia, have all died guiltless or forgiven. Late, and under the strong compulsion of approaching death, he has done, and well done, the inevitable task from which his gentle nature shrank. Why then any further thought, in the awful presence of death, of crimes, conspiracies, vengeance? Think that he has been slain in battle, like his Sea-King forefathers; and let the booming cannon be his mourners" (M.).

---

## ADDENDUM.

THE "TIME-ANALYSIS" OF THE PLAY.—This is summed up by Mr. P. A. Daniel (*Trans. of New Shaks. Soc.* 1877–79, p. 214) as follows:

"The time of the Play is seven days represented on the stage—or eight if the reader prefers to assign a separate day to the last scene—with two intervals.

Day 1. Act I. sc. i. to iii.
" 2. Act I. sc. iv. and v.
*An interval* of rather more than two months.
" 3. Act II. sc. i. and ii.
" 4. Act III. sc. i. to iv., Act IV. sc. i. to iii.
" 5. Act IV. sc. iv.
*An interval*—a week?
" 6. Act IV. sc. v. to vii.
" 7. Act V. sc. i. and ii."

RICHARD BURBADGE (p. 275).

# INDEX OF WORDS AND PHRASES EXPLAINED.


a (=one), 274.
about, 214.
abridgment, 209.
absolute, 262, 271.
absurd (accent), 222.
abuse (=deceive), 215.
abuse (noun), 255.
act (=action), 186.
addition (=title), 193, 199.
admiration, 230.
adulterate, 195.
aery, 207.
afeard, 274.
affection, 210.
affections, 220.
affront (=meet), 216.
afoot, 223.
against (of time), 176, 211, 236.
aim (=guess), 247.
a-making, 191.
amaze, 213.
ambition, 233.
amble, 219.
amiss (noun), 247.
an end, 195.
anchor (=anchorite), 227.
angle (=fish-line), 269.
annexment, 232.
another, 199.
answer, 240, 242, 272.
antic, 198.
antique, 275.
any the most, 180.
apart (=aside), 242.
apoplexed, 237.
appointment, 253.
approve (=commend), 271.
approve (=prove), 171.
appurtenance, 208.
argal, 259.
argument, 207, 225, 227, 246.
arm you, 232.
arras, 204.
art, 203.
article, of great, 271.
as (=as if), 200, 249, 255.
as (=for so), 244, 258, 275.
as (=namely), 193.
as's, 268.
aspect (accent), 213.
assay (=proof), 202, 233.
assay (verb), 216.
assays of bias, 200.
assigns, 272.
assurance, 262.
assure you, 202.
at, 244.
at foot, 244.
at height, 193.
at point, 186.
attent, 185.
attribute, 193.
authorities, 243.
avouch (noun), 172.
a-work, 211.
ay (dissyllable), 199.

back (=reserve), 257.
bak'd meats, 185.
Baptista, 228.
bare (=mere), 217.
barred, 177.
barren, 222.
bate (=blunt), 257.
bated (=excepted), 268.
batten, 236.
be, 174.
be it either which, 254.
beaten, 205.
beautied, 216.
beautified, 203.
beaver, 186.
beck, at my, 219.
bedded, 238.
belike, 225.
bended, 200.
be-netted, 268.
bent, 202.
beseeched, 216.
beshrew, 201.
bespeak, 203.
bestow, 212, 240.
beteem, 183.
bethought, 190.
better, you were, 212.
bettered, 274.
bilboes, 266.
bisson, 212.
blank (=target), 243.
blanks (=blanches), 227.
blastments, 188.
blench, 215.
bloat, 240.
blood, 187, 223, 246.
blown, 220.
board (=accost), 204.
bodkin, 217.
bodykins, 212.
bonnet (=cap), 270.
Bonny Sweet Robin, 252.
bore of the matter, 253.
borne in hand, 202.
bound, 195.
bourn, 218.
brainish, 242.
brave, 205.
bravery (=bravado), 270.
breathe (=speak), 199.
breathing time, 272.
broad (=free), 235.
brokers, 191.
brooch, 256.
bruit, 182.
brute (play upon), 224.
bugs (=bugbears), 267.
bulk (=breast), 200.
but (=except), 174.
buttons (=buds), 188.
buz, buz! 208.
buzzers, 248.
by and by, 231.
by (=with), 250.

can (=can do), 233, 255.
candied, 222.
canker, 188.
canonized (accent), 194.
capable, 239.
cap-a-pe, 186.
card or calendar of gentry, 271.
card, speak by the, 262.
carouses, 275.

carnal, 277.
carry it away, 208.
cart (=chariot), 225.
cast, 201.
cat will mew, etc., 266.
cautel, 187.
caviare, 210.
cease (noun), 232.
censure (= opinion), 190, 193, 221, 224.
centre, 204.
chameleon's dish, the, 224.
change (=exchange), 184.
changeling, 269.
chanson, pious, 209.
character (accent), 189, 255.
charge (=cost), 246.
charge (=load), 268.
chariest, 188.
check at, 255.
cheer, 226, 227.
chief (adverb), 190.
chopine, 209.
chorus, 228.
chough, 270.
cinkapase, 222.
circumstance, 197, 234.
clepe, 193.
climature, 175.
closely (=secretly), 216.
closet, 200, 230.
coagulate, 211.
cockle-hat, 247.
coil (=turmoil), 217.
cold (=chaste), 258.
coldly set, 245.
colour, will want true, 239.
columbines, 251.
come in further evil, 269.
come tardy off, 221.
come your ways, 191.
comma, 268.
commendable (accent), 180.
comment of thy soul, 223.
commerce, 218.
commune (accent), 252.
commutual, 225.
compact (accent), 173.
compare with, 272.
compelled, 253.
complete (accent), 194.
complexion, 193.
comply with, 208, 273.
compulsative, 174.
compulsive, 237.
comrade (accent), 190.
conceit (=conception), 213.
conceit (=imagination), 238, 248.
conceit, liberal, 272.
concernancy, 271.
concernings, 241.
conclusions, 241.
condolement, 180.
confederate, 228.
confine (accent), 176.
confines, 205.
confront, 233.
conjunctive, 254.
conscience, perfect, 269.
contagion, 257.
content (=please), 216.
continent, 246, 271.
contraction, 235.
contrary (accent), 227.
contrive (=plot), 257.
converse, 199.
convert my stern effects, 237.
convoy, 187.
coped withal, 222.
corrival, 170.
coted, 206.
couch (verb), 264.
count (=account), 254.
countenance, 243.
counter, 249.
counterfeit, 236.
couplets, golden, 266.
cousin (=nephew), 179.
cracks, 276.
crants, 264.
credent, 188.
crescent, 187.
cried in the top of, 210.
crimeful, 253.
crocodile, eat a, 266.
crow-flowers, 258.
crowner's quest law, 259.
cry (=company), 229.
cue, 213.
cullison, 222.
cunnings, 257.
curb, 239.
curiously, 263.
currents (=courses), 233.
cutpurse, 238.

daintier, 261.
daisy, 252.
Dane (=King of Denmark), 170.
Danskers, 199.
dead-men's-fingers, 258.
dear, 185, 223.
dear a halfpenny, 205.
debate (=decide), 245.
debatement, 268.
decline upon, 196.
declining, 211.
deeply-sworn, 227.
defeat (=ruin), 214.
defeated (=marred), 177.
defeature, 177.
defence, 256.
definement, 271.
deject, 219.
deliver (=relate). 186, 277.
demanded of, 243.
demonstrated (accent), 175.
Denmark (=King of Denmark), 181.
denote, 180.
deprive, 195.
desires (=good wishes), 202.
dexterity, 184.
didest, 255.
difference, with a, 252.
differences, 271.
dilated, 178.
disappointed, 196.
disaster, 175.
disclose (=hatch), 220, 266.
discourse of reason, 183.
discourse, such large, 246.
discovery, 205.
disjoint, 175.
dispatched, 196.
disposition, 194.
disprized, 217.
distempered, 229.
distract, 246.
distrust, 226.
divulging, 242.
document, 251.
dog will have his day, the, 266.
doom (=doomsday), 236.
doublet, 200.
doubt (=disbelieve), 203.
doubt (=suspect), 187, 202, 220.
douts, 259.
down-gyved, 200.
dram of eale, 193.
dreadful, 186.
drift of circumstance, 215.
drive upon, 211.
duke (=king), 228.

eager, 192, 196.
eale, 193.
easiness, 261.
eat (=eaten), 244.
ecstasy, 201, 237, 239.
edge, 216.
effects (=action), 239.
eisel, 265.
eldest, 232.
Elsinore, 169.
emulate (=envious), 173.
enact (=act), 224.
enactures, 226.
encompassment and drift, 199.
encumbered, 198.
engaged, 233.
enginer, 241.
entreatments, 191.
enviously, 247.

erring (=wandering), 176.
escoted, 207.
espials, 216.
estate (=rank), 264.
eternal blazon, 195.
even (=honest), 205.
even-Christian, 260.
event (=issue), 246.
exception, 274.
excrements, 238.
expostulate, 203.
express, 206.
expressed in fancy, 190.
extent, 208.
extravagant, 176.
eyases, 207.

fair (proleptic), 219.
falls (=happens), 255.
fanged, 241.
fantasy, 171.
fardels, 218.
fares (play upon), 224.
farm (=lease), 245.
fashion, 187, 220.
favour, 252, 263.
fay, 205.
fear (=fear for), 188, 235, 249.
fear (=object of fear), 232.
feature, 220.
feeds on his wonder, 248.
feelingly, 271.
felicity, 276.
fennel, 251.
fetch of warrant, 199.
fierce, 175.
figure, 203.
find (=detect), 220.
fine, 210, 262.
fingered, 267.
fire (dissyllable), 191.
first, 202.
fit (=ready), 273.
fitness, 273.
flaw (=gust), 264.
flush, 234.
flushing, 183.
fond (=foolish), 197.
fond and winnowed, 273.
for (=as for), 181, 187, 240.
for (=instead of), 264.
for and, 261.
for to, 220.
fordo, 201, 264.
fore, 211.
forestall, 233.
forged process, 195.
forgery, 256.
Fortinbras, 173.
forward, 187, 216.
fox (=sword), 244.
frame, 229.
free (=guiltless), 213, 228.
free (=willing), 244.
French falconers, 210.
fret, 230.
fretted, 205.
friending, 198.
from (=away from), 221.
front (=forehead), 236.
fruit (=dessert), 202.
full of bread, 234.
function, 213.
fust, 246.

gain-giving, 273.
gait, 178.
galled eyes, 184.
general (=people), 210.
general gender, 254.
gentle entertainment, 273.
gentry, 202.
germane, 272.
get thee, 219.
gib, 240.
gins, 197.
giving out, 198.
globe (=head), 197.
go about, 230.
go to, 191, 260.
God-a-mercy, 204.
God 'ield you! 247.
good kissing carrion, 204.
good now, 173.
gorge, 263.
grace (=honour), 181.
gracious (=blessed), 177.
grained, 237.
grating, 216.
green, 190.
greenly, 248.
gross, 246.
grossly, 234.
groundlings, 220.
grunt (=groan), 218.
gules, 211.
gulf, 232.
guts, 241.

hairs (=hair), 238.
handsaw, 208.
handsome, 210.
hangers, 272.
happily (=haply), 175, 208.
haps, 245.
haste (transitive), 195.
hatchment, 253.
haunt, out of, 242.
have (=find), 254.
have after, 195.
haviour, 180.
havoc, 276.
head (=armed force), 249.
health, 255.
hearsed, 194.
heaven (plural), 240.
heavens, 202.
hebenon, 196.
Hecate (pronunciation), 228.
hectic, 245.
hent, 234.
Hercules, 183, 208.
hernshaw, 208.
Herod, 221.
hey-day, 236.
hide fox, etc., 244.
hillo, ho, ho, 197.
him (=he), 199.
his (=its), 193, 194, 233.
hoar, 258.
hobby-horse, 225.
hoist, 241.
hold up, 260.
holds quantity, 226.
hold'st at aught, 244.
honest (=virtuous), 218.
hoodman-blind, 237.
how (=however), 231.
how purposed? 245
how say you by that? 204.
hugger-mugger, in, 248.
humorous, 206.
humour, 201.
husbandry, 190.
hush (noun), 211.
Hyperion, 183, 236.
Hyrcanian beast, 211.

idle, 224.
ill-breeding, 247.
illume, 171.
image, 227.
immediate, 181.
impartment, 194.
impasted, 211.
imperious, 264.
implorators, 191.
imponed, 272.
important, 238.
importing, 178, 267.
importuned (accent), 190.
imposthume, 245.
impress, 173.
imputation, 272.
in (=into), 203, 237, 266.
in (= in the thought of), 266.
in all my best, 181.
in few, 191.
in happy time, 273.
in little, 208.
in pause, 232.
in that, 178.
in the ear, 220.
in this consequence, 199.
incapable, 258.
incorporal, 238.
incorpsed, 256.
incorrect, 180.

indentures, 262.
index, 236.
indict, 210.
indifferent, 205.
indifferent (adverb), 219.
indifferently, 221.
indirections, 200.
individable, 209.
indued, 258.
inexplicable, 220.
infusion, 271.
ingenious sense, 265.
inheritor, 262.
inhibition, 207.
inky, 180.
insinuation, 269.
instances (=motives), 226.
instant, 196.
interpret, 228.
intil, 261.
investments, 191.
it (=its), 186, 264.

jade, 228.
jangled out of tune, 220.
jealousy, 247.
jig, 212, 219.
jig-maker, 225.
John-a-dreams, 213.
jowls, 261.
jump (=just), 172, 277.

keep (=dwell), 199.
keeps himself in clouds, 248.
kept short, 242.
kettle (=drum), 274.
kibe, 262.
kill dead, 226.
kindless, 214.
knowing (noun), 268.

laboursome, 179.
lack, 198.
Lamond, 256.
lapsed in time and passion, 238.
lapwing, 272.
larded, 247, 267.
law and heraldry, 173.
law of writ and liberty, 209.
lazar-like, 196.
leans on, 244.
leave (=cease), 183, 226, 236.
leave (=leave off), 199.
leave (=part with), 237.
lenten, 206.
let (=hinder), 195.
let the galled jade wince, 228.
let to know, 253.
Lethe wharf, 195.
liberal, 258.
lies, 233.
lightness, 204.
like (=likely), 186.
like (=uniform), 256.
like as, 186.
likes (=pleases), 202, 274.
limed, 233.
list (=boundary), 249.
list (=roll), 174.
littlest, 226.
loam, 263.
loggats, 261.
long purples, 258.
look through, 257.
loves (=love), 177, 187.
luxury (=lust), 196.

machine, 203.
maimed, 264.
main, the, 202, 245.
majestical, 176.
make (=do), 185, 205.
make assay, 233.
make love to, 269.
make mouths, 246.
manner, 192.
many many, 232.
margent, edified by the, 272.
market of his time, 245.
mart, 173.
marvellous, 229.
mass, 260.
massy, 232.
masterly report, 256.
matin, 196.
matter, 204, 250.
mazzard, 261.
me (=for me), 214.
means, 253.
meddle (=mingle), 223.
meed (=merit), 272.
merely, 182.
miching mallecho, 225.
might (=could), 172.
milch, 212.
milky, 211.
mincing, 212.
mineral, 242.
mobled, 212.
model (=copy), 268.
moiety, 174.
moist star, the, 175.
mole of nature, 193.
monument, living, 266.
mope, 237.
more above, 201, 203.
more considered time, 202.
more nearer, 199.
moreover that, 201.
mortal (=deadly), 257.
most (=greatest), 198.
motion (=impulse), 237.
mountebank, 257.
mouse, 240.
mouth (verb), 266.
mows, 208.
much (=great), 170.
muddy-mettled, 213.
murthering-piece, 248.
mutes, 276.
mutine (verb), 237.
mutines (noun), 266.

napkin (=handkerchief), 275.
native, 178, 258.
nature, 196.
near my conscience, 269.
neighbour (adjective), 242.
neighboured to, 201.
Nemean (accent), 195.
Nero, 231.
nerve (=sinew), 195.
neutral, 211.
new-lighted, 236.
nickname (=misname), 219.
nighted, 179.
nill, 259.
Niobe, 183.
nobility, 181.
nomination, 271.
nonce, for the, 258.
Norway (=King of Norway), 172, 245.
not (transposed), 227.
note (=attention), 223.
nothing (adverb), 178.
noyance, 232.

obscure (accent), 252.
obsequious, 180.
occulted, 223.
occurrents, 276.
o'er-crows, 276.
o'er-raught, 216.
o'er-reaches, 261.
o'ersized, 211.
o'erteemed, 212.
o'ertook, 199.
of (=about), 198, 248.
of (=because of), 246.
of (=by), 171.
of (=from), 201.
of (=on), 252.
of (=over), 202.
of (=upon), 205.
of (=with), 265.
of wisdom and of reach, 199.
offendendo, 259.
omen, 175.
on (=in consequence of), 277.
on (=of), 172.
on a roar, 263.
on brood, 220.

once (=ever), 197.
opened, 202.
operant, 226.
opposite, 227.
or (=before), 183, 185.
ordinant, 268.
ore, 242.
orisons, 218.
ostentation, 253.
outstretched, 205.
overlooked, 253.
overpeering, 249.
over-top, 210.

packing, 241.
paddling, 240.
paddock, 240.
painted (=unreal), 216.
panders (transitive), 237.
pajock, 229.
pansy, 251.
pardon (=leave), 179, 230.
parle, 172.
partisan, 176.
pass (=thrust), 269.
passage (=death), 277.
passion, 212.
pat, 233.
patience, 224.
pause, 244.
pause, give us, 217.
peace-parted, 265.
peak, 213.
pelican, 250.
perdy, 229.
periwig-pated, 220.
perpend, 203.
persever, 180.
perusal, 200.
peruse, 257.
pester, 178.
petar, 241.
picked (=refined), 262.
pickers and stealers, 230.
pigeon-livered, 214.
pioner, 198.
plausive, 193.
pluck, 255.
plurisy, 256.
ply his music, 200.
Polack, 172.
pole (=pole-star), 171.
politician, 261.
porpentine, 195.
posset, 196.
posy, 225.
pound (singular), 229.
powers (=troops), 245.
practice (=plot), 255, 257, 275.
precedent, 237.
precurse, 175.
pregnant, 205, 222.
prenominate, 199.
presence, 274.
present, 245.
presently, 204, 222.
presentment, 236.
pressure, 197, 221.
prevail (=avail), 180.
prevent (=anticipate), 205.
primy, 187.
probation (=proof), 176.
prodigal (adverb), 191.
profound, 242.
progress, 244.
pronounce, 230.
proof, 235, 256, 257.
proper, 201.
property, 213.
proposer, 205.
Provincial, 228.
puffed, 188, 246.
purgation, 229.
purport (accent), 200.
pursy, 239.
put on (=incite), 257, 277.
put on (=tried), 277.
put on me, 190.

quaintly, 199.
quality, 207.
quantity, 237, 265.
quarry, 276.
question, 207.
questionable, 194.
quick (=living), 262.
quiddits, 262.
quietus, 217.
quillets, 262.
quintessence, 206.
quit (=requite), 269.
quoted, 201.

rack (=clouds), 211.
ranker, 245.
rashly, 266.
ravel out, 240.
razed, 229.
reckon, 203.
record (accent), 197.
recorder (accent), 197.
recorders, 229.
recover the wind of, 230.
rede, 188.
re-deliver, 272.
reechy, 240.
region (=air), 211, 214.
relative, 215.
relish of, 219.
remember your courtesy, 270.
remiss, 257.
remorse (=pity), 211.
removed (=remote), 195.
repast (verb), 250.
replication, 243.
residence, 207.
resolve, 182.
respect (=motive), 217.
respects (=considerations), 226.
rests (=remains), 233.
retrograde, 181.
revenue (accent), 222.
revolution, 261.
re-word, 239.
rhapsody, 235.
Rhenish, 192.
rheum, 212.
rights of memory, 277.
rivality, 170.
rivals (=partners), 170.
romage, 174.
rood, 235.
rosemary, 250.
rough-hew, 267.
round (=directly), 203.
round (=plain), 220, 235.
rouse, 181, 192.
row (=stanza), 209.
rub, 217.
rue, 251.

sables, 225, 255.
sallet, 210.
sans, 237.
sat me down, 268.
satyr, 183.
saw (=maxim), 197.
sayest (=sayest well), 260.
'sblood, 208, 230.
scape, 188.
scarfed, 267.
school (=university), 181.
scourge, 244.
scrimers, 256.
sea-gown, 267.
season, 185, 190, 199, 227.
secure (=careless), 196.
seeming, 224.
seeming-virtuous, 195.
seized of, 173.
semblable, 271.
sense, 235, 237.
sensible, 172.
sensibly, 250.
sequent, 269.
sergeant, 276.
several (=separate), 267.
shall (=will), 198, 220.
shapes our ends, 267.
shards, 264.
share, 229.
sharked up, 174.
sheen, 225.
shent, 231.
shook, 254.
shoon, 247.

should (=would), 195, 205, 229.
shrewdly, 192.
shriving-time, 268.
siege (=rank), 255.
silence, 235.
simple (=foolish), 180.
simples, 257.
sith, 201, 246, 253
sits (of the wind), 189.
sized, 226.
skyish, 265.
slander, 191.
sledded, 172.
slips, 199.
sliver, 258.
so (=if), 255.
so (omitted), 253, 257.
so please you, 220.
soft (=hold, stop), 196, 218.
softly (=slowly), 245.
soldiers (trisyllable), 197.
sole, 234.
solicited, 276.
solidity, 235.
something-settled, 220.
sometime (adjective), 177, 218.
sometimes ( = formerly), 172.
sort (=suit), 174.
soul (gender), 213.
speak fair, 242.
spendthrift sigh, 256.
sphere, 254.
spies (=scouts), 248.
spirit (monosyllable), 176.
spite, 198.
splenitive, 265.
springes, 191.
spurns, 247.
stand me upon, 269.
star, 193.
star, out of thy, 203.
station, 236.
statists, 268.
stay (=wait for), 234, 268.
stay upon, 224.
stick fiery off, 274.
still ( = always), 175, 202, 256.
stithy, 223.
stomach (=courage), 174.
stoup, 260.
straight (adverb), 210, 235, 259.
strewments, 265.
strike (of planets), 177.
strucken, 228.
stuck (=thrust), 258.
subject (=people), 173, 178.
succession, 207.
sum of parts, 255.
supervise, on the, 267.
suppliance, 187.
supply and profit, 202.
sweet, 270.
Switzers, 248.
swoopstake, 250.
sword, upon my, 197.
'swounds, 214, 265.
synod, 212.

table (=tablet), 197.
tables (=note-book), 197.
taints, 199.
take (=bewitch), 177.
take arms against a sea, etc., 217.
tarre, 207.
tax him home, 232.
tell (=count), 186.
tempered, 276.
temple (of the body), 187.
tenable in your silence, 187.
tend (=attend), 190, 244.
tender (=regard), 244.
tenders, 190.
tent (=probe), 215.
Termagant, 221.
that (=such), 185, 196.
thee (=thou), 171, 196.
theft, 224.
thereabout, 210.
thews, 187.
thieves of mercy, 253.
thinks't thee, 269.
thou, 239.
thought ( = anxiety), 218, 252.
thought-sick, 236.
throughly, 249.
tickle o' the sere, 206.
time (=the times), 217.
tinct, 237.
to (=for), 177.
to (in comparisons), 183, 196, 216.
to-do, 207.
toils (transitive), 173.
too-much, 256.
too much i' the sun, 179.
too much proved, 216.
too, too, 182.
top of my bent, to the, 231.
top of question, 207.
topped, 256.
touched, 252.
toward ( = at hand), 173, 277.
toy (=trifle), 247.
toy in blood, a, 187.
toys (=freaks), 195.
trace (=follow), 271.
trade, 230.
trick (=habit), 259.
trick (=knack), 261.
trick of fame, 246.
tricked, 211.
tristful, 236.
tropically, 227.
truepenny, 198.
trumpet (=trumpeter), 176.
truster, 185.
turn Turk, 228.
two days old at sea, 253.
tyrannically, 207.

umbrage, 271.
unaneled, 196.
unbated, 257, 275.
unbraced, 200.
uncharge, 255.
undergo, 193.
uneffectual, 197.
unfortified, 180.
ungartered, 200.
ungored, 274.
ungracious, 188.
unhouseled, 196.
unimproved, 174.
union (=pearl), 274.
unlimited, 209.
unmastered, 188.
unpregnant of, 213.
unprevailing, 180.
unproportioned, 189.
unreclaimed, 199.
unshaped, 247.
unsifted, 190.
unsinewed, 254.
unsmirched, 249.
untimely (adverb), 243.
unyoke, 260.
upon (adverbial), 185.
upon (=just at), 170.
upshot, 277.
upspring, 192.

vailed, 179.
valanced, 209.
validity, 226.
vantage, of, 232.
vast, 186.
ventages, 30.
vice (=clown), 237.
vigour, 196.
virtue (=power), 250.
vouchsafe your rest, 208.
vulgar, 189.

wag, 235, 265.
wanned, 213.
wanton, 275.
warrantise, 264.
wash (=the sea), 225.
wassail, 192.
watch, 204.
water-fly, 270.

well be with you, 208.
well-took, 202.
wharf (=bank), 195.
what (=who), 253, 260.
what make you? 185.
wheel, 250.
whether (monosyllable), 202.
whiles, 188.
who (=which), 180.
who (=whom), 185, 204.
wholesome, 230.
wildness, 216.
will, 237.
windlasses, 200.
wit (=wisdom), 203.
withal, 188, 205.
withdraw with you, to, 230.
within's, 225.
woe is me, 225.
wonder-wounded, 265.
woodcock, 191, 275.
woo't, 265.
word (= watchword), 197, 249.
worser, 239.
would, 172, 234.
wrack, 201.
wretch, 204, 259.
writ, 178, 186.
writ (=commission), 268.

Yaughan, 260.
yaw, 271.
yeoman's service, 268.
yesty, 273.
yond, 171.
Yorick, 263.
your, 198, 220, 244.

THE INFANT SHAKESPEARE.